SEXUAL ARTIFICE

GENDERS
EDITORIAL BOARD

Ann Kibbey, EDITOR IN CHIEF
Kayann Short, ASSOCIATE EDITOR

Amittai Avirma	Anne Higonnet
Ellen Berry	Annamarie Jagose
Nancy Campbell	Paul Mattick
Mary Wilson Carpenter	Marta Sánchez
Kate Cummings	James Saslow
Samir Dayal	Jane Shattuc
Desley Deacon	Elaine Showalter
Abouali Farmanfarmaian	Carol Siegel
Thomas Foster	Alan Sinfield
Ann Gibson	Jeffrey Weeks
Lynda Hart	Jonathan Weinberg
Anne Herrmann	Kath Weston
Gail Hershatter	Carol Zemel

GENDERS 19

SEXUAL ARTIFICE

Persons, Images, Politics

Edited by Ann Kibbey,
Kayann Short, and Abouali
Farmanfarmaian

NEW YORK UNIVERSITY PRESS
NEW YORK AND LONDON

NEW YORK UNIVERSITY PRESS
New York and London

Copyright © 1994 by New York University
All rights reserved

New York University Press books are printed on acid-free paper, and their binding materials are chosen for strength and durability.

Manufactured in the United States of America

10 9 8 7 6 5 4 3 2 1

Contents

Preface   vii

PART ONE
Not the Person S/he Conceived Me

1. "Not the Person She Conceived Me": The Public Identities of Charlotte Charke   3
   Jones DeRitter

2. Posing *Orlando*   26
   Talia Schaffer

3. Fetishism and Parody in Stein's *Tender Buttons*   64
   Elisabeth A. Frost

4. Anita Hill, Clarence Thomas, and the Culture of Romance   94
   Margaret A. Eisenhart and Nancy R. Lawrence

PART TWO
Violating Images

5. Plastic Man versus the Sweet Assassin   125
   Leah Hackleman

6. The Anti-Body in Photomontage: Hannah Höch's Woman without Wholeness   148
   Lora Rempel

7. Something's Missing: Male Hysteria and the U.S. Invasion of Panama   171
   Cynthia Weber

8. Gendered Troubles: Refiguring "Woman" in
   Northern Ireland   198
   Heather Zwicker

PART THREE
How Political Is Identity Politics?

9. The Crisis of Femininity and Modernity in the Third World   223
   Rajeswari Mohan

10. Zero-Degree Deviancy: *Lesbians Who Kill*   257
    Lynda Hart

11. Macho Sluts: Genre-Fuck, S/M Fantasy, and the Reconfiguration
    of Political Action   265
    Ian Barnard

12. Ideology, Poststructuralism, and Class Politics: Rethinking Ideology
    Critique for a Transformative Feminist Politics   292
    Mas'ud Zavarzadeh

Contributors   325

Guidelines for Prospective Contributors   329

Preface

Dear Reader,

Beginning with 1994, *Genders* is taking a new shape! To increase the number of essays we print, we will now be publishing twice a year instead of three times a year. Each *Genders* will now be much larger—a volume of essays in its own right—and we will be arranging the contents topically. We hope this new form will help you find the essays of greatest value for you and, at the same time, suggest other essays that might be related to your primary interests. As usual, we haven't tried to tell you what to think of our essays. We haven't tried to make them say the same thing or sound alike. We leave you to decide for yourself which contributors offer the most persuasive and valuable insights for you.

By making these changes in our publication form, we also hope to make *Genders* available to the many general readers and students who have expressed an interest in the publication. Since we publish on topics of general interest to the public, we have now arranged for each *Genders* to be available for sale through bookstores of all kinds. If you prefer, you may still order in advance by writing directly to the publisher (New York University Press, Bobst Library, 70 Washington Square South, New York, NY 10012). For those of you who teach, we believe the new *Genders* will be much more accessible to students and much more suitable for your courses. Each *Genders* will remain in print for several years, so you can reorder easily for each semester.

People often ask where we get our essays. *Genders* draws its contributors from a wide spectrum of readers who also write. Because we want to provide a wide range of opinions on current debates, and because we think it's important to be open to new ideas and approaches, we select the best essays we receive regardless of the author's personal and professional identity. Guidelines for contributors appear at the back of the volume.

We hope you will enjoy the new *Genders* and that you will find it exciting reading.

Ann Kibbey
Editor in Chief

SEXUAL ARTIFICE

PART ONE

Not the Person S/he Conceived Me

ONE

"Not the Person She Conceived Me": The Public Identities of Charlotte Charke

Jones DeRitter

Charlotte Charke, the youngest daughter of the actor and playwright Colley Cibber, was born in 1713. By the time she began her stage career in 1730, her father was one of the patent-holders of Drury Lane Theatre, and he was named poet laureate later that year. After a disastrous marriage and five years spent mostly with acting companies controlled to a great extent either by her father or by her brother Theophilus, Charke joined Henry Fielding's company at the New Haymarket Theatre; soon afterward she broke off relations with her family, and shortly after that the Stage Licensing Act cast her abruptly into unemployment and poverty. From 1737 to 1745 she eked out a precarious hand-to-mouth existence in London; she became notorious during this period for wearing men's clothes on the streets of the city, and in her masculine disguise she held several jobs, including those of a street peddler, a gentleman's valet, and a tavern bouncer. After 1745 she went into the English countryside, where she spent nearly a decade alternately performing with strolling companies and trying to establish a place for herself in the small towns between London and Bristol; her autobiographical *Narrative* suggests that for much of this period she presented herself in public as Mr. Charles Brown. By the time she returned to London in 1754 she had given up cross-dressing; she set herself up as a novelist and memoirist, but neither pursuit made her rich, and she died alone and destitute in 1760.

Most of the critical attention that has been paid to Charke over the past decade has emphasized the schizophrenic nature of the *Narrative*, which presents its author as both a resourceful female rogue and a penitent prodigal daughter.[1] This essay, however, will focus primarily on Charlotte Charke's stage career and on her efforts to define herself through performances of various kinds. Actors are neither free agents nor puppets; the control they exercise over themselves is compromised and contested by the controls imposed on them by other people – playwrights, directors, fellow performers, spectators – and by a variety of circumstances representing the material effects of social, literary, and historical contexts. Although both Charke's relatively brief career on the London stage and the public record of her intermittent celebrity status in later years provide a number of interesting opportunities for investigating the dynamics of this struggle, my essay deals with only three of the characters played by Charlotte Charke on the London stage between 1731 and 1737 and with an equally small number of printed accounts concerning these and other performances both on- and offstage. My goal, then, is not to produce a coherent and comprehensive account of Charlotte Charke's life and career, but rather to explain how four clearly delimited moments from that career illuminate this struggle between certain producers and consumers of culture as it was staged in England during the 1730s and 1740s.

The theoretical underpinnings for my discussion are derived in part from an essay by Elin Diamond in which she defines what she calls "gestic feminist criticism"[2] and from a book by Bruce Wilshire titled *Role Playing and Identity*.[3] Diamond's analysis provides a way of focusing on crucial moments in performance, where the issue of the actor's self-creation becomes entangled with those of social and literary production; her model combines feminist theories of spectacle and spectatorship with the Brechtian concept of the gestus – a word, gesture, action, or image through which "the social attitudes encoded in the playtext become visible to the spectator" (89) – in order to "highlight sex-gender configurations as they conceal or disrupt a coercive or patriarchal ideology" (91). Wilshire combines phenomenological insights with more literary kinds of performance theory to argue that role-playing on stage is analogous to role-playing in real life – that the ways in which actors and spectators construct and construe the meaning of their shared experiences correspond to similar processes that figure in human relations in the world at large (44).

Two of Wilshire's terms, *authorization* and *engulfment*, will be of particular value in this discussion. According to Wilshire, theater audiences always begin by assuming that there is a fundamental connection between the onstage and offstage worlds; the presence of an audience authorizes specific actors to "stand in" for specific characters, and each individual spectator also authorizes each character to stand in on some level for him- or herself (40, 43). This does not mean that the spectators must adopt every character's feelings and motives as their own, but it does mean that they have to find a place for each character within their collective horizon of expectations.[4] Because, like the audience, the actor must also authorize the character to stand in for him- or herself, the emotional connection between the actor and the character is (like the character itself) always at risk; if the character is rejected, some part of the actor's identity has also been condemned. This condemnation can take at least two different shapes: the spectators can either simply refuse to authorize the performance, in which case they might choose either to leave or to seek some way to disrupt it; or they can pursue the course Wilshire describes as engulfment, by which a character is more or less deliberately misinterpreted and made to serve an agenda set not by those who are staging the production, but rather by their audience (44). Each of the four sections of my argument show Charlotte Charke searching for authorization and finding only refusal or engulfment.

Perhaps more importantly, each of these episodes raises questions about the social and institutional functions of eighteenth-century gender categories, particularly insofar as they are related to the evolution of the London stage. Kristina Straub has recently argued that between 1660 and 1800 the London theater community was increasingly concerned with the perceived need to establish clear and effective boundaries between the spectacle and the spectator. Drawing on the work of Nancy Armstrong and Michel Foucault, Straub suggests that, as the eighteenth century wore on, the role of the spectator came to be seen as more exclusively and essentially masculine, while that of the spectacle was viewed as more passive, more submissive, and therefore, according to the social conventions of the early modern period, more essentially feminine (4–5). Such a change represented a considerable departure from the plasticity of

Renaissance performance conventions, and it was not accomplished quickly or without human costs. At least in retrospect, the lifelong struggle of Charlotte Charke to stake out and claim her own discursive space in an increasingly rigid specular economy provides a striking example of how agonizing and disorderly — not to mention unjust and destructive — this process could be.

Early in her *Narrative*, Charlotte Charke suggests that she had been impersonating men since she was four, but her claim cannot be verified,[5] and even if it is true, her first three seasons at Drury Lane provided her with no opportunities to display this talent; before the summer of 1733, her only breeches role on stage was a rather anemic female adventurer named Clarinda in Colley Cibber's comedy *The Double Gallants*.[6] Given both the kind of character she became and the extraordinarily large number of breeches roles available in the eighteenth-century repertory, she seems almost exceptionally reserved in this respect.[7] Nevertheless, the surface calm of this period was interrupted on at least one occasion by an incident that foreshadowed some of the conflicts that burst into the open later in her career. Charles Johnson's *Caelia* was performed only once, on the night of December 11, 1732; the play apparently upset its audience so much that the actors refused to stage it a second time. In his preface to the printed text of his domestic tragedy, Johnson blamed the disaster on his portraits of a brothel madam named Mother Lupine and her prostitutes; in fact, he stated quite frankly that "I should not have made 'em necessary to my design."[8]

When she stepped on stage that night to play Mother Lupine, Charlotte Charke was a nineteen-year-old single mother.[9] She apparently already knew what brothel madams looked like and how they behaved; in the *Narrative* she claims that even during the first year of her marriage she had found herself "tracing [my] Spouse from Morn to Even through the Hundreds of Drury."[10] She also had firsthand experience of economic exploitation as it was practiced by her estranged husband Richard Charke, who in 1732 continued to exercise his legal right to claim his wife's earnings despite the fact that he had abandoned her and their infant daughter more than a year earlier. Finally, as a woman who later succeeded in presenting herself in public as another woman's husband, Charke might also have been able to infuse Mother Lupine's predatory gaze with a threatening and "unnatural" erotic interest in Johnson's virtuous heroine.

It is difficult even to speculate about what Charke might have been willing or able to do with her personal experiences in the context of early-eighteenth-century acting styles,[11] but there is some circumstantial evidence that suggests that Johnson might have been happy to have those elements brought into Charke's portrayal of Mother Lupine. When Mother Lupine first appears on stage, the text tells us that she should size up the pathetic heroine "as a Horse-Courser does a Filly" (act 1). A horse-courser at an auction was both an entrepreneur and a voyeur; his financial success depended on his ability to produce and manage a particular public spectacle, and on his ability to look carefully at what he was about to buy. By analogy, Mother Lupine's gaze implicated the spectator in the exploitation of women in general and female actors in particular; it demonstrated that the economic value of both Caelia and the woman who played her (Jane Cibber, the much-abused first wife of Theophilus) depended entirely upon their shared status as objects of desire. As Straub's analysis suggests, by the fourth decade of the eighteenth century such a gaze would also have been seen as a transgression of conventional gender boundaries, if only because it attempted to appropriate to itself a prerogative that by that time was generally presumed to belong exclusively to men. To the extent that Charke's personal background led her to enact this stage direction effectively, the spectators' reaction meant that they would authorize neither her erotic interest nor her awareness that the desires of others could be exploited for financial gain — neither her appropriation of masculine assurance and worldliness nor the implication of complicity that was derived from Mother Lupine's dispassionate inspection.

Eight months after the *Caelia* debacle, Theophilus Cibber and a group of veteran actors revolted against Drury Lane manager John Highmore and set up shop at the New Haymarket Theatre. Charlotte Charke walked out along with her brother and played a number of important parts with the rebel company, including many breeches roles.[12] Her new characters included Fainlove in Richard Steele's *The Tender Husband*, Charlotte Weldon in Thomas Southerne's *Oroonoko*, and Silvia in George Farquhar's *The Recruiting Officer*;[13] unlike Clarinda, each of these characters spends a significant amount of stage time in breeches, and none of them relies on a male rescuer to preserve and protect her double identity. In addition to the breeches roles, Charke also played a few ambiguously gendered monsters. For example, Theophilus had begun his season at the New Haymarket with Nicholas Rowe's *Tamerlane*, a patriotic tragedy that pitted solid English heroism against baroque Oriental villainy; in this production Charke played Haly, a eunuch whose chief purpose seems to have been to procure innocent female victims for his evil master. She also played Mrs. Otter — a termagant wife who shared Haly's exotic ethnic background — in the company's revival of Ben Jonson's *Epicoene, or the Silent Woman*. Of the eighteen roles credited to Charke in *The London Stage* summary of this season, ten required either cross-dressing or behaving in what was presumed at the time to be an inappropriately masculine fashion, or both.

Given this collection of roles, we might expect Charke to have encountered more reactions like the one that greeted Mother Lupine; in general, however, the rebels were kindly received, and Charke seems to have shared in their good fortune. This treatment may have been due largely to the advertising strategy of Theophilus Cibber, who presented the company as being engaged in the glorious task of defining a national repertory; in practice, this amounted to little more than deciding to produce the well-known plays mentioned above, but Theophilus was a good publicist. Unfortunately, this public image did not make it any easier for Charke to control the responses to the characters she played; the appeal to conventional tastes might have reduced the chances that the spectators would refuse to authorize a particular performance, but it seems on occasion to have predisposed those spectators toward the kinds of engulfment that reflected a conventional, essentialist approach to matters of gender — even when the play itself tended in another direction. Perhaps the best illustration of this process can be found in the rebel company's revival of Ben Jonson's *The Silent Woman*.

First, however, a bit of background. Jacobean audiences believed that otters were hermaphroditic,[14] and on that basis they would have assumed that Mrs. Otter's name alluded directly to her jarring combination of masculine language and behavior with feminine costume. Indeed, for Jonson's audience, Mrs. Otter's dress defined her transgression; since the character would have to have been played by a male actor during this era, it could be said that Mrs. Otter's costume provided the single most important means of defining "her" monstrosity. It might be objected that because such transvestism was one of the defining characteristics of Jacobean public theater, audiences of this period would have been slow to make anything of a particular instance of that fact. This claim cannot, however, be applied to *The Silent Woman*, because the end of the play focuses the spectator's attention directly on this issue. The climax of the comedy occurs when Epicoene (the title character) is revealed to be "a gentleman's son."[15] The effect must have been especially unnerving to Jonson's audience, because no one besides Dauphine (one of the play's protagonists) and his accomplice knows Epicoene's secret before he is unmasked; nothing is said to anyone about the possibility that she is a he until Dauphine removes "her" wig. Dauphine's trick confronts Jonson's audience with the fact that none of the ostensibly female figures on stage were actually women; rather, they were all male enactments of female characters. Although Jonson's script ridicules every one of his female characters, the animosity directed toward those characters is undermined to some degree by a gestus that forces the audience to recognize its own complicity in a performance style that effectively reduced all women to silence.[16]

Shortly after Charles II reopened the public theaters in 1660, he decreed that female roles should be played only by women; when the king issued the patents that licensed two new theatrical companies, the patents expressed the hope that if women's roles were indeed enacted by women, the plays themselves would soon be "esteemed not only harmless delights but useful and instructive representations of human life."[17] Lesley Ferris has recently pointed out that Charles believed that this new policy would help to differentiate the theater of his era from the all-male Renaissance stage, which he saw as promoting homosexuality;[18] since the court of his grandfather James I had been publicly attacked on the ground that it tolerated openly homosexual relationships, Charles II also stood to benefit politically from what amounted to an ostentatious display of his and his court's heterosexuality. Since women were first allowed on the London stage partly in order to involve them in an effort to stage a return to gender normalcy, it is ironic that Restoration playwrights and performers turned so quickly to the transvestite tricks of earlier times. Of course, the female-to-male cross-dressing of the Restoration and eighteenth-century stage was qualitatively different from the male-to-female cross-dressing of the Renaissance era. After the Restoration, theatrical cross-dressing by men seems to have been limited to cases of obvious parody, while women on the Restoration and eighteenth-century stage wore breeches for a variety of reasons. Although the "breeches part" on the Restoration stage seems to have come into vogue largely in order to put the bodies of the leading female performers on display, the acceptance of cross-dressed women under these conditions apparently created an opening for other, less exploitative uses of this practice. In her recent study of this issue, Kristina Straub suggests that by the middle of the eighteenth century most instances of female theatrical cross-dressing could be read as challenges to the process by which the masculinist specular economy came to be established as a social and aesthetic norm (127–35).

It took the two Restoration companies three years to determine how the king's decree should be applied to Epicoene, but they finally decided that the title character should be played exclusively by women, and the play was cast that way between 1663 and 1776.[19] As a result – and here we return at last to the species of engulfment mentioned earlier in this section – the gestus described earlier was emptied of its original contents and invested with a significance that ran directly counter to that which it had offered to Jonson's audience. Instead of showing the audience that Epicoene and the other female characters shared a common and somewhat suspect means of production, the Restoration and eighteenth-century versions of the play separated Epicoene from her onstage sisters, thereby allowing the hostility toward Mrs. Otter and the "collegiate ladies" (her colleagues in shrewishness) to continue unabated. The eighteenth-century productions of *The Silent Woman* also avoided the male-to-female cross-dressing of an earlier era by pretending briefly that one of the female actors on stage was a male character. But where the supposed maleness of these Epicoenes helped to clear them of the charge of violating standards of feminine decorum and virtue, no such license was extended to the actors playing Mrs. Otter and the collegiates, because in those cases the correspondence between the sex of the actors and the gender of the characters directed the audience's attention away from the act of impersonation and toward each character's unseemly language and behavior.

This effect was heightened by certain circumstances connected with the Drury Lane actors' rebellion. By the 1730s, both male-to-female and female-to-male cross-dressing were a staple of farces and other kinds of experimental drama, and theatrical travesties of this sort coexisted with more traditional deployments of the breeches part; however, such travesty performances were generally the province of the more marginal companies, and the Drury Lane rebels did not wish to be mistaken for a second-class troupe. Judith Milhous has argued that throughout the Restoration era, the use of breeches parts and other gender-bending theatrical tricks had been used as a cost-cutting measure by companies who could not hope to lure spectators into the boxes and galleries with the promise of more extravagant visual effects;[20] given this tendency, the fact that the newspaper and poster advertising for the rebel company announced that the audience at the Haymarket would see "All the Characters entirely new drest. With new Scenes and Decorations"[21] can be read as a signal that these plays would not challenge conventional assumptions about how men and women should dress and behave. To the extent that the rebels succeeded in presenting themselves as the true guardians of the English theatrical tradition — and they succeeded so well that when they returned to Drury Lane in the spring of 1734, Highmore was forced to sell his share of the patent, and many of the rebels had their salaries increased — they also succeeded in presenting the gender transgressors played by Charke as safely marginalized figures. (This tendency presumably held true regardless of whether a particular transgressor appeared on stage in breeches or simply misbehaved; Mrs. Otter, who apparently wore some sort of "Chinese" costume, could be included under either category, or both.) Stigmatized by the mainstream ideology to which Theophilus had pledged his allegiance and (unlike her Renaissance predecessor) denied the recuperative influence of Jonson's original gestus, the eighteenth-century Mrs. Otter became more monstrous as the performance itself became more respectable.

Because many Restoration and eighteenth-century spectators apparently believed that the onstage world could, should, and did in fact mirror some offstage reality in a simple and straightforward manner,[22] female performers of this era often found themselves characterized by the characters they enacted. In Charke's case, she had been driven off the stage as Mother Lupine but allowed to remain a part of the company as Mrs. Otter — an altogether less threatening presence. That she had also lost a degree of power in her professional life was made evident by her struggles when the rebel company returned to Drury Lane in the spring of 1734. Despite her successes at the Haymarket, Charke soon found herself competing with two or three other actors for roles that she considered to be hers alone. She blamed her brother and the new Drury Lane manager, Charles Fleetwood, for the apparent demotion, and she tried to fight them that summer by ridiculing both of them with a company of her own at the Haymarket.[23] With some assistance from her usually negligent father she returned to Drury Lane in September of 1734, but the following summer she was on her own again; then it was back again to Drury Lane and finally, in the spring of 1736, back to the Haymarket, where the Great Mogul's company had just struck it rich with Pasquin. The company's manager, Henry Fielding, hired Charke at a good salary to play Lord Place — a parody of the poet laureate and former Drury Lane patent holder who also happened to be her father.

Lord Place was only one of a number of male characters Charke played for Fielding at the Haymarket; the list also included Mr. Hen (a caricature of high-society auctioneer Christopher Cock) in *The Historical Register*, Spatter (one of Fielding's ubiquitous broken-down author figures) in *Eurydice Hissed*, and a minor role or two in *Tom Thumb* and other, more ephemeral pieces. These roles are much different from the kind of breeches roles Charke had played with the Drury Lane company, where female characters adopted masculine costumes and identities temporarily, only to be returned to their original gender shortly before the curtain fell. In her essay "Performative Acts and Gender Construction" Judith Butler compares the experience of seeing a transvestite onstage to that of sitting next to a transvestite on a bus and asserts that the second experience "becomes dangerous, if it does, precisely because there are no theatrical conventions to delimit the purely imaginary character of the act."[24] Breeches roles like those of Clarinda or Silvia are doubly insulated from offstage reality, because in each case the reinscription of gendered normalcy at the end of the play suggests that such transformations are inherently unstable (and therefore less threatening) even within the imaginary world onstage; the new characters in Charke's repertoire could not be dismissed so easily, although they of course were still circumscribed by the limits of the stage itself.

From Charke's perspective, the shift from Mrs. Otter to Mr. Hen allowed her to regain some measure of control over her public identity; playing masculine roles emphasized her skills as a performer and reduced the risk that she would be identified with the characters she portrayed. At the same time this greater freedom carried with it a more or less explicit challenge to the conventional equivalence of gender with sex, which meant that the body of the actor was still an issue. In a 1989 essay Joseph Roach uses the examples of castrati opera singers and acting virtuosos to argue that "the history of performance since the eighteenth century is the history of the ever more rigorous subjection of the body to forms of internalized control" (101–2). Although I believe that this claim is generally valid, I also believe that it is somewhat misleading with respect to the phenomenon of eighteenth-century theatrical cross-dressing, if only because it suggests that London theater audiences invariably approved such virtuosity. Charlotte Charke's success with Fielding at the Haymarket (like her later offstage successes) confirms the notion that an actor who portrayed a character of the opposite sex could achieve the same level of self-mastery that was attributed to the castrati and the acting virtuosos of her era; her fate, however, suggests that the response to that mastery could sometimes be determined not by what was displayed, but rather by what was masked.

At least one of the roles Fielding wrote for Charke seems to have been designed to emphasize this difference; even the name of Mr. Hen is calculated to focus the attention of the Haymarket audience on the phallus she did not possess, and the impersonation itself clearly showcased her ability to reproduce masculinity without maleness.[25] As Roach points out, the self-mastery displayed by the castrati was an easily recognizable product of an elaborate training regimen (109), but regardless of the aesthetic discourse that was invoked to justify this program, its effect was to produce an exterior that clearly identified the body in question as that of a castrated male. On the other hand, transvestite portrayals demonstrated that masculine and feminine behaviors were every bit as stylized and artificial as the vocabulary of gestures and inflections that identified the castrato, even as they challenged the hegemony of the "natural" that was apparently reinforced by the correspondence between the castrato's body and his style.

When Fielding integrated Charlotte Charke's talent for cross-gender impersonations into his social satires, he gave her access to a degree of social and financial stability that had been unavailable to her while she was working for more conventional companies. The Great Mogul's company might have been marginal in an ideological and an aesthetic sense, but the taste of the town conferred a degree of legitimacy on the group in the form of cold hard cash. At the same time, however, he helped to create a rift between Charke and her father that was never mended. Before she joined the Great Mogul's company, she had developed a reputation as an eccentric; she had not, however, dared to confront her father openly.[26] The authorization she had achieved at this point in her career was effectively revoked by the provisions of the Stage Licensing Act; soon afterward, just to add insult to injury, the stage historians of the following decade even managed to impose a kind of retroactive engulfment on her performances with the Great Mogul's company. Apparently as a result of her association with Fielding, Charke was disowned by her father in the spring of 1736;[27] then, in May of 1737, the passage of the Stage Licensing Act recapitulated her family situation on an institutional level. Because her father was no longer willing to mend fences for her at Drury Lane, she was thrown suddenly into unemployment and poverty. For reasons that will be addressed shortly, she began appearing in men's clothes on the streets of London soon after the public stage was closed to her; as soon as contemporary stage historians and controversialists connected this fact with her onstage breeches roles and with the well-known antagonism between Fielding and Cibber, they began to cite her in print as an eccentric, rebellious child whose primary goal was to embarrass her father.

In 1742, for example, an anonymous pamphlet attempted to embarrass Cibber by describing a blustering "Daughter CHARK" who had been "celebrated for her Performances in the Hay-Market Theatre, where, in the Farce of Pasquin, the Historical Register &c. she play'd off her Father and Brother with surprising Humour."[28] Five years later John Mottley asserted in his *List of Dramatic Authors* that Charke had opened *The Historical Register* with a parody of Cibber's most recent *New Year's Ode*, delivered in her father's "own Character."[29] There is only one problem with these summaries; the first is only half-true, and the second is not true at all. In fact, although *The Historical Register* contains at least three distinct Cibber parodies, none of them was enacted by Charke.[30] Notwithstanding its shaky grasp of the facts, Mottley's account encapsulates what was to become the general perception of Charke's role in Fielding's company; it serves, in other words, as the imaginary gestus that might have defined that largely imaginary role. These accounts imply that Charke joined Fielding's company in order to ridicule her father and that she also chose her roles with that goal in mind; in fact, however, the first claim must be viewed as partially true but probably misleading, while the second can be disproved simply by looking at *The Historical Register*. In essence, Mottley's anecdote shows us that sudden implementation of the Licensing Act allowed other writers to define her work with Fielding solely in terms of Lord Place; her skill as a performer was obscured by an exaggerated public interest in the challenge to her father's authority, and the issues raised by her transvestite stage portrayals were subsumed under the same heading. Her time with the Drury Lane rebels had cast her as an ambiguously gendered monster — as an eccentric but not (given the fate of characters like Mrs. Otter) a dangerous figure. On the other hand, the standard summaries of her time with Fielding presented her as openly antagonistic, not only to (usually unspecified) standards of public decency, but also and more importantly, to her famous father. In her recent study of transvestism and popular culture, Marjorie Garber argues that the interpreters of narratives by and about transvestites frequently distort the contents of those narratives by trying to normalize the phenomenon;[31] the willingness on the part of Mottley and others to reduce Charke's cross-dressing to a tactic employed solely for the purpose of embarrassing her father provides a striking example of this tendency. If these commentators can explain Charke's cross-dressing more or less exclusively in terms of her family conflicts, they can avoid the social and ideological issues raised both by that behavior and by the public response to it. By the time she undertook her *Narrative*, Charke herself was not above attempting to normalize her own activities in this fashion, but her family seems to have been convinced that there was something more going on; as Charke herself acknowledges, "my being in Breeches [offstage] has been alleged to me as a very great Error" by family members who sought to keep her and her father apart (139).

Charlotte Charke apparently began wearing men's clothes in the streets of London shortly after the Licensing Act was passed, and the *Narrative* implies that she impersonated a man almost continuously while she was gone from London between 1746 and 1753. There are a number of reasons why Charke might have chosen this particular course of action:[32] as an actor seeking employment she needed to be able to walk the streets after dark; as a debtor she needed a way to throw the bailiffs off her trail; as a sometime street peddler or tavern-keeper she needed to be able to protect herself. Finally, as a woman who for a number of years shared her life and ill fortunes with another woman (known in the *Narrative* only as

"Mrs. Brown") she needed a way to protect herself and her family — in addition to her wife, she kept her daughter with her throughout her troubles — not only from all of the difficulties already mentioned, but also from the prying eyes of moral authorities, self-appointed and otherwise. Charke makes no effort in the *Narrative* to deny her cross-dressing; instead, she tries to achieve a reconciliation with her father by presenting herself as both misunderstood and repentant. As part of this effort she concocts a small fable, set during the seven-year period when she was wandering the English countryside as a strolling player, which comments explicitly on her sense of the relationship between role-paying and identity.

Charke writes that shortly after she left the city to join one of the strolling companies, she found herself on a ramshackle stage in a town just outside of London. In the audience for this unnamed production is "an orphan Heiress" (106) who proceeds to fall desperately in love with the dashing Mr. Brown. When Mr. Brown learns of this infatuation, he meets with the heiress to apprise her of her error, eventually revealing to her that he is not in fact a man. The wording of this announcement is particularly significant; instead of identifying herself as a woman, an actor, or as Mrs. Charke, she presents herself as "actually the youngest daughter of Mr. Cibber, and not the person she conceived me!" (111). When Charke returns to her company, she continues to emphasize the distance between her current surroundings and what she wishes to present as her essential self:

On my Return Home, the Itinerant-Troop all assembled round me to hear what had passed between the Lady and me — when we were to celebrate the Nuptials? — Besides many other impertinent, stupid Questions; some offering, agreeable to their villainous Dispositions, as the Marriage they supposed would be a Secret, to supply my Place in the Dark to conceal the Fraud: upon which I looked at them sternly and, with the Contempt they deserved, demanded to know what Action of my Life had been so very monstrous, to excite them to think me capable of one so cruel and infamous? (112–13)

Then, for good measure, she also reveals her true identity to the townspeople in general — thereby insuring, she hopes, that "in Case [the heiress's mistake] was spoke of, it might be regarded as an Impossibility" (113).

Like much else contained in the *Narrative*, this episode can be neither verified nor disproven, but even if something very like this took place, the basic situation would still almost certainly have been recognized as a convention of transvestite biographies.[33] It seems to me, however, that Charke's account of this particular incident is designed not to connect, but rather to distance herself — not only from that tradition, but also from the previous incarnations of herself that separated her from her father. Charlotte was the only one of Cibber's children who was born after he had made his fortune, and the first installment of the *Narrative* concludes with her blaming herself for falling in love with Richard Charke against her father's wishes (50). She also presented herself as a swashbuckling male figure on more than one occasion, and the fact that her desperate circumstances had forced her to go strolling was well known. These details suggest that the episode should be treated as a kind of private myth about fragmentation and recuperation; the foolish but tenderhearted heiress (Charlotte Cibber) falls in love with the dashing actor (Charles Brown) who does the honorable thing by abandoning both his persona and the loot and by rejecting his disreputable companions (Charlotte Charke) as well. Finally, of course, the whole incident is organized around her hope of being reincarnated as Charlotte, the youngest daughter of Mr. Cibber.

Taken as a whole, the heiress anecdote sends a curiously mixed message. On the one hand the story seems to celebrate once again her ability to create and sustain the image of masculinity; on the other hand the position occupied by "Mr. Cibber's youngest daughter" suggests that Charke wanted to believe that family ties could be used to establish an identity that somehow transcended all this role-playing. At the same time, however, the passage begs the question of whether the situation can in fact be defused. Charke presents the father-daughter relation as an absolute, but Cibber's decision to disown her had already demonstrated that this, too, could be considered performative rather than essential; and if that were true, what could possibly make the identity defined by the phrase "Mr. Cibber's youngest daughter" any more stable than any of the other identities that are presented and discarded in these few pages?

Ultimately, Charke's fable suggests that the morality of any specific impersonation depends not on the degree to which it conforms to a predetermined natural order, but rather on the assumption that both the actor and the spectator understand exactly where the line is being drawn between the onstage and offstage worlds; in a sense she anticipates Butler's discussion of the difference between the transvestite on stage and the transvestite on the bus, with the crucial exception that her formulation is couched in ethical rather than emotional terms. Presented with an ethically dubious and potentially dangerous situation,[34] Charke extricates herself by establishing new boundaries for herself and her audience. No character can stand in for either an actor or a spectator without the consent of both: on the one hand Charke does not have to be Charles Brown unless she chooses to be, and she doesn't have to define herself as a strolling player unless she chooses to do so; on the other hand she needs to be absolved of blame by the heiress and the townspeople, and she cannot be Mr. Cibber's daughter unless he allows her to play that role. The wording of Charke's confession to the heiress is also suggestive in this respect, because it hints at a connection between an "actual" reality and an enacted role, and because the double meaning of the verb *conceived* can be construed as an allusion to the role played by an audience in creating and authorizing a particular identity.

I suggested in my introduction that actors were neither free agents nor puppets, but at that point I had established neither my interest in the consequences of performances nor the analogy between performers and individuals seeking authorization from the world at large. We can now develop the original point by suggesting that actors (and individuals) maintain their tenuous grasp on freedom only to the extent that they succeed in shaping and obtaining the authorizations they seek. Further, I would argue that, if and when they fail, they may find themselves constrained by circumstances to serve as characters in a script authored by someone else. This is not to suggest that either performers or individuals do in fact become those characters; one of the defining characteristics of performance is the material presence of human beings who are clearly not who they pretend to be, and each individual's identity is always more than a simple conglomeration of the roles s/he is playing at a particular moment (see Wilshire, 226–27). Performers and individuals can be distinguished in this respect from fictional characters, and even from textual constructs of real people; to put it another way, there is no engulfment quite so complete as that of being absorbed into someone else's narrative.

With regard to Mother Lupine, Mrs. Otter, and Mr. Hen, our sense of how each character means must take into account the disjunction between the material presence of Charlotte Charke's female body and the character and behavior she enacted. However, when the Stage Licensing

Act and her family situation conspired to deny her any further access to the London stage, Charke found herself unable to insist on that presence, that prior claim of shared humanity. On the printed page the body becomes just another verbal construct; its undeniable significance onstage is easily engulfed by various units of symbolic discourse, including those that seek explicitly to devalue the physical aspect of human experience. When Charke was forced into the world of texts, her material presence was supplanted by the figure of her displeased father; it was her relation to Colley Cibber, not her enactments and critique of eighteenth-century masculinity, that in retrospect defined her time with the Great Mogul's company, and it was the prospect of reconciliation with him that shaped or mis-shaped much of the *Narrative*.[35]

To finish this thought, we might look at how Mother Lupine fared in her transition from the London stage to the pages of the eighteenth-century realistic novel. Much of the plot of Richardson's *Clarissa* is taken directly from *Caelia*; in the novel, Mother Lupine becomes Mrs. Sinclair, and the animus generated against her on stage is worked out in the novel as one of the most lurid and overheated death scenes anywhere in English literature.[36] I suggested earlier that Charke as Mother Lupine might have sought to implicate her audience in the exploitation of Johnson's innocent heroine. The Drury Lane audience refused to tolerate this implication, but they could not deny the material presence of the character; their only alternative was to stop the performance itself. During the sixteen years between the premiere of *Caelia* and the publication of *Clarissa*, the London stage had become increasingly respectable — that, in fact, was the stated goal of David Garrick, whose star rose so rapidly during the 1740s — and on that basis had become thoroughly inhospitable to the kind of gender-bending tricks that had been the stock in trade of the Great Mogul's company. Richardson's treatment of the Mother Lupine character type suggests that in the eyes of her eighteenth-century audience her engulfment could not be accomplished until her physical presence had been not merely shouted down, but rather completely expunged. And if that is indeed the case, the novelist's gleefully pornographic account of Mrs. Sinclair's inarticulate howls and her physical deterioration might be best understood as the achievement of this long-deferred goal — that is, as a kind of ritual execution in prose, the justification for which had been shaped and reinforced over the previous two decades by the same social and institutional processes that had driven Charlotte Charke from the London stage and placed her, like her literary descendant, on the wrong side of the spectator's controlling gaze.

NOTES

For their assistance and encouragement throughout the process of writing this essay, I would like to express my gratitude to Rick Barr, Peter Burgard, Pat Gill, Leslie Gossage, and Sylvia Schmitz-Burgard.

1. See, for example, Sidonie Smith's chapter-length discussion in *A Poetics of Women's Autobiography: Marginality and the Fictions of Self-Representation* (Bloomington: Indiana University Press, 1987), 102–22, and Patricia Meyer Spacks's brief but valuable commentary in *Imagining a Self* (Cambridge: Harvard University Press, 1976), 75–77. Felicity Nussbaum's "Heteroclites: The Gender of Character in the Scandalous Memoirs," in *The New Eighteenth Century*, ed. Laura Brown and Felicity Nussbaum (New York: Methuen, 1987), 144–67, helps to place Charke's autobiography in its generic context. The most recent biographical study of Charke is Fidelis Morgan's *The Well-Known Troublemaker: A Life of Charlotte Charke* (London: Faber and Faber, 1988); Morgan reproduces Charke's *Narrative* side by side with the author's attempts to document the details of her account. For an opinionated summary of many earlier references to and comments on Charke, see Morgan, *The Well-Known Troublemaker*, 205–12; see also her bibliography, 218–19. Kristina Straub's *Sexual Suspects: Eighteenth-Century Players and Sexual Ideology* (Princeton: Princeton University Press, 1992), which was published after the initial work on this essay was completed, represents a significant exception to the generalization in my text; although her study focuses exclusively on Charke's print narratives, she does read Charke's efforts at self-fashioning and her depictions of homosexual characters in her novels in terms of their respective relationships to various eighteenth-century examinations of theatrical cross-dressing. Subsequent references to these works will appear in the text.
2. Elin Diamond, "Brechtian Theory/Feminist Theory: Toward a Gestic Feminist Criticism," *Drama Review* 32, no. 1 (Spring 1988): 82–94. Subsequent references to this essay will appear in the text.
3. Bruce Wilshire, *Role Playing and Identity* (Bloomington: Indiana University Press, 1982). Subsequent references will appear in the text.
4. Wilshire's assertions seem to imply that Brecht's notion of the Verfremdungseffekt — a crucial element of the gestus (see Diamond, "Brechtian Theory," 84–85) — is wrongheaded in some sense, but in fact this contradiction is more apparent than real. Despite Brecht's assertions to the contrary, there is no logical reason why the spectator's identification with a character should cease

merely because the mechanisms employed to construct that character are brought into the open (see also Wilshire, *Role Playing*, 14, 14n).
5. Although many critics and biographers have taken these statements as fact, Morgan notes that no records of the Cibber family for this period have survived (*The Well-Known Troublemaker*, 27).
6. In its entry on Charlotte Charke, the *Biographical Dictionary of Actors, Actresses, Musicians, Dancers, Managers, and Other Stage Personnel in London, 1660–1800* (Carbondale: Southern Illinois University Press, 1975–) claims erroneously that she played Mustacha in Fielding's *Tom Thumb* on May 1, 1730 (III:167). However, an examination of the primary sources by William Burling and Robert Hume ("Theatrical Companies at the Little Haymarket, 1720–1737," *Essays in Theatre* 4 (1986): 98–118) has since confirmed the earlier attribution of this part to a Mrs. Clark or Clarke (115 n. 43).
7. With the exception of court masques and other private entertainments, English women had not been allowed on English stages before the Restoration; this is perhaps the primary reason why the voyeuristic elements of the theatrical experience were especially prominent during the late seventeenth and early eighteenth centuries. Many seventeenth- and early-eighteenth-century playwrights took pains to provide their audiences with female characters in men's clothes; in *All the King's Ladies: Actresses of the Restoration* (Chicago: University of Chicago Press, 1958), John Harold Wilson has estimated that nearly a quarter of the plays first performed between 1660 and 1700 provided occasions for actresses to dress up in this fashion (73). It is possible that Charke wished to perform in breeches from the very beginning and that her status as a novice performer prevented her from getting the roles she wanted during those early years, but there is nothing in either her *Narrative* or the public record that would support this claim.
8. Charles Johnson, *Caelia, or the Perjured Lover* (London, 1733). Subsequent references will appear in the text; since this edition does not include page numbers, those references will indicate the location of the passage by act number only.
9. She had married Richard Charke two months after her seventeenth birthday, and he had abandoned her less than a year later. A musician employed by the Drury Lane company, he had been introduced to Charlotte Cibber by Theophilus when she was only sixteen; he apparently married her only because he thought she would help him gain the approval and assistance of the influential Colley Cibber. The failure of the marriage forced her to appeal frequently to her father and her brother for help, with predictably disappointing results.
10. Charlotte Charke, *A Narrative of the Life of Mrs. Charlotte Charke*, ed. Leonard R. N. Ashley (Gainesville: University of Florida Press, 1969), 53. Subsequent references will be to this edition and will appear in the text. The work was originally published in London in 1755.
11. See Katharine Eisamann Maus, "'Playhouse Flesh and Blood': Sexual Ideology and the Restoration Actress," *ELH* 46 (1979): 595–617, and Joseph

Roach, "Power's Body: The Inscription of Morality as Style," in *Interpreting the Theatrical Past: Essays in the Historiography of Performance*, ed. Bruce McConachie and Thomas Postlewait (Iowa City: University of Iowa Press, 1989), 99–118. Subsequent references to these works will appear in the text. Although Maus has argued that "Restoration theater . . . provided, at least for the leading players, manifold opportunities for self-expression" ("Playhouse," 599), it would be unwise to apply this generalization either to Charke or to secondary roles like that of Mrs. Otter. Charlotte Charke was not a Restoration but an eighteenth-century actor; in his essay Roach noted the astonishing proliferation of what he calls " 'how-to' manuals on the mastery of bodily expression" during the period in which she lived and worked ("Power's Body," 100). To obtain an impression of exactly how prescriptive and restrictive these manuals could be – how much they might do to forestall any attempt on the part of the performer to express him- or herself – see Roach, "Power's Body," 109–15.

12. There is no way to tell whether the increasing number of breeches roles reflected a conscious choice on Charke's part; it is at least possible that she stumbled onto this specialty accidentally, because the actors who had performed these roles for the Drury Lane company in the early 1730s (Theodosia Mills, Sarah Thurmond, and Elizabeth Wetherilt) had died or moved on to other venues before the actors' revolt.

13. In *The Tender Husband* Lucy Fainlove disguises herself as a man in order to assist one of the male leads with the project of reforming his wife; at the end of the play, she is married off to a country bumpkin. In *Oroonoko* Charlotte Weldon marries a wealthy widow for her money and allows a male accomplice to take her place on the wedding night, but she eventually resumes her female identity and marries her accomplice's older brother; in *The Recruiting Officer* Silvia disguises herself as a man so that she can join Captain Plume in his recruiting escapades and persuade him to love her in her apparent absence.

14. See Robert E. Knoll, *Ben Jonson's Plays: An Introduction* (Lincoln: University of Nebraska Press, 1964), 110–11.

15. Ben Jonson, *Epicoene, or the Silent Woman*, ed. L. A. Beaurline (Lincoln: University of Nebraska Press, 1966), V.iv.182ff.

16. For a discussion of some related issues, see Phyllis Rackin, "Androgyny, Mimesis, and the Marriage of the Boy Heroine on the English Renaissance Stage," *PMLA* 102, no. 1 (1987): 29–41, and Herbert Blau, *The Audience* (Baltimore: Johns Hopkins University Press, 1990), 215–17. Although Rackin makes a persuasive case for the claim that the thematic argument of *Epicoene* is fundamentally misogynist ("Androgyny," 33, 36–37), I would still argue that the oddly aggressive ending of the play subverts the argument of the text to some degree. Blau speculates that Jonson's eventual decision to abandon the public theater for more easily controlled contexts reflected his awareness that stage mechanisms like these tended to undermine the hierarchies he sought to establish in his scripts.

17. This passage is quoted in a variety of texts, including Maus, "Playhouse," 598, and Wilson, *All the King's Ladies*, 4.
18. Lesley Ferris, *Acting Women: Images of Women in Theatre* (New York: New York University Press, 1989), 70.
19. See Robert Gale Noyes, *Ben Jonson on the English Stage, 1660–1776* (New York: Benjamin Blom, 1935), 177.
20. Judith Milhous, *Thomas Betterton and the Management of Lincoln's Inn Fields, 1695–1707* (Carbondale: Southern Illinois University Press, 1979), 93.
21. See Arthur H. Scouten, ed., *The London Stage: 1660–1800*, pt. 3 (Carbondale: Southern Illinois University Press, 1961), I.321.
22. For an extended discussion of this point insofar as it pertains to female performers of this period, see Ferris, *Acting Women*, 72–74.
23. Judging from the tone and content of the puffs and other publicity Charke provided for her summer season at the Haymarket in 1734 (see Morgan, *The Well-Known Troublemaker*, 54–58), the roles she had played with the Drury Lane rebels during the 1733–1734 season had earned her a reputation for eccentric tastes and behavior. There is, however, no way to determine whether this image reflected her offstage behavior at this point in her life, primarily because the *Narrative* is (uncharacteristically) silent on the subject. In any case, I do not believe that her willingness to capitalize on this reputation necessarily indicates that she accepted the characterization.
24. Judith Butler, "Performative Acts and Gender Construction," in *Performing Feminisms: Feminist Critical Theory and Theatre*, ed. Sue-Ellen Case (Baltimore: Johns Hopkins University Press, 1990), 278.
25. For a detailed analysis of Mr. Hen, see Jill Campbell, "'When Men Women Turn': Gender Reversals in Fielding's Plays," in *The New Eighteenth Century*, ed. Brown and Nussbaum, 66–67, 74–77.
26. Before she joined Fielding, Charke had imitated her father only once, on June 19, 1735, when she had played Lord Foppington in Cibber's *The Careless Husband*; certain circumstances connected with that performance suggest that she was angry with her father at that point, but either the difference was patched up quickly or Cibber himself was angry enough to insist that Charke give up the role immediately. Since both Charke and Fielding had good reasons to be displeased with Cibber, it is impossible to determine whether he sought her out in order to exploit her private conflicts for his own purposes, or whether she was drawn to the Great Mogul's company by the prospect of striking back at her father for his years of neglect. Since Charke was definitely a cut above the other actors in the company, it is also just barely possible that both she and Fielding looked on the change merely as a matter of professional advancement – a way to get her better roles and to improve the level of acting in his plays. For further discussion of this point see Robert Hume, *Henry Fielding and the London Theatre, 1728–1737* (Oxford: Clarendon Press, 1988), 207–8.
27. According to the *Narrative*, Colley Cibber summoned his daughter to a family meeting that quickly degenerated into a shouting match; the confer-

ence ended with the old actor's announcement that he was cutting her off completely (124–25). A letter from Cibber to Charke that is now generally believed to deal with her connection with Fielding tells her in so many words that she will receive nothing from her father as long as she refuses to "dissociate [her]self from that worthless scoundrel" (quoted in Morgan, *The Well-Known Troublemaker*, 87).

28. *Sawney and Colley*, ed. W. Powell Jones (Los Angeles: Clark Memorial Library, 1960), 4, 4n. (originally published in London in 1742).
29. This passage is quoted in Martin Battestin, *Henry Fielding: A Life* (London: Routledge, 1990), 219.
30. Fielding's cast includes a playwright named Ground-Ivy, who satirizes Cibber's revision of Shakespeare; a blustering actor named Pistol, who obviously caricatures Theophilus; and a playwright named Medley who presents an imitation of Colley Cibber's poetry. This last is written ostensibly as a prologue for his new production (*The Historical Register* is a rehearsal play) and delivered in full before the play is five minutes old. All three roles were played by men.
31. Marjorie Garber, *Vested Interests: Cross-Dressing and Cultural Anxiety* (New York: Routledge, 1992), 68–69. Subsequent references will appear in the text.
32. In *Sex and Gender: On the Development of Masculinity and Femininity* (New York: Science House, 1968), Robert Stoller notes that there is no adequate psychoanalytical explanation for female transvestism (194–205); Garber points out quite rightly that this silence probably says more about psychoanalysts and sex researchers than it does about women who cross-dress (*Vested Interests*, 44–45, 94–99). Historically, some "female soldiers" dressed up in order to be near their (male) lovers, while others were apparently male-identified individuals who sought to emulate the swashbuckling rakes who served as role models for numbers of men throughout this period. Nor should it be assumed that the motive for female cross-dressing was always predominantly a matter of sexual identity and appetite. Even if such information were available, it would have to be weighed in each case against the possibility that a decision to adopt a male identity was based on material considerations rather than sexual preferences; impersonating a man would invariably grant the woman involved higher wages, greater mobility, and a degree of immunity from certain kinds of persecution. For further discussion see Kathleen Crawford, *The Transvestite Heroine in Seventeenth-Century Popular Literature* (Ph.D. diss., Harvard University, 1984); Lillian Faderman, *Surpassing the Love of Men: Romantic Friendship and Love between Women from the Renaissance to the Present* (New York: William Morrow, 1981); and Lynn Friedli, "Passing Women," in *Sexual Underworlds of the Enlightenment*, ed. Roy Porter and G. S. Rousseau (Chapel Hill: University of North Carolina Press, 1988), 234–60.

I am firmly convinced that Charlotte Charke was (in modern terms) either lesbian or bisexual, but that is neither a sufficient nor even a necessary condition for predicting her transvestism; a full explanation would have to

consider not only her sexual preferences and the historical context, but also her professional history, her financial troubles, and the abuse she suffered at the hands of virtually every man she was close to.
33. Morgan could not find any trace of the incident Charke describes, and it is at least conceivable that she had heard a story very similar to this one told about Mlle. de Maupin, the seventeenth-century French performer whose transvestism, like Charke's, was not limited to the stage. Mlle. de Maupin actually eloped with a girl and was later arrested and briefly imprisoned under a sixteenth-century antisodomy law (see Faderman, *Surpassing the Love of Men*, 57).
34. Faderman has identified several female transvestites who were arrested, tried, and punished during this period for marrying or plotting to marry other women; the most famous English case was that of Mary Hamilton, whose trial prompted the publication of Fielding's *The Female Husband* in 1746. The time scheme of Charke's *Narrative* is very vague, but it is possible that the placement of the orphan heiress episode was inspired by the well-publicized Hamilton case.
35. In the early part of the *Narrative*, Charke presents herself as a four-year-old who cross-dresses in her father's wig and brother's waistcoat; the episode is presented as comic, the result of an innocent child's wish to emulate her famous father (17–18). As Straub argues, this episode loses some of its innocence in the context of the autobiography, because it seems to ridicule Cibber by reminding Charke's readers that her father's trademark periwig could be read as a signal that his masculinity was somehow suspect (*Sexual Suspects*, 139–40). At the same time, Charke's willingness to introduce the phenomenon of cross-dressing to her audience as the misguided escapade of a small child can be viewed as a different version of the normalizing tendency reflected in the accounts that described her behavior as an attempt to embarrass her father. Charke's pursuit of this trope is only temporary; when she finally concludes, midway through the *Narrative*, that Cibber will not in fact respond to her overtures, the accounts of her adventures in men's clothes become more obtrusive and more obviously aggressive — as, for example, when she recounts the story that she had, while disguised as a (male) fishmonger, come upon her father in the streets of London and slapped his face with a flounder (115–16).
36. Samuel Richardson, *Clarissa*, ed. Angus Ross (New York: Penguin, 1985), 1387–93.

TWO

Posing *Orlando*

Talia Schaffer

I feel like one of those wax figures in a shop window, on which you have hung a robe stitched with jewels.... Darling, I don't know and scarcely even like to write it, so overwhelmed am I, how you could have hung so splendid a garment on so poor a peg.
— Vita Sackville-West, *The Letters of Virginia Woolf: Volume III, 1923–1928*

To most of these [female] writers that fundamental sexual self for which, say, Yeats uses nakedness is itself merely another costume.... For the male modernist, in other words, gender is most often an ultimate reality, while for the female modernist an ultimate reality exists only if one journeys beyond gender.
— Sandra M. Gilbert, "Costumes of the Mind: Transvestism as Metaphor in Modern Literature"

CRITICAL HISTORY

Woolf's *Orlando* is a biographical account, including documentary photographs, of a gender-changing four-hundred-year-old character. This combination is so strange that most critical strategies attempt to assimilate it to more conventional narrative forms, reading it either in realist terms (a biography of Vita Sackville-West) or in postmodernist terms (an anarchic Shandean antinovel). The novel's photographs, however, which have been almost universally ignored, demand another reading. *Orlando* shows that the categories by which we locate ourselves (gender, identity, history, language) are perpetual performances, proliferating self-reproductions. The photographs provide a counterdiscourse to the novel's text. They superimpose a personal history upon the fictional biography by introducing private jokes that only Woolf, Vita Sackville-West, or Vanessa Bell might find legible and that often contradict the narrative in strategic ways. When Orlando's photographs allude to famous artists like Sir Peter Lely and Julia Margaret Cameron, the effect is not to exalt Orlando but to reduce the artists' work to a series of mere mannerisms that can be facilely invoked, repeatedly reproduced, affectionately parodied, made into an easily recognizable cultural cliché. The act of imitation does important ideological work, for it constructs the present as an endless performance of a past that it constructs as essentially empty of meaning. The present, in other words, reiterates a past that is nothing more than a collection of stylistic quirks, and that past in turn reveals itself to be a performance of some previous style no more solid than itself. Judith Butler's term for this series of performances is *masquerade*, and her *Gender Trouble* will help guide us through the mazes of Woolf's great costume party. *Orlando*'s photographs constantly show their subjects masquerading as someone else, for the living sitter must pretend to be a fictional character, and the photographed character must look synonymous with the novel's character. The performance never works. (For instance, when Sackville-West poses as "Orlando as Ambassador," not only does the female sitter clash with the male character, but the photograph also contradicts Orlando's ambassadorial persona as described in the novel.) These strategic mistakes keep unsettling the truth of identity for the reader of *Orlando*. In *Orlando* identity is a transparently artificial pose. The gender-changing antics of *Orlando* allow Woolf to explore the rather different ways in which men and women perform their genders. In fact the model of male performance implicit in *Orlando*'s illustrations covertly challenges Butler's methodology and revises Butler's ideas. What is finally so important about the novel's eight photographs is the fact that they form a strange narrative themselves, constituting a countertext that contradicts, refines, supports, and satirizes the written text's assertions. If a narrative is intended to show the consistent development of a character through time, then the photographs are antinarratives: inconsistent, contradictory, stuck in a particular moment of time. The photographs thus wage a peculiarly modernist attack on the novel form — yet, as we have already seen, they also provide a peculiarly traditional biographical guarantee. No reading of *Orlando* can be viable unless it interprets the illustrations, for *Orlando* gets its meaning from precisely the conflicted, complex relation between image and narrative.

Biography, novel, or antinovel? The photographs support all three. The biographical school of *Orlando* criticism matches the novel's characters with their real counterparts. The novel's several photographs of Vita Sackville-West prove that Woolf carried out her biographical intention: "But listen: suppose Orlando turns out to be Vita; and it's all about you and the lusts of your flesh and the lure of your mind."[1] Orlando's house is based on Knole, the Sackvilles' ancestral home. Orlando's history comes from Vita's volume, *Knole and the Sackvilles*.[2] This biographical approach also provides us with a feminist reading of *Orlando:* we can see it as the courageous publication of a lesbian love story in juxtaposition to the contemporary *Well of Loneliness*. By "proving" that Orlando is Vita, the photographs let us agree that *Orlando* is "the longest and most charming love letter in literature."[3] However, trust in biography will undo us. "Do you think any history is even faintly true?"[4] Woolf asked. For Woolf found that writing *Orlando* made her doubt truth, personality, and history. As she told one correspondent, "I'm so glad you like *Orlando* in spite of its being so untrue. However I agree with you that truth is not very important in that particular book."[5] Fictionalizing Sackville-West as Orlando made her realize that her model might have been fictional all along. In a letter to Sackville-West Woolf wrote, "I've lived in you all these months — coming out, what are you really like? Do you exist? Have I made you up?"[6] (Sackville-West was "absolutely terrified" by this question. She responded, rather strangely, "I *won't* be fictitious.... So write quickly and say I'm still real.")[7] How did Woolf "come out"? Was Woolf coming out of Sackville-West like a child emerging from its mother? Did she mean that Sackville-West was entering the world in the form of a character, Orlando? Or did "coming out" have yet another meaning, one that would well account for Sackville-West's "terror": the problem of lesbian self-revelation and (quite literally) self-publication, which frames with startling clarity the questions of real, fictitious, masquerading, and original selves?

Significantly, biographical critiques of *Orlando* often end up replicating Woolf's uneasy shift from biographical intention to doubts about the possibility of biography itself.[8] Elizabeth Cooley asserts, "In *Orlando* she succeeded by dressing her biographical portraiture in the vestiges of fiction."[9] The emphasis on dress and portraits is significant as a metaphor for the novel, which remarks that "clothes ... change our view of the world and the world's view of us."[10] Similarly, Suzanne Raitt's sophisticated reading of *Orlando* comments, "*Orlando* unmasks Sackville-West, despite its high-spirited masquerade; it overcomes her, taking over the telling of her story and allowing her no quarter."[11] Woolf refigures "biographical portraiture" precisely by disguising it in fictional clothes, or stripping the clothes away – and this vestimental metaphor is not coincidental but necessary to understanding *Orlando*'s project.

This view of *Orlando* as a textual rebellion, an antinovel, agrees with several contemporary poststructuralist readings of the novel. Orlando's sex change destabilizes the idea that anyone has a "real" gender identity, while Orlando's comic difficulties with femininity puncture the notion of "natural" gender roles.[12] Rather, gender becomes an endlessly shifting intersection of sartorial signs that have no relation to any genital referent. As Nancy Armstrong says, "her radically fanciful biography of Orlando can be considered a history of gender differences and of the forms of subjectivity these differences engender, as well as a history of fashion."[13] Orlando's speech and life constitute "a history of the various transformations required to keep the truth of his or her desire concealed."[14] As a consequence of this constant disguise, Orlando's character becomes the compilation of sloughed selves, rather than a natural original being.[15] Neither identity nor language can be fixed; there is no reference to anything outside language; and *Orlando* does not present a vision of history's essential truth but "a play of forms ... a bistable vision, not a univocal theory."[16] This approach is succinctly summarized in Mary Jacobus's influential reading, which maps the convergence of gender and writing in *Orlando*. She argues that "though she lightheartedly takes issue with essentialist notions of gender ... Woolf's underlying concern is with questions of writing."[17] Jacobus shows that the narrator's soliloquies about writing biography mirror the precisely contemporary biographical events in her subject's life. "Orlando and her biographer, in other words, create each other by mutual substitution; the masquerade – Orlando's transvestite progress through the literary ages – is that of writing, where fictive and multiple selves are the only self, the only truth, the writer knows."[18] We might wonder how *mutual substitution* relates to masquerade; are the terms themselves substitutable? I would argue that they are neither synonymous nor substitutable. Like *transvestite*, masquerade implies successive layers, hiding an original self. Substitution means a clean exchange, rather than an economy of disguising and self-fashioning. In this passage the equivalence of a mutual substitution slips into the more complex dynamic of originary identity projecting itself into an array of disguises that in turn replace that original self. Jacobus locates that layered subjectivity in writing, whereas Armstrong placed it in costume. Could writing and costuming be disguises for each other, however? The sartorial metaphor creeps into Jacobus's text (masquerade, transvestite), in layers of metaphor that argue that substitution can be understood as a masquerade, which is transvestism, which is writing. The sentence itself masquerades; the "original" idea of substitution undergoes a profusion of metaphors that disguise it and displace its original meaning.

The metaphor of costuming significantly recurs in these discussions of *Orlando*'s writing. For it is difficult to argue that "Woolf's underlying concern is with questions of writing" when Woolf's letters show that she imagined the novel as primarily pictorial. In her letters Woolf wrote about the vicissitudes of acquiring *Orlando*'s photographs much more often than she mentioned writing the novel. Indeed, the very letter that first announces the idea of *Orlando* to Sackville-West also contains the apparently unrelated question of whether Woolf should allow Cecil Beaton to photograph her. "And shall I go and be done?" she asks, as if the invitation to "do" Sackville-West in the form of Orlando were somehow offset by the equivalent possibility that Woolf would be "done" by someone else.[19] Four days later, Woolf used the photographs as a way of characterizing the novel and extending her relationship with Sackville-West. "Look here, I must come down and see you, if only to choose some pictures.... *Orlando* will be a little book, with pictures and a map or two."[20] Woolf's letters to Sackville-West are highly self-censored — so invitations to photographs had to substitute for more erotic invitations. A typical example: "Look, dearest, what a lovely page this is, and think how, were it not for the Screen and the [Mary] Campbell, it might all be filled to the brim with lovemaking unbelievable: indiscretions incredible: instead of which, nothing shall be said but what a Campbell behind the screen might hear." The "screen" reveals Campbell, rather than hiding her, for in Woolfian logic disguises exhibit identity rather than concealing it. The photographs provided an excuse for Woolf's and Sackville-West's meetings. "You'll lunch here at *one sharp* on Monday won't you: bringing your curls and clothes."[21] The photographs forced Sackville-West to disguise herself, as the photographs themselves disguised unwritten desires.

Since the invention of the camera, photographs have been imagined as holding a mirror up to nature – quite literally, since the camera aims a mirror at the scene.[22] Thus the photographs seem to bring a real history into the novel form. They assert that Orlando lived in the reader's world rather than in a remote fictional space. They declare that Orlando had a physical body. As Roland Barthes says, "Photography's inimitable feature ... is that someone has seen the referent ... *in flesh and blood*, or again *in person.*"[23] A photograph can be an interpretation but never a fiction. The ordinary viewer of a photograph believes that photography "does not invent; it is authentication itself."[24] Susan Sontag agrees that "a photograph passes for incontrovertible proof that a given thing happened" and even goes so far as to argue that "photographed images do not seem to be statements about the world so much as pieces of it, miniatures of reality."[25] Thus the photographs uncomfortably conflate the fictional with the biographical and question the opposition between truth and fantasy. Even more problematically, however, *Orlando*'s images are nothing like "miniatures of reality." They actually indulge in artifice, satire, masquerade, and self-contradiction. We expect this sort of behavior from textuality, not photography.

Orlando's photographs record successive layers of masquerade. They show figures in costume. The presence of these photographs explains why sartorial metaphors leak into both biographical and poststructuralist accounts – and an analysis of the photographs may enable us to combine Jacobus's and Cooley's critiques by starting from the one metaphor they share, the image of the disguise.

THE MASQUERADE

Woolf's letters show how *Orlando*'s photographs conceal, enact, and document an ongoing masquerade – leading us to inquire how far we can extrapolate the masquerade and whether masquerade might be the logic of photography itself. The idea of a real, hidden self is a phantasm that the masquerade actually constructs, for the layers of disguise produce the desire for a "real identity" on the part of the bewildered reader. One example, "Sasha," will show how masquerade logic produces yet conceals a real identity. The character is a mysterious, androgynous figure marked by doubleness, as she is a Russian living in England, speaking French. "English was too frank, too candid, too honeyed a speech for Sasha. For in all she said, however open she seemed and voluptuous, there was something hidden; in all she did, however daring, there was something concealed" (47). Sasha's gender, nationality, motivations, and history all remain ambiguous. Instead of fixing Sasha's appearance, her photograph adds new layers of mystery. "The Russian Princess as a Child" makes the reader wonder. Why photograph her as a child, when she appears in the story as a grown woman? Why was the photograph apparently taken in summer, when the facing page has Sasha describing "winter in Russia" (54)? Why is Sasha, whose trademark costume is form-fitting fur, photographed in loose draperies (fig. 2.1)?

The history of the photograph shows how complicated the construction of a figure who is all masquerade might be. Woolf needed a photographic subject to resemble a mysterious character who was a portrait of a living woman (Violet Trefusis, Sackville-West's first female lover, is Sasha's biographical correlative). She asked Sackville-West if one of her current lovers would — to use again that ambiguous word — "do." "D'you think Valerie Taylor would do for the Russian Princess, if disguised?"[26] However, Woolf finally asked her sister Vanessa to photograph Vanessa's daughter Angelica. Indeed, this picture encodes a private family joke. Angelica writes, "As a child my favorite vice was dressing up."[27] *Vanessa Bell's Family Album* records a history of Vanessa photographing Angelica's elaborate disguises. Angelica's devotion to the masquerade makes it almost impossible to know what she really looked like as an adolescent, since each photograph of her shows her posing in costume.[28] In this case she managed to perform an almost excessively pouting sensuality for her mother's camera. The resulting images sparked an enthusiastic letter from Woolf to Vanessa: "The photographs are most lovely ... a trifle young, thats all, but I'm showing them to Vita, who doesn't want to be accused of raping the under age. My God — I shall rape Angelica one of these days."[29] Angelica performs sensuality for her mother and her aunt, thus impersonating the lesbian object of desire, an image whose arousing potential is both evoked and punctured by the letter's bravado. The presence of Angelica's photograph is itself a trace of Woolf's desire for violent control of Angelica's body. According to Sontag, "the act of taking pictures is a semblance of appropriation, a semblance of rape."[30] Her performance also gives Woolf a way to "come out" yet again to her sister. To alleviate Sackville-West's concerns, Woolf captioned the photograph "The Russian Princess as a Child." This image is remarkably complex: a "disguised" Valerie Taylor is replaced by Angelica Bell, who masquerades

Fig. 2.1 The Russian Princess as a Child

as Sasha, who is really a disguise for Violet Trefusis. Ironically, Woolf thanked Angelica in her preface "for a service which none but she could have rendered," as if Angelica were the only possible model for Sasha (viii–ix). But each element of the masquerade is "wrong." Valerie Taylor is absent. Angelica is too young. Her costume and climate do not match the character's. The character herself obfuscates rather than clarifies her original.

"The Russian Princess as a Child," which is the novel's only photograph of a female lover, is produced as a series of deliberate mistakes, misstatements, and misrepresentations. Between the historical reality of Violet Trefusis, the textual reality of Sasha, and the photographic reality of Angelica, impossible gaps intervene. Thus "The Russian Princess as a Child" exemplifies Judith Butler's claim that gender identity is produced through repetitions (which can fail strategically in order to produce new identities):

> The abiding gendered self will then be shown to be structured by repeated acts that seek to approximate the ideal of a substantial ground of identity, but which, in their occasional *dis*continuity, reveal the temporal and contingent groundlessness of this "ground." The possibilities of gender transformation are to be found precisely in the arbitrary relation between such acts, in the possibility of a failure to repeat, a de-formity, or a parodic repetition that exposes the phantasmatic effect of abiding identity as a politically tenuous construction.[31]

We can find no original identity when Woolf has a prepubescent niece impersonate a seductive Russian princess who in turn poses "as a child" and whose textual self disguises a real lover's self. Yet the character of Sasha is precisely produced by the combination of these various poses.

JUDITH BUTLER: GENDER TROUBLE IN *ORLANDO*

In many ways, *Orlando* seems like a case study designed for *Gender Trouble*. Butler uses the linguistic concept of the *performative* — a term that enacts what it expresses, like "I bet" or the marital "I do."[32] She argues that maleness and femaleness are performatives because our gestures both describe and enact our gender. We institute "femaleness" by behaving in a way we consider to be "female." "Gender is an identity tenuously constituted in time, instituted in an exterior space through a stylized repetition of acts."[33] For Butler, there is no original access to the natural body, but only encounters with an already mediated discursive construct.

Drag performances are pleasureable precisely because they reveal normative gender construction: "*In imitating gender, drag implicitly reveals the imitative status of gender itself — as well as its contingency.* Indeed, part of the pleasure, the giddiness of the performance is in the recognition of . . . sex and gender denaturalized by means of a performance which avows their distinctness and dramatizes the cultural mechanism of their fabricated unity."[34]

The theory of gender performativity also opens up the possibility of political action to alter gender identities. We can destabilize gender identity by performing it to excess — by parodying it, just as Angelica's pose parodies the sultry glare of the practiced siren. "Practices of parody can serve to reengage and reconsolidate the very distinction between a privileged and naturalized gender configuration and one that appears as derived, phantasmatic, and mimetic — a failed copy, as it were."[35] By overperforming, in other words, Angelica exposes the "siren" as an unnatural, learned behavior. Woolf's letter to Vanessa registers her uneasiness at Angelica's parody by producing her own parody, the excessive arousal that exaggerates a heterosexual male's "natural" response to the siren's photograph. This sophisticated game reveals the whole dynamic of female seductivity and male enthrallment as a set of acquired mannerisms, which can be enacted by a young girl and her aunt.

Judith Butler never differentiates male performance from female performance, because she argues that biological sex is already shaped by language. The two categories of male and female have no primary validity.[36] Problematically, however, her methodology relies solely on female gender although her philosophy tries to rethink gender difference for both males and females. Discussions of female gendering often slide into analyses of gender itself. For instance, when she quotes Simone de Beauvoir's dictum, "One is not born a woman, but rather *becomes* one," she almost immediately paraphrases it: "No one is born with a gender — gender is always acquired."[37] Butler's exciting work on the sexual ideologies implicit in language has some shaky moments as a result of her elision of gender difference. For instance, she asks: "What circumscribes that site as 'the female body'? Is 'the body' or 'the sexed body' the firm foundation on which gender and systems of compulsory sexuality operate? Or is 'the body' itself shaped by political forces with strategic interests in keeping that body bounded and constituted by the markers of sex?"[38] One might further inquire what presuppositions guide an argument that can make "the female body" synonymous with "the body." By ignoring male gender, Butler risks reifying gender difference, for she makes female gender performative while leaving herself open to the accusation that she views male gender as natural.[39]

Butler offers another explanation for her emphasis on gender rather than genders when she argues that one should not "identify the feminine through a strategy of differentiation or exclusion from the masculine. Such a strategy consolidates hierarchy and binarisms through a transvaluation of values by which women now represent the domain of positive value."[40] But if Butler had shown how masculine difference informs performativity, she could have analyzed both genders within the context of performance, whose iterability and parodic function deny "value." Instead, she offers an explanation of femininity that only reinforces the binary opposition between femininity and masculinity by implying that the two genders are so different that she can only discuss one of them.

Moreover, Butler's refusal to discuss maleness and femaleness limits her discussion of drag, an important consideration for its applicability to *Orlando*'s transvestite dramas. Drag usually means a male performing a female, whereas masquerade usually means a male disguised as another sort of male (or a female as another female). The pleasure of drag lies partially in seeing a man surrender the supposed "natural" of the male body.[41] According to drag, femaleness lies in costume — cosmetics, dresses, wigs — whereas maleness needs no artificial costumes, for a man is known by his minimality. "The natural" signifies maleness: the body devoid of ornamentation, without accessories, shorn of decorative excresences like long hair and nails. Drag layers the female masquerade atop a natural male original body. That original male body is what drag emphasizes, for the viewer constantly looks for signs of maleness, thereby learning that the male body is the underlying reality that manifests its presence through its own irreducible truth. Thus drag shows *female* gender to be a performance but does not challenge male gender's naturalness at all.

PERFORMING *ORLANDO*

How does *Orlando* perform drag? Butler's theory can help us expand Jacobus's and Cooley's shared insight into *Orlando*'s sartorial economy. The novel is about costuming, precisely because costuming is what gender is all about. Orlando learns to be female because her flowered paduasoy skirt teaches her dependence, chastity, flirtation. The novel's famous meditation on clothing demonstrates exactly how masquerade produces identity. "There is much to support the view that it is clothes that wear us and not we them; we may make them take the mould of arm or breast, but they mould our hearts, our brains, our tongues to their liking" (188). The next passage appears to support an essentialist view of bodily sex but actually undermines it: "Clothes are but a symbol of something hid deep beneath: It was a change in Orlando herself that dictated her choice of a woman's dress and of a woman's sex" (188). Clothes symbolize a prior and deeper identity — but sex and gender are also clothes, selected voluntarily and worn to advertise that deeper identity. This original self is not the bourgeois individual "human" self, but a constitutive confusion of genders. "In every human being a vacillation from one sex to the other takes place, and often it is only the clothes that keep the male or female likeness, while underneath the sex is the very opposite of what it is above. Of the complications and confusions which thus result every one has had experience" (189). Orlando's costume reveals her gender, while her gender determines her costume choice. Yet *Orlando* admits those Butlerian moments of parody, when the apparently clear substitution of dress for gender breaks down and costume no longer matches sex. These are the moments when Orlando, without changing clothes, is suddenly in drag.[42]

In Orlando's unique yet symptomatic androgyny the character sees both masculinity and femininity as performances. The most notable example of the character's bilingualism occurs when Orlando dresses as a man and hires a prostitute. In a black velvet suit Orlando recollects and utilizes the performances of a nobleman: "Orlando swept her hat off to her in the manner of a gallant paying his addresses to a lady of fashion in a public place" (216). Yet, with a strange sense of disappointment, Orlando finds he can only see women's actions as performances too. "Having been so lately a woman herself, she suspected that the girl's timidity and her hesitating answers and the very fumbling with the key in the latch were all put on to gratify her masculinity" (217).

Conscious that gender is a performance, Orlando finds herself exhausted by constantly acting. Thus Woolf appears to retain the concept of an ungendered original body, which Butler rejects. The prostitute drops her performance and acts naturally with Orlando. When Orlando is being courted by the Archduke Harry, "they acted the parts of man and woman for ten minutes with great vigour and then fell into natural discourse" (179). However, these passages really argue that "discourse" is constitutively unnatural and Orlando's ungendered body impossible. Orlando's supposed pregendered "self" is excessively gendered; "it was this mixture in her of man and woman, one being uppermost and then the other," that produced her physical sex alterations (189). The prostitute's "natural manner" consists in telling stories (218–19). The Archduke's supposedly natural discourse is "interspersed with tee-hees and haw-haws of the strangest kind," while it contains alliterative clichés, like "the Pink, the Pearl, the Perfection of her sex" (179). Woolf's novel generates the fantasy of an original speech and body, only to discover that they are fossilized remains of older performances.

THE NATURAL MAN

The novel shows how Orlando and the Archduke perform their female genders, but it seems to imply that maleness works without performance altogether. Only as a woman does Orlando have to adopt an artificial discourse and costume. As a man, Orlando always seems to know what to do – maleness comes "naturally" to her. After costuming herself as a lady Orlando disgustedly whips away her pearls and satin and stands "in her neat black silk knickerbockers of an ordinary nobleman" (186). Maleness is the antidote for performance. It is "ordinary," the original and natural state of being – maleness is the reality beneath the female masquerade. The Archduke's normal male discourse is broken by its unnatural femininity – its giggling "tee-hees." As he expresses his love for Orlando, femininity again interrupts the heterosexual declaration, for tears form in his eyes and run down his cheeks. Orlando "was beginning to be aware that women should be shocked when men display emotion in their presence, and so, shocked she was" (180). His courtship ends because he blushes, weeps, and finally "broke down completely" (183). Women's clothing and gestures, which were once a mere disguise, have now become constitutive parts of the Archduke's identity. These female performances corrupt his masculine declarations with artifice.

Similarly, Orlando's fluent femininity may mask a real masculinity. "The curious of her own sex would argue how, for example, if Orlando was a woman, did she never take more than ten minutes to dress? And were not her clothes chosen rather at random, and sometimes worn rather shabby?" (189). The very efficiency of Orlando's disguise gives him away; women would not don women's clothing so easily.

Orlando's characters get exhausted trying to become women, for maleness is their original, normal, and natural state of being. (Orlando's characterization of Sasha might stand for all women's masquerades: "faithless, mutable, fickle, he called her" [64].) From the beginning Orlando's history, memory, and expectations assume a homosocial male world. In the novel's first sentences Orlando strikes at a male Moor's head handed down to him by his father or grandfather. "Orlando's fathers had ridden in fields of asphodel, and stony fields.... So too would Orlando, he vowed" (13). His attic is hung with a tapestry embroidered with images of male riders. His genealogy is entirely male. "His fathers had been noble since they had been at all. They came out of the northern mists wearing coronets on their heads" (14). The only female figure in Orlando's childhood is his mother, whom he flees to the attic to escape; he is "disturbed" by seeing her from the window. Even the landscape is almost entirely masculine: "that was his father's house; that his uncle's" (18). He revels in his connection to a patriarchal world of hunters, noblemen, and property owners. Nothing made him male; he already is.

Nobody sees his male activities as performances. Queen Elizabeth loves him for his "ignorance," "simplicity," and "innocence," and she finds him completely transparent: "she read him like a page" (which, of course, he is in both senses) (23–25). Being male, he is also completely natural: "he was young; he was boyish; he did but as nature bid him" (28). His affair with Sasha progresses by means of Orlando's increasing self-revelation: "as the days passed, Orlando took less and less care to hide his feelings" (43). In other words, as a perfect nobleman, Orlando's actions correspond precisely with (and reveal) his inner feelings. He becomes truer to his inner self. No costuming mars his masculinity. Though Orlando dons a grey cloak for his surreptitious visits to the London prostitutes, the cloak does not change his identity, as her dresses do later. Rather, his clothing only serves to emphasize the natural body beneath it: "Guessing that something out of the common lay hid beneath his duffle cloak, [the women] were quite as eager to come at the truth of the matter as Orlando himself" (29). At the core of masculinity lies "truth," and costumes conceal but do not change that essentiality.

THE ARTIFICIAL MAN

But *Orlando*'s photographs unsettle the text's guarantees. The pictures of men say what the text does not say; that maleness, far from being the normative universal condition, is produced entirely through artifice. Woolf represents men through photographs of statues or paintings. Even "Marmaduke Bonthrop Shelmerdine," who appears after the historical invention of photography, is represented by a painting. Even the "Archduchess Harriet," who is a man in drag, gets a painting. On the other hand, Woolf represents women through photographs of their living bodies. "The Russian Princess as a Child," who must have been a child in the late 1500s, stares directly from a photograph in a grinning, joyful anachronism. Thus Orlando's original male body, far from being his real identity, becomes the always-already-interpreted aesthetic icon, whose original cannot be found. Meanwhile, her acquired female body, which she feels to be comparatively "unnatural," appears to be the unmediated visual truth of her identity.

For instance, "Orlando as a boy" and "Orlando as Ambassador" show men as costumed aesthetic productions, not "real" individuals. The males' Renaissance costumes, disturbingly androgynous to twentieth-century readers, enhance our sense of their surreal artificiality. Orlando is posing "as" a boy or an ambassador. The term suggests a certain doubt, a possibility of performance rather than authenticity. By contrast, images of Orlando as a woman are real photographs of Sackville-West, with direct captions ("Orlando about the year 1840," "Orlando on her return to England," "Orlando at the present time"). Women's photographs are fixed in time and space. They are records of living beings. Men's photographs are ambiguously captioned and are photographic interpretations of preexisting artistic interpretations. According to the photographs, women are real, while men are masquerading. *Orlando* mobilizes the binary terms *natural* and *artificial* in parodic ways, because the novel cannot escape this dichotomous reading. But text and photographs strategically contradict each other, keeping "authentic" and "performed" in flux, forbidding us to apply either adjective to either gender permanently. By portraying men as artificial and doubly mediated, women as directly accessible and real, *Orlando*'s photographs propose a new reading of gender performance.

According to *Orlando*, male naturalness is most appropriately challenged by art. Men have to celebrate natural maleness to be able to denounce feminine artifice. Men therefore need to portray themselves in this comfortable state of unself-consciousness. In literature and art men's naturalness can be recorded, to serve as an example for women. But this profusion of self-serving industries destroys the masculinity it was designed to preserve; men pose rather than act "naturally," they sit for their portraits according to the artificial requirements generated by hundreds of previous portraits, and they appear in literary forms worn into recognizable contours by multitudes of previously written male characters.[43] Thus art, which is produced by men's need to validate their normality, ends up reproducing them as fictional, artificial, and masquerading.

Orlando slyly shows how male artists produce art to disguise their own costuming. The novel cites the most powerful male critique of the artificial feminine, Pope's "Or stain her honour, or her new brocade" and Addison's "I consider women as a beautiful, romantic animal, that may be adorned with furs and feathers, pearls and diamonds, ores and silks" (209–10). But their interest in their own clothing belies their attention to female decoration. "They wore plum-coloured suits one day and grey another. Mr. Swift had a fine malacca cane. Mr. Addison scented his handkerchiefs" (208). The men's critiques of female costume evidently come from their need to repudiate their own evident interest in costuming. Men need to (re)produce themselves as natural, precisely because they are already costumed. Art both reinforces male naturalness and reveals male artifice; art paradoxically "constructs" men as "natural."[44]

On the other hand, art only reveals what everyone already "knows" about women – their artifice. When art validates our cultural conceptions of femininity, we believe that these images of women are "true." For instance, a painting of an elaborately dressed woman positioned to best advantage reinforces the viewer's impression that women naturally do dress elaborately and pose for a viewer's attention. Men artificially pose as natural, while women's daily artifice runs with seamless continuity from life to art. We are not surprised when female Orlando poses for her photographs, since women are always already posing. We are, however, surprised when the photographs reveal male Orlando as poseur, since men supposedly never pose. Art can unsettle our opposition between natural and artificial by proving men to be artificial. As art increasingly shows male artifice, men need to produce even more admiring portraits of themselves being natural. But since portraits necessarily show people posing, the portraits only reinforce male artifice. Maleness is founded on this circular paradox.

Indeed, Orlando's lover is a wholly artificial man, whose constant straining for "natural" maleness produces his identity. His photograph makes him seem like a copy of Orlando, and the text denies him any independent subjectivity when it obscures his origin, family, class, region, and even gender. The reader of *Orlando* notices how much he, with his feminine visage, resembles the portrait of "Orlando on her return to England"[45] (figs. 2.2, 2.3). Both photographs show a subject with short dark hair curled on the right side and large dark eyes, wearing dark cloth around the shoulders and exposing a bare white space of neck crossed by pearls or scarf. Only the caption reveals that "Marmaduke Bonthrop Shelmerdine, Esquire" is not in fact a portrait of Orlando. Whereas the portraits of Harriet and Sasha represent Sackville-West's and Woolf's families, respectively, the portrait of Orlando's male lover has no known origin. It is a photograph of an 1820s portrait of an unidentified man, by an unknown painter.[46] The painting's unidentifiability makes us unable to read either the history of the subject (his family, class, or personal history) or the history of the artist's work (his development as artist). Similarly, the automatic guarantors of male natural privilege, which taught Orlando to be so confident as a boy — family name, lineage, property — have been erased or destroyed for Shelmerdine, whose family's ancestral castle is a ruin (251). Thus character and image both lie outside the ordinary narratives of male identity.

In lieu of this history the text provides a new heritage for Shelmerdine; he succeeds to Orlando's male wishes. "Orlando on her return to England" has projected her male desires into the shape of "Marmaduke Bonthrop Shelmerdine, Esquire." Just as Orlando had vowed to ride on battlefields when he grew up, Shelmerdine does indeed become a soldier (251). Just as Orlando loved foreign cultures (Turkey, the gypsies), Shelmerdine becomes an explorer. Orlando had spent much of his youth on ships (sleeping with women among the treasure sacks); Shelmerdine is a sailor. The photographs' similarity establishes this succession. Shelmerdine is the man the text positions as its hero; he fulfils the traditional "poses" of intrepid explorer and passionate lover. Yet Shelmerdine's heroism is unmasked as mimetic. Shelmerdine simply performs Orlando's desires, thereby demonstrating that all the "poses" designed to remind

POSING *ORLANDO* 43

Fig. 2.2 Marmaduke Bonthrop Shelmerdine, Esquire

Fig. 2.3 Orlando on Her Return to England

the viewer of male natural desire and courage are merely performances of preordained roles. "It's about all a fellow can do nowadays," as he says (252).

Even Orlando himself is no natural, original man. Orlando's masculine activities are continually, comically, deferred. He cannot lead armies into battle because Queen Elizabeth cannot "bear to think of that tender flesh torn and that curly head rolled in the dust" and because he falls asleep when Turkish rebellion erupts (25). He cannot marry because Sasha deserts him, his aristocratic lovers hate him, and "Rosita Pepita" disappears from both the novel and Orlando's memory. He cannot demonstrate property ownership or class status because he lives in Turkey, away from his estates and the English class system. Ironically, Orlando turns female during his moment of greatest masculine opportunity — just as he "marries" Rosita Pepita, sees rebellion, and becomes a duke. But his imminent sexual, military, and economic adventures are impossible for a woman to perform. As a woman, Orlando cross-dresses to perform the manhood she could have once possessed; as a man, Shelmerdine imitates Orlando's dreams of manhood. The man Orlando, in other words, is a phantasmatic projection that both the woman Orlando and Shelmerdine endlessly try to imitate. And that man Orlando, in his brief existence, was an imitation of his "fathers" (13). *Orlando* shows that the concept of male naturalness is a cultural myth that all men try to approximate in an endless series of performances. No man possesses natural masculinity; every man tries to live up to it as his gender ideal. Thus when men wear no decoration, drab colors, and practical garb, they are masquerading as men.

THE ART OF THE PHOTOGRAPH

Orlando's photographs may show men as artifacts, but we must be careful not to treat the photographs as windows into the truth of male identity. *Orlando*'s photographs, like all photographs, are mediating interpretations, part of whose pleasure comes from the fact that the viewer has to overcome the photograph's apparent guarantee of authenticity. In fact, the photograph functions in the masculine economy. It pretends to be natural, simple, and direct, but really it is a mimetic performance of naturalness. The photograph mimics both the "real" subject and the history of art, for it reproduces both the "real" scene and the theory of composition. It chooses its subject "naturally" (whatever happens to be in front of the lens) and "art/ificially" (whatever subjects are sanctioned as properly artistic images). The viewer of the photograph is oddly aware of both the photographer's artistry and the subject's reality. "In photography ... one encounters a new and strange phenomenon ... something that cannot be silenced, that impudently demands the name of the person who lived at that time and who, remaining real even now, will never yield herself up entirely into *art*."[47] The photograph names a tension between art and "nature" — just as Orlando names a conflict between maleness and femaleness.

This aesthetic dilemma leads us to the rather eccentric fact that Vanessa Bell took some of *Orlando*'s photographs. Bell disliked portrait painting and often refused to achieve verisimilitude in her portraits.[48] "Vanessa Bell thus goes beyond the superficially representational portrait in two ways: she attempts to capture her subject's essential character, and she subordinates human figures to her interest in light, color, and overall composition."[49] By photographing her daughter Angelica as "The Russian Princess" and her friend Vita as "Orlando about the year 1840," Bell seems to have violated her own artistic principles (fig. 2.4). Indeed, Bell's circle seemed to believe that photographs are not art:

This impetus is in direct line of descent from the desire of Bell and Fry, early in this century, to free art from concerns "not peculiarly its own." [Clive] Bell, writing in 1913 ... complained of those who "treat created form as if it were imitated form, a picture rather than a photograph." In the same movement in which, in the West, the issue of representation in art became a dead issue, photography became consigned to the far side, the "wrong" side, of that divide which Cubism had opened up between the nineteenth century and the modern period.[50]

Yet Clive Bell, Roger Fry, Vanessa Bell, and Virginia Woolf were all deeply interested in one photographer and publicly campaigned to have her photographs recognized as legitimate art. Julia Margaret Cameron, the pioneering female photographer of the 1860s and 1870s, significantly influenced *Orlando*'s philosophy as well as its photographs. Cameron managed to use the camera's uncompromising realism to produce a costumed, unfocused, artificially posed, surreal portrait of her subject — an artistic philosophy whose contradictions probably appealed to Bell.

Virginia Woolf and Vanessa Bell were both extremely close to Cameron's work, not least because Cameron was their great-aunt. They inherited a collection of Cameron photographs, including a series Cameron

POSING *ORLANDO* 47

Fig. 2.4 Orlando about the Year 1840

took of their mother. One year before she began *Orlando*, Woolf wrote a lively and humorous biographical sketch of her great-aunt. She enjoyed the biography greatly, writing "I might spend a lifetime over her," and informing Sackville-West, "Cameron moving, not fast, but with the dignity of a battleship taking the water."[51] Earlier, in 1923, Woolf wrote a play called *Freshwater* about her redoubtable relative. "The idea is to have masses of Cameron photographs, shawls, cameos, peg-top trousers, laurel trees, laureates and all the rest," she explained.[52] Cameron seems to conjure up all the typical Victorian commodities for Woolf — which perhaps explains why she drew on Cameron's legacy for her illustration of "Orlando about the year 1840." Photographs visibly encoded family history for Woolf; her great-aunt took them, her mother sat for them, her sister owned them. Woolf could position this artistic family inheritance against Sackville-West's ancestral collection of priceless portraits. In *Orlando*, three illustrations are reproductions of Sackville-West's paintings, but four are photographs that members of Woolf's family took. Thus *Orlando*'s illustrations confirm that the novel chronicles both Woolf's family and Sackville-West's, and perhaps suggests a covert rivalry between the two histories. In 1923 Woolf began her relationship with Sackville-West by insisting that Sackville-West view the family's collection of Cameron photographs, as if asserting her own distinguished past against the intimidating heritage of *Knole and the Sackvilles* (her letters reveal her self-doubt whenever Sackville-West invited her to Knole).[53] Since 1923 was also the year of *Freshwater*, Woolf's and Sackville-West's affair began under the shadow of Woolf's humorous fascination for her ancestor. "The Russian Princess as a Child" and "Orlando about the year 1840," with their deliberate Cameron allusions, may encode a private, shared memory of the women's first year together.

"The Russian Princess as a Child" is a deliberate imitation of Cameron's style. The subject's pose, looking straight into the camera with a sulky expression, resembles the attitudes of Cameron's sitters (who often had to hold the same pose for ten minutes). The "Princess" wears layers of vaguely medieval/Eastern garments, a favorite look of Cameron's, and her pearls signify her royal wealth rather than her individual personality. She poses against a dark background with an artificial wall and shrub. This backdrop closely approximates Cameron's favorite settings, dark spaces punctuated only by bunches of flowers or the furniture on which the subject rested. Similarly, "Orlando about the year 1840" is Cameronian in its muted background, its formal portrait-like pose, and its use of a strange costume that does not relate to the subject's own life. Woolf and Bell deliberately posed and costumed their subjects in imitation of Cameron's. We might say that the photographs are masquerading as Cameronian.

Copying Cameron was not new to Vanessa Bell, for on June 2, 1926, Woolf had commented on Bell's "Aunt Julia photograph." Woolf did not like the photograph's proportions but was interested in the attempt to reproduce Cameron's style.[54] As *Vanessa Bell's Family Album* points out, Bell was an avid amateur photographer who enjoyed taking carefully posed pictures of her costumed daughter as well as spontaneous shots of family vacations, and this practice explains why Woolf asked her to take photographs for *Orlando*. Woolf clearly identified Bell with Cameron, equating them in the most straightforward of ways by actually casting Bell as Cameron in *Freshwater*. She also considered her sister a Cameron expert, informing Bell "you are urgently needed . . . to get up a book of Aunt Julia's photographs."[55] Whether or not Bell actually selected the photographs for *Victorian Photographs of Famous Men and Fair Women By Julia Margaret Cameron*, the book was certainly a family affair. In 1926, one year before *Orlando*, Woolf wrote its biographical introduction, and Bell's ex-lover Roger Fry wrote its artistic preface.

By choosing a photographer and a setting she identified with Cameron, Woolf seems to have deliberately made her novel's photographs Cameron-like. She did so because Cameron's photography had a very particular meaning for Bloomsbury. In *Victorian Photographs of Famous Men and Fair Women By Julia Margaret Cameron*, Roger Fry's introduction constructs photography as a surprisingly radical genre that challenges received ideas of history, art, and even gender. In these respects, his description of photography parallels (and probably influenced) Woolf's descriptions of *Orlando*. For Fry, photography is really the best way to transmit history, for photographs show us how people perceived their own identity in each era.[56] Perhaps Woolf drew on Fry's remarks when she decided to illustrate Orlando's life with photographs, agreeing that photography best preserves and reveals the cultural images of each era. Similarly, Fry claims that photography's faithful depiction of reality will make painted portraits useless, while Woolf claims that *Orlando*'s representation of reality will revolutionize biography overnight. Victorian women, according to Fry, "were more interested in the art which moulded and celebrated them" than Victorian men, a curious statement that implies that Victorian women were actually made by their photographs, which shaped and named them.[57] This is not too far from *Orlando*'s supposition that clothes "mould our hearts, our brains, our tongues" (188). Fry's ideas were so influential within Bloomsbury that twenty-two years later, Clive Bell rewrote them; in the course of another article on Cameron, he reiterated Fry's central ideas that photography has a strange relation to art and constitutes a privileged point of history ("a photograph is, or should be, a record").[58] He even repeated Fry's declaration that the National Portrait Gallery should replace its paintings with photographs. Did Woolf use Fry's revolutionary manifesto of photography to help her produce *Orlando*'s philosophy of art, history, and gender? Did Woolf's, Fry's, and Clive Bell's critical appreciation of Cameron represent a shared theory of Cameron's photography and of photography in general?

The Bloomsbury circle was fascinated with the relationship between photography and history. They recognized how photographs disrupt our sense of the past by preserving that past not wisely but too well. The men, Roger Fry and Clive Bell, praised photographs' privileged ability to record moments of history and to confront us with history's irreducible alterity. The women, Angelica and Vanessa Bell, hoped to recreate historical moments by composing carefully posed photographs in archaic settings and borrowed styles. For Virginia Woolf, who utilized both men's and women's traditions in *Orlando*, photography implied not only a very personal family history, but a very large component of the concept of history itself. To the Bloomsbury reader, then, the mere presence of photographs signaled the novel's desire to upset normative cultural expectations about history and art.

THE TEXT AND THE PHOTOGRAPH

One of the first expectations the photographs upset is our sense that the novel tells the truth. The photographs chart their own history of Orlando, which frequently contradicts the history of Orlando enshrined in the text. For instance, Woolf includes a portrait of the Archduke dressed as a woman (fig. 2.5). She mischievously entitles it "The Archduchess Harriet" and presents the Archduke in full female costume. All the accoutre-

Fig. 2.5 The Archduchess Harriet

ments of seventeenth-century upper-class female costume appear: corset, panniers, ruff, jewels, lace, embroidery. But when we put the "Archduchess" with the "Russian Princess" we notice elements of the costume that subvert the Renaissance subject's intentions. Both "The Archduchess Harriet" and "The Russian Princess as a Child" are draped in pearls and wrapped in elaborate cloaks. They decorate their bodies to make themselves desirable, and they entice the viewer with an identical facial expression. Their eyelids drooping, their rouged lips pouting, the Archduchess and Sasha seem to perform femininity in excess, giving campy portrayals of grand ladies. Though Angelica deliberately overacted Sasha for the camera, the "Archduchess" is an authentic portrait of a Sackville ancestor who doubtless imagined her portrait to signify splendor, economic might, class status, the dignity of birth. Yet in spite of these discrepancies between the portraits' origins, eras, and intentions, the similarity between the two images shows that femininity is a performance with remarkable continuity. Across the centuries, femininity is marked by recognizable props like pearls and pouts.

Like Sasha's photograph, the Archduchess's portrait follows masquerade logic by misperforming the text. The novel has the Archduchess in "old black riding-habit and mantle" and wearing an antiquated headdress (177, 114). The photograph, on the other hand, puts the Archduchess in an elaborately patterned pale brocade, with her hair dressed with pearls in lieu of headdress. The gap between the portrait's aggressively female, richly dressed woman and the novel's ambiguously male/female, shabbily dressed character makes us read both images as offset copies of each other.

The photographs of Orlando as a woman are among the most unsettlingly unfaithful portrayals in the novel. When Vita Sackville-West posed for these photographs, Woolf carefully designed her appearance. She asked Sackville-West to bring along "curls and clothes," and inquired, "should I hire a wig for you? Or can you make up?"[59] Yet not one photograph shows Sackville-West wearing a wig, makeup, or Orlandoesque clothes. Woolf selected cosmetics, coiffure, and clothing with no reference to the novel. If Sackville-West did not dress as Orlando, whom exactly did she impersonate?

Perhaps she was masquerading as a masquerader. In "Orlando about the year 1840," she resembles nothing so much as a woman dressed for a fancy dress ball. The Cameron-like image also alludes to the masquerade Cameron forced her sitters to adopt, as she draped them in "Eastern" or "Renaissance" robes indiscriminately. For Cameron, and perhaps for Woolf, costumes signified the subject's symbolic role, not her individual personality; for instance, an unmusical writer might nevertheless pose with a violin to signify his adherence to the arts. Orlando's flowered gypsy blouse, plaid kilt-like skirt, and soft velvet Renaissance cap do not match;

they seem to refer to three different cultures, implying Orlando's difficult multiple identities as male and female, gypsy and Englishwoman, Elizabethan and Victorian, aristocrat and bourgeoise, loyalist and spy, writer and patron. Ironically, this garb that alludes to men's kilts, that conceals hair and body, is Orlando's disguise precisely during the century that makes her consolidate her femininity by marrying. Though she adopts the crinoline, "heavier and more drab than any dress she had yet worn," made from "black bombazine," her photograph shows her in a light plaid skirt without hoops (244, 235). Thus the picture accuses the novel of lying, just as the Archduchess's portrait disproves the fiction of her black riding habit. Orlando writes herself as a falsehood, but a falsehood revealed by the photographs of herself. There is no "original" Orlando to tell us whether the black crinoline or plaid drapery would be correct. Even a biographical appeal to Woolf's letters only gives us an image of Sackville-West disguised. Even a historical reading only tells us that "Orlando" is disguised as a Cameron subject who is, in turn, wearing costumes that Cameron selected from her closet of props.

Images of men are equally subversive. The painting of "Orlando as a Boy" is probably the first photograph Woolf acquired for *Orlando*[60] (fig. 2.6). She would have had it while she wrote the story of Orlando's boyhood. The photograph's prominence is underscored by its status as a frontispiece. Yet, given the photograph's historical and textual importance, it is surprising what sort of information the image imparts. The novel emphasizes Orlando's red cheeks, almond teeth, small ears, dark hair, large eyes, and "brow like the swelling of a marble dome" (15). In the frontispiece image, Orlando's cheeks are colorless, his teeth invisible, his ears large, his hair full of light streaks, his eyes noticeably small, and his forehead hidden by his unruly hair. But Woolf evidently copied her description of Orlando's clothes from the photograph with great care. His "crimson breeches, lace collar, waistcoat of taffeta, and shoes with rosettes on them as big as double dahlias" matches the painting point by point (20–21). Woolf wants to emphasize the boy's costume, not his "natural" self. Though the biographer claims "directly we glance at eyes and forehead, thus do we rhapsodise," the novel's metalevel hints that Orlando's clothing is far more important than his eyes (15).

Similarly, the picture of "Orlando as Ambassador" (fig. 2.7) pays no attention to the text's rhapsody over Orlando's beautiful legs. Nell Gwyn mourns "that such a pair of legs should leave the country," and eventually

Fig. 2.6 Orlando as a Boy

Fig. 2.7 Orlando as Ambassador

sends him a dukedom, when "the envious said that this was Nell Gwyn's tribute to the memory of a leg" (118, 125). The Ambassador has "such a leg!" (129). But "Orlando as Ambassador" shows no legs at all. Though Sackville-West posed for "Orlando as Ambassador," she deliberately impersonated a painting style, rather than an identity. As Nicolson puts it,

Woolf dragged Sackville-West "to a London studio to have her photographed as a Lely" — not as an ambassador. It seems especially significant that the only image of Sackville-West as a man actually has her posing as artifact.[61] Woolf was probably inspired by the Lely portraits of Sackville ancestors with which Sackville-West had grown up. "Orlando as Ambassador" does not recreate a particular Lely portrait but instead parodies the long hair, draped shoulders, and three-quarter face that characterize many Lely portraits of gentlemen.[62] Orlando masquerades as "a Lely" or "a Cameron," a visitor to the novel from a wholly different artistic tradition.

Whenever we try to fix Orlando's photographic identity, we find ourselves staring blankly at those impossible captions. The caption is a peculiarly unclassifiable species. It acts as the seam that sews text into photograph. Because the caption makes the photograph meaningful, it seems an integral part of the photograph. But as written text, the caption seems part of the novel.[63] Nevertheless, the caption differs from the novel — it appears on a separate page, written in italics and phrased in incomplete sentences. Inasmuch as they refer to pictures, the captions deny Jacobus's claim that this novel is solely a text about writing. The caption must identify a subject and designate a date, thus working against the rest of the novel's attempt to undo fixed gendered and historical norms. In fact the captions frequently violate the plot, including "Orlando as a Boy," "The Archduchess Harriet," "Orlando as Ambassador," and "Orlando about the year 1840." Orlando as a boy turns into a girl. The Archduchess Harriet turns out to be really the Archduke Harry. Orlando's ambassadorial functions are notoriously undocumented, and the narrator hints that he actually fomented rebellions. The particularity of "Orlando about 1840" contradicts Orlando's sense of the nineteenth century as a timeless stagnant fog. Therefore, the captions belong neither to the novel, whose claims they confound, nor to the photographs, whose real subjects' identities they obviously mystify. In other words, they deny both poststructuralist emphasis on writing and biographical stress on reality. They constitute a third sort of discourse, one that might possibly, in Woolf's terms, "revolutionize biography in a night."[64]

By juxtaposing the certainly fictional text with the positively real photograph, Woolf produces a crisis of faith. Readers usually resolve it by deciding that Woolf has recaptioned real photographs, and they recall the biographical aspect of the novel. But the text and the photographs occasionally refer to each other convincingly, even authoritatively. Thus Orlando's emerald ring, a gift from Queen Elizabeth, appears on her photographed hand. Orlando's phosphorescent pearls and the elkhounds she bought from the king of Norway are also photographically documented. History and fiction (re)produce each other; the real history of Sackville-West's lifestyle may have generated the fictional history of Orlando's, but Orlando's fiction may have made Sackville-West reinvent herself. Did Woolf invent Orlando's emerald ring because it figures in the photograph Vita Sackville-West sent her? Or did she deliberately dress Sackville-West in Orlando's costume for her photograph? The photograph holds the mirror up to nature, and nature looks back at itself in an infinite regression of reflected images and costumes: Orlando performs Sackville-West performing Orlando.

The photograph contradicts itself precisely because it poses two "authentic" subjects, Orlando and Sackville-West. No matter which subject we choose, the photograph remains the site of "reality" for the novel because it implies a living subject. The text is fiction; the photograph is "real." In fact, *Orlando*'s performative constitution of gender lies precisely in the continuing contradiction between text and photograph — text mimics photograph in the same way that gender constantly tries "to become 'real' and to embody 'the natural.' "[65] The text produces itself in the spaces between photographs, always trying to achieve the reality of those photographs. The text chases the photographs, just as gender performance chases the ideal of real gender. Furthermore, by appearing to repeat each other, text and photograph only emphasize their failure to reproduce each other exactly. Butler might say that text and photograph engage in "strategies of subversive repetition."[66]

PHOTOGRAPHIC CRITICISM

In fact, the photographs challenge the linguistic category of performativity. Photographs seem to be perfect performative utterances, which according to Barthes enact the statement "this was alive, this posed live in front of the lens."[67] Photographs both do and describe. "Ultimately, having an experience becomes identical with taking a photograph of it."[68] Photographs also satisfy Derrida's redefinition of the performative as simultaneously unique and reiterable, for the photograph is a singular image that, thanks to its negative, can be reprinted an infinite number of times. On the other hand the photograph is no performative. Austin said that the performative fails if its speaker jokes.[69] In *Orlando* photographs lie and pun by claiming simultaneously to represent both Orlando and Sackville-West. But there is a disturbing difference between a photograph of Orlando and a photograph of Sackville-West, which we can read either as a historical relation (the tension between written biography and its original subject) or a linguistic problem (the gap between sign and referent). In other words, we cannot tell who the photograph "really" shows, a difficulty we can transform into a difficulty with the whole biographical genre or a difficulty with the nature of the sign itself. Hence we can see how the photographs of *Orlando*, by their challenge to "reality," motivate both the biographical and the poststructuralist schools of *Orlando* criticism.

Thus we cannot read *Orlando* as merely either a masquerade in writing or a biographical mimesis of Sackville-West. Rather, *Orlando* shows us that writing is a performance that endlessly reaches toward the biographical goal, "reality." Writing, indeed, constitutes itself by its inability to become reality. However, within the novel, "text" and "photograph" become local replacements for "writing" and "biographical realism." They are not substitutions but masquerades; the photograph pretends to be biographical realism but gleefully diverges from this "real" "identity" into textual fictions, while the "text" cannot ever perform "writing" adequately because it keeps distractedly referring to its other, the photograph. In short, the photograph can never prove the image to be "really" Orlando or "really" Sackville-West, because it keeps producing unsettling images that settle into neither Orlando nor Sackville-West, like the photograph of a masquerader in kilts. Nor can the text ever be a self-referential icon of writing about writing, since it generates photographs to which it refers incorrectly; Orlando as a boy has the right clothes but the wrong face. Fiction and photographs disguise themselves as each other, chase each other, and try to perform each other's identity. The two critical schools, the biographical and the poststructuralist, keep reproducing themselves in contrast to each other, precisely because the text of *Orlando* sets the two tendencies into an endless chase. Each seems to function as each other's truth. As Woolf says, the photographs and the text fit each other like "a glove."[70] Never able to attain the authenticity its own photographs seem to guarantee, *Orlando* strives endlessly to reach the reality of gender, enjoying itself mightily in the impossible journey to reach the ever-receding goal.

Orlando famously ends with a wild-goose chase: "'It is the goose!' Orlando cried. 'The wild goose...'" (329). The novel urges that the endlessly futile chase is precisely what constitutes gender. The wild-goose feather is associated with both Marmaduke Bonthrop Shelmerdine (his name reminds Orlando of a steely blue feather) and the goose quill, which produces poetry. Both desired objects — maleness and writing — travel away from Orlando's control, floating in planes, dissolving in blots. She achieves her gender identity by chasing them continually. In the futurist nightmare of the ending there is no more "natural." She cannot return her poem to the earth, for Nature refuses to accept the book when Orlando tries to bury it. Her house turns silver; her pearls glow in fluorescent brightness, and a rushing aeroplane sweeps through the night. But Orlando produces identity as both female and artist by perpetually trying for the impossible natural. And perhaps the "phosphorescent flare" of her pearls is the last glare of the flash bulb, snapping on the camera that eternally pursues Orlando to record her incessant chase, the photograph, her partner in the masquerade.

NOTES

I would like to thank Molly Hite, Misha Kavka, George Musser, Pam Thurschwell, and the anonymous readers for *Genders* for their generous help with various versions of this article.

1. Virginia Woolf, in *The Letters of Virginia Woolf: Volume III, 1923–1928*, ed. Nigel Nicolson and Joanne Trautmann (New York: Harcourt Brace Jovanovich, 1977), 428–29.
2. Thomas S. W. Lewis, "Combining 'the advantages of fact and fiction': Virginia Woolf's Biographies of Vita Sackville-West, Flush, and Roger Fry," in *Virginia Woolf: Centennial Essays*, ed. Elaine K. Ginsberg and Laura Moss Gottlieb (Troy, N.Y.: Whitston, 1983), 300.
3. Nigel Nicolson, *Portrait of a Marriage* (New York: Atheneum, 1973), 202.
4. Woolf, *Letters*, 465.
5. Ibid., 561.
6. Ibid., 474.
7. Vita Sackville-West, *The Letters of Vita Sackville-West to Virginia Woolf*, ed. Louise DeSalvo and Mitchell A. Leaska (New York: Morrow, 1985), 266.
8. Like Woolf, writers of biographical articles often contradict themselves.

Thomas S. W. Lewis claims that Archduke Harry was based on Vita's mother's lover, not (as Woolf maintained) Vita's, yet argues that Woolf faithfully "maintained the essence of truth" in *Orlando* (Lewis, "Virginia Woolf's Biographies," 303). Sherron E. Knopp argues that Woolf had *The Well of Loneliness* in mind when writing *Orlando*, yet Woolf's letters show that she first read *The Well of Loneliness* in November 1928, after *Orlando* was already published. He claims Woolf treats lesbianism as a "simple natural fact" — which, however, involves the decidedly complicated and unnatural mediation of an overnight spontaneous sex change. Woolf's decision to switch Orlando's sex both ignores real female-female relationships and manages to heterosexualize Orlando's affairs with both men and women. These articles show the impossibility of viewing *Orlando* in any kind of straightforward historical context. Perhaps Archduke Harry is both Lascelles and Murray; Woolf probably had *The Well of Loneliness* in mind before she actually read it. But the critic of *Orlando* must view history not as the straightforward truth but as a pun — a fictitious history that can contain mutually incompatible ideas just as Orlando contains mutually impossible genders (Sherron E. Knopp, "If I Saw You Would You Kiss Me? Sapphism and the Subversiveness of Woolf's *Orlando*," *PMLA* 103, no. 1 [1988]: 31).

9. Elizabeth Cooley, "Revolutionizing Biography: *Orlando, Roger Fry*, and the Tradition," *South Atlantic Review* 55, no. 2 (May 1990): 72.
10. Virginia Woolf, *Orlando: A Biography* (San Diego: Harcourt Brace Jovanovich, 1956), 187. All further citations will refer to this edition and will be noted parenthetically in the text.
11. Suzanne Raitt, *Vita and Virginia* (Oxford: Clarendon Press, 1993), 38.
12. See Rachel Bowlby, *Virginia Woolf* (London: Longman, 1992), who argues that the novel positions gender as culturally contingent.
13. Nancy Armstrong, *Desire and Domestic Fiction: A Political History of the Novel* (Oxford: Oxford University Press, 1987), 244.
14. Ibid., 57.
15. Also see Judy Little, "(En)gendering Laughter: Woolf's *Orlando* as Contraband in the Age of Joyce," *Women's Studies* 15, nos.1–3 (1988): 179–99, and Pamela L. Caughie, "Virginia Woolf's Double Discourse," in *Discontented Discourses: Feminism/Testual Intervention/Psychoanalysis*, ed. Marleen S. Barr and Richard Feldstein (Urbana: University of Illinois Press, 1989), 42.
16. Caughie, "Virginia Woolf's Double Discourse," 50.
17. Mary Jacobus, *Reading Woman: Essays in Feminist Criticism* (New York: Columbia University Press, 1986), 22.
18. Ibid., 22–23.
19. Woolf, *Letters*, 427–29. Interestingly, Sackville-West advised Woolf to get photographed by Beaton, but Woolf refused (Sackville-West, *Letters*, 239 n.4).
20. Woolf, *Letters*, 430.
21. Ibid., 435.
22. Allan Sekula gives a history of the "evidentiary" use of photography — the

way the police utilized photographs to identify persons or events. See Allan Sekula, "The Body and the Archive," *October* 39 (Winter 1986): 3–64.
23. Roland Barthes, *Camera Lucida: Reflections on Photography*, trans. Richard Howard (New York: Hill and Wang, 1981), 79.
24. Ibid., 87.
25. Susan Sontag, *On Photography* (New York: Farrar, Straus and Giroux, 1973), 5, 4.
26. Woolf, *Letters*, 434.
27. *Vanessa Bell's Family Album*, ed. Quentin Bell and Angelica Garnett (London: Jill Norman & Hobhouse, 1981), 81.
28. See, for instance, *Family Album*, ed. Bell and Garnett, 124.
29. Woolf, *Letters*, 497.
30. Sontag, *On Photography*, 24.
31. Judith Butler, *Gender Trouble: Feminism and the Subversion of Identity* (New York: Routledge, 1990), 141.
32. In its original formulation by J. H. Austin, the performative is a unique event. If you have to say "I bet" twice, one of those utterances must have failed to perform. "A performative utterance will be *in a peculiar way* hollow or void if said by an actor upon the stage." But Jacques Derrida argues that inasmuch as the performative is part of language it has to be repeatable; language's reiterability is the condition for our understanding it. Derrida responds, "What Austin excludes as anomaly, exception, 'non-serious,' *citation* (on stage, in a poem, or a soliloquy) is the determined modification of a general citationality — or rather, a general iterability — without which there would not even be a 'successful' performative." This paradoxical construct, the repeatable performative, is what Butler means by the term *performance* (J. H. Austin, *How to Do Things with Words* [Cambridge: Harvard University Press, 1962], 22; Jacques Derrida, "Signature Event Context," *Limited Inc* (Evanston: Northwestern University Press, 1988), 17).
33. Butler, *Gender Trouble*, 140.
34. Ibid., 137–38.
35. Ibid., 146.
36. Butler also suggests that the very ideas of masculinity and femininity are constructed by unresolved homosexual cathexes (Ibid., 54).
37. Ibid., 111.
38. Ibid., 129.
39. Though Butler discusses several theories that distinguish between maleness and femaleness, she critiques only their construction of homosexuality, not their specific treatment of maleness and femaleness. Thus we do not know whether Butler accepts the theories she carefully summarizes, like Monique Wittig's theory that the male is always the normative speaking subject, by whose side the female appears strange and artificial, or Joan Riviére's (and Stephen Heath's) argument that womanliness is itself a masquerade that hides the woman's natural and desired male identity.
40. Butler, *Gender Trouble*, 126.

41. By calling maleness "natural," I mean that it seems normative. I do not mean "nature-like," which implies fecundity, passivity, and beauty. The latter sense of "natural" is notoriously reserved for femaleness.
42. The definitive analysis of Orlando's costuming is Sandra M. Gilbert's "Costumes of the Mind: Transvestism as Metaphor in Modern Literature," *Critical Inquiry* 7, no. 2 (Winter 1980). Gilbert argues that female modernist writers treat the self as a series of costumes, while male modernists treat costuming with distrust and urge a return to an original naked truth. For instance, Orlando's sex change is all about clothing. "Orlando's metamorphosis is not a fall; it is simply a shift in fashion" (Woolf, *Orlando*, 405).
43. In literature a man can be a hero, a rake, a boy growing into man, a good man, a villain, a lover, or everyman. In art, men can pose on charging steeds, with hunting dogs, wrapped in Roman garb, reading tomes, leading armies, draped in academic robes, or against a backdrop of vaguely Mediterranean ruins, dusky study, or plunging torrent.
44. On a daily level, we see this contradiction at work in the fashion term "unconstructed men's jacket," which denies the careful process of artificial construction necessary to create a "natural" men's jacket. For the last few years "feminine" has been one of the most common adjectives in women's fashion columns, matched in men's fashions not by "masculine" but by "natural" (frequently used to describe colors as well as cuts). The term *natural* oddly stands in for *masculine*, as if the two were synonymous. If women dress up to look like women, men dress up to look like they didn't.
45. The Hogarth Press edition of *Orlando* emphasizes the image's painted quality, even including a sort of painted frame around the subject's head.
46. Woolf, *Letters*, 484.
47. Walter Benjamin, "A Short History of Photography," *Screen* 13, no.1 (Spring 1972): 7.
48. Diane Filby Gillespie, *The Sisters' Arts: The Writing and Painting of Virginia Woolf and Vanessa Bell* (Syracuse: Syracuse University Press, 1988), 162–68.
49. Ibid., 168.
50. Victor Burgin, "Photography, Phantasy, Function," in *Thinking Photography*, ed. Victor Burgin (London: Macmillan Education, 1982), 209–10.
51. Woolf, *Letters*, 280, 307.
52. Ibid., 72–73.
53. Ibid., 4, 18-19.
54. Ibid., 271.
55. Ibid., 276.
56. Roger Fry, *Victorian Photographs of Famous Men and Fair Women By Julia Margaret Cameron*, ed. Tristram Powell (1926; Boston: David R. Godine, 1973), 23.
57. Ibid., 25.
58. Helmut Gernsheim, *Julia Margaret Cameron: Her Life and Photographic Work*, intro. by Clive Bell (1948; New York: Aperture, 1975), 7.
59. Woolf, *Letters*, 435, 434.

60. Only four days after she began the novel, she asked Sackville-West for a portrait of a male Sackville from the time of James I (Woolf, *Letters*, 430).
61. Nicolson, *Portrait*, 208.
62. For examples, see "Sir William Temple" and "Portrait of the Artist" in Oliver Millar, *Sir Peter Lely* (London: National Portrait Gallery, 1978), 52, 56. A painting at Knole, with which Sackville-West would have been familiar, is "Second Earl of Sutherland," in R. B. Beckett, *Lely* (Boston: Boston Book and Art Shop, 1955), pl. 71.
63. Benjamin points out that the caption makes the image into a precise text. "At this point the caption must step in, thereby creating a photography which literarises the relationships of life and without which photographic construction would remain stuck in the approximate" (Benjamin, "Photography," 25).
64. Woolf, *Letters*, 429.
65. Butler, *Gender Trouble*, 146.
66. Ibid., 147.
67. Barthes, *Camera Lucida*, 94.
68. Sontag, *On Photography*, 24.
69. Austin, *How to Do Things With Words*, 9.
70. Woolf, *Letters*, 442.

THREE

Fetishism and Parody in Stein's *Tender Buttons*

Elisabeth A. Frost

> Poetry is concerned with using with abusing, with losing and wanting, with denying with avoiding with adoring with replacing the noun.
> — Gertrude Stein, "Poetry and Grammar"

> This way of dealing with reality [fetishism] ... almost deserves to be described as artful.
> — Sigmund Freud, "Splitting of the Ego in the Process of Defence"

Kin to her inimitable styles, Gertrude Stein's theory of the noun, and of language in general, is like no one else's, and *Tender Buttons*, which is like no other text, is Stein's great experiment with the noun. Stein writes in "Poetry and Grammar" that "the noun must be replaced ... by the thing in itself."[1] *Tender Buttons* enacts a wish to get back to the object, to substitute not a symbol for a thing but a thing for an outworn symbol. Yet the presence of erotic lesbian experience in *Tender Buttons* suggests as well another type of substitution that I would like to explore as a textual practice that sets Stein's poetics apart from avant-garde and modernist writing of her day. In *Tender Buttons* Stein practices what I will define as female fetishism. Stein's scopic and erotic investments in the objects named in *Tender Buttons* parallel fetishism as theorized by Freud. And her play with the materiality of language suggests as well what has been called the "perverse strategy" of the fetishist, a double consciousness of something at once absent and present, of language as both symbol and "object."[2] Yet Stein alters the Freudian notion of fetishism by using objects in her text to parody the male fetishist's anxiety and disavowal and to suggest instead another kind of object-love — one based on plenitude rather than loss.

For Freud, fetishism is strictly a male perversion. It begins in response to the boy's devastating loss of belief in the mother's phallic power and his attendant anxiety about his own possible castration. For some this trauma is so profound that a deliberate self-deception ensues. The fetishist forges a strategy: he substitutes an object for the mother's missing penis. Stein's textual "substitutions" are also strategic. But the object-love in *Tender Buttons* evokes a pleasure that involves neither denial nor fixation. To explain Stein's linguistic strategy, and her parody, I would like to follow Naomi Schor and others in exploring the notion of a female fetishism (impossible in Freudian terms) that would counter Freudian assumptions about female sexuality while still retaining an attitude of "undecidability" regarding the material world.[3] This "oscillation" is the defining feature of fetishism: the male fetishist oscillates between denial of the mother's castration and acceptance of it, and the object he chooses is both "itself" and the phallus. In an altered form this same oscillation is the source of Stein's poetics. I will argue that *female* (and specifically lesbian) fetishism is the basis of Stein's linguistic practice, while *male* (Freudian) fetishism is the target of her parody. What many critics see as the erotic plot of *Tender Buttons*[4] involves a parody and lesbian re-vision of the male fetishist's sexual pleasure in his personal objective world. In her playfully erotic and multiply-punning treatments of objects, Stein retells the Freudian story with a crucial difference — that of the female sexuality absent from Freud's theory of the fetishist.

THE "UNDECIDABLE": FEMALE FETISHISM AND LANGUAGE

According to Freud, the (male) fetishist, who cannot accept the mother's "castration," chooses an object in which to see both the maternal phallus and, implicitly, its absence from the mother, evident in his substitution of this object (a shoe, for example) for the "missing" phallus: "the fetish is a substitute for the woman's (the mother's) penis that the little boy once believed in and . . . does not want to give up." He empowers the fetish with symbolic significance, so that its presence allows him to retain his belief in the phallic mother even as he acknowledges her "lack." Freud calls this maneuver "a very ingenious solution of the difficulty" of confronting reality and still minimizing castration fear. Girls, however, share the mother's anatomy. They would derive no benefit from disavowing her castration; hence the impossibility of female fetishism.[5]

The gender specificity of this model has led several feminist theorists to appropriate its "perversion," to turn Freud's theory against itself. In a 1985 article – which she has recently reassessed – Schor first suggested the political benefits of ideas proposed by Sarah Kofman. For Kofman "what is pertinent to women in fetishism is the paradigm of undecidability that it offers. By appropriating the fetishist's oscillation between denial and recognition of castration, women can effectively counter any move to reduce their bisexuality to a single one of its poles." Here is "a *strategy* designed to turn the so-called 'riddle of femininity' to women's account." Schor elaborates with what she calls "bisextuality": "a refusal firmly to anchor woman – but also man – on either side of the axis of castration."[6] Elizabeth Grosz has used the same concept of undecidability to explore female, and specifically lesbian, fetishism as both possible in Freudian terms and useful as a potential basis for lesbian theory – a meeting-point of feminist politics and psychoanalysis. For Grosz, undecidability captures the "cultivated ambivalence" feminists need to take toward Freud in order to salvage his theory's usefulness and also acknowledge its inadequacies in describing female sexuality.[7]

Schor and Grosz both make strong cases for exploring female fetishism. But there is a fundamental problem. Fetishism in *any* form seems to rely on what Freud called "genital deficiency," the notion that women's bodies lack what is apparent in the male anatomy.[8] Luce Irigaray argues that Freud is "able to picture the little girl becoming a woman only in terms of *lack, absence, default,*" and that "pleasure boils down to being plus or minus one sex organ." Penis-envy – which besets the little girl as the boy wrestles with castration fear – is "a remedy for man's fear of losing one. If *she* envies it, then *he* must have it."[9] Schor points out that appropriating fetishism might reinstate this phallic norm in feminist discourse and create only "the latest and most subtle form of 'penis envy.'"[10] Reevaluating her first, important article, Schor has recently proposed that "What needs to be appropriated by women is irony, but an irony peeled off from fetishism, a feminist irony that would divorce the uncertainty of the ironist from the oscillations of the fetishist" – in other words, an appropriation that doesn't rely on castration fear.[11]

It's safe to say that female fetishism evokes an understandable anxiety in feminist critics. Yet by revising the phallicism of Freudian theory, we can reject castration while still claiming the fetishist's intriguing oscillation. Combining Freud's concept of object-love with feminist critiques of Freud's theory — criticisms of its reliance on castration anxiety and of its refusal to theorize female sexuality — I would like to suggest that it is indeed possible to recuperate fetishism for feminist theory, by recasting its gender specificity. I propose that Stein combines object-love with an alternative view of female sexuality, one based on the experiences of the female body rather than on the phallus, and on joyful multiplicity rather than on the perception of absence. I see in her work a female fetishism freed from the yoke of castration fear, a reconfiguring of Freudian difference that assumes a nonphallic view of the objective world, sexuality, and language. The female fetishist, by my definition, projects desire polymorphously, onto diverse objects, rather than choosing a substitute that alone will assure the subject of the mother's phallic power. Within an economy of plenitude the female subject experiences the sensuality of the objective world without the threat of castration or the need to invest the fetish with purely symbolic potency. I use the term "female fetishism" as opposed to "lesbian fetishism" because I see this psychic economy, as well as the linguistic strategies I will detail, as not necessarily exclusive to lesbian experience. Even Grosz, who uses fetishism to explore "the possibility of 'lesbian theory,' theory of and for lesbians," alternates in her usage between "female" and "lesbian" fetishism. For her "lesbianism provides [the] most manifest and tangible expression" of female fetishism. Similarly, I would like to imagine that a poetics of linguistic plenitude is available to all women intent on "playing" with the word.[12]

With this concept of female fetishism I am attempting both to revise Freudian theory and to suggest an alternative to our usual orientation toward language. For in occupying the position of the fetishist, women can "master" the symbolic in an entirely different way from that of male subjects — by embracing *both* materiality and meaning. Reconfiguring (masculine) avant-gardism for a feminist politics, the concept of female fetishism provides a way to read experimental texts by women against the grain of Freudian theory and to cross the perceived divide between avant-gardism and feminist poetics.

Stein's altered fetishism reveals how this process can work. One reason early readers of Stein often assumed that she was writing mere nonsense is that she changes the rules of signification — the metaphoric use of words that Emerson expounded and that Harriet Scott Chessman, for one, sees Stein responding to.[13] As many readers have shown, Stein substitutes private codes, predominantly of erotic experience, to "signify" on a different level from that of transparent language. At the same time, however, she also makes use of the plasticity of words, explores their materiality, their relation to our bodies through the orality of speech; in *Tender Buttons* she "caresses" them as nonreferential objects. As Chessman and Lisa Ruddick both point out, Stein never completely abandons the signifying process, even in what seems to be a "bodily" poetics.[14] I would argue that, because of this doubling in the quality and function of her language, Stein's writing is fetishistic: at once signifying and palpably material, her words, like her objects, function on two levels — the symbolic and what Julia Kristeva calls the "semiotic," the prelinguistic experience of rhythm and sound through the body.

In *Tender Buttons*, Stein refuses to choose. She fetishizes words by engaging with their symbolic nature as well as with their materiality — the pleasure they offer through the physical experience of speech — yet without the anxiety or disavowal that Freud saw as fundamental to the male fetishist. As I will show later, this process is also the basis for Stein's parody, which shows up the "lack" in the male fetishist and substitutes lesbian pleasure for masculine anxiety.

The first step in uncovering Stein's female fetishism is, of course, to investigate the language of *Tender Buttons*. Lacan suggests a rapport between words and fetishes that applies in part to Stein's poetics. In Lacan's view the signifier does not merely represent the signified.[15] The word, which does not contain the thing referred to, is *itself* material. Yet for Lacan this materiality is predicated on a profound loss. Language, the "symbolic behavior *par excellence*,"[16] functions metonymically, as a substitute for the fantasized phallus of the mother. At the moment the child realizes the mother's castration, the phallus comes to be associated not just with the father but with the law and the symbolic order, marking a loss of union with the mother: "The phallus is the privileged signifier of that mark in which the role of the logos is joined with the advent of desire."[17] The link between the symbolic and desire means that language can be experienced only as lack, an *inadequate* substitution, in this negative way verging on fetishism: "the fascinating image of the fetish" appears "at the very suspension-point of the signifying chain."[18] Language, then, like fetishism, is born from lack and unsatisfiable desire.

Kristeva's account of fetishism and poetic language is less focused on lack; in spirit it is apparently closer to Stein. Kristeva describes a dialectic between the semiotic and the symbolic in poetry — the former erupting into the latter, breaking its logical, semantic relationships. As the poet injects the semiotic into the symbolic, he (the poet is male in Kristeva's theory) "reinvest[s] the maternal *chora* [the pre-Oedipal state of the body] so that it transgresses the symbolic order," and the "semiotic network gives 'music' to literature." In this process "the subject of poetic language clings to the help fetishism offers" — that is, the stability it affords in relation to the *chora* — and therefore poets "fall under the category of fetishism." But Kristeva finally rules out the possibility of textual fetishism: "The text is completely different from a fetish because it *signifies*; in other words, it is not a *substitute* but a *sign* . . . and its semantics is unfurled in sentences."[19] For Kristeva the very process of signification eliminates the possibility of fetishistic language. Furthermore, Kristeva is blind to the possibility of a feminine practice of textual fetishism because she conceives of the writing subject only as male, part of a phallic economy. Grosz points out that, in Kristeva's theory of avant-garde poetics, the return to the semiotic can be effected only by men because they occupy a position within the symbolic order — women risk hysteria or psychosis in releasing the semiotic: "Kristeva seems to accept that phallic subjects alone, only men, can re-present the unrepresented, subversive underside of the *chora* and the semiotic."[20] Stein's poetics, among others, counters Kristeva's conception.

In contrast to Lacan, Stein insists that the material "presence" of language need not rely on a profound, symbolic absence. And both in her explanatory prose and in *Tender Buttons* Stein fuses the semiotic and the symbolic, refusing to subordinate one to the other, a process that, as Marianne DeKoven has shown in her readings of Stein, is consonant with at least some of Kristeva's contentions about poetic language.[21] Yet, in contrast to Kristeva's view of fetishism, Stein develops a *bothness* that is, as I see it, fundamentally fetishistic: for the primary experience of male fetishism is having it both ways — seeing the fetish as maternal phallus while still acknowledging castration. In her play with the noun, Stein indeed rejects castration, but she nonetheless practices a similar strategy of having it both ways — by using language as "thing" and symbol at the same time. Rejecting a phallic economy, Stein writes with a sense of both the signifying function of language and the disruptive release of the semiotic. *Tender Buttons* shows us a female fetishism freed from an obsessive castration fear and a language that reflects both the female body and the diversity of an eroticized objective world.

FETISHIZING THE NOUN

In "Poetry and Grammar," Stein describes the materiality of language. At the same time she makes it clear that her interest is not just in an experience of pure sound. Stein dislocates the relationship between meaning and sound so that, through a process of fetishistic substitution, language becomes material. In her method one word-as-thing substitutes for another one whose meaning has been lost through overuse in expected contexts. In prose this tiredness of particular words means that nouns are essentially uninteresting:

A noun is a name of anything, why after a thing is named write about it. A name is adequate or it is not. If it is adequate then why go on calling it, if it is not then calling it by its name does no good. (LIA, 209–10)

But in poetry Stein's practice is to make the named thing new by renaming it, or rather, by circumventing the original name: "I too felt in me the need of making . . . a thing that could be named without using its name" (LIA, 236). The "need" is explored in the new kind of poetry Stein was to write:

And so in Tender Buttons . . . I struggled with the ridding myself of nouns, I knew nouns must go in poetry as they had gone in prose if anything that is everything was to go on meaning something. (LIA, 242)

The interest here is clearly in signifying — in engaging the reader in the process of "meaning something," not simply in the material pleasure of the signifier. As Chessman notes, Stein said that making sense of language while writing is inevitable: "Any human being putting down words had to make sense of them."[22]

At the same time, though, Stein refuses to give up the palpable existence of the noun as an object, physically felt: "poetry is . . . a state of knowing and feeling a name" (LIA, 233). And to know and to feel involves not just the intellect, which responds to the symbolic, but the body and its passions. Thus the difference between poetry and prose is that poetry involves being in love:

> if you love a name then saying that name any number of times only makes you love it more, more violently more persistently more tormentedly. Anybody knows how anybody calls out the name of anybody one loves. And so that is poetry really loving the name of anything. (LIA, 232)

The experience is fetishistic — a violent and persistent passion invested in the "name" as substitute. Clearly "saying that name any number of times" is a favorite device in Stein's earlier poetry[23] as well as in *Tender Buttons*, which is about names — the relationship between the things "one loves" (for Stein, the material world in general, and Alice Toklas in particular) and the "names" that they possess.

Stein recounts the anecdote of her older brother who fell in love and, as comical as the resulting poetry was, "he knew the poem was funny but he was right, being in love made him make poetry" (LIA, 236). Stein herself discovers, supposedly during the writing of *Tender Buttons*, that "passion" must be invested in the noun — and in the "things" one sees:

> I called them by their names with passion and that made poetry, I did not mean it to make poetry but it did, it made the Tender Buttons, and the Tender Buttons was very good poetry. (LIA, 235)

This emphasis on "passion," as well as on "names," clarifies the way we should read *Tender Buttons*: the logic of love in connection to words and objects makes "good" poetry. We should never stop making sense of *Tender Buttons* — for Stein never did in writing it; she made the word deliver a multiplicity of "sense." And yet the *sensuality* of the signifier is inescapable. Stein forces us to become fetishizers of the text, to experience it as sign and material "thing" at the same time.[24]

The constant play in *Tender Buttons* between sensuality and semantics, materiality and meaning, begins with the title and the subsequent disjunction between headings and text.[25] As title, *Tender Buttons* initiates the reader into Stein's fetishistic strategy. The near-paradox of a hard object that is "tender" is evocative on several planes. One apparent reference is to a domestic activity that seems to pay tribute to the Victorian sensibility: just as "boxes" and "dresses" pervade Stein's "Objects" section,[26] so "buttons" are the implements of the feminine activity of sewing; at the same time, the plurality of these small objects suggests her words themselves, and perhaps even the multiple geometrical shapes used in Cubist painting.[27] Yet these "buttons" also suggest parts of the female body (nipples, clitoris) that become multiple, pluralized, in pleasure, alive to the play of sameness and difference between physical selves.[28] These more conventional meanings cover over the female, sensual one in Stein's displacement of the erotic onto the objective world, the fetishized "buttons" of her domestic landscape. The same strategy is effected by the back-and-forth between the headings and the text. For the most part the headings bear witness to the transparent function of language; with a few exceptions ("A Little Called Pauline," "A Leave," "Suppose An Eyes"), objects are conventionally "named" in the headings. Oddly, though, they become the backdrop for disruptive texts in what would normally be a hierarchical relationship. Instead, the symbolic language in the headings merely provides the reader with a false sense of security, of "stable" ground that Stein will shift throughout the writing of *Tender Buttons*.[29]

Within the text the essence of Stein's female fetishism is the experience of reaching after fact and reason and of discovering pleasure at the same time. Contrary to the division between semiotic and symbolic central to Kristeva's theory of the avant-garde text — in which the semiotic disrupts the logical surface of the text, and therefore signification and sonic play are always at odds — Stein avoids any separation of meaning from the "language" of what Kristeva calls the *chora*. In "A Substance in a Cushion," for example, the text can be read only by experiencing the materiality of the language at the same time as the multiplicity of possible significations at play with one another:

A closet, a closet does not connect under the bed. The band if it is white and black, the band has a green string. A sight a whole sight and a little groan grinding makes a trimming such a sweet singing trimming and a red thing not a round thing but a white thing, a red thing and a white thing.[30]

Here language functions under two imperatives — polyvalent signification and semiotic release, impossible to separate from each other. Moments of "sense" introduce speculative ideas: "A closet, a closet does not connect under the bed" raises the question of what it means to "connect," in (or "under") the bed or elsewhere, as well as the pervasive issue in *Tender Buttons* of embeddedness and enclosure. At the same time the heading "A Substance in a Cushion" suggests needles and pins in their "cushion" (the passage continues, "The disgrace is not in carelessness nor even in sewing it comes out out of the way," creating syntactic ambiguity that multiplies meanings around the motif of sewing). The "band" surrounds a part of the piece of clothing, just as a "sash" (mentioned later) surrounds one's waist. Labor produces "a trimming" through arduous activity – "a little groan grinding." Briefly, then, the passage becomes a portrait of sewing. So the text is "readable," or rather, decipherable; if we want to push and pull at it, like a piece of cloth, we can cut it into shapes of meaning.

Yet these meanings cannot account for the materiality language takes on here. It is not simply that poetic devices create onomatopoeic effect or decorate a discursive content. Stein evokes the physicality of the words.[31] Rhythmic insistence and sonic repetition suggest sensual experience. As in other Stein texts (such as "As a Wife Has a Cow: A Love Story" and "Susie Asado"), this section is propelled by imperatives other than those of semantics, particularly in the long final sentence. Stein orchestrates phonemic shifts through which sounds evolve and resolve: "sight a whole sight" lightens into the short "i" of "trimming such a sweet singing trimming and a red thing," while the long "o" of "whole" and "groan" evolve into the diphthong of "round" and the higher sounds of "a red thing and a white thing." The recurrence of particular words ("sight," "trimming," "red," "white," "thing") exemplifies Stein's theory of the relationship between "love" and repetition: that "if you love a name then saying that name any number of times only makes you love it more" (LIA, 232). The sentence lightens into a kind of ecstasy of repetitive sound. There is no way to render such semiotic release in discursive terms; the multiple meanings work on a completely different plane from the eroticized "experience" of the words as sounds. Having become material "things," carrying not just symbolic but bodily "content," Stein's words are fetishes, even as the reader – forced to "see" doubly, through the lenses of the mind's meaning and the body's knowing – must become a fetishist to read *Tender Buttons*.

It is in this way that Stein's fetishization contrasts with Kristeva's account of avant-garde practice, in which the semiotic completely disrupts the symbolic function of the text. Stein instead refuses to choose. In "A Waist" she again suggests the motif of sewing, yet she also creates of language not a container for meaning but an emphatic physical presence:

A star glide, a single frantic sullenness, a single financial grass greediness.
Object that is in wood. Hold the pine, hold the dark, hold in the rush, make the bottom.

A piece of crystal. A change, in a change that is remarkable there is no reason to say that there was a time.
A woolen object gilded. A country climb is the best disgrace, a couple of practices any of them in order is so left. (TB, 471–72)

"A Waist" evokes feminine "dress." But the disjunction between the heading and the "content" (which, except for the word "woolen," evokes the natural world) forces the reader to examine individual words to "decode" the symbolic workings. The word "disgrace," for example, will recur in "A Petticoat," in a parodic version of lesbian transgression. And a "star," "crystal," and "gilded" may be drawn from Stein's lexicon of that which "shines" – a code word for sexual pleasure in *Tender Buttons*. "Grass" suggests the envy of "greediness," and the green of money ("financial"), conflating nature and the fiduciary, the natural object and symbol. Categories are dismantled, as in the heading, where the pun on "waste" questions distinctions between physicality and social coverings (the waist of a dress). There is also a different kind of meaning in the heightening of tone ("Hold the pine, hold the dark, hold in the rush"), which impels the writing toward emotional climax, only to end in bathos: "make the bottom."

And yet we need to curb our irritable reaching after fact and reason. Any efforts at "decoding" are complicated, if not foiled, by moments that refuse grammatical rules. "A couple of them any of them in order is so left" could be pinned down only with punctuation – a confusion similar to "object that is in wood" (a location, a material?). With such syntactic indeterminacy, no "single" meaning will yield itself. Instead, there are sonic repetitions: "a single frantic sullenness, a single financial grass greediness" uses sounds hypnotically (the liquid "l" for example), independent of semantic content. And while this is no ecstasy of the mellifluous, even discursive statements (like the much-cited "Act so that there is no use in a centre" [TB, 498] of "Rooms") provide only momentary resting points. It is tempting, for example, to read the following autobiographically: "in a change that is remarkable there is no reason to say that there was a time" (during a favorable change in one's life, there is no reason for nostalgia). Perhaps this is a cryptic allusion to the "change" of ménage when Alice moved in to 27, rue du Fleurus, and Leo eventually moved out. But such a reading, while possible, seems hopelessly reductive if asserted as a kind of "translation" – especially juxtaposed as the passage is with the more surreal "A woolen object gilded." Stein's breach of our expectations makes her play apparent: the pleasure of this text is in the continuous doubling of words as "names" or symbols and as material things.

It is this ability to see and to write "both ways" that makes *Tender Buttons* so disruptive a text, an attack on the systematization of language. Stein's fetishism of language (in contrast to Lacan's view of language as a sign of lack, verging on the fetishistic because it stands for the absent phallus) involves not trauma but irreverence. Hers is a strategy that overturns literary conventions and defies any division between what we now call the semiotic and the symbolic. For this reason – the subversive nature of *Tender Buttons* – a description of Stein's revisionist fetishism must take into account the other register of doubleness in her text: the parody that similarly redefines fetishism itself.

FEMALE FETISHISM AND PARODY

The allure of female fetishism as a model for Stein's poetics is precisely its impossibility in Freudian terms, a gender specificity Stein can be seen working against parodically in the domestic landscape of *Tender Buttons*. Stein was certainly cognizant of Freudian theory; in addition to an extensive connection to William James and his lectures on psychology at Harvard, Ruddick has documented Stein's familiarity with Freud before the writing of *Tender Buttons*.[32] Passages of *Tender Buttons* provide evidence that, complementing her fetishization of words, Stein was "playing" with male fetishism, along with a female variant of it – a version of object-love that is multiple and playful, rather than fixated on the singularity of the (one) "thing." In *Tender Buttons*, Stein both parodies male fetishism and, at the same time, evokes an experience of lesbian pleasure. Relying on both signification and the semiotic, Stein's parody emerges from her fetishization of language.

In its overturning of an established scenario, Stein's parody anticipates Irigaray's concept of mimicry, which, in turn, sheds light on *Tender Buttons*. Mimicry combats the masquerade of femininity, that process by which women "recuperate some element of desire, to participate in man's desire, but at the price of renouncing their own." In masquerade, "the woman loses herself, and loses herself by playing on her femininity." One response to this compulsory masquerade is a willed, self-conscious, and ironic version of it: mimicry. Why not "convert a form of subordination into an affirmation, and thus ... begin to thwart it," to "recover the place of [our] exploitation by discourse"?[33] Stein's parody does just that, attacking and distorting masculine views of the feminine, just as Irigaray's "speculum" can "disturb the staging of representation according to too-exclusively masculine parameters."[34] Yet it is important to note that Stein comes to writing with less difficulty in expressing feminine pleasure. Desiring another woman, Stein is not the object of masculine desire; in Irigaray's words, (heterosexual) women "are there as objects for sexual enjoyment, not as those who enjoy." In affirming lesbian sexuality, Stein experiences what Irigaray calls for — a nonphallic, multiple sensuality. She is free to express, through lesbian love, the feminine desire that, in heterosexual love, can only be mimed: "from the time of the Oedipus complex, [women] are exiled from themselves, and lacking any possible continuity/contiguity with their first desires/pleasures, they are imported into another economy." Attacking this Freudian economy, Stein asserts the difference of feminine pleasure.[35]

Tender Buttons as a whole is clearly parodic, and not just where sexuality is concerned. In Elizabeth Fifer's view, Stein both encodes sexuality and offers us moments of parody, including a parody of romanticism.[36] Throughout *Tender Buttons*, Stein takes shots at the Victorian earnestness that directly reflects sexual roles. In the "Objects" section, "A Time to Eat" is a parody of Victorian domestic ritual in which the voice of the patriarch betrays its reliance on strict order:

A pleasant simple habitual and tyrannical and authorised and educated and re-sumed and articulate separation. This is not tardy. (TB, 472)

The whole notion of creating a "time" to eat suggests a need to control the raw energy of the appetite; in appointing a time for the consumption of food, the patriarch places limits on the satisfaction of desire. The notion of control over the body is reinforced by the "tyranny" of Latinate adjectives here. (Stein condemned the adjective as "not really and truly interesting" [LIA, 211]). "Pleasant" and "simple" suggest the psychologi-cal need for decorum; like Edith Wharton's Mrs. Welland, whose life strategy was to avoid anything "unpleasant," the paternal figure institutes a ritual of decorum, "resumed and articulate," to protect himself and those he is responsible for. In defense of the importance of honoring this "time" to eat, the patriarch chides the members of the family that "This is not tardy," that the law is to be respected and that, at the same time, the ritual itself is not "tardy" — outmoded. And yet, amid what is "authorised" appears the protest, the renaming of the father as "tyrannical" and the notion of "time" as "articulate," in opposition to a more organic sense of the body and to time as Bergsonian (or Jamesian) duration. The humor of "A Time to Eat" lies in its combination of parody with quick shifts in voice that alter the tone even from one word to the next.

Yet this parodic word-play is most cutting in those crucial passages where Stein contrasts masculine and lesbian views of sexuality. The erotic encodings in *Tender Buttons*, as I have noted, have been explored extensively. Yet Stein's parody in these same passages has often been overlooked. *Tender Buttons* metonymically substitutes eroticized "objects" for the female body and yet also "impersonates" the masculine perspective on both lesbian and heterosexual sexuality. The fetishistic functioning of language in *Tender Buttons* provides the means of achieving this kind of double seeing.

One of the densest examples is the close of the "Objects" section. "This Is This Dress, Aider" signifies on multiple levels, parodying a masculine view of heterosexual intercourse, as well as representing lesbian sex and one kind of masculine response to its "perversion." It demonstrates Stein's use of puns and linguistic play to parody one thing and pay tribute to another:

THIS IS THIS DRESS, AIDER
   Aider, why aider why whow, whow stop touch, aider whow, aider stop the muncher, muncher munchers.
   A jack in kill her, a jack in, makes a meadowed king, makes a to let. (TB, 476)

William Gass astutely points out the contrast between male and female sexuality that emerges in the space between the first sentence and the second.[37] What Gass and others have noticed fits the model of Stein's textual fetishism, for the multiply signifying — punning — heading sets up an even broader range of meanings. "This Dress" is often read as "distress," and "Aider" as both a pun on "Alice" ("Ada" was one of Stein's names for Alice Toklas),[38] and an elision of "aid her." Thus the possibility of both distress and pleasure emerge right away, coupled inextricably in the same signifiers. "This Is This Dress" also picks up on the domestic motif of sewing for a final time in "Objects" and implies a play with identity and difference ("this is this"), central to all sexuality.

Given the confusion between calling for "aid" and receiving pleasure from "Aider" (evoked in the ecstatic sounds of "why whow, whow stop touch"), Gass, despite his cogent reading of the movement from female orgasmic pleasure to more violent (male) sexuality ("A jack in kill her"), misses the double perspective Stein creates. The second sentence, as Ruddick points out, critiques the male sex act in which a "jack," who, through patriarchal law becomes a "meadowed king," "makes a to let" — a "toilet" or a rented or used vessel — out of the female body. The second sentence seems less polyvalent than the first; clearly the "meadowed king" is crowned at the expense of the female, "her."[39] In this sense, Stein satirizes the "meadowed king."

Yet the same kind of parody occurs from the very beginning of "This Is This Dress." The play between lesbian sexuality and "distress" clearly calls up the patriarchal law; since "Aider" is the source of pleasure, "distress" would be felt only by the *male* onlooker — who, fetishistically, "watches" and labels what he sees with a symbolic value, one he associates with a threat. The lesbian experience of pleasure — which doesn't have to involve a phallus at all — causes "distress" to the "king" who, as patriarch, longs to "aid" the female gone astray. He displaces his phallic anxiety (for the two women represent the insignificance of his own sexuality) onto chivalric concern for a woman in "distress." There is a fetishistic substitution of castration fear with paternalistic regard, which Stein brilliantly parodies through punning — sheer signification.

Meanwhile, however, the text registers on the "other" level as well — that of lesbian *jouissance*. "Aider, why aider why whow, whow stop touch" presents several possible "decodings." "Aider" is the lover's name (and "saying that name any number of times" makes one "love it more" [LIA, 232]), but it is also a question: "Aid her?" The response is, in fact, "*why* aid her?" That is, the lovers don't need the intervention so anxiously posited by the patriarchal onlooker. As the sentence unfolds, the masculine perspective drops out, giving way to female pleasure ("whow stop touch"), and ending with a humorous version of mutual satisfaction (a single "muncher" — suggesting oral gratification — becoming plural, "munchers"). The final reflection that occurs in the second sentence "interprets" the male response to the lesbian exclusion of the phallus and ends the "Objects" section with what is at once a satire of masculine panic and, at the same time, a representation of an orgasmic lesbian experience. Stein's invention of a fetishistic language — at once satiric and shot through with *jouissance* — thus "aids" her in creating a parody of the very fetishism she appropriates and renews.

Such elaborate encodings of female sexuality occur throughout "Objects" and continue in "Food" and "Rooms."[40] Yet the first part of *Tender Buttons* exemplifies most clearly Stein's parodic versions of male fetishism that, at the same time, represent the "difference" of lesbian sexuality. Stein's very process of composition involved a consciously fetishistic relationship to the objects she chose to paint in prose.[41] Her strategy was to focus on an object and through this scopic relationship liberate herself to "name" it without using its already-given name. Three times in "Portraits and Repetition" Stein describes the importance of "looking" in *Tender Buttons:* "I was trying to live in looking, and looking was not to mix itself up with remembering" (LIA, 189); and later, "I did express what something was, a little by talking and listening to that thing, but a great deal by looking at that thing" (LIA, 190). She even goes so far as to explain the substitution of objects for living subjects: "I had the feeling that something should be included and that something was looking, and so concentrating on looking I did the Tender Buttons because it was easier to do objects than people if you were just looking" (LIA, 198–99; no italics in original). Stein deliberately repeats the fetishist's scopophilia ("love of looking") that invests the object with erotic significance and then focuses on it to achieve orgasm, or, in Stein's appropriation, a pleasure of the text.[42]

This fetishistic process at once mimics *male* fetishism and substitutes a female version — a release into the sensuality of the material world and of language. Within an economy of plenitude, the female fetishist is able to see language not as lack but as presence. She is liberated to experience the sensuality of the objective world without fearing castration. Irigaray imagines such a feminine economy, based on multiplicity, on "exchanges without identifiable terms, without accounts, without end."[43] Stein's poetic practice coincides as well with Cixous's vision of writing the female body:

I don't want a penis to decorate my body with. But I do desire the other for the other, whole and entire, male or female; because living means wanting everything that is, everything that lives, and wanting it alive. Castration? Let others toy with it. What's a desire originating from a lack? A pretty meager desire.[44]

This passage seems a prototype for Stein's poetics of *fulfilled* desire; one need only substitute the material world for Cixous's "everything that lives" to identify Stein's fetishistic practice as well as her rejection of the notion of language as "lack." But we can also hear in Cixous's irreverent tone Stein's appropriations. Instances of parodic fetishism in *Tender Buttons* demonstrate Stein's "toying" with castration. Many of the "objects" are fetishistic favorites — items metonymically associated with the female body, such as pieces of clothing — including "A Box," "Mildred's Umbrella," "A Long Dress," "A Red Hat," "A Purse," "A Petticoat," "A Handkerchief," "Shoes," and "A Shawl."

The most clearly parodic of these sections is simple enough, and its very clarity is, in this case, a result of its reliance on a predominantly symbolic use of language. Here signification supplies the tools for parody:

A PETTICOAT
A light white, a disgrace, an ink spot, a rosy charm. (TB, 471)

In Freudian terms, a petticoat would be a perfect candidate for a fetish, since it is likely to be the last object glimpsed before the boy discovers his mother's "castration"; then, too, there is a metonymic logic to the choice of the petticoat, encircling as it does the female body, even bearing its traces, its shape. Stein plays on the likelihood of male fixation on feminine clothing, much as she does in "This Is This Dress, Aider" (and, clearly, the petticoat is part of the study of "dress" in *Tender Buttons*) through the word "disgrace," akin to the pun in "distress" in the later section. Ruddick points out the specifically female nature of this "rosy charm," for, in her important reading, the "disgrace" that taints the "light white" of the undergarment is, on one level, menstrual blood. Yet, as in "This Is This Dress," the event is only a disgrace from a masculine point of view; it is a feminine perspective that could see the "grace" in "this" happenstance event — that the red token of the body has its own "charm," and, as Ruddick suggests, that the "white" of the garment has in fact been "written" on, touched by "an ink spot." Quite literally, Stein is providing a parable of "writing the body," equating the processes of the female body with the act of writing; on another level, the supposed violation (of the "white" cloth) and the breach of decorum ("a disgrace") are metaphoric of the woman's transgression onto the male-dominated domain of letters.[45]

The implied narrative, then, functions doubly. For a moment, in Stein's rendering of the male fetishist's perspective, the fetish is ruined —

stained by the female genitals that the fetishist finds loathsome. At the same time, Stein "substitutes" a female narrative of the body, one that rejoices in the erotics of "disgrace," of a mistake that becomes "charming" because it represents a transgression of the virginal white of the petticoat (as a double for the page). For Stein, the petticoat does, in fact, take on an erotic charge; just like the "Red Hat" (TB, 467) that becomes eroticized through the fact of its color, this tainted garment is a source of joy to the lover who identifies its color as her own. The male, on the other hand, sees blood as "other," perhaps even a sign of the castration he has sought to forget through the process of fetishizing a newly beloved object. In the paratactic list of "A Petticoat," Stein at once creates a male fetishist's nightmare and a female fetishist's revision: taking pleasure in the "rosy charm," the feminine economy recovers (or avoids in the first place) the loathing of the body that motivates the male fetishist.

At once parodic and erotic, using both semantics and suggestion, "A Petticoat" represents the female laugh in *Tender Buttons*, what Cixous might see as a version of the "Medusa," an image she appropriates to recast male castration fear. For Cixous, castration should only elicit women's laughter:

> Too bad for them if they fall apart upon discovering that women aren't men, or that the mother doesn't have one.... Wouldn't the worst be ... that women aren't castrated, that they have only to stop listening to the Sirens (for the Sirens were men) for history to change its meaning? You only have to look at the Medusa straight on to see her. And she's not deadly. She's beautiful and she's laughing.[46]

Just as Cixous takes Freud's classic interpretation of the Medusa as a figure for male castration fear (the head enveloped by phallic snakes) and reinvests the image with "beauty," not horror, Stein reinvests female blood with the potency and the delight of a "charm." The act of laughing — at once joyous and vengeful — is part of Stein's strategy as well. In the case of "A Petticoat," Stein's feminine laughter mocks and celebrates at once, "cutting" both ways. We could well apply Freud himself, on the function of humor: "Humour is not resigned; it is rebellious. It signifies not only the triumph of the ego but also of the pleasure principle, which is able here to assert itself."[47] Stein's strategy bears out Freud's insights, "asserting itself" against masculine anxiety and domination, and by so doing, Stein's becomes an exemplum of Cixous's feminine practice, fomenting "rebellion" and a "triumph of the [feminine] ego."

EROTICIZING LANGUAGE

Stein's alternative to masculine object fixation emerges as well in several other sections that contrast male and female sexuality, all of which suggest the difference of women's engagement with both language and the material world. In "Shoes," as in "This Is This Dress," Stein uses the relatively simple structure of two sections to create a marked contrast:

SHOES
    To be a wall with a damper a stream of pounding way and nearly enough choice makes a steady midnight. It is pus.
    A shallow hole rose on red, a shallow hole in and in this makes ale less. It shows shine. (TB, 474)

The object is common to male fetishists because of the boy's (supposed) act of glancing up the mother's skirt only to discover her "lack" and substituting, for the phallus, her shoes. Stein contrasts male and female anatomy, reversing the polarity by displaying a disgust for the former and celebrating the latter. The first section contains the phallic images of "a stream of pounding," and its residue of seminal "pus." There is a resistance to motion, a stifling of the body (a version of the patriarch's control of the appetite in "A Time to Eat"). A "wall with a damper" suggests the hindering of fluid movement, while violent "pounding" leads only to "a steady midnight," a (spiritual) obscurity. The shoes, as fetishes, represent fixation — the lack of "choice" characteristic of the male fetishist. Whatever pleasure might be taking place in the closet, its climax is quickly deflated.

By contrast, brightness and multiple punning erupt in the second section as Stein substitutes female pleasure for the male fetishist's unappealing phallic relationship to the shoes. Crucial to the reversal of the male fetishist's mechanism is a bilingual pun. Ruddick points out that the French "chose" is slang for "vagina,"[48] punning on both "shoes" and "shows." The substitution of the feminine perspective, then, takes place on the level of the signifier itself: the same "object," and the same word, are perceived from different points of view. "A shallow hole rose on red" serves as an alternative depiction of the "chose," one that rejects the male fear of the female genitals. The sensory and symbolic qualities of "red" and "rose" — attributes of the female body — are "played" with rather than feared, while assonance and alliteration return the language to its materiality. The repetitions Stein delights in ("a shallow hole," "in and in") link the love of words to a delight in the "rose" of the female body. And of course the code for Alice ("ale less") evokes Stein's difference from the male paradigm. In this movement from male to female and from fear to *jouissance*, "midnight" becomes "shine" — a term that, along with other words for brightness in *Tender Buttons*, signifies sexual satisfaction. Using sonic play, Stein again makes use of the semiotic in the interest of a fetishistic plenitude.[49]

"Shoes" substitutes one kind of fetishism for another: rejecting the male's fixation on the object in the closet, Stein brings the shoes into the light. Even as she retains a private textual code, Stein takes pleasure in the heterogeneity of the material world, the attributes of the female body, and the particular appeal of the word itself. Stein merges "fetishistic" observation with her own fetishization of the word, connecting language as a medium to the lesbian pleasure *Tender Buttons* describes.

The same eroticization of language and the material world appears in "A Little Called Pauline," one of the few headings that is as disjunctive as the text itself. The act of naming ("calling") with affection (the diminutive "little") results in a new name — Pauline, the feminized version of the masculine (perhaps apostolic) Paul. Stein evokes several different objects in the game of naming what one desires; the plurality (rather than the fetishist's singular choice) suggests a polymorphously perverse pleasure, an erotics precedent to Oedipal anxiety. The sexual image with which the section opens ("A little called anything shows shudders" [TB, 473]) can be glossed by Stein's comments on the noun, revealing a conflation of language, love, and object in Stein's poetic world. Since poetry is "really loving the name of anything" (LIA, 232), the act of naming an object ("a little called anything") is an act of love — it "shows shudders." Like "it shows shine," this phrase links climactic pleasure to the objective world, and to the material that is language. Despite the absence of a heading that "names" a chosen object, this formulation explains Stein's fetishistic economy.

Throughout this section — unlike "Shoes" or "A Petticoat" — Stein refuses to choose one particular object. There are phallic reminders — the "pope," scourge-like "boils," and the penetration of "a tight head" ("jam it not") — which parody masculine anxiety about castration and punishment. Yet we are also invited to child-like enjoyment through the intonations of nursery rhyme: "Come and say what prints all day" links pleasure to language both rhythmically and through the pun on "prints" that suggests painting and writing. Rejecting patriarchal authority ("There is no pope"), Stein evokes objects that seem to escape the obsessive singularity of the male fetishist. There is a punning reprise of "Shoes": "little dressing and choose wide soles and little spats really little spices." From "soles" and masculine "spats" come "little spices," elements of a (feminine) oral pleasure that refuses to be limited by the singular.

Stein evokes fetishism ("A little lace") and its possible punishment (it "makes boils"), only to shed such fear ("This is not true"). This dismissal of obsession and punishment is linked to the feminine: "A peaceful life to arise her, noon and moon and moon" associates the moon with sexual "arousal." Perhaps the most explicit "clue" is "I hope she has her cow." Fifer has noted that "cow" denotes orgasm in Stein's lexicon, here associated with "Bidding a wedding" and thus with Stein's own domesticity.[50] The unnamed "she" places "A Little Called Pauline" in the realm of the personal, the world of concern for — rather than objectification of — a loved woman. For Grosz, such an "object" choice might itself represent a form of lesbian fetishism.[51] Here Stein suggests, indeed, a *female* version of fetishism — one based on love, not loathing, of the female body.

Such an embrace is also suggested in "A Shawl," an item of warmth and security, of comfortable intimacy, that counters the male fetishist's fixation on feminine dress: "A shawl is a hat and hurt and a red balloon and an under coat and a sizer a sizer of talks" (TB, 475). Here Stein recapitulates her terms for the female body and, at the same time, evokes items that are all in some way fetishistic. The "hat" has already emerged as an element of Stein's erotic lexicon, especially in being "red," while the word "hurt" is itself a metonym for shades of red (in "A Carafe, That Is a Blind Glass," it suggests the color of wine). A "red balloon" becomes an eroticized female shape, while the "under coat" recalls Stein's "petticoat" and puns as well on "udder" (which returns in the "Milk" section of "Food" as "utter," conflating the female body and the act of writing).[52] Most significantly, "A sizer" reads as "a scissor," a feminine aid to sewing that can be both a threatening instrument to the male fearful of castration and, conversely, a potent tool for the fetishist who cuts women's hair. The entire list, then, is simultaneously a summation of the feminine code and an elaborate reference to male fetishism.

Yet the reflexive quality of the language here bears further examination, as in the following: "It was a mistake to state that a laugh and a lip and a laid climb and a depot and a cultivator and little choosing is a point it." The "mistake," like the fortuitous "disgrace" in "A Petticoat," is a matter of language ("a mistake to state"). And in this list of items the "depot" (a point of departure) and the "cultivator" (agricultural or familial) find company with the body ("a laugh and a lip"). It is a "mistake" to state that this list "is a point it," that is, "disappointed" or, possibly, has a "point" or logical closure. "Point" suggests a directive; Stein returns to the questions with which "Objects" began – the carafe, an object that is "an arrangement in a system of pointing" (TB, 462). From an initial naming of fetishized objects and a suggestion of feminine difference, we move to a comment on Stein's own practice of "caressing" the noun. Meditating on her relationship to the "covering" of language, Stein refuses to rely simply on meaning (a "point"); at the same time, she is not "disappointed" with the nouns she "addresses and caresses." Stein suggests her divergence from the male fetishist's rejection of the female body, and her self-reflection also points to her distance from disavowal. Instead, Stein takes joy in language, linking body to word – as she does throughout *Tender Buttons*.

Like Irigaray, Stein is aware that the expression of feminine pleasure is "the greatest threat of all to masculine discourse."[53] In *Tender Buttons*, the object of Stein's desire is, in fact, a word spoken through the body. Developing a new language, as well as bearing witness to a different sexuality, *Tender Buttons* as a whole is both formative and revisionist. It demonstrates Stein's willingness to take on the emerging Freudian notions of her time. Stein's female fetishism attests to her belief in the intersections among the objective world, the symbolic system of language, and sexuality, in contrast to the fascination with the power of the inanimate, and the ambivalence about the human body, that spurred the writing of so many male avant-garde poets of her day.

Equally important, Stein shows us that there is a place for female fetishism within feminist conceptions of language and sexuality, despite feminists' recent fears that fetishism might either erase the lines of difference altogether (Apter, for example, is hesitant to embrace Kofman's sexual and textual indeterminacy)[54] or simply reassert a phallic norm. *Tender Buttons* might serve as a complement to critiques such as Marjorie Garber's in her astute "Fetish Envy." Garber sees what she calls female fetishism as the invisible norm of heterosexual culture, since the penis is itself the fetish object of heterosexual women.[55] Stein shows us a very different way of fetishizing. *Tender Buttons* reveals that female fetishism, seen as originating *not* from a phallic norm but from a feminine sense of plenitude, can be an assertion of difference, particularly the difference of lesbian sexuality. Stein's combination of a fetishized language with a parody of Freudian sexuality expresses her liberation from the masquerade of femininity and announces a distinctly different kind of pleasure in both language and the material world.

NOTES

I would like to express my appreciation to Lucia Re for her generous support and many readings of this essay. I would also like to thank Calvin Bedient and Stephen Yenser for their advice and encouragement.

Grateful acknowledgment is made to Random House, Inc., for permission to quote from *Lechres in America* by Gertrude Stein, copyright © 1935 and renewed by Alice B. Toklas, and from *Selected Writings of Gertrude Stein* by Gertrude Stein, copyright © 1946 by Random House, Inc.

1. Gertrude Stein, "Poetry and Grammar," in *Lectures in America* (New York: Random House, 1935), 246, cited subsequently within the text as LIA.
2. See Louise J. Kaplan's *Female Perversions: The Temptations of Emma Bovary* (New York: Doubleday, 1991) for some definitions and typologies: "A perversion is a mental strategy that uses one or another social stereotype of masculinity and femininity in a way that deceives the onlooker about the unconscious meanings of the behaviors she or he is observing" (9).
3. See Naomi Schor's "Female Fetishism: The Case of George Sand," in *The Female Body in Western Culture: Contemporary Perspectives*, ed. Susan Rubin Suleiman (Cambridge: Harvard University Press, 1985), 363–72, on "undecidability."
4. See, especially, William Gass's "Gertrude Stein and the Geography of the Sentence" in his *The World within the Word* (New York: Knopf, 1978), 63–123; Catharine R. Stimpson's "The Somagrams of Gertrude Stein," in *Critical Essays on Gertrude Stein*, ed. Michael J. Hoffman (Boston: G. K. Hall, 1986), 183–96; Elizabeth Fifer's "Is Flesh Advisable? The Interior Theater of Gertrude Stein," *Signs* 4, no. 3 (1979): 472–83; and Lisa Ruddick's "A Rosy Charm: Gertrude Stein and the Repressed Feminine," in *Critical Essays*, 225–40. See also Margueritte S. Murphy, " 'Familiar Strangers': The Household Words of Gertrude Stein's *Tender Buttons*," *Contemporary Literature* 32 (Fall 1991): 383–402, for an exploration of Stein's desire to "reinvest domestic

labor with value, to make household tasks into code words for stability in her new domestic arrangement and for erotic lesbian love" (388).
5. Sigmund Freud, "Fetishism," *The Standard Edition of the Complete Works of Sigmund Freud*, trans. and ed. James Strachey (London: Hogarth Press, 1961), 11:152–53; "Splitting of the Ego in the Process of Defence," 23:275. John Matlock ("Masquerading Women, Pathologized Men: Cross-Dressing, Fetishism, and the Theory of Perversion, 1882–1935" in *Fetishism as Cultural Discourse*, ed. Emily Apter and William Pietz [Ithaca: Cornell University Press, 1993], 31–61) shows that cases of female fetishism were in fact documented in the 1880s in France, but that the emerging discourse of "perversion" ultimately gendered fetishism as a male phenomenon. He speculates that the suppression of female fetishism kept alive a crucial "story of primal difference" (58) along gender lines. In *Feminizing the Fetish: Psychoanalysis and Narrative Obsession in Turn-of-the-Century France* (Ithaca: Cornell University Press, 1991), 102–4, Apter summarizes Schor's assembling of such case histories in her "Female Fetishism," 263.
6. Apter, "Female Fetishism," 368–69. Schor also cites Sarah Kofman's "Ça Cloche," in *Les Fins de l'homme: A partir de Jacques Derrida*, ed. Philippe Lacoue-Labarthe and Jean-Luc Nancy (Paris: Gallilée, 1981), 83–116.
7. Elizabeth Grosz, "Lesbian Fetishism?" *Differences* 3, no. 2 (1991): 52, reprinted in *Fetishism as Cultural Discourse*, ed. Apter and Pietz, 101–15. For Grosz, the choice of another woman as loved "object" could constitute, in Freud's own terms, a kind of female fetishism. In *Feminizing the Fetish*, Apter also uses female fetishism to stress gender flexibility. She reconceives of the idea of masquerade as a "sartorial female fetishism," part of a theory of "materialized social construction" (Apter, *Feminizing the Fetish*, 98). She also proposes the category "gynotextual fetishism," "a female fetishism traversing literary and psychoanalytical boundaries and defined from a woman's point of view" (Apter, *Feminizing the Fetish*, 100). In this context she examines the "feminine relic" as female fetish (Apter, *Feminizing the Fetish*, 121). Apter retains a focus on loss that I am trying to move away from in my analysis of Stein's female fetishism.
8. Freud, "Femininity," *The Standard Edition*, ed. Strachey, 22:134, cited by Apter, *Feminizing the Fetish*, 105.
9. Luce Irigaray, *Speculum of the Other Woman*, trans. Gillian C. Gill (Ithaca: Cornell University Press, 1985), 41–42, 52, 53.
10. Schor, "Female Fetishism," 371.
11. Naomi Schor, "Fetishism and Its Ironies," *Fetishism as Cultural Discourse*, ed. Apter and Pietz, 98.
12. Grosz, "Lesbian Fetishism," 40 and 39. I feel that the question remains open as to whether the "difference" of lesbian sexuality requires as well a separate theory of fetishism and/or parody.
13. See Harriet Scott Chessman, *The Public Is Invited to Dance: Representation, the Body, and Dialogue in Gertrude Stein* (Stanford: Stanford University Press, 1989), 82–87. Margaret Homans's *Bearing the Word: Language and Female*

Experience in Nineteenth-Century Woman's Writing (Chicago: University of Chicago Press, 1986) also provides a fascinating account of woman and the literal in Romantic ideology.

14. Chessman, *The Public Is Invited to Dance*, 4. In *Reading Gertrude Stein: Body, Text, Gnosis* (Ithaca: Cornell University Press, 1990), 241, Lisa Ruddick uses the word "oscillation" to describe the movement between "the newly unearthed maternal dimension" and "the paternal/symbolic." Marianne DeKoven makes a similar point about what she calls Stein's "lively words" style, but she stresses the "presymbolic *jouissance*" of *Tender Buttons* (see Marianne DeKoven, *A Different Language: Gertrude Stein's Experimental Writing* [Madison: University of Wisconsin Press, 1983], 68 and 76).
15. See Jacques Lacan, "The Agency of the Letter in the Unconscious or Reason since Freud," in *Ecrits*, trans. Alan Sheridan (New York: Norton, 1977), 150.
16. Jacques Lacan and Wladimir Granoff, "Fetishism: The Symbolic, the Imaginary and the Real," in *Perversions: Psychodynamics and Therapy*, ed. Sandor Lorand (New York: Random, 1956), 287.
17. Lacan, "The Signification of the Phallus," in *Ecrits*, 287.
18. Lacan, "The Agency of the Letter in the Unconscious or Reason since Freud," in *Ecrits*, 167. See also Lacan, "The Signification of the Phallus": "it should not be forgotten that the organ that assumes this signifying function [the phallus] takes on the value of a fetish" (290).
19. Julia Kristeva, *Revolution in Poetic Language*, trans. Margaret Walker (New York: Columbia University Press, 1984), 63–65. Kristeva also cites Jean Pouillon: "If words were merely fetishes, semantics would be reduced to phonology" ("Fétiches sans fétichisme," *Nouvelle Revue de Psychoanalyse* 2 [Autumn 1970]: 39). See Kristeva, *Revolution*, n. 80, 249.
20. Elizabeth Grosz, *Jacques Lacan: A Feminist Introduction* (New York: Routledge, 1990), 164.
21. DeKoven uses Kristeva's notion of "musicalization" occurring *along with* signification to illuminate Stein's difficult language. As Kristeva points out, "No text, no matter how 'musicalized,' is devoid of meaning or signification; on the contrary, musicalization pluralizes meanings" (*Revolution*, 65), a process Stein was well aware of. See chapter 1 of DeKoven, *A Different Language*.
22. Chessman, *The Public Is Invited to Dance*, 91, citing an interview of Stein in *A Primer for the Gradual Understanding of Gertrude Stein*, ed. Robert B. Haas (Los Angeles: Black Sparrow, 1971), 18.
23. DeKoven distinguishes Stein's early style of repetition and "insistence" from that of the "lively words" of *Tender Buttons*. See DeKoven, *A Different Language*, 63ff.
24. Roland Barthes's concept of textual "pleasure" is relevant (in *The Pleasure of the Text*, trans. Richard Miller [New York: Farrar, Straus and Giroux, 1973]). Barthes asserts that significance "is meaning, *insofar as it is sensually produced*" (*The Pleasure of the Text*, 61) — a truth for Stein as well — and that "the text of pleasure is a sanctioned Babel" (4). In addition, perversion is "the realm of

textual pleasure" (Barthes, *The Pleasure of the Text*, 9–10): "language in pieces. ... Such texts are perverse in that they are outside any imaginable finality" (51–52). Barthes also addresses fetishism: reading is "perverse" in that "the reader can keep saying: *I know these are only words, but all the same*" (*The Pleasure of the Text*, 47). Barthes, however, associates both "bliss" (*jouissance*) and fetishism with loss, not plenitude: although he "perversely" reverses sexual polarities ("The text is a fetish object, and *this fetish desires me*" [*The Pleasure of the Text*, 27]), he posits the "text of bliss" as one "that imposes a state of loss" (14): "it is the abrupt loss of sociality ... everything is lost" (39). While verging on a Steinian sort of textual pleasure, Barthes maintains the Lacanian reliance on a phallic economy and on *jouissance* as loss.

25. I will call these capitalized phrases "headings" because I think it is misleading to use the word "title." Among other possibilities, each of the sections of *Tender Buttons* is itself a "button" in Stein's box, as words are buttons, too — or, simultaneously, each is a figure-in-words for a female body-part; but each is not an independent "poem" that begins with an extratextual title. As *Tender Buttons* is *sui generis*, its divisions are parts of a larger, serialized whole. Each heading provides a focus of attention, a moment — a "title" would have more pretensions. DeKoven uses the term "subtitles" (*A Different Language*, 77).

26. My focus will be on the "Objects" section, because it is here that the material world and the fetishistic strategy are most apparent. Stein's fetishism of language occurs, of course, throughout *Tender Buttons*.

27. For criticism on Stein and Cubism, see Randa Dubnick, *The Structure of Obscurity: Gertrude Stein, Language, and Cubism* (Chicago: University of Illinois Press, 1984), 28–44; and Stephen Scobie, "The Allure of Multiplicity: Metaphor and Metonymy in Cubism and Gertrude Stein," in *Gertrude Stein and the Making of Literature*, ed. Shirley Neuman and Ira B. Nadel (Boston: Northeastern University Press, 1988), 98–118.

28. Chessman elaborates on "the 'tenderness' of these 'buttons' [as] a human and bodily one." She also observes that, as words, "these buttons call our attention to the value they hold outside of their capacity to represent: their sound, their shape, their rhythm and length" (91). This important reading of Stein's bodily play is crucial to my model of fetishism in *Tender Buttons*.

29. William Gass describes how Stein "exposed the arbitrary conventionality" of title and chapter headings in *Four in America*. See Gass, *World with the Word*, 67–68.

30. Gertrude Stein, *Tender Buttons*, in *Selected Writings of Gertrude Stein*, ed. Carl Van Vechten (New York: Random, 1962), 462. Further references will appear within the text as TB.

31. What Barthes calls an "éclat du mot" ("an explosion of words") in such writers as Mallarmé is relevant, as it provides a vocabulary with which to describe the nonreferential uses of language. The difference, as I see it, between an awareness of the materiality of language and Stein's practice is that Stein evokes "doubleness" in language, rather than subverting significa-

tion. See "Is There Any Poetic Writing?" in *Writing Degree Zero*, trans. Annette Lavers and Colin Smith (New York: Farrar, Straus and Giroux, 1968), 41–52 (esp. 46).

32. In *Reading Gertrude Stein*, Ruddick documents Stein's familiarity with Freud (and William James) during the time of the writing of *The Making of Americans*, between 1906 and 1908 (92–116) and argues that at the time Stein wrote *Tender Buttons*, "her evolving feminism distanced her from Freud. The very gender relations that Freud explains but simultaneously naturalizes, Stein now denaturalizes, showing how the categories 'male' and 'female' are violently made" (Ruddick, *Reading Gertrude Stein*, 2). Stein must have been aware of the new categorizations of various "perversions" — including lesbianism — by the sexologists then coming into vogue; but the concept of fetishism was current as early as Marx's "Commodity Fetishism" of 1847 (though the usage there is less relevant to the erotics of the Freudian plot). And, while Freud's essay "Fetishism," in which he describes the fetish as "a substitute for the [mother's] penis" (152) was not published until 1927, versions of the theory appear as early as 1905, in "Leonardo da Vinci and a Memory of His Childhood," *The Standard Edition*, ed. Strachey, 11:59ff. Here Freud provides the same explanation of the castration complex and the possibility of emergent fetishism: "the fixation on the object that was once strongly desired, the woman's penis, leaves indelible traces on the mental life of the child. . . . Fetishistic reverence for a woman's foot and shoe appears to take the foot merely as a substitutive symbol for the woman's penis which was once revered and later missed" (96). The dates for Stein's beginning work on *Tender Buttons* range from 1910 to 1912. See Ruddick, *Reading Gertrude Stein*, 190.

33. Luce Irigaray, *This Sex Which Is Not One*, trans. Catherine Porter (Ithaca: Cornell University Press, 1985), 133, 84, 76.

34. *This Sex*, 155. Chessman, *The Public Is Invited to Dance*, 94–95, makes a similar point about the speculum, applied to Stein's resistance to conventional vision in *Tender Buttons*.

35. *This Sex*, 133–34. Joan Riviere first described the notion of masquerade — an exaggerated femininity that she found in a female patient. For Riviere, this parading of the feminine helped the woman compensate for her intellect, particularly because it followed her public lectures; it was an effort to placate the "father" for her theft of phallic power. Lacan offers his own version of the masquerade, one that Irigaray criticizes for its reinscription of a Freudian phallic norm: "It is for that which she is not [the phallus] that she wishes to be desired as well as loved" ("Signification," 290). Among the important recent responses to Riviere's — and Irigaray's — elaboration of the masquerade of femininity are Mary Ann Doane's "Film and the Masquerade: Theorising the Female Spectator," *Screen* 23 (1982): 3–4, 74–87, and her later "Masquerade Reconsidered: Further Thoughts on the Female Spectator," *Discourse* 11 (1988–89): 1, 42–54, as well as Matlock's "Masquerading

Women" and Apter's chapter "Unmasking the Masquerade" in *Feminizing the Fetish*.
36. Fifer, "Is Flesh Advisable?" 477–79.
37. See Gass, *World within the Word*, 101–4. For other explications of this passage, see Ruddick, *Reading Gertrude Stein*, who identifies the "Aider" section with "a scene of sacrifice and communion" (215); Neil Schmitz, "Gertrude Stein as Post-Modernist: The Rhetoric of *Tender Buttons*," in *Critical Essays*, ed. Hoffman, 123–24; Richard Bridgman, *Gertrude Stein in Pieces* (New York: Oxford University Press, 1970), 129–30, who interprets the passage more broadly; and Catharine R. Stimpson, "Gertrude Stein and the Transposition of Gender" in *The Poetics of Gender*, ed. Nancy K. Miller (New York: Columbia University Press, 1986), 15–16, who sees a Jack the Ripper figure in the final section.
38. Bridgman (*Gertrude Stein in Pieces*, 93) points out (as Ruddick notes in *Reading Gertrude Stein*, 215) that Stein wrote her portrait of Toklas called "Ada" between 1908 and 1912.
39. As Gass argues, there could be a pun on "kill" as "dying," or achieving orgasm, in which case this final image is, he insists, a dildo (*World within the Word*, 103).
40. In "A Rosy Charm," 226, Ruddick points to the uses of "red" to suggest the female body, the motif of "boxes" or enclosures as figures for female sexuality, and the encoding of what is "dirty" as a parodic naming of lesbian "perversion."
41. Kaplan mentions Robert Stoller, *Observing the Erotic Imagination* (New Haven: Yale University Press, 1985), 16–17, because he details "the infinite variability of the fetishistic objects or erotic preferences" (*Female Perversions*, 36n). The heterogeneity of possible points of focus or object choices illuminates Stein's textual practice.
42. Kaplan explains that in numerous cases, voyeurism or intensive looking is part of the sexual "performance" of fetishism. According to Freud, the child "begins to display an intense desire to look, as an erotic instinctual activity" even before he discovers the mother's "castration," and the awareness of castration is based on his visual encounter with the female body. See "Leonardo da Vinci and a Memory of His Childhood," *The Standard Edition*, ed. Strachey, 11:96. Kaja Silverman's *The Acoustic Mirror: The Female Voice in Psychoanalysis and Cinema* (Bloomington: Indiana University Press, 1988) provides a fascinating account of fetishism and the visual in film. (Silverman cites Christian Metz, *The Imaginary Signifier: Psychoanalysis and the Cinema*, trans. Celia Britton, Annwyl Williams, Ben Brewster, and Alfred Guzzetti [Bloomington: Indiana University Press, 1982].) The fact that "cinema is founded on the lack of the object" (Silverman, *The Acoustic Mirror*, 4) makes the viewer into a fetishist, simultaneously believing and not believing what he sees on the screen. As Silverman notes – relevant to Stein's scopic investments – "even outside the cinema, the fetishist always begins as a voyeur,

requiring of the erotic prop that it function as a spectacle prior to any tactile convergence" (Silverman, *The Acoustic Mirror*, 6). Silverman also points up the "lack" in Freudian theory, the point of departure for Stein's parody: "looking at Freud's theory of castration . . . one is struck by its single-mindedness, its refusal to accommodate any lack except that which it attaches to the female genitals" (Silverman, *The Acoustic Mirror*, 14). Silverman counters that "this refusal to identify castration with any of the divisions which occur prior to the registration of sexual difference reveals Freud's desire to place a maximum distance between the male subject and the notion of lack" (Silverman, *The Acoustic Mirror*, 15).

43. Irigaray, *This Sex*, 197. "This Sex Which Is Not One" emphasizes that female sexuality is always "*plural*" (28), and "When Our Lips Speak Together" explores that which is "never finished" (210) in the feminine economy. Irigaray also points out in "Commodities among Themselves" that female homosexuality "is recognized only to the extent that it is *prostituted to man's fantasies*" (196).

44. Hélène Cixous, "The Laugh of the Medusa," in *New French Feminisms: An Anthology*, ed. Elaine Marks and Isabelle de Courtivron (New York: Schocken Books, 1981), 262. In Cixous's formulation, "Because the 'economy' of [woman's] drives is prodigious, she cannot fail, in seizing the occasion to speak, to transform directly and indirectly *all* systems of exchange based on masculine thrift" ("The Laugh of the Medusa," 252). It is interesting to note, in the context of this passage, Stein's repeated use of the words "change" and "exchange" in *Tender Buttons*, which I take to be part of her erotic code of lesbian sexual "exchange."

45. See Ruddick, "A Rosy Charm." Ruddick stresses the conversion from "disgrace" to "charm," "ugliness or distaste to pleasure" (Ruddick, "A Rosy Charm," 227), in this and other passages.

46. Cixous, "The Laugh of the Medusa," 255.

47. Freud, "Humour," *The Standard Edition*, ed. Strachey, 21:163.

48. Ruddick, *Reading Gertrude Stein*, 226.

49. Chessman's comments on another passage in *Tender Buttons* apply to "Shoes" as objects of female fetishism. The passage is "A Carafe, That Is a Blind Glass," in which the word "difference" and the phrase "a system to pointing" are prominent: "Otherness ('difference') is not celebrated; the hole, or lacuna, which in a Freudian 'system' 'points' to such difference can now be sensed to be, not a locus of absence at all, but a rich and indefinable presence" (Chessman, *The Public Is Invited to Dance*, 93).

50. See Fifer, "Is Flesh Advisable?" 480–81.

51. See Grosz on the masculinity complex associated by Freud with lesbianism: the lesbian woman "displaces phallic value onto an object outside the mother's (or her own) phallus; but in contrast to the fetishist, her love-object is not an inanimate or partial object, but rather another subject. Her 'fetish' is not the result of a fear of femininity but a love of it" (Grosz, "Lesbian

Fetishism," 51). In this sense Grosz embraces the possibility offered by the concept of "lesbian fetishism."
52. See Ruddick, "A Rosy Charm," 240, for the connection between "utter" and "udder" in Stein's "Milk" section.
53. Irigaray, *This Sex*, 157.
54. See Apter, *Feminizing the Fetish*, 109–10.
55. See Marjorie Garber's "Fetish Envy," *October* 54 (1990): 45–56.

FOUR

Anita Hill, Clarence Thomas, and the Culture of Romance

Margaret A. Eisenhart and Nancy R. Lawrence

On October 8, 1991, in an extraordinary circumstance on the eve of a scheduled vote, the U.S. Senate decided to postpone for a week its decision on the confirmation of a Supreme Court justice. The delay was caused by public outcry, especially from women's groups, that the Senate, 98 percent male, was not taking seriously an allegation that the judicial nominee had sexually harassed one of his former employees. The outcry came after the allegation, made in confidence to senators by the former employee, was obtained by the press, and the employee went public at a press conference to tell her side of the story. A three-day hearing, before the Senate's Judiciary Committee, was then scheduled to air the allegations of sexual harassment brought by the former employee, Anita Hill, against the nominee, Clarence Thomas. Sen. Joseph Biden (Democrat – Delaware) presided over the hearing in his role as chairman of the Judiciary Committee.

On October 11 Senator Biden officially opened the hearing by announcing, "This is a fact-finding hearing. And our purpose is to help our colleagues in the United States Senate determine whether Judge Thomas should be confirmed to the Supreme Court."[1] Biden continued,

There are two things that cannot remain in doubt after this hearing is over: first, that the members of this committee are fair and have been fair to all witnesses, and second, that we take sexual harassment as a very serious concern in this hearing, and overall. So, let us perform our duties with a full understanding of what I have said and of our responsibilities to the Senate, to the nation, and to the truth.[2]

Using less formal but more prophetic language, Biden had been quoted earlier that week: "This ain't about Anita Hill and this ain't about Clarence Thomas. . . . This is about a power struggle going on in this country between men and women. This is the biggest thing you can imagine."[3]

So began three days of allegations and denials, inferences and speculations that jolted the U.S. Senate and the American people out of complacency about sexual harassment in the workplace. During the three days Anita Hill, a black woman and a law professor, who alleged that Clarence Thomas had sexually harassed her ten years earlier when she had worked for him, would be asked to make sense of her allegations for the fourteen all-white and all-male members of the Senate Judiciary Committee and before a television audience. Clarence Thomas, a black man and a federal court judge, who denied any improprieties, would be asked to defend himself against her charges. Supporters and detractors would be asked to tell what they knew about the character and conduct of each. After the hearing the Judiciary Committee members, along with the full Senate, would vote to confirm, or not, Clarence Thomas's nomination to the Supreme Court.

From the day of Hill's press conference until the hearing began, Hill was widely portrayed as a "credible witness." Eleanor Holmes Norton, Democratic Congresswoman from the District of Columbia, wrote of Hill:

Her press conference revealed a woman of awesome credibility, not to mention brains, dignity, attractiveness of person, and a personality so compelling that the official Thomas advocates never dared to attack her personally.[4]

Reporting on the same press conference, *Newsweek* said, "She was credible, she was articulate, she was poised."[5] " 'She didn't seem like a flake or an idiot and she presented herself with extreme sincerity and honesty,' said Carl Hempe, an aide to Senator Simpson"[6] (Republican – Wyoming), a strong Thomas supporter.

In the Senate, the fact that Hill was so credible became a reason for Thomas supporters to seek a delay in the confirmation vote. Trying to make up his mind about a delay, Sen. Hank Brown (Republican – Colorado) decided to telephone Hill. He wanted to assess her and her story for himself. After the call, Brown sat thoughtfully for a while and then said, "She tells a very credible story."[7]

By the afternoon of October 8, Hill – whom the Senate and public had come to admire as a black woman who rose out of poverty in Oklahoma to become a high school valedictorian, a graduate of Yale Law School, an appointee to important government positions, a law school professor, and an articulate and composed public speaker — was considered so eminent and reliable that Thomas supporters believed she would doom what had been a certain vote for his confirmation. Timothy Phelps and Helen Winternitz, in their book *Capitol Games*, described the force of Hill's credibility on the Senate as follows:

On Friday [Oct. 4], Clarence Thomas had had a solid sixty senators ready to vote for his confirmation, with a chance of getting more.... By midafternoon Tuesday [Oct. 8], ... Thomas could count on only forty-one senators to definitely vote for him. An equal number were ready to vote against his confirmation, and as many as nineteen senators were undecided or calling for a postponement. The victory that had seemed so close just a few days before had evaporated....

The Republicans ... knew Thomas would lose if the vote proceeded as scheduled.[8]

Thus the Senate decided to delay the confirmation vote and to open a public hearing into Hill's allegations.

But despite her awesome stature at the time the hearing began, Anita Hill's prestige and credibility soon began to crumble. By the end of the hearing, she had been transformed from an eminent and reliable woman into someone most people disbelieved. At the same time Clarence Thomas was changed from a beleaguered and bewildered nominee to a proud man whom most people believed. This determination was not, however, based on facts presented at the hearing. All observers agreed that the "truth" was never found. The accounts by Hill and Thomas were irreconcilable. One of them had to be lying. The Senate and the public had to decide which one. After the hearing ended, the Senate voted to confirm Thomas (although by only a small margin, 52–48), and a poll taken immediately after the hearing by the *New York Times*/CBS News showed that only 20 percent were willing to say they believed Anita Hill.[9, 10]

Many questions have been raised about this situation. Why did so many of us disbelieve Anita Hill? Why did so many of us, especially so many women, choose to ennoble Clarence Thomas rather than Anita Hill? Why was such an ambiguous dispute so unambiguously decided, at least at the time?

Numerous explanations have been offered. Some believe that an organized and alert coalition of Thomas's supporters, led by the power and resources of the George Bush White House, manipulated the hearing and the press to consistently portray Thomas in a positive light. They also believe that the lack of an organized opposition to Thomas, occasioned by blacks' and white liberals' hesitancy to oppose any black man, created a situation in which damaging information about Thomas was never vigorously pursued.[11]

Within the black community many scorned Hill as a traitor to her race and to the cause of racial solidarity.[12] About this, black author Barbara Smith wrote:

> any woman who raises the issue of sexual oppression in the black community is somehow a traitor to the race, which translates into being a traitor to black men. It is particularly disheartening knowing that probably a lot of black people took this stance despite believing Anita Hill. They ... decided that standing behind a black man — even one with utter contempt for the struggles of African Americans — is more important than supporting a black woman's right not to be abused.[13]

In other words, although blacks may have believed Hill's story, they were not willing to support her in a confrontation with a black man.

Judith Resnick, a law professor who provided legal advice to Hill, suggests that the presumption of credibility lay "naturally" with the employer, as is common in sexual harassment cases, and not with the employee.[14] And Susan Estrich, former campaign manager for Michael Dukakis's failed presidential bid in 1988, suggests that entrenched sexism caused both women and men to be uncomfortable with the specter of women's power raised by Hill and its potential to harm men.[15] According to Estrich, the suggestion that a woman might have the power to derail the career of a prominent man was simply too threatening for most people to entertain.

These explanations for Hill's fall are powerful, but they leave a curious aspect of this case virtually unexplored: how to explain the precipitous fall from credibility that Hill suffered during the three days of the Senate hearing. Regarding this, Susan Garment suggests that the (erroneous) framing of the hearing as a trial, in which the presumption of innocence was given to Thomas, encouraged both senators and the public to apply a potent but irrelevant standard to Hill's testimony.[16] Others have argued that Thomas, in labeling the hearing "a high-tech lynching," turned the proceedings and public sentiment to his advantage.[17] When Thomas used this so-called race card, he drew attention to white privilege and guilt, away from male privilege and guilt, and away from Anita Hill and her allegations.

In this essay we will argue that another plausible account of Hill's fall from credibility, and of the hearing's outcome, can be developed by reference to a widely shared "cultural model"[18] about the world of male/female relationships in the United States. Cultural models, or taken-for-granted sets of ideas about how the world is supposed to work, are frames of reference that people use to make sense of, and debate, the meaning or interpretation of events. Before moving on to our main argument, we must first say a few things about cultural models.

When a cultural model is invoked, it establishes one way of interpreting an event, and in so doing it limits and simplifies the interpretations that people are likely to give to the event. Thomas invoked a cultural model of racism when he played his race card. By summoning familiar American cultural imagery in which black men are destroyed by white men, Thomas (purposefully or not) created the impression that the hearing was racist — that he was being treated shamelessly by the white male Senate committee, and by extension by white society, because of his race (and not because of his sex). As this example illustrates, actual events are not determined or dictated by a cultural model, but experiences are anticipated, extrapolated, or evaluated in light of it. When someone acts or speaks in such a way as to evoke a familiar aspect of the model, people are likely to assume that other aspects of the model apply as well.

The other explanations given (above) for the hearing's outcome draw their power from various cultural models. Each one connects the Hill/Thomas confrontation to other taken-for-granted assumptions about how political and class power, racism, or sexism "work" in the United States. These cultural models of power, class, racism, and sexism frame much contemporary debate about topics ranging from Supreme Court nominations to household chores. Although in this essay we will stress the explanatory power of one particular cultural model, we recognize that there are numerous, overlapping cultural models that can be brought to bear on the Hill/Thomas case. Together, they will provide the grounds for ongoing discussion and dispute about what happened and why. In Toni Morrison's words about the hearing: "To know what took place summary is enough. To learn what happened requires multiple points of address and analysis."[19]

In this essay we focus on a cultural model that was not directly invoked during the hearing and has not, to our knowledge, been explored since, one that seems to have cut to the quick of Hill's prestige and made her especially vulnerable to public doubt. We will argue that Hill's initial credibility was undermined because the story she had to tell and the way in which she and others thought she should tell it rendered her a woman of limited attractiveness and low prestige against the backdrop of a pervasive "culture of romance" — a cultural model of ideas about how the world of male/female relationships is supposed to work, at least in the United States.

Psychologist Louise Fitzgerald has observed that sexual harassment is mostly about power, rarely about sex, and "never about romance."[20] We disagree. With reference to the culture of romance, we will attempt to show how sexual bad treatment is in fact linked to romance and to the status of women, both black and white, in U.S. society. Our understanding of the culture of romance derives from an anthropological study, conducted by Margaret Eisenhart and her colleague Dorothy Holland, of black and white college women at two U.S. universities.[21] We turn now to a brief discussion of this study and its findings, after which we will return to the story of the hearing and our interpretation of it.

THE STUDY[22]

Holland and Eisenhart's work began in 1979, when they received funding to study why so few women were going into math and science careers. They focused on the experiences of women at two southern universities: a predominantly black, publicly supported university called "Bradford," and a predominantly white, publicly supported university called "Southern University" (SU).[23] Twenty-three women — twelve at Bradford and eleven at SU — were closely followed through their freshman and sophomore years of college (1979–1981). During this time the researchers got to know the women well as friends and confidants.[24] Researchers and students met regularly (at least twice a month) to do things together on campus and to talk. The same women were then interviewed in 1983 when they were about to graduate from college and again in 1987, four years after they left college.

In 1979 Holland and Eisenhart hoped that their in-depth and longitudinal study would reveal some previously hidden dynamic in the experiences of college women — some dynamic that could help explain why, despite the removal of legal barriers and the establishment of affirmative action programs, talented young women were not pursuing high-paying, high-status careers in fields such as science, mathematics, computer science, and engineering. As it turned out, the study went beyond the question of why so few American college women were going into the high-paying, traditionally male-dominated fields of math and science. It revealed, further, young women's paths into traditional female positions in society in general. When the women in the sample began their college careers, they had at least a B+ high-school average, above-average Scholastic Aptitude Test (SAT) scores, and approximately half said they would major in a math- or science-related field. At that time all stated emphatically that they expected to build an occupational career upon their college major after graduating from college. Yet from following these twenty-three women's unfolding lives, the researchers found that less than a third of these bright and privileged women met their own expectations for the future. By the time they left college, two-thirds had arrived at practices that served to sustain their subordinate positions in society. Most ended up with intense involvements in romantic relationships, weak career identities, and poor preparation for supporting themselves financially or emotionally.

The central argument of the book is that this outcome can be explained, at least in part, by the existence of a peer-supported culture of romance that dominates and organizes the students' campus life in such a way as to encourage women to invest time and energy, and to construct their identity, primarily in traditional romantic relationships with men, and not in career plans and preparation. The peer system on the campuses studied encouraged women to invest heavily in romantic relationships and in so doing to make themselves both financially and emotionally dependent on men.

THE CULTURE OF ROMANCE[25]

According to Holland and Eisenhart, the culture of romance is a set of background assumptions about the world of romantic relationships. Like other cultural models, the culture of romance defines a simplified world of prototypical characters, ways of acting, and social contracts that are expected or assumed (taken for granted) in romantic affairs. Because

Holland and Eisenhart's culture of romance is derived from research among heterosexual women primarily, it should be considered one way of interpreting male/female relationships from women's point of view.[26]

The culture of romance hinges first on a particular conception of who should be involved in a romantic relationship with whom. Ideally, attractive men are drawn to equally attractive women and vice versa. Similarly, unattractive men deserve unattractive women. In other words, the culture of romance makes "attractiveness" a commodity of value in romantic relationships. But the prestige gained from attractiveness is calculated differently for women and men. Women acquire attractiveness – and their prestige – in two ways: by being judged physically attractive by others and by demonstrating that they can attract the attention of desirable men. Although women may expend considerable time and money on their physical appearance, it alone does not establish their attractiveness or prestige. Women's attractiveness – or symbolic capital – in the culture of romance depends on the kind of attention they receive from men. When a man demonstrates romantic interest in a woman, she gains attractiveness. For a woman to have high social prestige, then, she must have attracted the romantic attention of an attractive man.

Men acquire some of their prestige from their physical appearance and their ability to attract attractive women. But their prestige is calculated more broadly to include their special talents, earning potential, and sensitivity to women. Thus, men can acquire prestige from more sources than can women, and they can be judged prestigious without the favorable attention of women. For these reasons a man's prestige is much less vulnerable to women's treatment of him than is a woman's prestige to men's treatment of her.

This gender-differentiated system for determining prestige is not new. Helen Horowitz writes about its beginnings on college campuses in the early part of the twentieth century:

> As dating entered the college scene, it fundamentally reshaped the college lives of coeds.... It established the key way that women gained status. College men vied for positions on the [sports] field or in the [campus] newsroom; college women gained their positions indirectly by being asked out by the right man. Their primary contexts became those of beauty and popularity, won not because of what they did, but because of how and to whom they appealed.[27]

It is also not restricted to campus social life or romantic relationships per se. The calculation of women's prestige in classrooms and workplaces is often made on the basis of their ability to please men.[28] When a prestigious man is attentive to a woman — whether on a date, in the classroom, or at work, he thereby creates and confirms her attractiveness, and her prestige is elevated.

The culture of romance also hinges on a particular conception of exchange. In a prototypical romantic relationship — when the man and the woman are matched in attractiveness, the woman is expected to offer affection and intimacy in exchange for the man's attention, his sensitivity to her concerns, and his gifts as well as the access he provides to various social activities. Couples judged to be poorly matched, that is, when one person is considered more "attractive" than the other, were the targets of endless analysis and debate in the women's informal peer groups studied by Holland and Eisenhart. Discrepancies were rationalized in terms of the ideas about exchange, so that unmatched romantic partners came to be matched. If a woman is romantically involved with a man judged more attractive than she is, she will be expected to provide extra affection, sexual intimacy, or other favors in exchange for the privilege of being with him. The higher the man's prestige relative to the woman's, the more she is expected to give and the more intimacy and other favors he can demand. Discrepancies in which the man's prestige is higher, then, can empower him to treat a woman harshly, especially sexually. On the other hand, when a woman's prestige is higher than the man's, he is expected to show exceptional attentiveness or sensitivity, offer lavish gifts, and take her special places. Discrepancies in which the woman's prestige is higher empower her to treat the man harshly too, but emotionally or financially, rather than sexually.

In such a system, a woman's demands for and expectations of good treatment are claims about her own prestige. Correspondingly, a man's demands for physical intimacy are claims about his prestige. Bad treatment, especially if it persists, becomes a sign of low prestige for both women and men. For this reason, both women and men will try to hide any evidence of bad treatment.

But because a woman's prestige is so dependent upon men's response to her, her prestige is especially vulnerable if it becomes public knowledge that a man is treating her badly. Because she has no other major source of social worth, a woman must be treated well by the men around her if she is to acquire and keep high prestige. If it becomes known that she has been treated badly by a man, she will lose prestige, both among women and among other men who might have been attracted to her. Thus it is especially important for women to conceal bad treatment from men.

The women in Holland and Eisenhart's study also expected women to be able to protect themselves against bad treatment from men. If a man treated a woman badly once, she was expected to take some action against him. In college relationships, the woman might stop dating the man or otherwise take control of the relationship in order to demand better treatment. If a woman did not take action and the bad treatment persisted, her failure to stick up for herself was taken as evidence that she accepted her low prestige relative to the man's. Women are placed at great — and disproportionate — social risk when others find out about bad treatment that has gone unchallenged or uncorrected.

Rape is the ultimate form of bad treatment for a woman. In *Educated in Romance*, the authors say about rape:

The man disregards the woman's feelings completely. He treats her as though she deserves nothing, or worse yet, abuse. In the logic of the culture of romance . . . , he claims physical intimacy from her with nothing given in return. In effect, he states with his act that her prestige is so low that he does not need to win her affection at all. And, because attractiveness is attested to by the treatment women receive from men, rape *creates* the victim's low prestige.[29]

In the remainder of this essay, we will argue that although Anita Hill was not literally raped, her low prestige was similarly created during the hearing. With reference to the culture of romance, Hill's prestige could be eroded and her allegations dismissed by virtue of: the requirement that she publicly describe Thomas's treatment of her as a sexual object; the fact that she did not or could not provide evidence that other men found her attractive; and her failure to take obvious steps to defend herself against (more) bad treatment from Thomas.

THE HEARING

Anita Hill finally went public with her allegations after ten years of agonizing about what to do, after moving to Oklahoma to stay out of the limelight, after repeated refusals to talk to Senate staffers or reporters about Clarence Thomas during the summer of 1991, and after she tried in vain to get the Judiciary Committee to take her confidential statement seriously.[30] With rumors flying that she had made such a charge and a leak to the press of the contents of her confidential statement, Hill came forward to defend herself, to tell her story in her own words, because she thought it was her civic duty. Ironically, by exercising the duty to tell, her attractiveness and prestige could be exposed to public interpretation in terms of the culture of romance. In the logic of this interpretive system, once Hill explained how badly Thomas had treated her and that she had endured this treatment for some time, her prestige as a woman sank. The questioning of Hill during the hearing served to play out the script of her demise in a way perhaps unimagined but nonetheless familiar to the senators who did it and the public who watched it. From this perspective, the questioning and testimony of Thomas mattered very little. As her prestige fell, his was automatically raised.

The hearing itself began with introductory remarks by Senator Biden, the committee chairman, and Sen. Strom Thurmond, the ranking Republican from South Carolina. Then Thomas read an opening statement of bewilderment and victimization. He began by expressing his "shock," "surprise," and "hurt"[31] upon hearing of Hill's allegations. He denied all the allegations and went on to express his dismay that such mistaken charges would be brought by "a person I have helped at every turn in the road since we met."[32] He had never felt anything other than respect for her. Their relationship was always "cordial and professional."[33] He had considered it a working relationship only. Apparently, he said, she had grossly misunderstood something he had done. He never referred except in the most general terms to the nature of the charges against him.

What Thomas was specific about was how much he had been hurt by the hearing and disclosures. He said he had been irrevocably harmed; he was at the lowest point of his life; he (not Hill) was the victim here.

Mr. Chairman, I am a victim of this process. My name has been harmed. My integrity has been harmed. My character has been harmed. My family has been harmed. My friends have been harmed. There is nothing this committee, this body, or this country can do to give me my good name back. Nothing.[34]

In the logic of the culture of romance, though, the allegations against Thomas reflected more negatively on Hill than they did on him. If he had, in fact, treated her badly, this treatment affirmed his higher status relative to hers. If he had not treated her as alleged, his reputation had certainly been impugned, but not as badly as hers. At least with reference to the culture of romance, he was already in the more powerful position, and Hill's allegations could not change that.

After Thomas concluded his statement, he left the hearing without being questioned. Hill was then called to make her opening statement and to be questioned first. Hill's opening statement recounted the history of her association with Thomas.

In 1981, I was introduced to now Judge Thomas by a mutual friend. Judge Thomas told me that he was anticipating a political appointment, and he asked if I would be interested in working with him. He was, in fact, appointed as Assistant Secretary of Education for Civil Rights. After he had taken that post, he asked if I would become his assistant, and I accepted that position. . . .

During this period at the Department of Education, my working relationship with Judge Thomas was positive. I had a good deal of responsibility and independence. I thought he respected my work and that he trusted my judgment. After approximately three months of working there, he asked me to go out socially with him. . . .

I declined the invitation to go out socially with him and explained to him that I thought it would jeopardize what at the time I considered to be a very good working relationship. I had a normal social life with other men outside of the office. I believed then, as now, that having a social relationship with a person who was supervising my work would be ill-advised. I was very uncomfortable with the idea and told him so.

I thought that by saying no and explaining my reasons my employer would abandon his social suggestions. However, to my regret, in the following few weeks, he continued to ask me out on several occasions. He pressed me to justify my reasons for saying no to him. These incidents took place in his office or mine. They were in the form of private conversations which would not have been overheard by anyone else.[35]

With this statement, only a few minutes into her testimony, Hill's relationship with Thomas was cast in a romantic light. According to Hill, Thomas had asked her for a date several times. The stage was now set for the committee and the public to consider what kind of relationship they really had.

The idea of a romantic interest between them was not hard to imagine. Separated from his wife at the time, an appointee to a high government position, and one of a small circle of influential blacks in the Republican administration, Thomas commanded respect and was "eligible." Hill appeared to be a physically attractive woman. She traveled in the same social circles, and she was single. They should, or at least could, have been well matched: a prestigious man and a physically attractive woman.

But something was wrong with this romantic picture. He said he never made any romantic overtures and (later) that he never asked her out (apparently contrary to his earlier statement to the Federal Bureau of Investigation), that she must have mistaken some innocent remark for romantic interest. She said she had refused his invitation to date (on the grounds that a romantic relationship would interfere with their working relationship). His testimony suggested that he was not at all attracted to her. Her testimony suggested that he found her attractive but that she was not attracted to him. How could the senators and the public decide which one to believe?

Hill's statement continued with her description of the alleged instances of harassment that followed. Apparently, she felt the need to provide details.

> His conversations were very vivid. He spoke about acts that he had seen in pornographic films involving such matters as women having sex with animals and films showing group sex or rape scenes. He talked about pornographic materials depicting individuals with large penises or large breasts involved in various sex acts. On several occasions, Thomas told me graphically of his own sexual prowess....[36]
>
> One of the oddest episodes I remember was an occasion in which Thomas was drinking a Coke in his office. He got up from the table at which we were working, went over to his desk to get the Coke, looked at the can and asked, "Who has pubic hair on my Coke?" On other occasions, he referred to the size of his own penis as being larger than normal, and he also spoke on some occasions of the pleasures he had given to women with oral sex.[37]

According to the logic of the culture of romance, Hill's statement could be interpreted as revealing that Thomas considered his prestige considerably higher than hers, that he considered himself more powerful than she — so much more powerful that he could treat her like a sexual object. Later, in response to a question from Senator Heflin (Democrat — Alabama) about a line in her affidavit, Hill made this interpretation herself.

> SEN. HEFLIN: You describe ... the working relationship and the various conversations which you say were very vivid and very graphic pertaining to pornographic materials and films and other statements of that nature. Then you end that paragraph with these words: "However, I sensed that my discomfort with his discussions only urged him on as though my reaction of feeling ill at ease and vulnerable was what he wanted." ... What do you mean by that? How do you conclude that?
>
> MS. HILL: Well, it was almost as though he wanted me at a disadvantage — to put me at a disadvantage so that I would have to concede to whatever his wishes were.

SEN. HEFLIN: You think that he got some pleasure out of seeing you ill at ease and vulnerable?
MS. HILL: I think so, yes.
SEN. HEFLIN: Was this feeling more so than the feeling that he might be seeking some type of dating or social relationship with you?
MS. HILL: I think it was a combination of factors. I think that he wanted to see me vulnerable, and that if I were vulnerable, then he could extract from me whatever he wanted, whether it was sexual or otherwise — that I would be at his — under his control.
SEN. HEFLIN: Now, as a psychology major [Heflin had earlier established that Hill had an undergraduate degree in psychology], what elements of human nature seem to go into that type of a situation?
MS. HILL: Well, I can't say, exactly. I can say that I felt that he was using his power and authority over me, was exerting a level of power and attempting to make sure that that power was exerted. I think it was the fact that I had said no to him that caused him to want to do this.[38]

In the culture of romance, if a woman has more prestige than a man, or roughly the same amount, then her refusals should end his advances. But according to Hill, they did not. Thomas did not take her objections seriously; he did not leave her alone.

There can be no doubt that Hill's statements about Thomas portray wrongdoing by reference to workplace standards, but they also draw attention to Hill's prestige. In presenting her case by revealing his bad treatment and invoking his power and authority, she also had to reveal her lower prestige as defined by the culture of romance.

As chair of the Judiciary Committee, Biden then began the questioning of Hill.[39] Biden began by asking Hill to recount briefly her background, how she came to know Thomas, and the circumstances in which she worked with him. Then he requested that she retell the instances of alleged sexual harassment and include even greater detail.

SEN. BIDEN: Now I must ask you now to describe, once again, and more fully, the behavior that you have alleged he engaged in while your boss. Which you say went beyond the professional conventions and were unwelcome to you.
    Now I know these are difficult to discuss. But you must understand that we have to ask you about them.[40]

Biden proceeded to go over each incident.

SEN. BIDEN: Would you describe it once again for me, please? . . .[41]
SEN. BIDEN: Do you recall what the first time was and, with as much precision as you can, what he said to you? . . .[42]

SEN. BIDEN: Can you tell the committee what was the most embarrassing of all the incidents that you have alleged? . . . [43]

SEN. BIDEN: You have described the essence of the conversation . . . can you tell us in his words what he said? [44]

And finally,

SEN. BIDEN: Now again, for the record, did he just say, "I have great physical capability and attributes," or was he more graphic?
MS. HILL: He was much more graphic.
SEN. BIDEN: Can you tell us what he said? [45]

In every case, Hill replied patiently, calmly, and in detail, sometimes suggesting possible wording by Thomas that was not included in her earlier statements. By this time she had, unwittingly perhaps, made very clear how extraordinarily badly she had been treated.

Then Senator Specter took his turn to question Hill. After some preliminaries, Specter quickly returned to Hill's descriptions of Thomas's sexual interests. Again she was asked to describe all the incidents and all the details. Specter's strategy was to show that Hill's original statement to investigators from the FBI (prior to the hearing and in confidence) differed from her opening statement to the committee, which in turn differed from her statements in response to Biden's questions. The differences were in the level of graphic detail provided and her speculations (given at Biden's request) about such things as what words Thomas might have used. More graphic details were provided in her opening statement and more speculations were given in response to Biden's questions. Specter smugly argued that these differences constituted "inconsistencies" in Hill's testimony, evidence that her "facts" had changed, and support for the view that she should not be believed. But there was more going on than that.

By the time Specter had finished his interrogation, Hill had spent close to three hours talking about the details of Thomas's alleged sexual harassment of her. It began when she gave her own account in her opening statement to the committee. It continued when, in response to Biden's questions, she was forced to repeat her description of the incidents, to add more graphic details to them, and to speculate about them. Then, in response to Specter's questions, she was asked to make sense of versions that included different amounts of detail and to provide support for (admitted) speculations. By this time the image of Hill as a poised and articulate woman was firmly established. Her answers to the questions were quick and to the point. She did not appear nervous or confused by the setting, the cameras, or the scrutiny. Despite her statements of how difficult the hearing was for her, never once did she choke; never once did she cry. Never once did she visibly indicate turmoil or weakness. Yet for all her composure, she had methodically just participated in a legalistic exercise that also undermined her prestige.

In sexual harassment cases such as Hill's, where no witnesses, photographs, or other tangible evidence exist, lawyers have tried to establish harassment by eliciting precise descriptions of each instance from the complainant.[46] In the absence of corroborating evidence, graphic details are considered necessary to establish that harassment did in fact occur. Thus the nature of the evidence that Hill had to provide and the style of questioning used by Senator Biden[47] and others — evidence and questioning that required her to expose her bad treatment, with all its attendant liabilities for her prestige — were rooted in legal precedent.

Once the graphic details had been aired, Hill could have trouble regaining her prestige for two reasons. Because a woman's prestige is so dependent on a man's in the logic of the culture of romance, Hill could conceivably have regained some prestige if prestigious men had supported her. At the least, she needed a husband or a male romantic partner to come forward and affirm, by his reflected prestige, that she also was a prestigious person. She had neither. She found no senator on the Judiciary Committee prepared to come to her aid.[48] And she had little support in the black community. About this, Stephen Carter, a law professor at Yale, wrote, "A lot of black people saw Clarence Thomas as a black man under attack and therefore decided to rush to his aid. What made me very sad was that not many people saw Anita Hill as a black woman under attack and rushed to her aid."[49]

Two of the four witnesses who later spoke on Hill's behalf were men: John Carr, a lawyer who had dated Hill in the past, and Joel Paul, a law professor who knew her. Both men were considered "solid" witnesses and confirmed Hill's story by reporting that she had told them years ago about Thomas's harassment of her. In another ironic twist, their confirmation may have done Hill more harm than good.

Despite their support for her story, they did not as clearly support her prestige. Neither they nor the senators who questioned them dwelled on Hill's attractiveness as a woman or as a romantic partner. Further, their confirmation of her story underscored another problem with Hill's credibility: If she, a poised and articulate lawyer, had been harassed, had been so upset, and had told a few trusted confidants about it, why had she stayed? Why had she continued to work under Clarence Thomas? Why had she never before aired her allegations?

As the hearing continued, Hill was pilloried for her "inability" to make sense of her actions regarding Thomas during the ten-year interim between the first instance of alleged sexual harassment and her public disclosures. She was repeatedly asked why she had not filed charges against Thomas at the time, why she had never kept any notes on his objectionable behavior, why she had followed him when he took another job, why she had never previously expressed reservations about him in public, why she had made "friendly" visits and calls to him after she left his employ. Senator Simpson dealt her a hard blow with regard to these issues when he concluded his five-minute questioning.

> SEN. SIMPSON: Well, I just — it just seems so incredible to me that you would not only have visited with him twice after that period and after he was no longer able to manipulate you or to destroy you, that you then not only visited with him, but took him to the airport and then 11 times contacted him [by telephone]. That part of it appalls me. I would think that these things which you describe are so repugnant, so ugly, so obscene, that you would never have talked to him again. And that well — is the most contradictory and puzzling thing for me.[50]

Hill's efforts to keep the bad treatment to herself are understandable in terms of the culture of romance. To preserve her prestige (and her job), she tried to handle Thomas's behavior on her own. As she said, she did not intend to pursue litigation against him. She thought she could stop the behavior by herself.[51] Because she did not want to address the suspicions that an abrupt departure from a good job or a less-than-flattering statement about the respected boss would inevitably raise, she dealt with her knowledge on her own.[52] Some of what seemed so puzzling to Simpson and his male colleagues in the Senate would have been understandable to the women, especially the black women, in Holland and Eisenhart's study. To avoid the scorn and exploitation of one's status that can result when information about bad treatment from men is public knowledge, the campus women kept such matters to themselves.[53]

However, because Hill did not immediately stop her work with Thomas or her association with him, she could not demonstrate that she had taken any steps to defend herself against his treatment of her. In the logic of the culture of romance, her failure to protect herself served to corroborate his treatment of her.

By the time Hill's testimony before the committee ended, she had spent nearly eight hours trying to explain Thomas's alleged harassment of her and her response to it. Although she was poised and articulate throughout, the graphic details she was forced to provide about bad treatment and her failure to provide evidence that she had tried to defend herself against repeated bad treatment would have compromised her prestige, and thus her credibility, in the logic of the culture of romance. Now it was Thomas's turn to face the committee's questions. If Hill was discredited in the way we have suggested, the demands on Thomas's testimony and performance would be low. If Hill's prestige sank by reference to the culture of romance, his was correspondingly raised. In his testimony and answers to questions, he had only to deny the allegations and present himself as a decent man. In this he got plenty of help from the Senate.

When Thomas returned, he made another opening statement in which he reiterated the themes he had presented earlier in the day, and he played the famous "race card."

JUDGE THOMAS: Senator, I would like to start by saying unequivocally, uncategorically, that I deny each and every single allegation against me today that suggested in any way that I had conversations of a sexual nature or about pornographic material with Anita Hill, that I ever attempted to date her, that I ever had any personal sexual interest in her, or that I in any way ever harassed her.

A second, and I think more important point, I think that this today is a travesty.... The Supreme Court is not worth it. No job is worth it. I'm not here for that. I'm here for my name, my family, my life and my integrity. I think something is dreadfully wrong with this country when any person, any person in this free country would be subjected to this.... This is a circus. It's a national disgrace. And from my standpoint as a black American, as far as I'm concerned, it is a high-tech lynching for uppity blacks who in any way deign to think for themselves, to do for themselves, to have different ideas, and it is a message that unless you kowtow to an old order, this is what will happen to you. You will be lynched, destroyed, caricatured by a committee of the US Senate rather than hung from a tree.[54]

There have been numerous analyses of how powerfully Thomas and the committee relied on and were affected by this racial image from this point on during the hearing.[55] Of special interest to our analysis, however, is the difference between the ways Thomas and Hill were questioned. During the earlier questioning of Hill, the senators had made her tell her story and all its sordid details three times. They had roughly interrogated her about its inconsistencies and harshly attacked her for failing to adequately explain her actions to them. The questioning of Thomas was quite different: The questions allowed him to collude with the committee in a character assassination of Hill that further undermined her credibility.

Senator Hatch began the questioning of Thomas.

SEN. HATCH: Judge Thomas, I've sat here and I've listened all day long, and Anita Hill was very impressive. She is an impressive law professor. She is a Yale law graduate. And when she met with the FBI, she said that you told her about your sexual experiences and preferences. Now I hate to go into this, but I want to go into it because I have to. And I know it's something that you wish you'd never heard at any time or place. But I think it's important that we go into it. And let me just do it this way. She said to the FBI that you told her about your sexual experiences and preferences, that you asked her what she liked, or if she had ever done the same thing, that you discussed oral sex between men and women, that you discussed viewing films of people having sex with each other and with animals, and that you told her that she should see such films, and that you liked to discuss specific sex acts and the frequency of sex. What about that?

JUDGE THOMAS: Senator, I would not want to — except being required to here — to dignify those allegations with a response. As I have said before, I categorically deny them. To me, I have been pilloried with scurrilous allegations of this nature, I have denied them earlier, and I deny them tonight.[56]

At this point Hatch recounted each specific allegation. Thomas had only to say "no." He never had to stain his reputation by using any dirty language. After denying that he had ever asked Hill out, Thomas was never asked to discuss his romantic interest in Anita Hill.

Hatch and Thomas then proceeded in concert to create the image of federal Equal Employment Opportunity Commission procedures by which sexual harassment charges were treated seriously and sensitively,[57] of Thomas as a man who had worked successfully with "hundreds of women in different capacities,"[58] who had been terribly wronged by the lone voice of a single woman who was known for, as Thomas said, "storming off or throwing a temper tantrum of some sort, that either myself or the chief of staff would have to iron out."[59]

In addition to being portrayed as unconvincing (earlier), Hill was now described as emotional and irrational, as a woman whom others like Thomas, presumably more level-headed, had to tame. Hatch later suggested some vivid imagery that made Hill's statements about Thomas seem preposterous.

SEN. HATCH: I have to say cumulatively these charges, even though they were made on all kinds of occasions — I mean, they're unbelievable that anybody could be that perverted. I am sure there are people like that but they are generally in insane asylums.[60]

Thomas, for his part, continued to express outrage at the actions of the committee and the process that had treated him so badly. Biden, in defense of the committee, tried to explain its position.

SEN. BIDEN: When a respectable, reasonable, upstanding person, professor of law, someone with no blemish on her record, comes forward, this Committee has the obligation to do exactly what you would have done at EEOC [Equal Employment Opportunity Commission, where Hill had followed Thomas after they had worked together at the Department of Education], investigate the charge.[61]

Senator Hatch, however, insisted on a different interpretation.

SEN. HATCH: I hope that nobody here, either on this panel or in this room is saying that Judge, you have to prove your innocence because I think we have to remember and we have to insist that Anita Hill has the burden of proof, ... and not you, Judge.
  The fact of the matter is the accuser, under our system of jurisprudence and under any system of fairness, should have to prove the case.[62]

With Hatch's statement the hearing became like a court of law in which the burden of proof was placed on Hill. She now had legal imagery as well as romantic, emotional, and irrational imagery stacked against her.

The pattern of collusion between Thomas and the senators continued the next day when Thomas returned to complete his testimony. When Specter began his questioning, his tack was to "cover" with Thomas four inconsistencies in Hill's testimony, the existence of which, Specter argued, seriously undermined Hill's credibility and indicated that she might have committed perjury.[63] Specter's approach allowed Thomas simply to agree with Specter's speculations that Hill's explanations for her actions regarding Thomas were incomprehensible, and thus they lacked credibility.

SEN. SPECTER: Now, my question to you is this, Judge Thomas, when she says she's concerned about being fired, and she says that she is taking precautions and writes down the details of work assignments, if she's looking for retaliation from you, is it credible that had the statements been made that she would not make a written notation of those statements in the context where she writes down notes on all these other matters?
JUDGE THOMAS: Senator, it doesn't sound credible to me.[64]

And then,

SEN. SPECTER: Judge Thomas, *The Washington Post* reported on this issue that, quote, "Ms. Hill called the telephone logs garbage and said that she had not telephoned Thomas, except to return his calls." And I questioned her about that at page 173 and 174 of the record. And then to abbreviate this, when confronted with the logs, I asked her, as it appears at page 175 of the record. "Then you now concede that you had called Judge Thomas 11 times?" Answer, following some other material. "I will concede that those phone calls were made, yes."

And my question to you, Judge Thomas, what impact do you think that has on her credibility?
JUDGE THOMAS: Senator, I think it's another of many inconsistencies that have occurred in her testimony.[65]

Intermittently throughout, Thomas continued to stress that he had always tried to help Hill and others like her with their careers. "I tend to be the proud father type who sees his special assistants go on and become successful, and feels pretty good about it."[66] And he ended his testimony by reminding the committee that he was a real (but sensitive) man: He would not be bullied by this process; he would remain a good father and husband no matter what.

SEN. HATCH: So you'd still like to serve on the Supreme Court?
JUDGE THOMAS: I'd rather die than withdraw from the process. Not for the purpose of serving on the Supreme Court, but for the purpose of not being driven out of this process. I will not be scared. I don't like bullies. I've never run from bullies. I never cry uncle and I'm not going cry uncle today, whether I want to be on the Supreme Court or not.[67]

Shortly after this, in responding to Senator DeConcini, Thomas said,

[If] I'm not confirmed, so be it — [I'll] continue my job as a court of appeals judge, and hopefully live a long life, enjoy my neighbors and my friends, my son, cut my grass, go to McDonald's, drive my car, and just be a good citizen, and a good judge, and a good father, and a good husband.[68]

DISCUSSION

Senator Biden had been right from the start: The hearing was a power struggle between men and women. It was an old, familiar struggle that women lost. Anita Hill, initially so credible that she caused an unprecedented delay in Senate proceedings, was conclusively discredited with astonishing speed. We are suggesting that Hill's loss of credibility was due in large part to the ease with which her public story could be interpreted negatively in relation to a prototypical image of male/female relationships in the United States.

In the logic of the culture of romance, prestigious men are "naturally" attracted to prestigious women. Slight differences in prestige can be negotiated if less prestigious men offer special attention and gifts, or less prestigious women offer extra intimacy and sexual favors. But if differences of prestige are too great, then bad treatment becomes likely. Because it is the woman's prerogative to give sexual intimacy,[69] attempts by a man to control her sexual decisions are a sign of bad treatment and very low prestige relative to the man. If this prototypical model of male/female relationships was the implicit, background knowledge that informed views of Hill and Thomas, then Hill's fall from credibility began at the moment she told her story. By admitting the evidence of bad treatment, Hill presented herself to other women (and men) as unattractive. The graphic detail she was forced to provide about Thomas's alleged sexual advances further subverted the image of her attractiveness. As she came to be perceived as an unattractive woman, she could be viewed as facing two choices: She could leave the relationship (and find a way to express her attractiveness somewhere else) or she could stay (and accept her low status in exchange for his favors). Hill chose to stay. Maintaining her positions and connections to him and her silence about harassment, she also could maintain the high prestige she gained by association with him, and she could hide the bad treatment, a sign of her low prestige. But once she went public with the bad treatment and implied her acceptance of it, she came to embody the low prestige it indicated. Thus Hill became an unattractive woman, a woman of considerably lower prestige than the man she was linked with, who chose to maintain her ties to him, presumably to retain her prestige by association with him.

As Hill's attractiveness and prestige were lowered, doubts were cast on her credibility. Interestingly (given that something similar seemed to occur in the black community but for different reasons), these doubts permitted people to discredit Hill without necessarily disbelieving her. If she were telling the truth about being harassed but had made the "choice" to keep silent about it in order to gain and preserve her public position and prestige, she had paid a price, but it was apparently a necessary price given her low prestige, and for it she had taken possession of the goods. Now she appeared to be reneging on her part of the deal. By such logic, it was not "fair" of Hill, once she had achieved a secure, good job and high professional status, to turn in Thomas.

Of course, it is also possible that Thomas was telling the truth. As Hill's attractiveness and prestige were diminished, it became easier to doubt her story and, as long as Thomas was not further impugned, easier to believe his. If Hill were such an unattractive woman, it would make more sense that she, rather than he, had tried to initiate a romantic relationship, and in turn, that he had spurned her. Perhaps she was lying now in order to get back at him.

Thus, by these means, as Hill's attractiveness and prestige — her symbolic capital — were discounted, the attractiveness and prestige of the man with whom she was linked were correspondingly increased. By such a transformation, Hill became a woman who did not deserve the attentions of a man like Thomas. She became someone whose "story" could be dismissed as the delusions or "sour grapes" of a relatively unattractive woman who did not understand that she was supposed to put up with, or find a way to avoid, this type of bad treatment in exchange for an attractive man's continued interest in and support of her.

This is the note on which we believe the hearings ended, and we believe that this way of interpreting Hill's actions, and the corresponding implications for Thomas, could lead to the confirmation vote and public opinion that went against Hill.

POSTSCRIPT: ONE YEAR LATER

But the end of the hearing and the vote was not the end of the story. More than a year has passed since the Senate and the nation sat watching the hearing and Thomas's swearing in as a Supreme Court justice. But debate has continued about what happened and why. Interestingly, the passage of time has brought a change in public opinion regarding Hill and Thomas. On the first anniversary of the hearing, *U.S. News and World Report* published a poll showing that 38 percent of respondents believed Hill, whereas another 38 percent believed Thomas. A *Wall Street Journal/NBC News* poll found 44 percent who believed Hill and only 34 percent who believed Thomas. These polls reflect a dramatic change from just a year earlier when public opinion heavily favored Thomas.

Appearing October 6, 1992, on the NBC "Today" program, Hill was asked by Katie Couric about the change in opinion polls after twelve months. Replied Hill, "I think people have just become more thoughtful about the hearing and about the issue itself and the theories that were just spun out of nothing that were thrown at them to explain my motives." We agree with Hill that public opinion has probably been affected by the question of motive, and we believe that the culture of romance may continue to be the background knowledge that informs peoples' thinking about this complex case.

During the hearing and afterward, there was much speculation about motives. If Thomas lied, why did he do it? If Hill lied, why did she? In Thomas's case, it seems obvious that he might lie to preserve his chances for a Supreme Court seat. Had he acknowledged any of Hill's allegations, his nomination would certainly have been doomed. His motive was as obvious during the hearing as it is a year later.

In Hill's case, things were less clear at the time of the hearing. Theories about her motives included suggestions that Hill was a spurned lover, that her allegations of sexual harassment were fantasies, and that she was motivated by greed and self-interest.

Hill is right that we are in a better position now to challenge several of the theories offered last year by senators, witnesses, and the media to "explain" why Hill should be disbelieved. A theory easy to discount is the suggestion that Hill was selfishly or politically motivated to come forward with her allegations against Thomas. Following the hearing, Hill returned to teaching law at the University of Oklahoma in Norman. Contrary to the expectations of many, Hill has not capitalized on the hearing. She has not written a book. She has granted few interviews. She is not on the lecture circuit. She was even tacitly criticized when she turned down offers from *People Magazine* to tell her story for money. Tania Modleski notes that in a 1991 *People Magazine* interview with Thomas's wife, Virginia Thomas, the piece was prefaced by the comment: "More than a dozen times *People* approached Anita Hill or her representatives for her account of her unwanted time in the spotlight, but she has declined to be interviewed."[70] In short, the hearing has not made Hill a rich woman.

It is also easy to dispute the charges that Hill was politically motivated to air allegations of sexual harassment against Thomas in the eleventh hour. Hill has resumed her private life. Although a record number of women ran for political office, at least in part as a response to Hill's situation, Hill herself has remained out of the political limelight. Further, no evidence of delusional behavior or spurned feelings has ever surfaced.[71]

In contrast, perhaps it has become more evident what an extraordinary risk Hill took in coming forward with her allegations. Framed against the backdrop of the culture of romance, as well as other cultural models of racism, sexism, and power, the risk to her was enormous. Like the women in Holland and Eisenhart's study, Hill must have sensed the risk to her prestige in making such public allegations. Surely she anticipated Thomas's denial of them and the public's negative reaction to them. To make the allegations after so long a time was to risk her prestige as a woman, her competence as a lawyer, her stature in the black community, her privacy, her job, and probably her future employment opportunities. With no apparent motive, why would she (or any other woman) take such a risk . . . unless she was telling the truth?

In conclusion, we submit that the culture of romance, supported by the legal and procedural requirements to establish sexual harassment, doomed Anita Hill's case against Clarence Thomas. By virtue of requirements to provide graphic and specific details of the harassment, the implications for women of acknowledging repeated harassment, and the consequences for women who do not rely on prestigious men to make their cases for them, it is easy to see how Hill lost her case. Perhaps the post hoc analyses of Hill's situation will make some people less comfortable with the status quo, but unless formal and informal ways can be found to protect women's prestige, status, and position during harassment proceedings, it is not likely that women who have been harassed will come forward or that they will win their cases if they do. As things stand, is it any wonder that Anita Hill, and others like her, never wanted to tell?

NOTES

We would like to thank Joe Harding, Dorothy Holland, and Ernest House for their comments on an earlier version of this essay.

1. Federal Information Systems Corporation, *Transcript of Proceedings of the United States Senate, Judiciary Committee*, October 11, 1991, 2. All excerpts from the Judiciary Committee hearing are taken from transcripts provided by the Federal Information Systems Corporation © 1992. Because sections of the transcripts were out of chronological order in the version received, page numbers for quotations used in this essay are not in sequence.
2. Ibid., 4.
3. Gloria Borger and Ted Gest, with Jeannye Thornton, "The Untold Story," *U.S. News and World Report*, October 12, 1992, 32.
4. Eleanor Holmes Norton, "And the Language is Race," *Ms. Magazine*, January/February, 1992, 43.
5. David Kaplan, "Anatomy of a Debacle," *Newsweek*, October 21, 1991, 26.
6. Timothy Phelps and Helen Winternitz, *Capitol Games: Clarence Thomas, Anita Hill, and the Story of a Supreme Court Nomination* (New York: Hyperion, 1992), 245.
7. Phelps and Winternitz, *Capitol Games*, 288; Borger et al., "The Untold Story," 32.
8. Phelps and Winternitz, *Capitol Games*, 270.
9. Borger et al., "The Untold Story," 28.
10. The question in the *New York Times*/CBS News poll asked, "Looking back on the charges Anita Hill made and Clarence Thomas's responses, whom do you believe more?" The results showed 60 percent believed Thomas and 20 percent believed Hill. Apparently, 20 percent were undecided or did not answer.
11. Phelps and Winternitz, *Capitol Games*, 197–225; Nina Burleigh, "Now That It's Over: Winners and Losers in the Confirmation Process," *The American Bar Association Journal* (January 1992): 51–52.
12. Public Broadcasting System, "Clarence Thomas, Anita Hill; Public Hearing, Private Pain," *Frontline*, October 13, 1992.
13. Barbara Smith, "Ain't Gonna Let Nobody Turn Me Around," *Ms. Magazine*, January/February, 1992, 38.
14. Judith Resnick, "Hearing Women," *Southern California Law Review* 65 (1992): 1333–45.
15. Susan Estrich, "What Went Wrong," *Southern California Law Review* 65 (1992): 1393.
16. Susan Garment, "Why Anita Hill Lost," *Commentary* (January 1992): 26–35.
17. See the articles in *Race-ing Justice, Engendering Power*, ed. Toni Morrison (New York: Pantheon Books, 1992).

18. Dorothy Holland and Naomi Quinn, *Cultural Models in Language and Thought* (Cambridge: Cambridge University Press, 1987).
19. Toni Morrison, "Introduction: Friday on the Potomac," in *Race-ing Justice*, ed. Morrison, xii.
20. Louise Fitzgerald, "Science vs. Myth: The Failure of Reason in the Clarence Thomas Hearings," *Southern California Law Review* 65 (1992): 1399.
21. Dorothy C. Holland and Margaret Eisenhart, *Educated in Romance: Women, Achievement, and College Culture* (Chicago: University of Chicago Press, 1990).
22. This section is adapted from Holland and Eisenhart, *Educated in Romance*, 1.
23. These names are pseudonyms.
24. Black researchers worked with the women at Bradford, white researchers with those at SU.
25. This section is adapted from Holland and Eisenhart, *Educated in Romance*, 94–106.
26. For a detailed explanation of how the cultural model of romance was derived, see Dorothy Holland and Debra Skinner, "Prestige and Intimacy: The Cultural Models behind Americans' Talk about Gender Types," in *Cultural Models in Language and Thought*, ed. Holland and Naomi Quinn (Cambridge: Cambridge University Press, 1987), 78–111.
27. Helen Horowitz, *Campus Life: Undergraduate Cultures from the End of the Eighteenth Century to the Present* (New York: Knopf, 1987), 208.
28. Holland and Eisenhart, *Educated in Romance*, 202–7. See also Linda Valli, "Becoming Clerical Workers: Business Education and the Culture of Femininity," *Ideology and the Practice of Schooling*, ed. Michael Apple and Lois Weis (Philadelphia: Temple University Press, 1983), 213–14.
29. Holland and Eisenhart, *Educated in Romance*, 101.
30. Phelps and Winternitz, *Capitol Games*, 227–45.
31. Federal Information Systems Corporation, *Judiciary Committee*, 8.
32. Ibid., 8.
33. Ibid., 6, 148.
34. Ibid., 10.
35. Ibid., 15–16.
36. Ibid., 16.
37. Ibid., 17.
38. Ibid., 50–51.
39. By prior arrangement, each political party designated two of its committee members to be the primary examiners (to begin after the chairman finished his questioning). These senators, Heflin (Alabama) and Leahy (Vermont) for the Democrats and Specter (Pennsylvania) and Hatch (Utah) for the Republicans, were given alternate thirty-minute examining periods until they had exhausted their questions. Then each member of the committee was allotted five minutes to ask questions.
40. Federal Information Systems Corporation, *Judiciary Committee*, 119.
41. Ibid., 120.
42. Ibid., 121.

43. Ibid., 122.
44. Ibid., 122.
45. Ibid., 123.
46. Marianne Wesson, personal communication, November 9, 1992.
47. Apparently, Biden at least had conferred with legal experts about sexual harassment cases before the hearings began (Borger et al., "The Untold Story," 33).
48. See Phelps and Winternitz, *Capitol Games*, for fascinating discussions of the many reasons various senators were disinclined to come to Hill's aid during the hearing.
49. Burleigh, "Now That It's Over," 52.
50. Federal Information Systems Corporation, *Judiciary Committee*, 101–2.
51. Ibid., 38.
52. Ibid., 43; see also Phelps and Winternitz, *Capitol Games*, 255 and 268, for evidence that Hill's reticence about Thomas was noticed by her friends.
53. Holland and Eisenhart, *Educated in Romance*, 111–17.
54. Federal Information Systems Corporation, *Judiciary Committee*, 138–39.
55. See, for example, Morrison, ed., *Race-ing Justice*.
56. Federal Information Systems Corporation, *Judiciary Committee*, 143.
57. Ibid., 146–47.
58. Ibid., 148.
59. Ibid., 151–52.
60. Ibid., 159.
61. Ibid., 164.
62. Ibid., 165.
63. The focus on inconsistencies that Specter so relentlessly pursued with Hill was never even raised with regard to Thomas's testimony, despite the fact that there were inconsistencies in the various statements he had made concerning Anita Hill.
64. Ibid., 55.
65. Ibid., 56.
66. Ibid., 157.
67. Ibid., 82.
68. Ibid., 89.
69. Holland and Skinner, "Prestige and Intimacy," 100.
70. Tania Modleski, "Melodrama and Memory," *Southern California Law Review* 65 (1992): 1353–55.
71. Since the writing of this essay, a book highly critical of Hill has appeared. Entitled *The Real Anita Hill*, by David Brock, this book reports that some of Hill's EEOC coworkers believe that she was upset about Thomas's inattention to her.

PART TWO

Violating Images

FIVE

Plastic Man versus the Sweet Assassin

Leah Hackleman

> Since I was shot, everything is such a dream to me. I don't know what anything is about. Like I don't even know whether or not I'm really alive or — whether I died. It's sad. Like I can't say hello or good-by to people. Life is like a dream.
> — Andy Warhol, *New York Times Magazine,* 10 November 1968

> SCUM is against half-crazed, indiscriminate riots, with no clear objective in mind, and in which many of your own kind are picked off. SCUM will never instigate, encourage or participate in riot of any kind or any other form of indiscriminate destruction. SCUM will cooly, furtively, stalk its prey and quietly move in for the kill.
> — *S.C.U.M. (Society for Cutting Up Men) Manifesto*

IF ONLY SHE HAD DONE IT WHILE THE CAMERA WAS ON

Valerie Solanas first met Andy Warhol when she gave him a copy of her script, variously entitled *Up Your Ass, Up from the Slime, The Big Suck,* and *From the Cradle to the Boat.*[1] Warhol recalled, "I looked through it briefly and it was so dirty I suddenly thought she might be working for the police department and that this was some kind of entrapment."[2] Warhol left the script lying around the Factory office where it became lost, and Solanas began calling him on the phone, demanding that he either return her script or pay her. One afternoon when she called Warhol was shooting *I, a Man* and invited her to earn twenty-five dollars by appearing briefly in the film, "instead of asking for a handout," and she did (Warhol and Hackett, 271). The phone calls tapered off, and Warhol wrote, "By now I'd decided she wasn't a lady cop after all. I guess enough people must

125

have told me that she'd been around for quite a while and confirmed that she was a bona fide fanatic" (Warhol and Hackett, 271).

Paul Krassner described her later in 1968 as "a cross between an early Rosalind Russell movie and the Ancient Mariner, only instead of plucking at the elbows of strange wedding guests on the street, you had the feeling she would much rather be breaking up the honeymoon itself by somehow managing to get into the marriage bed, replacing the wife with her albatross."[3] Solanas was born in 1936 in Atlantic City, New Jersey, and attended college at the University of Maryland, where she majored in psychology. Solanas received her status as a "fanatic" because of her mimeographed "S.C.U.M. (Society for Cutting Up Men) Manifesto," which she had peddled in Greenwich Village coffee houses and in the streets, charging women twenty-five cents and men a dollar (Bourdon, 287).[4] One of Warhol's biographers, David Bourdon, speculates that she showed "signs of a disturbed psyche since childhood," although her experiences working in an animal research lab in college, he surmises, "possibly helped prepare her for her later verbal and physical assault on Warhol" (Bourdon, 286–87).

On June 3, 1968, she had been waiting outside the Factory building for two hours, wearing a fleece-lined coat despite the heat. Warhol recalls, "She was wearing pants, more like trousers (I'd never seen her in a dress), and holding a paper bag and twisting it — bouncing a little on the balls of her feet. Then I saw that there was something even more odd about her that day: when you looked close, she'd put on eye makeup and lipstick" (Warhol and Hackett, 272).[5] She had recently begun "pestering" Warhol again about the return of her script. She accompanied Warhol and Jed Johnson, a worker in the Factory, into the building and up to the sixth floor. When they reached the Factory, Warhol immediately received a phone call from Viva, one of his "superstars." As Warhol listened to Viva recount the production of *Midnight Cowboy*, a movie she was involved in making, he heard a loud explosion. When he turned around, he realized Solanas had shot at him and missed: "I said, 'No! No, Valerie! Don't do it!' and she shot at me again. I dropped down to the floor as if I'd been hit — I didn't know if I actually was or not. She moved in closer, fired again, and then I felt horrible, horrible pain, like a cherry bomb exploding inside me" (Warhol, 273). Mario Amaya, a London art dealer and writer, assumed a sniper was shooting and dropped to the floor; Valerie shot at him twice, hitting him on the left side above his hip. She then pointed the gun at the remaining target in the room, Fred Hughes, Warhol's business manager, who begged her not to shoot. She hesitated and pushed the button for the elevator but then walked back closer to Hughes, aiming her gun. Just when it looked as if she might shoot, the elevator doors opened and Hughes yelled, "There's the elevator! Just take it!" and she left. The police arrived a half hour later to take Warhol and Amaya to Columbus Hospital, where Amaya convinced them to treat Warhol by assuring them he was a famous artist with a lot of money (Bourdon, 287).

After the news hit radio stations, the lobby of the Factory building was jammed with police, the media, and curious onlookers. Outside, police erected barricades to hold back the crowds that were gathering. About seven o'clock that evening, Solanas turned herself over to a policeman who was directing traffic, telling him, "I am wanted by the police. I am a flower child. He had too much control over my life,"[6] and relinquishing the .32 automatic she had fired and a .22 revolver from her coat pocket. In mid-August she was declared incompetent to stand trial and committed to a mental institution. Warhol remained in the hospital for nearly two months, recovering from his almost five-hour surgery that repaired the damage done to his liver, stomach, spleen, esophagus, and right and left lungs by the two bullets that hit him. One year later, on June 9, 1969, after being declared competent to stand trial, Solanas was sentenced to a maximum three-year prison term. Ten years later, in 1979, Warhol (with Pat Hackett) wrote *POPism: The Warhol '60s*, whose first sentence reads, "If I'd gone ahead and died ten years ago, I'd probably be a cult figure today" (Warhol and Hackett, 3).

Because his greatest creation was Pop Artist Andy Warhol, it was inevitable that the attempt on his life became an occasion to amplify the Andy Warhol image; for example, he later posed for a Richard Avedon photograph and for an Alice Neel painting of his surgical scars. Sales of his paintings increased dramatically after the shooting (Bourdon, 290). Even directly after the shooting he was concerned about its possible use. David Bourdon, who was an associate of Warhol's at The Factory, records his despair from the hospital: "In a voice that sounded weaker than ripping facial tissue, he lamented that the attempted assassination had not been recorded on film. 'If only she had done it while the camera was on!'" (Bourdon, 7).

Although biographers of Warhol note the importance of the attempted murder in their dramatizations of his life, none attempts to explicate the meanings of the event itself. For these writers it was an absurd, irrational, and entirely subjective moment in his life: they narrate it but do not analyze its importance except in terms of the change in Warhol. For me, however, Valerie Solanas's attack on Andy Warhol is a cultural event, replete with significance not only for art histories or biographies, but also for feminism. An analysis of the varied constructions of this episode can demonstrate the complex sexual politics at work in 1968 America. Both dominant and countercultural media perceived/manufactured Solanas as a hysterical madwoman, some feminists claimed her as an ally to the reinvigorated women's movement, and Solanas viewed herself as a revolutionary in her *S.C.U.M. (Society for Cutting Up Men) Manifesto*. What is at stake, then, in this struggle over meaning is cultural domination: whose interpretation becomes the official sermon? Even in this relatively localized incident we can grasp the relations of ruling at work: analyzing the various positions from which Solanas's action and identity were evaluated and invoked can demonstrate how gender domination is maintained and confirmed, even in the context of the late 1960s, through the figure of the woman out of control.

MEDIA RECONSTRUCTIONS

The mass media wallowed in the story of the shooting, for it suggested the ultimate example of what they had already constructed as Andy Warhol's violent and sick world. *Time* magazine practically gloated over the news under a headline that read, "Felled by SCUM":

Americans who deplore crime and violence might consider the case of Andy Warhol, who for years has celebrated every kind of licentiousness. Like some Nathanael West hero, the pop-art king was the blond guru of a nightmare world, photographing depravity and calling it truth[,] playing games of lust, perversion, drug addiction and brutality before his crotchety cameras. Last week one of his grotesque bit players made the game quite real.[7]

While the *Time* reportage exhibits a "we-told-you-so" attitude toward the event, *Newsweek*'s coverage explicitly links Warhol's shooting to Robert Kennedy's assassination:

It almost seemed as if the shooting on Monday of Andy Warhol, the foremost creator of Pop images, was a mad rehearsal, stage-managed by some diabolical cosmic impresario, for the shooting less than 48 hours later of Bobby Kennedy. ... Though the thought will shock many, Kennedy and Warhol are not unrelated in these out-of-joint times. Each in his own way is what is called a culture-hero, a force that defines reality for masses of people, whether they love or hate that reality.[8]

Both news stories, in recounting the event, seek also to convey with it the sense either that Warhol is implicated in the attack (that is, it is a logical extension of the world he created in his Factory and films) or that he helped to establish a culture, as "a shaper of the forms, styles and even behavior of the '60s," in which the violence would logically exist.[9] In linking Kennedy to Warhol, moreover, *Newsweek*, while carefully disavowing any serious political motive or meaning in the attack on Warhol, implies subtly that Warhol helped generate the "out-of-joint" culture that produced the recognizably political assassin Sirhan Sirhan.

Counterculture media, represented by the *Village Voice*, followed the dominant media's trend. Although the paper adopted a different (from the dominant media) stand vis-à-vis the Warholian subculture, it too searched for a meaning in the shooting that was personal, not political: "[S]uddenly [Solanas] turned savage, and people at The Factory searched for a motive. She was bitter, they said, because Warhol had refused for over a year to use a script she had written. She had also at one time accused Warhol — absurdly, his associates said — of dubbing in over her voice in the film, 'I, a Man.' Neither clue seems sufficient to explain the horror that shattered the Velvet Underground."[10] Although the June 6 *Voice* article appeared on the front page next to a report about the Paris student and worker demonstrations, there is little mention of politics in the attempted assassination. Despite noting that her life "revolved around her 'manifesto,' " the article makes no attempt to link Solanas's political views with her motive, instead opting to focus on her alleged psychological state. Its follow-up story, "A Winter Memory of Valerie Solanis [sic]," an interview with Solanas that was conducted prior to her shooting of Warhol, is focused on the *S.C.U.M. Manifesto* and her work in promoting it. In spite of the ostensibly objective reporting style, the writer infuses his own evaluations that once again serve to redirect attention to her psychology: "I had a momentary urge to shake her hand, wish her luck (not for her organization but for herself). I figured she would have none of that 'crap' so I didn't bother."[11] Describing her as "a not unusual looking woman with clear brown eyes and a restless mind," the article quickly points out a contradiction for its readers, that "[s]he has dedicated the remainder of her life to the avowed purpose of eliminating every single male from the face of the earth."[12] Clearly, printing this story on the heels of the Warhol shooting (which is not mentioned in this interview but does appear as a brief note on the first page of the interview, directly below Solanas's explanation of the need for violence) draws attention to the personal rather than the political purposes.

In choosing to focus on the status of her mental health, the media deflected difficult questions about the meaning of the attack by constructing Solanas as a lunatic whose preposterous motives are beyond the grasp of saner, logical people. Arguably, the media could have been following the lead of the New York justice system: during her first appearance in court, reported on June 5, Solanas attempted to explain her objectives, but the judge ordered her remarks stricken from the record and held her without bail for a psychiatric examination.[13] However, in reporting the shooting on June 4, the *New York Times* article raised the issue of her oddities by quoting Solanas directly and by interviewing the night telephone operator at the Chelsea Hotel about her eccentric habits.[14] Other national media quickly pounced on this aspect of the story: *Time* described her as a "grotesque bit player" in Warhol's entourage of "freakily named people," and *Newsweek* intoned, "Among the idiosyncratic rebels and one-person parties of New York's new Bohemia, she is one of the strangest.... [I]ndeed, she is the Village's most notable female panhandler."[15] One reviewer of the *S.C.U.M. Manifesto*, for example, calls it a "daft diatribe" that contains "nothing unusual, given the author's particular kind of sickness," without identifying precisely from what it is that Solanas suffers.[16] Solanas contended she was mistreated by the media at the time, and even nine years later, after an interview with the *Village Voice*, she insisted that the media as a whole created, through editorial decisions, inconsistencies that misrepresented her state of mind.[17]

Paul Krassner continues the discourse about her "absurd" state of mind in recounting, in the afterword to the published *S.C.U.M. Manifesto*, that he had seen Solanas earlier on June 3, 1968: "If I had known, I might have been able to talk Valerie out of her act. Had she actually been asking for help from me? Or did she simply want company? It was a switch. She usually charged lonely men on the street six dollars for an hour of conversation. Then again, she could've shot me, right there in the restaurant. 'What do you mean, I can't join you for lunch? ' Bang! That easy. That absurd" (Krassner, 94).

Krassner's remarks reflect the general construction of Valerie Solanas as crazy. He attempts to present her as a paranoid: "Valerie is a working paranoid. . . . She only wished she were relevant enough to cause others to want to manipulate her" (94). Yet later in the afterword, in another context, he remarks in a one-line paragraph, "Paranoia does not come out of a vacuum" (100). Despite this potentially fruitful observation, however, Krassner continues to dismiss Solanas as a lunatic. Both Krassner and Warhol describe her actions as irrational, as simply incomprehensible, even given her general misandry. Warhol remarks, "I couldn't figure out why, of all the people Valerie must have known, I had to be the one to get shot. I guess it was just being in the wrong place at the wrong time. That's what assassination is all about. 'If only Miles White had been home when I rang his doorbell,' I kept thinking, 'maybe she would've gotten tired and left' " (Warhol and Hackett, 277–78).

Krassner also questions Solanas's choice of victim: "It was poetic injustice that Warhol should be the first practical extension of her [man-hating] philosophy, for he is apparently *a*sexual. You'd have expected her to go after some exploitative stud" (Krassner, 94). Publisher Maurice Girodias laments, "At least, if she intended the shooting of a man as a symbolic gesture, she could have chosen a more representative male oppressor than . . . Andy Warhol!"[18] Although it is clear from Warhol's own narrative of the shooting that she planned it carefully, these men attempt to disavow any deliberate intention through their questions by defining Solanas's choice of subject as an irrational one.

Constructing Solanas as a hysteric allows various media to depoliticize her action; the word most often used to describe her is "absurd." The context can be especially important to understanding this gesture: the late 1960s were a carnivalesque period in U.S. history, in which the "enactments of popular protest, counterculture, experimental theater, and multimedia art were all together suggestive of the energies and possibilities of unlimited cultural and social transformation."[19] In popular imagination the 1960s are a radical break in the normal patterns of collective social psychology, a time when people (inexplicably) "went crazy." Fredric Jameson links the new "psychology" to the imperialist expansion of capitalism: "We have described the 60s as a moment in which the enlargement of capitalism on a global scale simultaneously produced an immense freeing or unbinding of social energies, a prodigious release of untheorized new forces,"[20] and commentators since the sixties have continued to reflect upon the ease with which capitalism commodified or consumed the social movements, rendering them ineffective. Within this context Valerie Solanas was constructed by the media and later reports as an emblem of that collective insanity that ultimately provides no enduring social change. At the time, the media construction of Solanas as a madwoman effectively removed her from the domain of the political. Just as the psychoanalyst understands his description of reality as truthful and sees the hysteric's narrative as disjunctive and incoherent, writings about Solanas assume their version of reality is in fact more accurate than hers: her hatred and distrust of men is seen as a "symptom" of her madness, rather than an indictment of the society in which they operate. The media constructs Solanas as insane in an attempt to recuperate her as a panacea for dominant bourgeois culture: they define an objective reality that contains the "insane" by rendering them powerless through mental institutions and the "justice" system. In this way her critiques can be readily absorbed into the context as merely examples of her insanity rather than as claims to take seriously.

Solanas did not succeed in creating the "utopia" she had envisaged in the *S.C.U.M. Manifesto*, but as Mary Russo points out, "The extreme difficulty of producing lasting social change does not diminish the usefulness of these symbolic models of transgression" (215). The figure of the woman out of control can be a powerful image for women to recuperate. This unruliness, as Natalie Davis suggests, may provide a release from traditional structures and embody "part of the conflict over efforts to change the basic distribution of power within society."[21] Feminists thus can seize upon this figure as an occasion for evaluating "hysteria" as a political protest rather than a psychological problem. Throughout *The Newly Born Woman*, for example, Hélène Cixous and Catherine Clément interrogate the political value of the symbolic figure of the hysteric: Is she a heroine or a victim? Does she contest or conserve?[22] Cixous asks, "Does the hysteric change / the Real? Desire, the Imaginary, class struggle — / how do they relate? What are the yields?"[23] Although they disagree on the correct answer to their questions — Cixous sees the hysteric as disruptive of the social economy, whereas Clément claims that that disruption is simply swallowed by the existing order — Clément alleges one possible link between the woman out of control and historical change: "The distinction between [different hysterics], between those who nicely fulfill their function of challenging with all possible violence (but who can enclose themselves afterward) and those who will arrive at symbolic inscription, no matter what act they use to get there, seems essential to me" (Cixous and Clément, 156). Clément calls, in fact, for the hysteric's construction of herself as a subject. She does not use "symbolic" here in the Lacanian sense but follows anthropologist Claude Lévi-Strauss in depicting culture as "symbolic systems" that "express certain aspects of both physical reality and social reality" (Cixous and Clément, 168). Valerie Solanas, then, enters "symbolic inscription" both through her cultural act of shooting Warhol and through her writing. Solanas insisted in interviews that reporters search for the meaning of her attack in her writing: "I have a lot of very involved reasons. Read my manifesto and it will tell you what I am."[24] In the *S.C.U.M. Manifesto* she signifies herself as a subject for other signifiers. S.C.U.M. does not offer a transparent, unmediated view into Solanas's psyche but provides an alternative construction of its author/narrator for analysis.

S.C.U.M. (SOCIETY FOR CUTTING UP MEN) MANIFESTO

In 1969 Robin Morgan issued an ultimatum for the members of the emerging Women's Liberation Movement to relinquish their nice-girl status: "Let it all hang out. Let it seem bitchy, catty, dykey, frustrated, crazy, Solanasesque, nutty, frigid, ridiculous, bitter, embarrassing, man-hating, libelous, pure, unfair, envious, intuitive, low-down, stupid, petty, liberating. We are the women that men have warned us about."[25] What is "liberating" is valuing as positive and potentially emancipatory traits the insults typically hurled at resisting women. Not only does she invoke Solanas's name, but she may also be following her lead. The *S.C.U.M. Manifesto* attempts to create a new woman operating outside the boundaries of traditional society by privileging the female who is "least embedded in the male 'culture' " as its point of departure. These females are the ones who are "the least nice," who are, in Solanas's words,

too childish for the grown-up world of suburbs, mortgages, mops and baby shit, too selfish to raise kids and husbands, too uncivilized to give a shit for anyone's opinion of them, too arrogant to respect Daddy, the "Greats" or the deep wisdom of the Ancients, who trust only their own animal, gutter instincts, who equate culture with chicks, whose sole diversion is prowling for emotional thrills and excitement, who are given to disgusting, nasty, upsetting "scenes," hateful, violent bitches given to slamming those who unduly irritate them in the teeth, who'd sink a shiv into a man's chest or ram an icepick up his asshole as soon as look at him ... in short, those who, by the standards of our "culture," are SCUM.[26]

Solanas constructs women who resemble Morgan's dictums; both are after a transformation in women's behavior that would shatter cultural conventions of proper womanhood. If *S.C.U.M.* can be seen as a call to arms, its goal is not only to eliminate men and male dominance but also to urge women to reject the standards of gentility. In doing so it also attempts to incite women's anger, for the key to this text is its valuation of the "untidy" emotions. Too long, it asserts, women have been taught through the example of their fathers to fear facing a reality that inspires strong emotion: "Fear of anger and hatred combined with a lack of self-confidence in one's ability to change the world, or even to affect in the slightest way one's own destiny, leads to a mindless belief that the world and most people in it are nice and that the most banal, trivial amusements are great fun and deeply pleasurable" (Solanas, 41). This response, which according to *S.C.U.M.* infects nearly everyone in different degrees, impedes change because it renders its holders unresponsive to the oppressive world around them. Anger, then, is valued as spurring political action. Rationalism itself is challenged in the valuation of emotionalism: "The male, although able to understand and use knowledge and ideas, is unable to relate to them, to grasp them emotionally" (Solanas, 53).[27]

The *S.C.U.M. Manifesto* asserts that the root of all the world's problems is men's inability to love. Because men are, in this way, "incomplete females," they seek to "complete" themselves by

seeking out, fraternizing with and trying to live through and fuse with the female, and by claiming as his own all female characteristics — emotional strength and independence, forcefulness, dynamism, decisiveness, coolness, objectivity, assertiveness, courage, integrity, vitality, intensity, depth of character, grooviness, etc. — and projecting onto women all male traits — vanity, frivolity, triviality, weakness, etc. (Solanas, 34)

Because men cannot become women, they cannot really feel, and so are responsible for, among other things, money, marriage, prostitution; "niceness"; prejudice; government; fatherhood; and mental illness, which the *Manifesto* defines as "fear, cowardice, timidity, humility, insecurity, passivity" (Solanas, 39). They create "Daddy's Girls," women who passively accept the characteristics of mental illness in order to please men at the expense of bonding with women. In fact, the *Manifesto* deliberates at one point, the real conflict may be between free-wheeling SCUM women (those who accept the principles of S.C.U.M.) and the approval-seeking "Daddy's Girls" (71–72). Yet, without the interference of men, most women can be "improved" out of their "Daddy's Girl" status: "Eliminate men and women will shape up" (77). Without the psychic and physical aggravation of men, women will create the true love that the male culture lacks: "[L]ove can exist only between two secure, free-wheeling, independent, groovy female females, since friendship is based on respect, not contempt" (56–57). But, as the text notes, love is impossible in the current cultural context, since it cannot flourish "in a society based on money and meaningless work" (57).

One result of men's inability to love is his creation of empty alternatives, such as "Great Art" and "Culture," artificial worlds that reinforce the status quo:

> The veneration of "Art" and "Culture" – besides leading many women into boring, passive activity that distracts from more important and rewarding activities, and from cultivating active abilities [–] allows the "artist" to be set up as one possessing superior feelings, perceptions, insights and judgments, thereby undermining the faith of insecure women in the value and validity of their own feelings, perceptions, insights and judgments. (59)

One objective of the movement of SCUM women will be to "destroy all useless and harmful objects – cars, store windows, 'Great Art,' etc" (73). Clearly, the text connects artistic production, reception, and evaluation with political control: "Lacking faith in their ability to change anything, resigned to the status quo, they have to see beauty in turds, because, so far as they can see, turds are all they'll ever have" (59). The *Manifesto* implies that SCUM women are the true artists because they are the least immersed in the veneration of male "Art" and "Culture." Reviewer Jayne Egerton links the text's hostility to these institutions to Solanas's attack on Warhol:

> Solanas's attempted assasination *[sic]* of Andy Warhol rather than any other "male great" makes perfect sense to me after reading Scum. Who else symbolised self-indulgent, pretentious, male, capitalist art to the extent that he did in the last decade? He was also an obvious target since the Warhol bandwagon carried many a drug-addicted, sexually exploited, "disposable" woman on it, some of whom are no longer alive.[28]

Because Egerton has read the *S.C.U.M. Manifesto*, she uses it to make sensible Solanas's choice of victim. Unlike the dominant media, she follows Solanas's own advice in grasping the argument of the text in order to construct its author as a woman who makes deliberate choices about the target of her attack, not a woman who is psychotic. In other words, Egerton constructs Valerie Solanas as a political being who is "out of control" only in the minds of the conservers of dominant culture.

Women who are out of control confront the larger society together as a political movement: as Solanas was seen as "ranting and raving,"[29] so she wants other women to be seen, and heard. The goal of the *Manifesto* is to create a movement that will overthrow the present social order — primarily through the elimination of men. Here Solanas's act converges with the text: "The elimination of any male is, therefore, a righteous and good act, an act highly beneficial to women as well as an act of mercy" (Solanas, 67). But such elimination of men (which, despite the requisite laboratory reproduction of babies, Solanas admits will eventually lead to the eradication of the human species) will take too long to achieve; if the majority of women were SCUM, they could instigate the immediate collapse of the government and economy simply by refusing to work or to have anything to do with men. A few men will escape the wrath of SCUM women if they purge themselves of male values, but the most harmful — rapists, politicians, landlords, police officers, disc jockeys, and "Great Artists," among others — will not be spared (71, 75–76). However, after the destruction of capitalism, there will be no need to keep slaughtering men; money is the only power they hold over psychologically independent females (81). Yet the text's vision does not rely on individual solutions but advocates a political movement of SCUM women who are actively promoting the ideas of SCUM in the dominant society. As opposed to the countercultural advocates of the time, the text instructs its readers to stay within institutions to annihilate them from within:

> Dropping out is not the answer; fucking up is. Most women are already dropped out; they were never in. Dropping out gives control to those few who don't drop out; dropping out is exactly what the establishment leaders want; it plays into the hands of the enemy; it strengthens the system instead of undermining it, since it is based entirely on the non-participation, passivity, apathy and non-involvement of the mass of women. (77)

Here again, the key to a revolution is the anger and action of a mass of women; women who are SCUM, who act on their transgressive desire for an entirely new social order. Hélène Cixous speculates that hysteria "starts with [the hysteric's] anguish as it relates to desire and to the immensity of her desire — therefore, from her demanding quality. She doesn't let things get by. I see the hysteric saying: 'I want everything' " (Cixous and Clément, 154–55). Solanas takes another step by attempting to construct the figure of the hysterical woman as the political icon for a wider movement, rather than solely as a goal for individual women. In doing so she jettisons earlier campaigns that promoted typically feminine attributes (nurturance, temperance) as a way to create a new world. Her call for women to make "scenes" in an era of outrageous public display like the late 1960s was at once congruent with and radically different from its cultural context. As Mary Russo notes, "The figure of the female transgressor as public spectacle is . . . powerfully resonant, and the possibilities of redeploying this representation as a demystifying or utopian model have not been exhausted."[30] In *S.C.U.M.*, the female transgressor is unequivocally linked to political action. What comes first is, must be, the text insists, women's emancipation from internalized cultural norms. What comes next is political action: "Life in this society being, at best, an utter bore and no aspect of society being at all relevant to women, there remains to civic-minded, responsible, thrill-seeking females only to overthrow the government, eliminate the money system, institute complete automation and destroy the male sex" (Solanas, 31). What Solanas constructs through the *S.C.U.M. Manifesto* is a vision of a world that will value the strong emotions and the free female while divesting men of power and of their lives. The political consciousness to fight for that world comes out of an emotional engagement with and healthy anger toward the dominant culture. Although psychoanalysts have suggested that one possible evolution of a hysteric is a public career as a savior,[31] Solanas's text insists that liberation and change will only be achieved through direct, sometimes violent, action by groups of women who identify themselves as SCUM. With this gesture she explicitly links her text and her construction of out-of-control women with the emergent Women's Liberation Movement.

S.C.U.M. AND FEMINISM

In the afterword to the *S.C.U.M. Manifesto*, Paul Krassner transcribes the actions of the first group to take Solanas seriously, a "revolutionary group called 'Up against the Wall, Mother-Fuckers' " that "considered the attempt on Warhol's life to be the cultural equivalent of a political assassination." The group leafleted the Village with a broadside that read,

VALERIE LIVES!
Andy Warhol shot by Valerie Solanas. Plastic Man vs. the Sweet Assassin — the face of plastic fascist smashed — the terrorist knows where to strike — at the heart — a red plastic inevitable exploded — non-man shot by the reality of his dream as the cultural assassin emerges ... the "hater" of men and the lover of man — with the surgeon's gun — NOW ... Valerie is ours and the sweet assassin lives.
— SCUM in Exile. (Krassner 103–4)

The group's assertion that "the terrorist knows where to strike" flies in the face of the puzzled men like Krassner and publisher Maurice Girodias who subtly attributed her choice of victim to her madness. In attempting not only a collective effort on Solanas's behalf but an explanation of her relevance, this group strives to create a political objective for her action, providing an interpretation opposing that of the dominant media.[32] The cadre saw her action as a direct assault on the empty consumer culture Andy Warhol exploited as art.

It was, in fact, radical feminists who took Valerie Solanas seriously immediately after the shooting. In the late 1960s feminist analysis was beginning to flower from women's experiences of sexism in the New Left, civil rights, and antiwar movements. The first Women's Liberation group in New York, the New York Radical Women, was formed by Shulamith Firestone and Pam Allen in 1967 as an alternative to the less radical National Organization for Women (NOW). Yet it was the actions of liberal feminists — picketing the *New York Times*, marching on Washington — that propelled the issue of feminism into mainstream media. Martha Weinman Lear writes in a March 1968 article for the *New York Times Magazine* that "feminism, which one might have supposed as dead as the Polish Question, is again an issue. Proponents call it the Second Feminist Wave."[33] Lear, no proponent of feminism, points out that the more radical feminists are the movement's "theoreticians — atypical, but they are interesting, because they are the movement's intellectual hip, the female version of Black Power" (51). New York radical feminists knew next to nothing about Solanas until she attempted to kill Warhol; then "Solanas's case became something of a cause célèbre among radical feminists. Ros Baxandall declared her 'our movement's Victoria Woodhull.'

[Roxanne] Dunbar [of Boston's Cell 16 revolutionary feminist group] visited her in jail, while Ti-Grace Atkinson [president of New York NOW] and others attended her trial."[34] In October of 1968 Atkinson, then president of New York NOW, resigned from the organization, listing "irreconcilable ideological conflicts" as her reason; one of those conflicts listed is "the bitter schism" over "the support of persons in the cause who have crossed the law (e.g., Bill Baird, Valerie Solanas)," both of whom Atkinson supported.[35] Atkinson later would call the *S.C.U.M. Manifesto* "the most important feminist statement written to date in the English language," and Dunbar proclaimed it "the essence of feminism" (Echols, 174, 104). Solanas became an important theoretician for a small segment of the emergent radical movement.

Less than two weeks after the shooting, the *New York Times* proclaimed "Valeria Solanis *[sic]* a Heroine to Feminists."[36] This article reports that two representatives from NOW, Atkinson and lawyer Florynce Kennedy, appeared in court to argue that Solanas was "being prejudicially treated because she was a woman. Her actions are politically, not sexually, motivated, they said." Their appearance on her behalf, which "cast [her] in the role of a heroine of the revitalized feminist movement," was apparently not greeted with the hostility Solanas had reportedly shown the (male) lawyers hired for her by Olympia Press publisher Maurice Girodias. According to the *Times* article, Solanas described herself as a "social propagandist," a "superfeminist," and a "revolutionary." The article ends with Kennedy's prediction that "[t]he woman thing is going to be like the campus thing. . . . Women may be the third force to link up with youth and black people." In fact, three months later feminists demonstrated against and interrupted the Miss America Pageant in "the first major action of the . . . Women's Movement,"[37] which put the Women's Liberation Movement (WLM) on the cultural map for the majority of Americans. Portions of the *S.C.U.M. Manifesto* were also included in *Sisterhood Is Powerful*, the earliest anthology of writings from the WLM to be distributed nationally by a commercial publisher. In the appendix of contributors, editor Robin Morgan writes

Valerie Solanis *[sic]* should be known primarily as an artist, not as someone who shot Andy Warhol. Her filmscripts and other writings have not received the attention they deserve. She is still being persecuted by police and "mental health" authorities for her "attempted murder" of Warhol, and has been in and out of prisons ever since. Interestingly enough, Norman Mailer was charged with the same crime when he almost fatally stabbed his wife. He was never imprisoned; all charges were dropped; his reputation was enhanced; he subsequently ran for Mayor of New York. Enough said.[38]

Morgan points out the similarities between Solanas's and Mailer's cases in order to demonstrate that women are subject to differential treatment by the state, an argument promoted by attorney Florynce Kennedy in her remarks to the court on Solanas's behalf.

Not all women were pleased that Solanas was conceived of as an important voice of the movement: book reviewer Claire Tomalin, writing in the *New Statesman*, called *S.C.U.M.* "a pathetic example of a distracted mind," asserting, "[i]t will give comfort to those who believe that feminism is a pathological condition, product of hysteria, sexual bitterness or perversion."[39] Betty Friedan later countered the notion that Solanas was backed by NOW: "No action of the board of New York NOW, no policy ever voted by the members advocated shooting men in the balls, the elimination of men as proposed by that S.C.U.M. Manifesto!"[40] S.C.U.M. seems to assume a larger connection with American feminism than is probably warranted; although after the shooting, the *S.C.U.M. Manifesto* was read by feminists, Solanas herself was not a known member of any feminist organization when she wrote it. S.C.U.M. continues to retain its reputation; for example, in a recent feminist theory text, Caroline Ramazanoglu states that "[s]ome radical feminist groups [of the 1960s took] a physically aggressive stance towards men (e.g. SCUM, the Society for Cutting Up Men)."[41] In a 1977 interview with the *Village Voice*, however, Solanas clarified that SCUM was "hypothetical. No, hypothetical is the wrong word. It's just a literary device. There's no organization called SCUM — there never was, and there never will be.... It's not even me.... I mean, I thought of it as a state of mind. In other words, women who think a certain way are in SCUM."[42]

FEMINIST POLITICS AND THE POLITICS OF CULTURE

Around the central event, the shooting of Andy Warhol, circle competing discourses attempting to construct Valerie Solanas for their own purposes. One strand, which includes Warhol, his biographers, the New York judicial system, and the mass media, tries to locate her actions in the figure of the hysterical, criminal woman who needs to be removed from the social sphere. I suggest that, without too much effort, this strand can be explicated as the reaction of the dominant culture seeking to preserve the status quo. A competing authority is radical feminism, then and now, which finds in Solanas a repository of the intertwined stories of women's oppression and resistance. Then we have the document created by Solanas herself, which echoes radical feminists' assertions of women's collective resistance. And, finally, we have my reconstruction, a fourth narrative, which appropriates Solanas's story to distill the myriad of issues involved when we speak of reactions to feminist cultural politics. All of the competing (re)constructions converge on one point: all describe her as out of control. Where they differ is in their judgment of the meaning in her actions. What is at stake in these competing interpretations?

As Sandra Harding has suggested, "at the moment feminist scholars begin to address themselves to women's experiences, their inquiry necessarily becomes concerned with questions of power and political struggle."[43] What happens to Valerie Solanas is instructive in that it marks the convergence of discourse and discipline in the dominant culture: the state intervenes and shuffles her from mental institutions to jail. The stories told by Warhol and the media are complicitous in justifying this consequence by pointing out that it was right for her to be incarcerated because, after all, her action was criminal. Yet as Robin Morgan pointed out in 1970, in comparing Solanas's situation with that of Norman Mailer, the consequences were much greater for Solanas because of her gender. For a man to attempt to kill a woman tallies with the established cultural codes of male domination and exploitation. For a woman to attempt to kill a man explodes the status quo. Regardless of the material differences between these cases, it is instructive that the state decided on punishment for the woman. The social consequences of the act are bound up with its symbolic meaning: in attempting to construct her as crazy and criminal, the dominant discourses avoid a discussion of her threatening political agenda. Yet they also unwittingly implicitly endorse the idea that her act is political when they end up agreeing that her act disrupts their version of a "normal" reality in which women love, not kill, men. Similarly, dominant media silenced Solanas except when her words could be used against her as evidence of her insanity. Although apparently she had given interviews to the media prior to shooting Warhol (because of the notoriety of the *Manifesto*), they went unpublished or unbroadcast because the dominant media did not like what she had to say.[44]

In contesting dominant media and judicial images of Solanas, radical feminists operated to deconstruct their reading of "out of control" as equaling dangerous-and-needs-to-be-silenced. They viewed the symbolic danger to patriarchal authority as a positive trait, worthy of extension to a wider political movement. Only they gleaned a meaning from the event that was thoroughly grounded in gender politics rather than in personal characteristics. Michele Barrett asserts that "[c]ultural politics are crucially important to feminism because they include struggles over meaning. ... We have asserted the importance of consciousness, ideology, imagery and symbolism for our battles."[45] In understanding Solanas's attempt on Warhol's life and her subsequent incarceration as connected to the oppression of women by men, radical feminists constructed an early heroine of women's struggle for liberation. Most did not advocate eliminating men. But many leaders of the burgeoning movement found in her both a confirmation of women's powerlessness (in relation to individual men and the state apparati) and the possibility of resistance to that oppression. Four years after the shooting Solanas's figure still captured feminists' imaginations: in 1972 Joanna Russ, writing for the *Village Voice*, appropriates her to justify the political use of misandry: "[F]or every Valerie Solanas, how many rapists, how many male murderers are there? What male reviewer found Hitchcock's 'Frenzy' one-20th as revolting as Solanas's 'Scum Manifesto'? Of course Solanas went out and did it, but then so do many, many men — in the small town I live in there were several incidents of rape last year, and a common response to them was laughter."[46] It is in relationship to this culture, which covers up real aggression against women with jingles like "battle of the sexes," that Russ says, "Solanas is Everywoman" (29). The meanings of Solanas's resistance gleaned by feminists is their equation of "out of control" with "free," confirming the radical critique feminism offers to the dominant culture. "Although the models, of course, change, there is a way in which radical negation, silence, withdrawal, and invisibility, and the bold affirmations of feminine performance, imposture, and masquerade (purity and danger) have suggested cultural politics for women,"[47] and Solanas delineated the boundaries of such "hysterical" politics for feminism.

Valerie Solanas also understood the role of the creation of cultural meaning in maintaining existing power relations: in the *S.C.U.M. Manifesto* she writes, "We know that 'Great Art' is great because male authorities have told us so, and we can't claim otherwise, as only those with exquisite sensitivities far superior to ours can perceive and appreciate the greatness, the proof of their superior sensitivity being that they appreciate the slop that they appreciate" (Solanas, 58). Her analysis exposes the supposedly truth-telling authorities' tautology in defending the truthfulness of the stories they tell. Only crazy women, according to these authorities, would shoot men; the proof of their insanity lies in the act itself. Michel Foucault, writing about the history of sexuality, formulates the kinds of questions we need to ask of historical events: "In a specific type of discourse ... in a specific form of extortion of truth, appearing historically and in specific places ... what were the most immediate, the most local power relations at work? How did they make possible these kinds of discourses, and conversely, how were these discourses used to support power relations?"[48] If we ascribe to Solanas only the marginal role of "that crazy woman who shot Andy Warhol," we undermine the valuable insights she can provide, both about her cultural context and about reactions to feminist political action. We can recuperate Valerie Solanas not to romanticize the lawless woman operating on a politics entirely free from that which it struggles against but to glean what answers were culturally available to explain her behavior — and how our explanations themselves support or challenge the maintenance of domination and control.

Even latter-day feminists of the 1980s (and 1990s) use Solanas as a touchstone. The radical feminist group Always Causing Legal Unrest (A.C.L.U.) advertises its handbook, *Nemesis: Justice Is a Woman with a Sword*, with reference to Solanas's text: "We wanted to create a nice little handbook on manhating that would make the S.C.U.M. Manifesto seem tame."[49] Like feminists of the late 1960s, most contemporary feminists do not advocate killing men as a way to hasten women's liberation. More likely, as the A.C.L.U. case indicates, women who refer to the *Manifesto* as a source of inspiration look to it for a confirmation of the power of women's anger that can spark movements for change, anger that is most dangerous to authority because it is uncontrolled or uncontrollable.[50] Jayne Egerton suggests, in a review marking the 1984 reissue of the *S.C.U.M. Manifesto* in England, that the text can provide the spark of anger spurring feminist thought: women will find in it "a refreshing antidote to both the scholarly, sleep-inducing style of much academic feminist writing and to the kind of feminism which would have us sweet talk and therapise men out of their nasty ways."[51] In an era of "backlash" against women and feminism, Solanas's act seems dangerous to our own rational goals; indeed, it seems unlikely that the majority of feminists will advocate violence against men in a period in which feminism has confronted the existence of other oppressions in our activism and theory, both of which suggest that an exclusive focus on sexual difference does not account for the variety of women's experiences.[52] Yet Egerton's remarks are suggestive of the usefulness of the *S.C.U.M. Manifesto* and more generally of such "hysterical" cultural interventions, because we are forced to examine the foundation upon which our feminisms are built, to find the meaning(s) of our actions in different cultural spheres. Even an incorporated version of feminism, within the academy, is subject to reprisal and dismissal — the common reactions to Solanas — for its alleged irrationality; one recently established popular culture journal financed by "conservative foundations," for example, featured a list of "The Ten Wackiest Feminists on Campus," to discredit and mock women in areas outside traditional academic boundaries.

Any feminist action is vulnerable to these attacks. As Audre Lorde points out, we never speak as political women without fear of reprisal, but that fear should not allow us to silence ourselves:

And it is never without fear — of visibility, of the harsh light of scrutiny and perhaps judgment, of pain, of death. But we have lived through all those already, in silence, except death. And I remind myself all the time now that if I were to have been born mute, or had maintained an oath of silence my whole life long for safety, I would still have suffered, and I would still die. It is very good for establishing perspective.[53]

It may be too simplistic to assert that the *S.C.U.M. Manifesto* can help us reclaim a healthy anger toward institutional structures and personal practices that oppress women. It may be detrimental, in some feminists' views, to examine Valerie Solanas's act as an event whose symbolic value lies in our analyses of the responses to her "insanity" and our appropriations of the figure of the woman out of control. But rather than explain Solanas's actions against Andy Warhol as the result of hysterical madness, we can understand that their basis was outrage at and frustration with the political system that Warhol represented. We cannot afford to let such actions and their consequences be defined outside of the realm of the political.

NOTES

I would like to thank the following colleagues for their comments on earlier drafts of this essay: William Grant, Denise Hartsough, Joy Rouse, Marilyn Motz, Le'a Kent, Patrice Neal, and Annette Taylor. In no way should this imply, however, that they are in agreement with everything I assert.

1. See especially David Bourdon, *Warhol* (New York: Harry Abrams, 1990), and Bob Colacello, *Holy Terror: Andy Warhol Close Up* (New York: HarperCollins, 1990). See also Victor Bockris, *The Life and Death of Andy Warhol* (New York: Bantam, 1989). Further references to these works will be made parenthetically in the text.
2. Andy Warhol and Pat Hackett, *POPism: The Warhol '60s* (New York: Harcourt Brace Jovanovich, 1980), 271 (hereafter cited in text).
3. Paul Krassner, afterword to *S.C.U.M. Manifesto*, by Valerie Solanas (New York: Olympia, 1968), 89 (hereafter cited in text).
4. Howard Smith, "The Shot That Shattered the Velvet Underground," *Village Voice*, June 6 1968, 54.
5. All biographical accounts mention the makeup.
6. Most sources agree that the "flower child" line must have been invented by someone else. Solanas was most definitely not a flower child, and she wrote very derisively about the flower power movement in her *Manifesto*. Apparently the policeman or the reporter had an ideological axe to grind.
7. "Felled by SCUM," *Time*, June 14, 1968, 25.
8. "Sweet Assassin," *Newsweek*, June 17, 1968, 86.
9. Ibid., 87.
10. Smith, "The Shot."
11. Robert Marmorstein, "A Winter Memory of Valerie Solanis [sic]," *Village Voice*, June 13, 1968, 20.
12. Ibid., 9.
13. *New York Times*, June 5, 1968, 50.
14. Ibid., June 4, 1968, 36.
15. "Felled by SCUM"; "Sweet Assassin."
16. Phoebe Adams, review of *S.C.U.M. Manifesto*, by Solanas, *Atlantic* 222 (November 1968): 144.
17. Howard Smith and Brian Van Der Horst, "Valerie Solanas Replies," *Village Voice*, August 1, 1977, 28.
18. Maurice Girodias, publisher's preface to *S.C.U.M. Manifesto*, by Solanas (New York: Olympia, 1968), 24.
19. Mary Russo, "Female Grotesques: Carnival and Theory," in *Feminist Studies/Critical Studies*, ed. Teresa de Lauretis (Bloomington: Indiana University Press, 1986), 215 (hereafter cited in text).
20. Fredric Jameson, "Periodizing the 60s," in *The 60s without Apology*, ed. Sohnya Sayres et. al (Minneapolis: University of Minnesota Press, 1984), 208.

21. Natalie Davis, "Women on Top," in *Society and Culture in Early Modern France* (Stanford: Stanford University Press, 1965), 124–52, quoted in Russo, "Female Grotesques," 215.
22. Jane Gallop, "Keys to Dora," in *In Dora's Case: Freud — Hysteria — Feminism*, ed. Charles Bernheimer and Claire Kahane (New York: Columbia University Press, 1985), 201, 214.
23. Hélène Cixous and Catherine Clément, *The Newly Born Woman*, trans. Betsy Wing (Minneapolis: University of Minnesota Press, 1986), 147 (hereafter cited in text).
24. Smith, "The Shot."
25. Robin Morgan, "Goodbye to All That," in *Going Too Far: The Personal Chronicle of a Feminist* (New York: Vintage-Random, 1978), 126.
26. Valerie Solanas, *S.C.U.M. (Society for Cutting Up Men) Manifesto* (New York: Olympia, 1968), 61–62 (hereafter cited in text).
27. For an interesting discussion of antirationalism as a political strategy, see Christine Di Stefano, "Dilemmas of Difference: Feminism, Modernity, and Postmodernism," in *Feminism/Postmodernism*, ed. Linda J. Nicholson (New York: Routledge, 1990).
28. Jayne Egerton, "For 'Thrill-Seeking Females' Only," *Trouble and Strife* 2 (Spring 1984): 23.
29. Girodias, publisher's preface to *S.C.U.M. Manifesto*, 19.
30. Russo, "Female Grotesques," 217.
31. Dianne Hunter, "Hysteria, Psychoanalysis, and Feminism: The Case of Anna O.," in *The M(O)ther Tongue*, ed. S. Gardner et. al (Ithaca: Cornell University Press, 1985).
32. For more information on the Motherfuckers, see Todd Gitlin, *The Sixties: Years of Hope, Days of Rage* (New York: Bantam, 1987, 1993), 239–40; he is, however, inaccurate here about the shooting (which he labels a stabbing) and dismissive of Solanas.
33. Martha Weinman Lear, "The Second Feminist Wave," *New York Times Magazine*, March 10, 1968, 24 (hereafter cited in text).
34. Alice Echols, *Daring to Be Bad: Radical Feminism in America, 1967–1975* (Minneapolis: University of Minnesota Press, 1989), 105 (hereafter cited in text). See also Sara Evans, *Personal Politics* (New York: Vintage-Random, 1979), 209.
35. "Resignation from NOW," reprinted in *Amazon Odyssey* (New York: Links, 1974), 9.
36. *New York Times*, June 14, 1968, 52.
37. Robin Morgan, "Women Disrupt the Miss America Pageant," in *Going Too Far* (1968; New York: Vintage-Random, 1978), 62.
38. Robin Morgan, ed., *Sisterhood Is Powerful* (New York: Vintage-Random, 1970), 645–46.
39. Claire Tomalin, "Liberty, Equality, Sorority," *New Statesman*, March 26, 1971, 430.

40. Betty Friedan, *It Changed My Life* (New York: Norton, 1985), 109, quoted in Echols, *Daring to Be Bad*, 168.
41. Caroline Ramazanoglu, *Feminism and the Contradictions of Oppression* (London: Routledge, 1989), 102. Perhaps she is thinking here of Cell 16, which advocated that women learn karate in order to protect themselves from men.
42. *Village Voice*, July 25, 1977, 32. When asked whether her views had changed since the publication of the *Manifesto*, she answered no.
43. Sandra Harding, paraphrased in Frances C. Mascia-Lees, Patricia Sharpe, and Colleen Ballerino Cohen, "The Postmodernist Turn in Anthropology: Cautions from a Feminist Perspective," *Signs* 15, no. 1 (1989): 23.
44. See Marmorstein, "A Winter Memory," 10, where Solanas explains her experiences with reporters interviewing her about the *S.C.U.M. Manifesto*.
45. Michele Barrett, "Feminism and the Definition of Cultural Politics," in *Feminism, Culture and Politics*, ed. Rosalind Brunt and Caroline Rowan (London: Lawrence and Wishart, 1982), 37.
46. Joanna Russ, "The New Misandry," reprinted in *Amazon Expedition*, ed. Phyllis Birkby, Bertha Harris, Jill Johnston, Esther Newton, and Jane O'Wyatt (Albion, Calif.: Times Change, 1973), 27 (hereafter cited in text).
47. Russo, "Female Grotesques," 211.
48. Michel Foucault, *The History of Sexuality*, vol. 1, *An Introduction* (New York: Vintage, 1980), 97–98.
49. Always Causing Legal Unrest, flyer (Rancho Cordova, Calif., 1992).
50. Interestingly, the creation of this group—a response to the "silencing" of women by the American Civil Liberties Union's support for the free speech of the pornography industry—was met with an attempt by the American Civil Liberties Union to take "every legal effort" to suppress its use of the acronym (Always Causing Legal Unrest, flyer, 1992).
51. Egerton, "For 'Thrill-Seeking Females' Only," 23.
52. See Ramazanoglu, *Feminism*; Elizabeth Spelman, *Inessential Woman: Problems of Exclusion in Feminist Thought* (Boston: Beacon, 1988); Gloria Anzaldúa, ed., *Making Face, Making Soul, Haciendo Caras: Creative and Critical Perspectives by Women of Color* (San Francisco: Aunt Lute, 1990).
53. Audre Lord, "The Transformation of Silence into Language and Action," in *Sister Outsider*, by Audre Lorde (Trumansburg, N.Y.: Crossing, 1984): 43.

SIX

The Anti-Body in Photomontage: Hannah Höch's Woman without Wholeness

Lora Rempel

The idea that a "nothing to be seen," a something not subject to the rule of visibility or of specula(riza)tion, might yet have some reality, would indeed be intolerable to man.

— Luce Irigaray, *Speculum of the Other Woman*

In Hannah Höch's photomontage *For a Red Mouth* (fig. 6.1) of 1967, a pair of coral-red shiny lips, with edges slightly raised, float between what appears to be a slice of a pink-hued subterranean landscape and a snow-white mass of ruffles embellished with gathered rows of fuchsia organza trim. Beneath this, algae-green tentacles protrude upward from an uneven plane and appear to sway side to side as if to catch and pierce the enormous cumulus cloud formation sashaying toward it. There is a lack of clarity in the depth of field, which makes any logical reading of the image impossible; the flat geological form on the left is overlapped by the volumetric satin skirt only to frame it on the opposite side and to be exposed again by its lifted hem. Another subterranean strip, articulated by bronze-colored crustation, is overlaid by a half-moon shape of its kind at the far right. Although there is no body, no bodily wholeness, represented, the disembodied painted lips — the commodified lips of patriarchal capitalist culture, the culture of the cosmetic industry and mass-circulation women's magazines — are metonymical signifiers of

Fig. 6.1 *For A Red Mouth*, 1967, Hannah Höch. Courtesy of the Artists Rights Society, © 1993 ARS, New York/VG Bild-Kunst, Bonn.

"woman" — signifiers that are far removed in relationship to their signified. The abundance of rich, trimmed, satiny fabric suggests a similar origin both in terms of reproduction, as an illustration from a magazine fashion spread, and of product, as a commodity for sale — but a commodity that belongs to no body. The various round amorphic shapes and the geological formations whose innermost ovoids are repeated by encircling rims of pale flesh tones echo in shape and in color both the floating, bodiless lips and the lines of ruffles on the celestial shirt that belongs to no body. It is in their suggestion of female genitalia that the inanimate striations of unearthed pinkish rock become suggestively animate, suggestive animations, of the private body that might exist if a body possessed the vacant space beneath the great floating skirt.

Borrowing the deadpan irony of Rene Magritte, I am compelled to state the obvious: "This is not a woman."

Some might, I suspect, question whether this is a photograph. After all, is not a photograph proper about as different from an assemblage of photographic fragments as, say, an authentic Renaissance portrait painting is from its replica or parody? Following from Roland Barthes's assertion that a photograph is "an emanation of the referent," a ratification of what once existed, photography might be considered as the epitome of a kind of "High Objectivity" and as the exemplary visual language of the Enlightenment idea, the Enlightenment ideal, of empirical truth and objective vision.[1] Photomontage, by contrast, seems more like the chaotic counterpart of photography: a monstrous hybrid of "truthful" photographic representations.

A vast array of photographic representations from various illustrated magazines provide the primary source material for the montages Höch produced between 1919 and her death in 1978.[2] From the "New Woman" — sprung from the ideological rib of Weimar Germany — to the primitivist artifacts and preindustrial-peoples-cum-ethnographical-curios in an empire without colonies, to the glamorous star of the silver screen, to the fashionable consuming woman of the postwar period, Höch grafts together limbs and features utterly disharmonious in their nature. The multitude of referential body parts and their ornaments, each loaded with its own message, overcodes and overkills the resulting pastiched composites. This is patently the case in *For a Red Mouth*, an image that invokes an abstract, disembodied "sense" of woman — an anti-body.

A comparison of George Platt Lynes's photograph of *Salvador Dali* [with "Venus"] (fig. 6.2) of 1939 with Höch's *English Dancer* (fig. 6.3) of 1928 illustrates how differently his photograph and her photomontage represent the female body and appeal to our sense of reason: the former as "document," and the latter as a kind of "antidocument." On the one hand, in Höch's montage the mismatched eyes, the skewed mouth, the

THE ANTI-BODY IN PHOTOMONTAGE 151

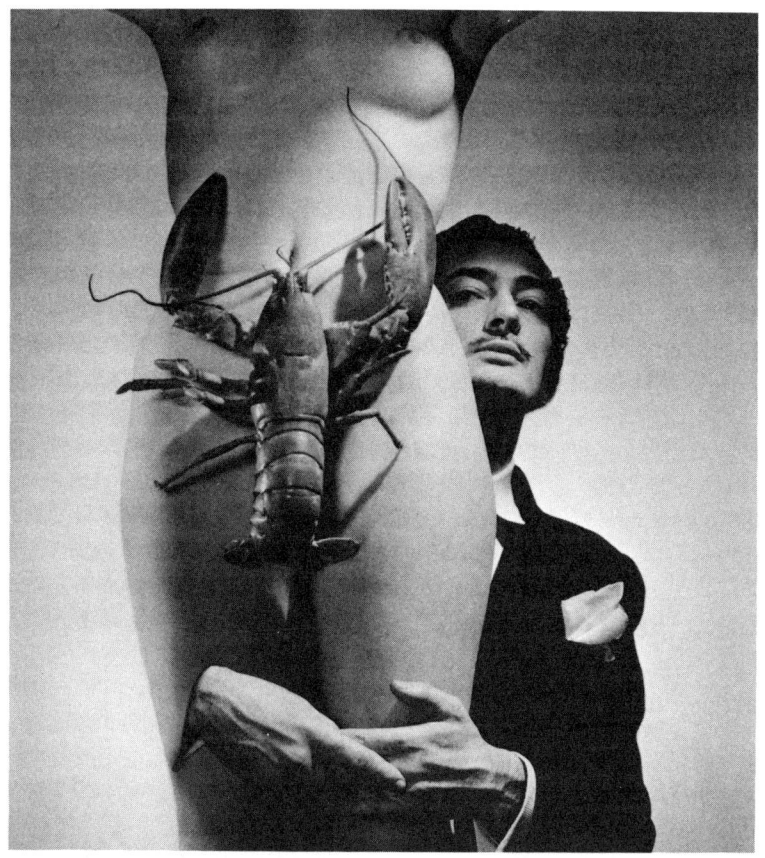

Fig. 6.2 *Salvador Dali* [with "Venus"], 1939, George Platt Lynes. Courtesy of the Metropolitan Museum of Art. All rights reserved.

assortment of foliage emerging from the top of the dancer's head, and the suspended dancing feet emerging from below add up to an image that does not purport to represent seeable reality. On the other hand, Lynes's photograph of Dali, bizarre as the sealife-as-body-ornament appears, is a document of what the artist brought together from material reality and composed into an object to be photographed, with the female body as the ridiculed and ridiculous locus of meaning. The constructed physical reality was first seen by the photographer, and its likeness can be seen again and again in its recorded, photographic form. Lynes's "Venus," as female body imaged, feminine sexuality imagined, and woman's identity con-

152 LORA REMPEL

Fig. 6.3 *English Dancer*, 1928, Hannah Höch. Courtesy of the Artists Rights Society, © 1993 ARS, New York/VG Bild-Kunst, Bonn.

structed, is predicated on a plethora of heterosexual male fantasies and allegories. Höch's "Dancer," while clearly also manipulated into an image, is conceived from images; it does not feed a desire to objectify and render submissive the female form, to construct the identity of woman as sex object and her sexuality as arcane, but rather feeds *from* such desires.

Like so many of Höch's images, it is an iconoclastic, cannibalistic feasting on the mythical body of femininity and the mass media's iconography of misogyny.

Clearly, these pictorial differences between Lynes's manipulation of model and props and Höch's assemblage of photographic fragments are in large part due to the self-evident disparities in medium. The implications of these differences are, however, less obvious and worth noting. For if representation feeds desire and constructs identity, can it not also steer, circumscribe, normalize, gender, and dichotomize both desire and identity? If there is an inequality between who looks and who is looked at — between who desires and who is desired, who is centered and who is pulled apart — what superpower determines and defines the sexual and psychic roles that pivot back and forth from the register of the eye?

In the phallocentric logic of Freud's theory of the Oedipal crisis, the eye discovers the original and organic difference, a discovery that will shape the psyche of the future woman, her body marked with otherness, as well as the psyche of the future man, against whose bodily mark of distinction the Other's difference is defined.[3] On the surface of the observed human body, the eye discovers, in a moment of crisis, what is merely physical difference — a different kind of body. Until the eye perceives anatomical difference, the psyche can conceive neither gender difference nor what it means to have one or the other kind of body. This vision of difference is endowed with meaning and essentializes signifying systems — systems of language (visual and linguistic) from which cultures and social structures precipitate. The eye, the psyche, and the body, eventually this human trinity will map the trilogy of sexual development from preadolescence to adolescence and finally to maturity. Difference is perpetually proclaimed in visions of the body. But there is no notion of bodily difference until the eye proclaims it — this speaking, telling eye.

What role, then, do representations of the body have in reaffirming and exaggerating the difference that was first proclaimed by the eye? How different, in fact, is a vision of bodily difference when one sees it, once removed, captured by the mediating eye of the camera? Can the body ever escape the visual truisms that the camera-eye — this modern, mechanical, speaking, telling eye — proclaims about it?

The photograph, to paraphrase Jonathan Crary, is a mechanical, mass-produced form of exchangeable "truth."[4] The question whether a photograph is in fact a slice of "truth" — a reality past — or whether photography is a manner of representing that tags onto the tradition or genre of pictorial realism verges on the metaphysical. Suffice it to say that, broadly speaking, photomontage undermines the concept of empirical truth, whereas important decisions continue to be based upon the empirical evidence photographs provide. Mug-shots, X-rays, and department store antitheft cameras, for instance, are trusted to divulge the unarguable evidence upon which final verdicts are based.

In the photomontage, furthermore, there is neither an agreement of time or of space between the assembler of the image and the photographic fragments she appropriates, nor an agreement among individual fragments internal to the image itself. Thus the photomontage is characterized by a double fissure: first, a fracturing of the unitary two-dimensional space of the photograph itself – what I will refer to as the body *of* the photograph – and second, a fragmentation of the photographic image – the body represented *in* the image. Although this double fissure is a key component of the medium of photomontage, the two separate acts of fracturing can be manifested in varying and disproportionate degrees. What I am proposing is that in Höch's photomontages both aspects of this double fissure are of equal, and of equally radical, intensity. Consequently, insofar as it negates bodily wholeness, her montage work is distinct from that of other Berlin Dadaists, who used the technique of photomontage but maintained sufficient order in their treatment of the represented body, as well as from Surrealist photographers, who ruptured the internal unity of imaged corporeality but ultimately upheld the ruling tradition of rational, empirical vision and much that is concomitant with that way of seeing as well.[5]

Still, the relationship Höch's photomontage work has with photography is in a number of ways a paradoxical one: one based on both dependence and rejection. Photographs are the necessary parents of her montages. But the offspring have been estranged from their progenitors – cut from the photographic materials and severed from the slice of time and space photographs claim to represent. Photographic images provide the primary visual materials for Höch's montages, but the technique of photography plays only a secondary role. For the maker of the photomontage is not required to use the mechanism of the camera but rather glue and sharp blades to (re)make fragments from once unified and autonomous photographs into an image that betrays its own disunity and sets aside all claims of mimesis – of iconicity – despite its appropriation of analogical representations. If new meaning emerges from between the spaces of Höch's oddly juxtaposed fragments, it is perceived anarchically, in the observer's suspension of disbelief — a willing disbelief liberated from the primacy of vision. Such anarchical experimentations in creative interpretation go against preordered expectations of objective vision and empirical truth, expectations that are always already impressed upon the beholder of photographic images. Moreover, as a product of a multiplicity of subverted past realities — of a multiplicity of radical acts of severing unity — "estrangement" from parental origins does not capture the intensity of this multiple fracturing. Aesthetic parenticide comes closer to describing the violation in Höch's montages of her photographic sources and of the principles inherent to the medium from which she borrows.

The act of symbolically killing one's aesthetic parents has been, historically and historiographically, an important initiation rite for entrance into the ranks of the artistic avant-garde — an expected impudence. In Hans Richter's book of 1965 entitled *Dada: Art and Anti-Art*, the Berlin Dadaists are remembered as heroic radicals, as avant-garde warriors against bourgeois art and bourgeois notions of the artist. Höch, who from 1915 to 1922 was a companion and artistic collaborator of Raoul Hausmann — the self-proclaimed "Dadasoph" of Berlin Dada — is, however, present only as a negative shadow within the characterizations of her larger-than-life male colleagues. "Her tiny voice," he writes,

would only have been drowned by the roars of her masculine colleagues. But when she came to preside over gatherings in Hausmann's studio she quickly made herself indispensable, both for the sharp contrast between her slightly nun-like grace and the heavyweight challenge presented by her mentor, and for the sandwiches, beer and coffee she managed somehow to conjure up despite the shortage of money.

On such evenings she was able to make her small, precise voice heard. When Hausmann proclaimed the doctrine of anti-art, she spoke up for art and for Hannah Höch. A good girl.[6]

Richter's description of Höch confines her to the outermost margins of the politicized aesthetic movement. She is a Dadaist by default, married into the radical clan rather than a member by right: a token in the totem of the masculinist historiographer of the Dada avant-garde. He relies on adjectival binaries, which describe the (non)physicality and passivity of Höch, who in turn is not treated as a historical entity but rather as a foil for the male Dadaists: shy versus bold, quiet versus roaring, graceful versus heavyweight, "nun-like" versus "masculine," an embodiment of bourgeois values and reverence for art as opposed to an antagonist intolerant of bourgeois society and artistic conventions. In short, Höch is given credit for her accessory role in filling the domestic task of supplying refreshments in the Dada drama in which all the protagonists are male.[7]

Richter's essay is a forceful example of the textual devaluation and ultimate exclusion of Höch, his mention of her notwithstanding, from the history of Dada.[8] It is a forceful and resonant example because Richter "was there"; he was a member of Berlin Dada and a participant in its events, and having been there ostensibly endows his text with a kind of historical truth value.[9] Richter's voice becomes the voice of the documenter that speaks the historical "documents," reciting them from memory. One and the same person experiences, remembers, and recounts the events. The experience, memory, and feeling of the individual author become, in and of themselves, the intimate and comprehensive facts that comprise a textual history, a body of historical knowledge that encompasses its oral and experiential prehistory and thus remains a continuous, stable whole. Or so it would seem. And from this body of knowledge Hannah Höch has been virtually left out.[10]

Richter's essay, which for the reasons noted above carries special status as a must read, must cite, Dada Ur-text, is not unrepresentative of the treatment of Höch in the literature on Dada.[11] In consequence of the negative textual construction of Höch in the historiography of Dada there is a devaluation of the woman Dadaist and her work that is strangely not unlike the recurring negation of the wholeness of "woman" in Höch's montages. She is there, but only in cameo, not as a pictured wholeness and not as a fully participating historical entity. "She" is not "real" — not really represented, not present. A "no-body."

Perhaps, however, Höch was less a marginal "no-body" of Dada than she was an "anti-body" within it. Richter's tacit affirmation that Höch does not fit his paradigm of the homogeneously radical, all-male Dada collective might in fact have validity. And it may not be quite right to assume that gender is the singular and absolute explanation for the lack of fit between Höch and Dada. She was introduced to Dada by Hausmann around 1918. Without this personal affiliation with the "Dadasoph" she may not have had access to the inner circle of the group. Her "tiny voice" in the midst of the "roars of her masculine colleagues" could well have been a consequence of her irresolution rather than her inability to engage wholeheartedly in Dada antics.[12] She may have known better than anyone else that she did not fit the Dada mold. More comfortable with making her pronouncements and criticisms "through the medium of art" rather than declaring them publicly and demonstratively, Höch was surely an outsider inside the group that fashioned itself as collectively anti-art.[13]

One of the unique visual characteristics of Höch's montages, as I have argued above, is that the recalcitrant incompleteness and radical fragmentation of juxtaposed secondhand body parts subtract from, rather than add up to, centered and whole representations of the female body. Consequently, there is no body left, no body left to be seen, and none can reemerge from the chaos of her montages.

There are exceptions in Höch's oeuvre, however. In *Hungarian Rhapsody* (fig. 6.4) of 1940, for example, a "body," hatted, feathered, flowered, and bejeweled, provides the focus. There seems to be an attempt to assemble a body: in terms of the scale of parts, the positioning of parts, and the single viewpoint, the figure seems to logically add up and offer the viewer a point of reference within the operating visual language system. Or does it? In any case, the image does not present us with a "Venus." The pleasure of looking, the expectation of recognizing, is arrested, confused, frustrated by the three-legged dancer. It is not the direct and obvious opposite of bodily wholeness, but rather an appeal to the tentativeness of representational wholeness.

This is in dramatic contrast to the photomontages of Höch's Dada colleague John Heartfield. In the latter's antiwar and antifascist work of the thirties, figures almost always refer back to recognizable individuals. Not unlike political caricature from the late eighteenth century to the present, understanding the intended message of Heartfield's photomontages hinges on the viewer's identification of individual "portraits" featured in the image. Manipulations and exaggerations of facial features must be kept in check in order to ensure that every character portrayed can be accounted for (or held accountable). In his well-known photomontages *The Meaning of the Hitler Salute*, of 1932, and *Goering the Executioner of the Third Reich*, of 1933, the familiar photographed faces of Hitler and Goering each refer back to a singular respective body, to a recognizable, once-seen, once-seeable, person. And even though individual identity has been stripped away along with the decomposed flesh from the carcasses

158   LORA REMPEL

Fig. 6.4 *Hungarian Rhapsody*, 1940, Hannah Höch. Courtesy of the Artists Rights Society, © 1993 ARS, New York/VG Bild-Kunst, Bonn.

that lay in the mud of war in Heartfield's *Rearmament Is Necessary* (fig. 6.5) of 1932, horrific as it is, we comprehend that these human remains were once the skeletal armature of living soldiers. Within the image itself there is no contradiction but rather a seamless unity: two bodies rotting in the ominous open graveyard of an abandoned battlefield. Before death there was life, before war there was peace, before the black-and-white photograph of bodies laid to waste there was the actual stench, scream, and sight of death. The tremendous power of *Rearmament*, and of many other equally chilling photomontages of Heartfield's, is precisely the invocation of the human narrative and the context of reality that the frame of the image cannot encompass. The meticulous erasing of seams that link piece with piece characterizes Heartfield's photomontages and makes them function in a way that is remarkably similar to unmanipulated photographic images in which the "real" is the assumed predicate of the picture.

The only apparent contradiction in Heartfield's photomontages is external to the pictorial image — between the grim photographic image and the attached imperative caption — and does not impinge on our reading of the bodies in the image or of the images themselves as bodies, as unities. Occasionally, superimposed slogans and captions are all that separate Heartfield's work from "straight" photographs. The reliance on words to convey, confuse, or complete the narrative meaning in Heartfield's work places these images solidly within the indexical, symbolic realm of language.

Rarely does Höch employ textual language in her photomontages.[14] Except for a few of her early Dadaist works, *Cut with the Kitchen-Knife Dada through the Last Weimar Beer Belly Cultural Epoch of Germany*, of 1919–1920, for example, there is a general nonreliance on words to complement or to linguistically complete her images. And when words are included, they occur as interrupted fragments that resist the sloganistic didacticism that is particularly characteristic of Heartfield's work. This rejection of textual language in Höch's images compels an altogether different kind of heuristic path, one that is not shaped by the domination of indexical clarity central to Heartfield's propagandistic photomontages, in which captions rule over image and direct the route of visual, intellectual, and political interpretation.[15]

The conspicuous absence of accompanying texts in Höch's photomontages is an important formal and iconographical element that markedly

Fig. 6.5 *Rearmament Is Necessary*, 1932, John Heartfield. Courtesy of the Artists Rights Society, © 1993 ARS, New York/VG Bild-Kunst, Bonn..

distinguishes her work from Heartfield's photomontages. The rejection, or overloading, of clear referents, which would create a smooth semiotic path from signifier to sign, in her work also contrasts with the salient, unambiguous signs or "emblems" in Heartfield's virtually seamless photomontages.

To apply a semiotic analysis to montages produced by a number of male artists in the interwar period is to discover that the propensity toward interpretive clarity evident in Heartfield's work persists in much of their work as well — except that concerns with the carnage of war are replaced by other carnal interests. For example, Georges Hugnet's untitled photomontage of 1936 (fig. 6.6) represents the female body as whole. Photographs of bodies are appropriated in strange ways in these images, but the resilient wholeness of the pictured body — as complete and as obvious referent — functions as the source of scopophilic pleasure in the surreal dream narrative.

There is a fundamental difference between the image by Hugnet described above, which remains tied to the culturally dominant empirical mode of looking despite the use of montage and the surrealist élan, and Höch's radically disordered "no-bodies." In *Never Put Both Feet on the Ground* (fig. 6.7) of 1940, we see not bodies but what remains of them below the engulfing pale blue haze. These are not bodies but disembodied legs, severed just below their biological sex: the legs of a whimsical hovering centipede that extends beyond either side of the frame. *On With the Party* (fig. 6.8), of 1965, provides another example of how the pastiched female body in Höch's montages resists the ordering logic of the patriarchal gaze. "Woman" is camouflaged by the glittery and reflective environment — "woman" is subtracted from, and added to. The remade profile of the head echoes the remade profile of the breast, articulated by a sharp, shiny red cone — not sexualized but rather roboticized, lobotomized. Not frightening but frozen in frightfulness. An unblinking, two-dimensional cyclops: an unwelcoming grotesque. Not threatening, but threatened by the acid green and electric blue crystalline bullets, one of which hangs directly above the single anxious eye.

Despite the employment of a pictorial medium that is essentially based upon the fragmentation of representation, there is an adamant refusal to jeopardize the unified body in the above-mentioned photomontages by Hugnet and Höch's fellow Dadaist Heartfield. The obverse of this equation between the fragmentary body of the photograph and the unified

Fig. 6.6 Untitled, 1936, George Hugnet. Courtesy of the Spencer Collection, New York Public Library, Astor, Lenox and Tilden Foundations.

Fig. 6.7 *Never Put Both Feet on the Ground*, 1940, Hannah Höch. Courtesy of the Artists Rights Society, © 1993 ARS, New York/VG Bild-Kunst, Bonn.

164 LORA REMPEL

Fig. 6.8 *On With the Party*, 1965, Hannah Höch. Courtesy of the Artists Rights Society, © 1993 ARS, New York/VG Bild-Kunst, Bonn.

body in the photograph is Hans Bellmer's *Doll (La Poupee)* photographs (fig. 6.9), which allow a glimpse of the apparent paradox that arises when the empirical, mechanical eye of the camera produces incongruous images of the body form. Bellmer's first and second doll series, which span the 1930s, depict radically fragmented, clearly gendered "dolls." In these photographs human-like doll parts, sometimes complete with shoes, hair, and makeup, are pulled apart and reassembled, in a way that is not entirely unlike Höch's cutting and pasting of photo-fragments of the body and its accoutrements. It is crucial, however, to recognize how medium impacts on readings of these images. Even though the doll configurations seriously hinder our reading of them as "whole," the photographs themselves remain singular, decipherable entities and conceivable extensions of the viewer's space. Precisely because the photographs can impinge on the viewer's space, they have the potential to pose a challenge on the level of *what* they show. Yet the initial horror we might have imagined at first glance is ameliorated by the evidential facts the photographs reveal when we look more closely: we see, and we know, after all, that these are dolls the artist has manipulated in shocking ways.

And if our eyes cannot discern the plasticity of the photographed figure, the title, "Doll," can reassure us of the inanimate nature of the human-like form, as well as of its traditional function as passive plaything with which a gendered destiny is enacted and reinforced. That gendered destiny, or gendered identity, is indeed played out by Bellmer in the preparation of the staged and sordid scenes and in the images that chronicle them. On the level of *how* they show — in their maintenance of photographic unity — they are conventional and in no way disruptive of the traditional, patriarchal mode of looking. In these images the female form is the vehicle-victim of the (male) photographer's idea. "He" looks (with initial shock) at her mutilated body — a body he has imagined-imaged.

Bellmer's *Doll* images do not depart from entrenched conventions of

Fig. 6.9 *The Doll*, Hans Bellmer. Courtesy of the Metropolitan Museum of Art. All rights reserved.

representing the female body in photography, though they do take it to an uneasy extreme. That tradition is one dominated by the objectification and fetishization of the female body, a tradition in the service of women's oppression and at war with the integrity of women. By remaining within this photographic tradition, Bellmer's photographs do not imperil the precedence of the "eye" to order visual fact according to the specular logic of patriarchy in which the "otherness" of woman is constantly reaffirmed. Despite vicarious bodily mutilation, the order of things is ultimately supported.

By contrast the negation of the objectified and illusionistically organic body of woman in Höch's photomontages is a subversive pictorial strategy with a double edge. First, the medium of photomontage, although perilously linked to the logic of vision by its dependence on photography, radically undermines the faith that vision confirms physical "reality." Second, the speaking, telling "eye" (either as the original eye that first discovers or as the mechanical eye that mediates and then duplicates an original, physical "sight") is denied its primacy over the body-object when the body is not (re)presented — when it is signified only in the most oblique and highly attenuated manner — and therefore not categorizable as either a body of difference or a body that defines difference. In this fashion Höch's "anti-body" is dislodged from the Enlightenment scopic regime of "high objectivity" — a regime that reassures knowledge by sight (that is, we know because we see it to be thus). Within this regime, to deny the eye its orientation is also to strip away the regime's power to orient — to differentiate and to subordinate.

How, then, are we to understand Höch's photomontages that feature signifiers of "woman" but negate the wholeness of woman as readable sign? Do they represent a kind of desperate protest against the erasure of woman from public spheres of life, except as commodified, fetishized, and spectacularized? On the one hand they can be interpreted as pessimistic pictorial accounts of how problematic representing the female body is within a culture that demands that that body obey its commands, fit its ideals, and succumb to the roles it has been assigned within the all-encompassing organism of late capitalism. (Late capitalism: a body greater and more voracious than all others.) On the other hand one could also suspect that there is a certain nihilism evident in these images, where it is not the problematic but rather the utter futility of representing the female body that is being called upon.[16] Born of the photographic material of the mass culture of capitalism, nurtured on the misogynist mythologies that find their most persuasive articulation in imagistic as well as textual representations, Höch's anti-bodies function as signifiers metonymically replacing the poisoned organism that the female body becomes in capitalist culture through substitution laterally — through parts for wholes. And as metonymical transformations of the female body in capitalist culture, they resist that culture's attempts at colonization. And in this resistance there is a glimpse of optimism.

Höch's montaged anti-bodies escape the visual truisms that the camera-eye speaks about bodily difference by negating the photographed body of difference — the female body — and leaving disarranged photo-fragments that retain only scant and aberrant traces of the pictorial signifiers that were previously one-half of the equation of the "female body."[17] Höch cuts from this "female body" and in the process transforms that mythically centered body into a "no-body" in her antiphotographs, and she twists both the phallocentric logic that defines woman as Other and the specular logic that articulates the social being of woman as "nobody." Beneath this pictorial approach of radically fragmenting and negating the female body, an anti-state — anti-statement — strategy can be discerned. The history of the state is indissociable from the evolution of patriarchal authority. Be it oppressively authoritarian or condescendingly benevolent, the state and its organs always harness the body to its all-encompassing, insidious logic. The female body can find no liberation under the laws of orthodox Freudian theory either, for under its regime the female unconscious is (dis)ordered into obeyance. Negating the female body from within visual systems of signification and representation is a way to elude the various strands of patriarchal logic that aim to tie that body down.

To loop back to the beginning of this essay, then, to Höch's *Red Mouth* — the image in which the body of "woman" is negated most, but at the same time most resonant — an unarticulated body (or, indeed, many bodies) emerges from between the collaged multiplicity of red- and flesh-colored shapes. This anti-body — "a something not subject to the rule of visibility or of specula(riza)tion" — can only be imagined in the blind spots and outermost margins of specular logic and visual reality. Even though Höch's images in fact (re)announce the (no)place, the (no)body of woman under capitalism, they encourage a reanalysis of the representation of women within our present culture by revealing the tentativeness of the sutures that join the secular faith in empirical "truth" with patriarchal myths. The represented female body is exploited by those myths — it is the body most often made to bear those sutures — whereas the anti-body, simultaneously negating and exposing these myths, dissolves them in pursuit of awakening.

NOTES

This text evolved from a seminar on photography at the Graduate Center of the City University of New York. I wish to thank Carol Armstrong for the helpful and provocative comments she provided on the original version. Later drafts benefited greatly from the suggestions made by Alex Alberro.

1. Roland Barthes, *Camera Lucida*, trans. Richard Howard (New York: Hill and Wang, 1981).
2. For more on Höch's sources, see Maud Lavin, *Cut with the Kitchen Knife: The Weimar Photomontages of Hannah Höch* (New Haven: Yale University Press, 1993).
3. Luce Irigaray's critique of Freud in *Speculum of the Other Woman*, trans. Gillian C. Gill (Ithaca, N.Y.: Cornell University Press, 1985), and Gilles Deleuze and Felix Guattari's *A Thousand Plateaus: Capitalism and Schizophrenia*, trans. Brian Massumi (Minneapolis: University of Minnesota Press, 1987), provide the main theoretical undergirdings of this essay, and I thus alert the reader at the outset to my indebtedness to these writings.
4. Jonathan Crary, *Techniques of the Observer: On Vision and Modernity in the Nineteenth Century* (Cambridge, Mass.: MIT Press, 1990), 99.
5. For an interesting discussion of how the radically cropped image of the body functions to connote "body" and to eroticize it, see Rosalind Krauss's discussion of Man Ray's *Monument a D.A.F. de Sade* of 1933 in "Photography in the Service of Surrealism," in *L'Amour fou: Photography and Surrealism* (New York: Abbeville, 1985), 19.
6. Hans Richter, *Dada: Art and Anti-Art* (New York: McGraw-Hill, 1965), 132.
7. See Griselda Pollock's chapter "Woman as Sign in Pre-Raphaelite Literature: The Representation of Elizabeth Siddall," in *Vision and Difference: Femininity, Feminism and Histories of Art* (London: Routledge, 1988), 91–114, in which Pollock discusses how gender differentiation is conveyed in texts by constructing binaries; see esp. 103.
8. Essentially, Richter's paradigm of the heroic, avant-garde, anti-art, antibourgeois Dadaist functions as a hermeneutic circle of exclusion: Höch is conveyed as lacking the fundamental characteristics of a Dadaist and thus as someone who cannot be cast in the role of the Dadaist. Höch is thereby excluded from the action of the Dada drama, where the fundamental characteristics of a Dadaist can be developed and exhibited.
9. By virtue of his having "been there," Richter's text is not a reconstruction of

a movement, its philosophies, and its practitioners, but rather a foundational construction of what the knowing author, privileged spectator, and entitled participant — all three embodied in the author-authority posing as a transhistorical anti-art Dadaist-cum-omniscient-art-historian — considers the key component parts that comprise an entirety, a textual body of an artistic movement.

10. I am interested in deconstructing Richter's text in order to expose the subtle ways in which his language functions to frame and circumscribe what for him does or does not fit into Dada. I am also interested in exposing the pretense of dispassionate, distanced objectivity in the voice of the historian who needs to construct his subject as an entity and to solve its internal contradictions. That entity is represented in textual form as a body of knowledge, a wholeness that, although unperceivable, is conceivable and knowable through the text in which it is reconstructed, or in the case of Richter's text, constructed.

11. The marginalization or exclusion of Höch in art historical literature is discussed briefly by Karin Thomas, "Hannah Höch — The 'Good Girl Who Works Hard': The Feminist Question Mark," in *Hannah Höch, 1889–1978, Collages*, ed. Götz Adriani, trans. Eileen Martin (Stuttgart: Institute for Foreign Cultural Relations, 1985), 71–81.

12. Ibid., 72–73.

13. See Suzanne Page's interview with Hannah Höch in the catalogue *Hannah Höch* (Berlin: Staatliche Museen Preussischer Kulturbesitz, 1976), 23ff. This is discussed in Eberhard Roters, "Pictorial Symbolism in Hannah Höch's Work," in *Hannah Höch*, 65–69. I am, however, interested in a different set of peculiarities in Höch's photomontages than is Roters.

14. The relationship between photography and language in the photomontage — what she calls the "language effect" of dada montage — is discussed by Krauss in "Photography," 25–28.

15. Ibid. Krauss mentions Louis Aragon's understanding of Heartfield's photo collages as "textual" in their insistence upon meaning and their potential to signify, or articulate, reality ("Photography," 25).

16. In asking this question, I have in mind the following passage from Deleuze and Guattari, *A Thousand Plateaus:* "You have to keep enough of the organism for it to reform each dawn; and you have to keep small supplies of significance and subjectification, if only to turn them against their own systems when the circumstances demand it, when things, persons, even situations, force you to; and you have to keep small rations of subjectivity in sufficient quantity to enable you to respond to the dominant reality. Mimic the strata. You do not reach the BwO [Body without Organs], and its plane of consistency, by wildly destratifying" (160)

Interpreting their caution against "wildly destratifying" as it might relate to Höch's "woman without wholeness," it seems to me that their warning might also be extended to Höch's virtual negation of the body. That is, it would be better to maintain some semblance of "wholeness" in order for the body to maintain its oppositional potential. However, as I have argued, the tradition of picturing the female body subordinates women to such an extreme that mimicking the strata — which is not a new venture in photography — is in itself an appropriatable strategy.

17. Maud Lavin's recent study of Höch contextualizes the artist's early work within the historical and political frame of Weimar Germany, with a particular interest in the gender politics of those years. In its thorough examination of the historical moment and of Höch's appropriation of mass media illustration sources and their significance in her photomontages, Lavin's book is provocative and useful. However, Lavin's use of Freudian theory, as well as her insistence on the utopian elements that she argues are manifested in Höch's treatment of representations of female athletes, dancers, and other feminine icons, play into patriarchal constructs of femininity that posit the feminine as always already Other. Though I do agree with Lavin's point that there is an empowering aspect to Höch's photomontages (I hesitate to call it utopian), this aspect resides precisely in the negation of the represented female body rather than in its appropriation and ironic rearrangement. See Lavin, *Cut with the Kitchen Knife*.

SEVEN

Something's Missing: Male Hysteria and the U.S. Invasion of Panama

Cynthia Weber

The best strategy for challenging the phallic authority of the penis is laughter.
— Elizabeth Grosz, *Jacques Lacan: A Feminist Introduction*

Analyzing the cause of the 1989 U.S. invasion of Panama, a White House advisor told the *New York Times* that the president "felt that Noriega was thumbing his nose at him."[1] Read symptomatically, Manuel Noriega's political gesture toward Bush is exposed as hysterical. The substitution of the unconscious impulse for the signifier — penis for thumb and the Central American isthmus for nose — suggests a geopolitical anatomy of frustrated desires.[2] Furthermore, it prompts a series of questions: Why did Noriega expose himself to Bush? What accounts for Bush's response (a military invasion)? And does this scenario as a summary statement of the Bush administration's position toward Noriega offer any insights about male hysteria as a motif for political leadership in the "New World Order?"

What follows is a symptomatic reading of geopolitical bodies (diplomatic and territorial) and body parts (sexual and strategic) that appear in the discourse surrounding the U.S. invasion of Panama. Among the bodies analyzed are those of Manuel Noriega and George Bush (diplomatic), Panama and the United States (territorial), and the Panama Canal (sexual as well as strategic body part).

This symptomatic reading of the invasion discourse draws upon the work of Luce Irigaray, particularly her books *Speculum of the Other Woman* and *This Sex Which Is Not One*, to make two theoretical moves.[3] The first move reads Noriega and Bush as hysterical males by examining them as isolated corporal signifiers and later relating them to the Panama Canal, their figural support. I suggest that both Noriega and Bush lack phallic power, and this lack is related to a lack of a feminine object (in this case, the Panama Canal). Noriega lacks the Panama Canal because he is denied access to the canal by the Bush administration. Noriega's lack may be read as a discourse of externally imposed celibacy. Bush, in contrast, controls the Panama Canal yet also lacks the canal. Bush's lack derives from his position as the leader of a state that is a declining hegemonic power in international affairs. Bush lacks the canal, then, because he and his state are nearly impotent. Both Noriega and Bush attempt to compensate for their lack by excessively miming masculinity in the invasion discourse.[4] The effect of their discursive practices is to uncode the male bodies of Noriega and Bush as men.

The second theoretical move concerns feminization rather than emasculation. Thanks to their emasculation (uncoding as men), Noriega and Bush are open to feminization (recoding as women). For Noriega, feminization both precedes the U.S. invasion of Panama and continues during and after the invasion.[5] I limit my reading to Noriega's feminization during the invasion, and even then, this is brief. I focus primarily on Bush because, as I suggest, it is the Bush administration's discursive invasion strategy of encirclement rather than penetration that leads to the feminization of Bush.

More importantly in terms of international relations theory generally and theories of state sovereignty and intervention specifically, the Bush administration's strategy of encirclement invites a deconstruction of two dichotomies upon which the invasion discourse relies. These dichotomies are domestic politics/international politics and the complementary engendering of domestic politics as feminine and international politics as masculine, resulting in a domestic = feminine/international = masculine dichotomy.[6]

The invasion discourse disrupts the logic whereby sovereign nation-states and their ultimate affirmation of manhood – intervention – are masculinely engendered. Rather than regarding posthegemon (postphallic) states simply as old, nearly impotent masculine bodies, this reading suggests that they might instead be interpreted as transvestites because in what is regarded as the masculine sphere of politics (international space), posthegemonic states rely upon simulated feminine modes of conduct.[7]

Irigaray's focus on miming, mimicry, or mimesis invites an analogical reading of the invasion discourse. This strategy of reading deliberately employs the metaphorical imagery found in Irigaray's work for two reasons. First, attending to the mimetic performance of engendered language enables one to refuse to position oneself either within or beyond symbolic and cultural codes of phallocentrism that value male terms over female terms. In this context, miming — like laughter — allows me to perform a parody of phallic authority. Following from this, one is positioned to bring gender dichotomies into question. Second, as Margaret Whitford explains, "The tactic of mimesis can be seen as a kind of deliberate hysteria, designed to illuminate the *interests* which are at stake in metaphors."[8]

Although this reading embodies profane treatments of "honorable" institutions (such as the presidency) and humorous analyses of "dishonorable" acts (rape and a bloody military intervention), the political implications of this reading should not be overlooked. By attending to these aspects of the U.S. discourse on the Panama invasion, I focus on a neglected feature of what enables such atrocities to occur and of their effects on institutions, events, and engendered representations of subjectivity. It is not my intention to divert attention away from other political implications of the invasion discourse; rather, in accordance with feminist readings of politics, I am attempting to explode the notion of politics.[9]

This reading of the invasion discourse equates de-authorization (the death of the author) with the hystericization of male subjectivity.[10] It deliberately engages the invasion discourse with humor. As Mikhail Bakhtin noted, "Laughter liberates not only from external censorship but first of all from the great interior censor."[11] Laughter defamiliarizes discourses and events for their readers, giving readers license to disobey common expectations about what meanings a given text ought to generate. Attention is drawn to subtexts and double meanings embedded in texts. By "liberating" the interpretation of a text from the sole domain of its author's intentions, texts are remotivated with plural interpretations.

MALE SUBJECTIVITY

In *Speculum of the Other Woman* Luce Irigaray observes, "We can assume that any theory of the subject has always been appropriated by the 'masculine'" (*Speculum*, 133). Irigaray's conclusion is based on a reading of psychoanalytic theory and what that theory necessarily overlooks. Her focus is on "a difference not taken into account" — the difference between the sexes (*Speculum*, 21). Turn, for example, to Freud's story of the Oedipal complex. During the Oedipal stage, the dual taboos of incest and masturbation act to transform bisexual children into heterosexual adults. But as Irigaray notices, becoming a woman is "'more difficult and more complicated' than becoming a man" (*Speculum*, 22). In the maturation process, the boy displaces his desire for his mother onto other women and substitutes the vagina for his hand as the organ that will satisfy his desires. For girls, the desire for the mother must be displaced first to the father and then to other men. The girl, motivated by her presumed "penis envy," also must abandon her clitoris or little penis in favor of her vagina, which can lodge a mature penis.

Her reconsideration of the Oedipal complex suggests to Irigaray that "[f]emale sexuality has always been conceptualized on the basis of masculine parameters" (*This Sex*, 23). Little girls are understood as castrated little men, and "normal" women satisfy male desires as a passageway (vagina) through which male subjects reach maturity and as a receptacle (womb) that assures reproduction. In other words, women are necessary in Freud's system to accommodate the penis.

Freud's system depends upon both an essential male/female dichotomy and a hierarchization of that dichotomy that produces oppositions such as: "be/*become*, have/*not have* sex (organ), phallic/*nonphallic*, penis/*clitoris* or else penis/*vagina*, plus/*minus*, clearly representable/*dark continent*, logos/ *silence* or idle chatter, desire for the mother/*desire to be the mother*, etc." (*Speculum*, 22; italics and parentheses in original). In each of these oppositions, the first and valued term is masculine, and the second, feminine term finds meaning only in relation to the masculine term. For Freud, it is the penis that is the standard of value and guarantee of meaning.

Lacan's theory substitutes phallus for penis as the psychoanalytic standard of value. For Lacan — who, like Freud, does not differentiate between males and females before the Oedipal stage — it is the mirror stage that is the formative moment of subjectivity. At the culmination of the mirror stage, the child leaves the Imaginary (in which the child views its body and the mother's body as one) and enters the Symbolic Order (in which the child sees itself as separate from the mother).[12] When the child can distinguish between the mother, who supports it as it gazes into the mirror, and itself, the formation of subjectivity is complete. For Lacan, the culmination of the mirror stage corresponds to the child's entry into language. The child completes its detachment from the mother when it announces "I am," which Lacan says is like saying "I am he (she) who has lost something" or "I am that which I am not."[13] What the child has lost/ lacks and what the child is not is the mother. Crucial to Lacan's theory and its value of the phallus is that it is the father, representing the threat of castration, who intervenes between the child and the mother. This intervention by the father enforces a split between the child and the mother, thus enabling the child to become a subject in the system of language. The Law of the Father is represented by the phallus in Lacan's system.[14]

The Lacanian phallus is a signifier that is not reducible to the penis. As Jane Gallop explains, "It [the phallus] is neither a real nor a fantasized organ but an attribute: a power to generate meaning."[15] The function of the phallus in the mirror stage is simultaneously to produce the Symbolic Order and to produce subjects who can make meaning within that order. The phallus is not possessed by either males or females. It appears in Lacan's theory as a transcendental signifier that is absolute Other to both males and females.[16] Even so, subjects can exercise phallic power as, for example, the father does during the mirror stage. Gallop suggests, "To have a phallus would mean to be at the center of discourse, to generate meaning, to have mastery of language, to control rather than to conform to that which comes from outside, from the Other."[17]

Whereas Lacan insisted that the phallus and penis were not the same, Gallop observes the phallus/penis opposition is difficult to maintain. "Of course, the signifier *phallus* functions in distinction from the signifier *penis*. It sounds and looks different, produces different associations. *But* it *also* always refers to *penis*. Lacanians might *wish* to polarize the two terms into a neat opposition, but it is hard to polarize synonyms."[18] Exercising phallic power, then, is related to having a penis. Maggie Berg explains, "Despite his claims that the speaking being can line up on whichever side of the phallus she chooses, Lacan renders it impossible for one born without a penis to be on the side of the phallus: gender, within the determinism of his discursive system, is ultimately linked to anatomy."[19]

Lacan's simultaneous distinction and association of the phallus/penis in part explain Lacan's claim that the phallus can function as a signifier "only as veiled, i.e., when it is not recognized as the penis."[20] In addition, the power of the veiled phallus as opposed to the unveiled penis is derived from locating the phallus beyond the Symbolic Order. The phallus derives its power precisely because it cannot be represented within the Symbolic Order. When the phallus is recognized as the penis — an organ that can be represented — the phallus functions as any other signifier in the Symbolic Order and cannot function as a transcendental signifier because a transcendental signifier necessarily must remain beyond representation. Naomi Schor explains: "To subject the penis to representation is to strip the phallus of its empowering veil, for . . . while the phallus can be said to draw its symbolic power from the *visibility of the penis*, phallic power derives precisely from *the phallus's inaccessibility to representation.*"[21] As Irigaray notes, "Exhibition is equivalent to announcing that the central postulate is in fact being called into question" (*Speculum*, 27).

For both Freud and Lacan, the central dichotomy of "have penis/lack penis" organizes the representational logic of psychoanalytic discourse. Representation is regulated by what can be seen (or more accurately, what can be seen but is veiled) — primarily the phallus. In this discourse, Irigaray argues, woman as woman cannot be represented for two reasons. First, woman's genitals appear to be absent. "[H]er sexual organ represents *the horror of nothing to see.* . . . [T]his nothing-to-see has to be excluded, rejected, from such a scene of representation" (*This Sex*, 26). Second, because woman has no penis, woman's role in the representational logic of psychoanalysis is to enable the representation of male subjectivity. Woman as object is the necessary complement to man as subject. Irigaray suggests that for Freud, woman is the object through which man realizes his mature subjectivity. For Lacan, the mirror stage not only separates the mother from the child but also transforms the feminine into the mirror. What the child sees is itself alone. Irigaray regards the disappearance of the mother in the mirror stage as an act of matricide. The feminine hereafter functions as a "faithful, polished mirror," which reproduces masculine subjectivity but which is not itself representable (*Speculum*, 136). Gazing into the mirror/woman, male subjects see only themselves and not the mirror that generates their reflection. In this phallocentric system, woman as woman has a function but no identity of her own. As Irigaray suggests, "She has no 'proper' name" other than that of the male she reflects (*This Sex*, 26).

The inability to represent woman in psychoanalytic discourse does not mean that some essential woman based on woman's anatomy is excluded from this system and must be recovered to take sexual difference into account.[22] Like Lacan, Irigaray holds that subjectivity is linguistically constructed. Therefore, there is no pre- or extra-linguistic subjectivity. The feminine is incorporated into the symbolic code of psychoanalysis, but always as an other "wholly in the service of the same [masculine] subject to whom it would present its surfaces [function as a mirror]" and not itself as a subject (*Speculum*, 136). Taking the metaphor of the whole/ hole further, Irigaray suggests that the feminine underwrites the masculine symbolic order because "in order to articulate a phallic whole," the feminine function "will be as *hole*" (*Speculum*, 231; italics in original).

The phallocentric economy of representation that reduces girls to little men and mature woman to complements of men effectively silences the representation of female desire.[23] Owing to woman's lack of a penis, female desire exceeds the terms of comprehensibility insured by the exchange value of the phallus. Because the symbolic code of psychoanalysis is guaranteed by the exchange value of the phallus, it reserves representation for masculine subjects only. Woman is "a use-value" or "commodity" exchanged among men (*This Sex*, 31–32). Thus, female desire is unrepresentable. The only way it can be intelligible in this economy is if it abides by the sign of the phallus. The clitoris or castrated penis becomes the only representation of female desire in Freud's system that counts.[24] The expression of feminine desire is only possible in masculine form. Woman, as lesser because castrated man, may act out or mime her own sexuality in masculine form to recover part of her own desire. Irigaray refers to a woman who mimes her sexuality in masculine form as a hysteric. And in the psychoanalytic system of representation, hysterical women are "condemned as so many 'bad' copies or gross caricatures of a 'good,' and valuable and valid, relationship to origin [phallus]" (*Speculum*, 60).[25] For by expressing her desire in masculine terms, woman is regarded as abnormal and immature – a little girl who failed to make a successful transition to womanhood during the Oedipal stage.

MALE HYSTERIA

The hysteric . . . cannot assume his/her own discourse; everything is referred for validation to the "you."
— Margaret Whitford, *Luce Irigaray: Philosophy in the Feminine*

While the statement "I am" expresses subjectivity, the question "Am I? " denotes hysteria. Hysteria has been defined as "a response in symptomatic form — that is, one made through a substitution of corporeal signifiers for unconscious impulses — to a sexual demand or urge that the subject cannot accommodate."[26] Lack and excess are the two complementary motifs of hysteria. Hysteria appears as the excessive miming of masculinity (subjectivity), which "stands in" for a lack of phallic power (inability to make meaning). In the case of female hysteria, this lack of phallic power follows from an anatomical lack of a visible penis.

Irigaray reminds us that hysteria is not an exclusively female pathology (*This Sex*, 46). Yet male hysteria takes a different form from female hysteria. While female hysteria illustrates the coding of women as men, "what male hysteria shows us is not so much the coding of men as women, as the uncoding of men as men."[27] Male hysteria is the emasculation of men (uncoding of men as men) rather than the feminization of men (coding of men as women).

One expression of emasculation is the exposure of the phallus. Exposure combines excessive display with a lack of phallic power. Exposing the penis (excess) demonstrates the absence of phallic power (lack). Thus, male hysterics, like female hysterics, excessively mime masculinity to compensate for a lack of phallic power; however, they do so not because they lack a penis but because their penis is exposed.

NOSE THUMBING AND SIGN POSTING

Noriega's nose thumbing at Bush, then, artfully combines excess and lack in the form of male hysteria. Referring to this gesture as the summary statement of why the United States invaded Panama, the White House advisor interviewed hints at a pervasive hysterical backdrop. Indeed, as they appear in the discourse concerning the invasion, both Noriega and Bush display hysterical symptoms.

To encounter Noriega is to encounter a symbolic excess of masculinity. Manuel Antonio Noriega's name — read as an acronym (M.A.N.), as a proper name ([Man]uel), or as a nickname ([Man]ny) — attests to his manliness.[28] So too do Noriega's possessions. Recounting the assets of Noriega's personal fortune, Lawrence Eagleburger, then deputy secretary of state, noted that Noriega had "Three large pleasure yachts, the Macho I, Macho II, and Macho III — now that's a lot of macho."[29]

Bush's hysterical excess is displaced from his physical body to his geopolitical body, from George Bush the man onto George Bush the commander in chief of a posthegemonic state.[30] The military invasion of Panama marks the attempted masculine projection of his stately authority not only into the international sphere but also into the territory of another domestic space, more specifically into the "canal zone." Once again, it is the phallus that is the masculine projection of authority internationally and the feminine "hole" — the Panama canal — that is its domestic and geopolitical underwriter.

In both of these cases, excess is tied to a lack of phallic power. For Noriega, phallic power is undercut by his lack of staying power. Shortly after the coup attempt of October 3, 1989, Noriega boasted that "Virility is proved by staying in [power]."[31] Noriega's staying power was to last a brief time after this. Noriega's difficulty with staying in was that he was left with nothing to stay in. He had no domestic space, no nation-state, no canal in which he could express his phallic power. Noriega became a man without access to a canal — a hysterical male who, in this case, could be read as a man with a useless phallus thanks to externally imposed celibacy.

Bush's lack (man)ifested itself differently. Rather than having no domestic space(s) in which to project his authority, Bush's projection of hegemonic authority was in decline. Like Noriega's excess, Bush's lack plays on the thumb metaphor. While Noriega was waving his thumb (penis) at Bush, Bush was attempting to revitalize his stately thumb (penis coded as hegemonic power). Touring Panama after the invasion, Representative Lee Hamilton observed that Panamanians would "come out and give us a thumbs up signal."[32] Apparently, the mission was a success.

Prior to the invasion, Bush's thumb did not speak so loudly in the region. To compensate for the impending impotence of the declining hegemon, a formal display of hegemonic power was offered by General Colin Powell, chairman of the Joint Chiefs of Staff. Powell "is reported recently to have said that we have to put up a shingle outside our door saying 'superpower lives here.' "[33] Powell's countervailing strategy of announcing the obvious contradicts the message he "posts." It is an act of exposure that, to recall Irigaray, calls the central premise into question. The announcement of hegemonic power unveils the phallus and displays the penis that cannot stand on its own. This accounts for Senator Sam Nunn's insistence in the joint hearings on the invasion that American "[l]egitimacy... is going to depend on... reduced American visibility."[34]

SPECULUM OF THE OTHER COUNTRY

Irigaray describes the relationship between the sexes in psychoanalytic discourse as "specularized." The word "speculum" refers to both an "instrument for dilating cavities of [the] human body for inspection" and to a "mirror, usu. of polished metal."[35] Both the masculine and the feminine share aspects of the speculum. The masculine instrument or tool (the penis) penetrates the formless empty cavity (the vagina) of the feminine, and the feminine acts as a mirror that reflects masculine subjectivity but not itself. The mirror (feminine) symbolized by the speculum depicts both the transformation of the mother into a ghost (specter) and the concavity of the mirror (speculum), which turns images upside down.[36]

Yet another meaning of speculum is a lens that focuses light on a hole. This understanding of speculum combines the masculine and feminine aspects of the term. Writes Irigaray of the speculum, "It may, quite simply, be an instrument to *dilate* the lips, the orifices, the walls, so that the eye can penetrate the *interior*" (*Speculum*, 144; italics in original). She goes on to explain that man's eye is "understood as substitute for penis" (*Speculum*, 145). It is by separating the vulva (lips) and penetrating the vagina with his penis (eye) that man sees his subjectivity reflected back at him in the concave mirror (woman).

The masculine ability to penetrate and the feminine ability to reflect images correspond to a hierarchy of solids and fluids found in psychoanalytic theory. Visible forms (penis) are privileged over formless voids (vagina). Irigaray traces this hierarchical relationship of solids over fluids to physics, in which matter was privileged long before a theory of fluids was expounded.[37] Irigaray's observation that gender is coded in terms of solids and fluids leads to her account of the potentially turbulent role the feminine may play in psychoanalytic discourse. The feminine as mirror only reflects masculine subjectivity if it is placid, unclouded, and fixed. Irigaray notes that in psychoanalytic discourse it is necessary to have a fixed feminine object. Otherwise, "the erection of the subject might thereby be disconcerted and risk losing its elevation and penetration. For what would there be to rise up from and exercise his power over? And in?" (*Speculum*, 133).

When the feminine ceases to function as a reflective pool, masculine subjectivity is in crisis. Writes Irigaray, "Perhaps for the time being the serene contemplation of empire must be abandoned in favor of taming those forces which, once unleashed, might explode the very concept of empire" (*Speculum*, 136).

THE PANAMA CANAL

Geopolitical bodies in international relations may be described in terms of gender. A sovereign nation-state, for example, is said to have a feminine domestic side and a masculine international side. Domestic refers to the private sphere of state relations that gives a particular state a unique national character.[38] International refers to the projection of this domestic identity into the public sphere of relations among states. And in international relations theory, as in Irigaray's account of psychoanalytic theory, the feminine (domestic) makes the masculine (international) possible. For without a clearly identified domestic sphere, a nation-state would have no voice to project into the international sphere.

Panama and the United States can be described as engendered geopolitical bodies. For each state it is a domestic citizenry and territory (the feminine) that provides the basis for international authority (the masculine). When these geopolitical bodies are conjoined with the bodies of their respective heads of state, what are highlighted are the sources of hysteria for Noriega and Bush. What comes into focus is the particular geopolitical lack each leader compensates for through a discourse of excess.

Each leader in a different way lacks the feminine object that will affirm his masculine subjectivity. For Noriega, the feminine is a domestic space (a nation-state) that he can claim as his own so that a Panama under his leadership will have a legitimate voice in international affairs. For Bush, the feminine object is an international space in which to project hegemonic authority. This space is also Panama. But in the Bush administration discourse, Panama does not compensate for Bush's lack of a domestic space; rather, Panama helps Bush compensate for his lack of the "vision thing," for it is in the canal zone that U.S. hegemonic authority is reflected. These two very different ways of understanding Panama as lack are combined in the discourse on the invasion through the Bush administration's attempt to project its authority internationally by withholding the feminine object from Noriega.

This feminine object shows up in the Bush administration discourse as both an anatomical and a geopolitical body. What these bodies have in common is that they are victims of attempted rape by the Noriega administration. In his speech to the American public outlining the justifications for intervention in Panama, Bush explicitly states that what all the fighting is about is sexual abuse. Panamanian "forces under his [Noriega's] command shot and killed an unarmed American serviceman; wounded another; arrested and brutally beat a third American serviceman; and then brutally interrogated his wife, threatening her with sexual abuse. That was enough."[39]

The anatomic body of the American serviceman's wife implies another body that, according to the Bush administration, Noriega sexually abuses. This feminine geopolitical body is the Panama Canal. Noriega's discourse inscribes the canal in similar terms to those used by Irigaray to describe how the feminine appears in psychoanalytic discourse. A few months before the invasion Noriega commented, "Panama [is] like a mirror in which all of America . . . — . . . see themselves."[40] The locus of Panama's reflective power is the Panama Canal. State sovereignty is symbolized by the flagged ships of various nation-states floating in this man-made passageway that spawned a nation-state.[41]

Noriega's rape of the canal seemed to be imminent to the Bush administration. The invasion occurred just eleven days before the administration of the canal was scheduled to be handed over to a Panamanian commission.[42] Panamanian administrative control of the canal troubled the United States because of Noriega's leadership style. In the Bush administration discourse, Noriega signifies a disruptive force who threatens to stir the still waters of the canal. Discussing the invasion, General Thomas Kelly remarks about Noriega, "He knows how to swim in that environment down there."[43] Another Bush administration official refers to Noriega's government and style of rule as "Noriega's (Tit)anic."[44]

A Bush administration official notes, "We must recognize . . . that

Panama's ability to responsibly pursue its own interest — and hence the long-term future of the canal — cannot be assured in the context of political instability." He goes on to stress that democracy is "an essential element of political stability on the isthmus." The "firm" position of the Bush administration is that "securing the long-term future of democracy in Panama and of the canal" are two elements that are "indissolubly linked." "Noriega's continuation in power is a threat. . . . And . . . it will be the canal's users who ultimately must face the burden of bearing the costs."[45]

Democracy is valued, then, for its stabilizing influence — for its ability to calm formless feminine fluids so they may serve masculine purposes. Until a democratic environment could be established in Panama — until the Endara government could be seated — the United States had to retain administrative control of the canal. So long as Noriega governs Panama, he endangers the U.S. "broad national interest" of maintaining "a safe, efficient, and neutral Panama Canal."[46] "Broad" in this context may refer to both the scope of U.S. interests and to a vernacular expression of the feminine component of U.S. interests.

Both interpretations are suggested by what became the epitome of the Bush presidency, "Read my lips." A symptomatic interpretation of this phrase replaces "lips" with "vulva." Bush's "lips," then, refer to the canal. "My" is his assertion of ownership of the canal, and "read" denotes the autistic character of the feminine.[47] So long as his lips (the Panama Canal) can be read but cannot speak, Panamanian stability is insured. But like General Powell's sign posting, Bush's challenge to his audience ("Read my lips") is as disempowering as it is empowering. Bush's lips at once claim the Panama Canal as a reflective pool of U.S. hegemonic power and display the feminization of the American president. Read as a sign of female reproductive ability more generally, Bush's lips silently announce that the president has egg on his face.

In the Bush administration discourse, a distinction is drawn between preserving Panamanian sovereignty and removing Noriega from power. What this suggests is that the Bush administration does not want to become the only user of the canal. Rather, the "neutrality" of the canal must be ensured so that the United States and Panama can be among the canal's users. The achievement of this goal entails separating the disruptive masculine subject (Noriega) from his feminine object (the canal). By denying Noriega his feminine object, the United States effectively denies

Noriega's masculine subjectivity. And as a head of state without a state, Noriega is no longer a threat to U.S. hegemony in the region. A joke by a senator at the Joint Congressional Hearings on Events in Panama explicitly links masculine subjectivity with the feminine object. When a man testifying before the committee announced, "I was confirmed in June," a senator added, "No pun intended."[48] Read as the proper name of a woman rather than as a month, "June" signifies the body in which masculine subjectivity is achieved. It is not so much the pun as it is the pun's structure that is of interest here. Notice that it is the U.S. senator who substitutes the unconscious impulse (confirmation of male subjectivity in a female body) for the corporal signifier (June read as a woman's body), thereby revealing the hysterical subtext of the hearings.[49]

Speculum turns to spectacle when the United States invades Panama to capture Noriega. And spectacle turns to farce while Noriega eludes the U.S. military. Even so, this moment of the invasion serves the U.S. "broad" national interest. William Bennett, the president's director of national drug control policy at the time, says of Noriega at this juncture, "He's not running drugs; he's not running Panama; he's just running."[50] The transformation of Noriega from solids to fluids guarantees that Noriega may no longer pose a threat to the canal. Indeed, as the Papal Nuncio remarks, Noriega is politically castrated. "The entire nation thinks [Noriega is] a man endowed with powers he doesn't have. I found him a man who, without a pistol [penis], could be handled by anyone."[51]

SPECULARIZED POLICY

Military intervention joins the affirmation of state sovereignty with violence. In international relations theory, intervention is defined as the violation of one state's sovereignty by an uninvited intruder.[52] It is rape on an international scale. A recent panel at the American Political Science Association meetings conveys the masculine inscription of intervention and its relationship to a feminine object. The panel is entitled "Dilemma of Protracted [Specularized?] Intervention," and the primary titles of the papers are "Getting In," "Staying In," and "Getting Out."[53]

Given this, the Bush administration's strategy of denying Noriega his feminine object (a nation-state and the canal) through the act of military intervention is consistent with the account of Bush as a hysterical male. If

Bush embodies the United States during a refractory period that signals the impending impotence of the United States (hegemonic decline), then the U.S. invasion of Panama exemplifies the excessive miming of masculinity. But this begs the question: Does a nearly impotent commander in chief have the capacity to "get in"? Put differently, is a declining hegemon able to project its masculine subjectivity internationally through an act of military intervention?

The answer to these questions appears to be both yes and no. A U.S. military operation clearly took place in Panama. However, it replaced penetration with encirclement as its modus operandi. Instead of internationally projecting U.S. hegemonic power into the domestic affairs of Panama, the United States domesticated Panama. That is, the U.S. discourse on Panama effectively subsumed Panamanian domestic affairs within the scope of U.S. domestic policy. Territorially, their domestic/international boundaries did not change; discursively, however, Panama was left with no domestic sphere distinct from that of the United States. The U.S. strategy of encirclement made the more common intervention tactic of penetration unnecessary. Thanks to this initial act of domestication, the invasion could be viewed as an internal act undertaken to consolidate one domestic space.

Two factors make the U.S. domestication of Panamanian space possible. The first is historical. Panama's history as a sovereign nation-state cannot be separated from U.S. history. It was the U.S. desire for a canal in Central America in the early 1900s that led the United States to support a Panamanian claim of independence from Colombia. To this day, this initial act of genesis lingers in U.S.–Panamanian relations. For it is the United States that controls the vital circulatory systems of Panama – the Panama Canal and the Panamanian currency (U.S. dollars).

Staged against a background of shared history is a second, more immediate factor: the U.S. discursive claim to Panama couched in terms of the "War on Drugs." While the Bush administration holds, "This is a war as deadly and as dangerous as any fought with armies massed across borders," the administration rhetoric on drugs erases any distinctions between what is domestic and what is international.[54] According to the administration, drug trafficking "is a worldwide problem" that "threatens the security of nations."[55] "The drug issue knows no national borders."[56]

The administration's refusal of the domestic/international dichotomy makes Noriega's drug-related indictments by two Florida grand juries less objectionable. Noriega is transformed from a head of state to a common domestic criminal. "The story these indictments tell is simple and chilling. It is the story of that same shameless excess in the criminal field that we have already seen in the political field."[57] Bringing Noriega to justice means bringing Noriega to trial in the United States. The community of judgment in this case was a jury composed of U.S. citizens. Justice here refers to U.S. domestic justice and not international justice.

Indeed, the Bush administration's discourse on the invasion of Panama always finds its point of reference in the U.S. citizenry. Unlike the U.S. intervention in Grenada in 1983, the United States did not direct its justification for intervention in Panama to some international community. No organization analogous to the Organization of Eastern Caribbean States was created so that it could ask for U.S. military assistance. A regional or international request for intervention was unnecessary because the U.S. invasion of Panama was an internal matter. Only the U.S. citizenry needed to be consulted and, in the event of a military action, offered an explanation. "Operation Just Cause," the administration's code name for the invasion, was just by U.S. domestic standards and was justified to the U.S. public.[58]

The U.S. invasion of Panama abides by a specularized logic both because it transforms a traditional account of intervention into its negative image and because the traditional locations of domestic and international policy appear upside down in the concave mirror of Panama. With respect to intervention the Bush administration's domestication of Panama reinscribes the meaning of intervention in this case. President Bush asks, "[W]hat, in God's name, would we ... call the international drug trade — and those who aid it and abet it — but intervention in our internal affairs?"[59] This notion is expanded upon elsewhere.

> There are times when good principles force us to defend bad men. Some argue that this is the case with Noriega and Panama. They argue as if the principle of nonintervention requires us to accept whatever Noriega does.
>
> But nonintervention was never meant to protect individual criminals. It was never meant to promote intervention by drug traffickers in our societies against our families and children. It was never meant to prevent peaceful and diplomatic action by sovereign states in support of democracy. And it was never meant to leave the criminals free to savage the good and the good powerless to react.[60]

Additionally, the strategy of encirclement specularizes the logic of the invasion by transposing domestic and international policy. The U.S. war on drugs encircles Noriega in a threefold sense — first by the domestication of Panamanian policy, second by surrounding the Vatican Embassy with rock-and-roll music, and third by encapsulating Noriega in a U.S. prison cell. Manuel Noriega — the head of state of an independent sovereign nation — became U.S. Federal Prisoner #41586. Looking at the discourse of the U.S. invasion of Panama, then, one finds foreign policy located in U.S. domestic space (Noriega in a U.S. prison) and domestic policy located in U.S. foreign space (the U.S. war on drugs fought in Panama).

THIS STATE WHICH IS NOT ONE

If male hysteria refers to the uncoding of men as men (emasculation) rather than the coding of men as women (feminization), this reading of the U.S. invasion of Panama suggests both emasculation and feminization. That Noriega and Bush lack phallic power and compensate for this lack with the excessive miming of masculinity indicates male hysteria. Yet it would be an oversight to stop analysis at this point. For in their moments of excess, the bodies of Noriega and Bush are femininely engendered. Recall, for example, Noriega's transformation from solids to fluids and Bush's display of female reproductive organs on his face. Furthermore, the name "Bush" announces the location of female genitalia. The most critical moment of feminization in the invasion discourse pertains to the Bush administration's strategy of encirclement. In this section I will focus on this move because it deconstructs masculine standards of "international" and "intervention."

For Bush and the United States, hysteria or the crisis in subjectivity is brought about by hegemonic decline. The Panama Canal functions in Bush's discourse as the reflective pool that can mirror back U.S. hegemonic subjectivity. Because the U.S. invasion of Panama secured the stability of the canal, one might conclude that the reflective function of the canal and therefore U.S. hegemonic subjectivity are rescued.

This conclusion overlooks the feminization of Bush and the United States. Specifically, it neglects to theorize the implications of an intervention strategy based on encirclement rather than penetration. As noted earlier, intervention in international relations theory is rape on an international scale. Rape commonly refers to an act committed by a male to a female or male. Considered from a psychoanalytic perspective, the U.S.

invasion of Panama might be said to include two different scenarios of rape — the first by a woman to a man and the second by a (male) transvestite to a woman. These unusual sexual pairings of rape — by female to male and by transvestite to female — are suggested by penis envy and the threat of castration as they appear in psychoanalytic discourse.

The first rape scenario — by female to male — symbolizes the threat of castration. In psychoanalytic discourse, the threat of castration is not reserved for the father. The woman too may pose this threat to a man, only differently. While the father's threat is to cut off his son's genitals, the woman's threat — owing to her penis envy — is to refuse to relinquish the penis that has penetrated her. Should the woman whose body encircles the penis refuse to surrender it, the male would experience a similar sense of loss as he would if he were actually castrated. Encirclement or entrapment, then, are the modalities of female rape of a male.

In the discourse of the U.S. invasion of Panama, it is the Panama Canal that threatens to encircle and symbolically castrate Noriega and Bush. Noriega never experiences this form of castration because the Bush administration denies him access to the canal and thus symbolically castrates him first. Bush also avoids castration by the canal — not because he is denied access to it but because even given access he is incapable of penetration. In this regard, the canal's threat of castration to Bush serves as an embarrassing reminder of Bush's lack of phallic power. For both Noriega and Bush, the threat of castration posed by the Panama Canal is never anything more than a threat.

Even though it is not actualized, this first rape scenario is important because it acts as an interpretive guide for the second rape scenario — by a (male) transvestite to female. A transvestite is a man acting and/or appearing as a woman. While the transvestite is anatomically male, his actions are those of a female. The transvestite is both emasculated (a man uncoded as a man) and feminized (a man recoded as a woman).

In the U.S. invasion of Panama, the transvestite is Bush and the female is the Panama Canal. Bush is a transvestite in international politics because in the masculine arena of international politics, his actions as commander in chief are feminine. The U.S. invasion of Panama is a feminine act because it is carried out via a strategy of encirclement. This act of encirclement takes on interesting implications when examined psychoanalytically. As noted earlier, encirclement may be interpreted as both the threat of castration and as female rape. When encirclement as rape occurs to a female, the threat of castration is canceled out because the female in psychoanalytic discourse is already castrated. The focus, then, is on female rape.

This act of female rape by Bush has two effects. First, it suggests that in the international arena where states project their masculine authority, the masculinely engendered United States is reengendered as feminine. The move from penetration to encirclement marks the uncoding of man as man as well as the recoding of man as woman. This first effect is emphasized by the second effect. Rather than miming masculinity directly (hysteria), Bush's miming of masculinity is once removed. What Bush mimes is female rape, specifically his own threatened rape or encirclement by the Panama Canal. In other words, thanks to the declining hegemon's inability to project its phallic power into international politics, Bush is only able to mime his own castration through the female model of rape. The U.S. invasion of Panama reminds Bush that he and his state have already been effectively castrated because they are impotent. They have already been rewritten as feminine. Because this reinscription of man as woman occurs in what should be the international sphere, which is reserved for actions by male subjects, Bush appears as a transvestite rather than as a woman.

Two final implications of the invasion are suggested by this reading. If, as Freud and Lacan argue, it is through the castration complex that subjects enter the symbolic order and become "civilized," then the castration of the former hegemon marks the end of one symbolic order and the beginning of a new order. During the invasion the United States confronts its own castration, which it then mimes through its intervention strategy of encirclement. This encounter with its castration and feminization in international politics leads the United States and Bush to reinscribe the symbolic order in terms that can accommodate the refigured United States. In this "New World Order" two quite different models of "civilization" or "meaning" are at work. For Panama the terms of the old international order are still meaningful. Although Noriega has been effectively castrated by the United States, Panama without Noriega appears in this order as simply "immature." It can reach maturity under the terms of the "old" world order when it receives possession of the Canal Zone at the turn of the century. The United States, in contrast, is mature but impotent. In its old age, it must go through a recivilizing process into a "New World Order" in which its international interactions will be expressed by the body of a man acting as a woman. The posthegemonic state is a postphallic state because it grafts female modalities of action onto a male subject.

The final implication has to do with how theorists think about intervention and sovereign statehood. Intervention may still be rape and the bodies that perform that rape may still be male, but the performance of the rape mimes the female threat of castration. Given this and given that intervention practices are only meaningful in the international arena, this analysis suggests that the old dichotomy of domestic = feminine/international = masculine may not be appropriate in a posthegemonic world order.[61] Intervention practices by posthegemonic states reengender sovereign statehood. The intervention practices of the posthegemonic United States deconstruct the terms "masculine" and "international" in this dichotomy. For contained in the masculine, international realm are feminine processes of intervention. Similar to women in psychoanalytic discourse, as Irigaray described them, a posthegemonic sovereign state engaged in intervention practices is both a state and a sex which is not one. Posthegemonic states are lesser, impaired states because they lack the ability to project phallic power internationally. Described in terms of sex, they are hysterical men. Furthermore, posthegemonic states are not *just* one but more than one. Their surplus again may be described in engendered terms. Internationally (or in what traditionally is regarded as the international realm), posthegemonic states are transvestites. With respect to intervention, posthegemonic states are cross-dressed men who abide by female modes of conduct.

Taking transvestite subjectivity into account leads to a rethinking of sexual difference because transvestites – subjects who combine male and female terms – disrupt the logic whereby sexuality can be managed with dichotomies.[62] This is so as much for some theories of psychoanalysis (those of Freud and Lacan, for example) as it is for theories of international relations.

Transvestite transgressions have the effect of destabilizing the subjectivity of singularly sexed bodies – both diplomatic and territorial.[63] Because the United States and its president do not represent stable, single-sexed subjects in this reading of the invasion discourse, they signify an erasure rather than a reinscription of gender dichotomies. It is a misreading to continue to describe these bodies as either males acting as women or women miming the actions of men because in a posthegemonic, postphallic world order the male/female dichotomy breaks down. This reading calls into question the practice in international relations theory of deploying a masculine/feminine dichotomy to write the domestic/international boundary. Transvestite subjectivity embodied in a state or a statesperson focuses attention on the artificial and arbitrary distinction between that which is male and that which is female and between that which is domestic and that which is international. In so doing, transvestite subjectivity suggests another series of possible inscriptions of gender that can be found in diplomatic practice but that have generally been neglected in international relations theory.

Returning to the title of this essay, "Something's Missing," this analysis concludes that what is missing from diplomatic practice is a stable, singularly engendered domestic subject — a masculine-only or feminine-only sovereign state — that can ground claims to legitimate international actions. Attending to how unconscious codes and presumed dichotomies hysterically mime this fundamental lack so that acts like military intervention become possible is as important for international relations theory generally as it is for this specific reading of a foreign (domestic?) policy.

NOTES

Presentations based on this essay were given at the Purdue University Women's Studies Brown Bag Series, the 1992 International Studies Association Meetings in Atlanta, March 31–April 4, the 1992 Midwest American Political Science Association Meetings in Chicago, April 4–7, and the Middlebury College Women's Lecture Series. I am grateful to many people who offered suggests at those meetings. In addition, thanks to Thomas Biersteker, Berenice Carroll, Barbara Hinckley, Alon Kantor, Lyn Kathlene, Ann Kibbey, Timothy Luke, Marianne Marchand, Tamar Mayer, Diane Rubenstein, William Stearns, David Sylvan, Gerard Toal, Michael Weinstein, and two anonymous referees for their comments and to Monica Monroe and Carol Pech for research assistance.

1. Brian Morton, "And Just Why Did We Invade Panama?" *Dissent* 37 (1990): 148–50.
2. In Saussure's system of semiotics, a signifier is what joins the object with its acoustic image. In the above example the signifier "thumb" joins the mental image of the material object thumb with the sound produced by the pronunciation of the word thumb. For a discussion of semiotics, see, e.g., Terry Eagleton, *Literary Theory: An Introduction* (Minneapolis: University of Minnesota Press, 1983); Vincent Descombes, *Modern French Theory*, trans. L. Scott-

Box and J. M. Harding (Cambridge: Cambridge University Press, 1980); and Kaja Silverman, *The Subject of Semiotics* (New York: Oxford University Press, 1983).

Regarding the substitution of a presidential nose for Central America, see Diane Rubenstein, "Oliver North and the Lying Nose," in *Rhetorical Republic: Governing Representations in American Politics*, ed. Frederick Dolan and Thomas Dumm (Amherst: University of Massachusetts Press, 1993).

3. Luce Irigaray, *Speculum of the Other Woman*, trans. Gillian C. Gill. (Ithaca: Cornell University Press, 1985), and Luce Irigaray, *This Sex Which Is Not One*, trans. Catherine Porter. (Ithaca: Cornell University Press, 1985). Further references to these works will be included parenthetically in the text.

4. Irigaray uses the terms *miming*, *mimicry*, and *mimesis* to refer to the practice of positioning oneself in relation to masculinity so that, at least superficially, the subject appears to be masculine. Subjects located in this space can be either male or female. See Irigaray, *This Sex*, 76.

Although Irigaray arrives at her characterization of hysteria through a focus on how females mime masculinity, nothing in her discussion of hysteria precludes males from having a similar relationship to masculine subjectivity. Of psychoanalytic representations of hysteria, Irigaray writes, "The hysteria scenario, that privileged dramatization of feminine sexuality, is condemned as so many 'bad' copies or gross caricatures of a 'good,' and valuable and valid, relationship to origin. Hysteria ... must be unmasked, interrupted, brought back to the reality of a repetition, a reproduction, a representation that is congruent to, consistent with, the original" (Irigaray, *Speculum*, 60). Transvestites who mime feminine positions have a similar relationship to origin — the phallus — as do female hysterics.

5. For example, Noriega's dependence on the United States prior to the invasion contributed to his feminization in the invasion discourse.

6. For accounts of how states are engendered in international relations theory, see, e.g., Jean Bethke Elshtain, *Public Man, Private Woman: Women in Social and Political Thought* (Princeton: Princeton University Press, 1981); Jean Bethke Elshtain, *Women and War* (New York: Basic, 1987); Rebecca Grant and Kathleen Newland, eds., *Gender and International Relations* (Bloomington: Indiana University Press, 1991); V. Spike Peterson, ed., *Gendered States: Feminist (Re)Visions of International Relations Theory* (Boulder, Colo.: Lynne Rienner, 1992); and Anne Sisson Runyan and V. Spike Peterson, "The Radical Future of Realism: Feminist Subversions of IR Theory," *Alternatives* 16 (1991): 67–106.

7. I am not the first to suggest that Bush can be read as a transvestite. See Diane Rubenstein, "This Is Not a President: Baudrillard, Bush and Enchanted Simulation," in *The Hysterical Male: New Feminist Theory*, ed. Arthur Kroker and Marilouise Kroker (New York: St. Martin's, 1991), 253–65.

Although this reading of Bush employs the term "transvestite" to refer to cross-dressed men, it should be pointed out that a transvestite could also be a

cross-dressed woman — a woman in men's clothing. Cross-dressing by women often goes unnoticed because its transgressive function for the most part has been reinscribed by symbolic and cultural codes as not "deviant" but "normal." See Marjorie Garber, *Vested Interests: Cross-Dressing and Cultural Anxiety* (New York: Routledge, 1992).
8. Margaret Whitford, *Luce Irigaray: Philosophy in the Feminine*. (London: Routledge, 1991), p. 71.
9. See, for example, Carol Cohn, "Sex and Death in the Rational World of Defense Intellectuals," *Signs* 12 (1987): 687–718.
10. For works that read the president as a sign, see for example Michael Rogin, *Ronald Reagan, the Movie* (Berkeley: University of California Press, 1987); Anne Norton, "The President as Sign" (paper presented at the annual meeting of the American Political Science Association, New Orleans, La., September 1985); and Diane Rubenstein, "The Mirror of Reproduction: Baudrillard and Reagan's America," *Political Theory* 17, no. 4 (1989): 582–606. For critical analyses of the president done through linguistic and symbolic categories, see Murray Edelman, *Constructing the Political Spectacle* (Chicago: University of Chicago Press, 1988); Roderick Hart, *The Sound of Leadership: Presidential Communications in the Modern Age* (Chicago: University of Chicago Press, 1987); and Barbara Hinckley, *The Symbolic Presidency: How Presidents Portray Themselves* (New York: Routledge, 1990).
11. Quoted in Murray Edelman, *Constructing the Political Spectacle*, 128.
12. Lacan's theorization of the mirror stage has been crucial to the reconceptualization of subjectivity and ideology. See, for example, Louis Althusser's "The Ideological State Apparatus," 127–86, and Althusser, "Freud and Lacan," 189–219, in *Lenin and Philosophy, and Other Essays*, trans. Ben Brewster (New York: Monthly Review, 1971); and Fredric Jameson, "Imaginary and Symbolic in Lacan: Marxism, Psychoanalytic Criticism, and the Problem of the Subject," *Yale French Studies*, nos. 55–56 (1977): 338–95.
13. Quoted in Toril Moi, *Sexual/Textual Politics: Feminist Literary Theory* (New York: Methuen, 1985), 99.
14. For a collection of Lacan's writings, see Jacques Lacan, *Ecrits: A Selection*, trans. Alan Sheridan (New York: Norton, 1977). For a discussion of Lacanian psychoanalysis, see Juliet Mitchell and Jacqueline Rose, *Feminine Sexuality: Jacques Lacan and the Ecole Freudienne*, trans. Jacqueline Rose (New York: Pantheon, 1985); Judith Butler, *Gender Trouble: Feminism and the Subversion of Identity* (New York: Routledge, 1990); and Kaja Silverman, *The Acoustic Mirror: The Female Voice in Psychoanalysis and Cinema* (Bloomington: Indiana University Press, 1988).
15. Jane Gallop, *Thinking through the Body* (New York: Columbia University Press, 1988).
16. A transcendental signifier is situated beyond a symbolic order from where it both produces the symbolic order and guarantees meaning within that order. A common example of a transcendental signifier is "God."

17. Gallop, *Thinking through the Body*, 126.
18. Ibid.; italics in original.
19. Maggie Berg, "Luce Irigaray's 'Contradictions': Poststructuralism and Feminism," *Signs* 17 (1991): 50–70.
20. Ibid., 57.
21. Naomi Schor, "The Portrait of a Gentleman: Representing Men in (French) Women's Writing," *Representations* 20 (1987): 113–33; italics in original.
22. For a discussion of the essentialist debate concerning Irigaray's work, see Naomi Schor, "This Essentialism Which Is Not One: Coming to Grips with Irigaray," *differences* 1 (1989): 38–58.
23. Freud's logic, which "*reduce[s] all others to the economy of the Same*" (Irigaray, *This Sex*, 74), is what Irigaray refers to as the law of the self-same. See Irigaray, *Speculum*, 32–34.
24. Freud's assertion that the penis is the only sex organ that counts has to do with its "oneness." The penis is visible as one organ. Irigaray plays on this notion of the penis counting when she notes that the female sex organ, "which is not *one* organ, is counted as *none*" (Irigaray, *This Sex*, 26). If the two lips (vulva) of which Irigaray speaks were to count, they would disrupt Freud's unitary system based on a single standard of value (the penis).
25. Irigaray does not end her discussion of Freud and Lacan here. Rather, with her introduction of specularization and her analysis of solids and fluids, she goes on to deconstruct the psychoanalytic system of representation. I will return to these aspects of Irigaray's work later in the section entitled "Speculum of the Other Country: The Panama Canal."
26. Thomas DiPiero, "The Patriarch Is Not (Just) a Man," *Camera Obscura* 25–26 (1991): 101–24, esp. 104.
27. Lynne Kirby, "Male Hysteria and Early Cinema," *Camera Obscura* 17 (1988): 115–31.
28. Because it is the Bush administration's encounter of Noriega that is of concern here, the English-language plays on Noriega's Spanish-language name are noteworthy. Had the acronym of Noriega's name spelled out "man" in Spanish *(hombre)*, it would not have announced Noriega's symbolic excess of masculinity so boldly to the English-reading Bush.
29. Lawrence Eagleburger, "The Case against Panama's Noriega," *Current Policy* 1222 (August 31, 1989): 1–6, esp. 3.
30. The U.S. status as hegemonic or posthegemonic is a matter of much debate in international relations. In this analysis I regard the United States as posthegemonic because a symptomatic reading of the invasion discourse suggests this interpretation. See below. For more on the hegemony debate see, e.g., Robert O. Keohane, *After Hegemony: Cooperation and Discord in the World Political Economy* (Princeton: Princeton University Press, 1984); Susan Strange, "The Persistent Myth of Lost Hegemonies," *International Organization*, no. 4 (Autumn 1987): 551–74; Paul Kennedy, *The Rise and Fall of the Great Powers* (New York: Random House, 1988); Joseph S. Nye, "The

Misleading Metaphor of Decline," *The Atlantic,* March 1990; and Isabelle Grunberg, "Exploring the 'Myth' of Hegemonic Stability," *International Organization,* no. 4 (Autumn 1990): 431–77.
31. *New York Times,* October 4, 1989.
32. U.S. Congress, "Rebuilding Broken Economy Will Strain Purse Strings," *Congressional Quarterly,* weekly report 48, January 6, 1990, 43–44, esp. 43.
33. *London Times,* December 22, 1989.
34. U.S. Senate Committee on Armed Services and Select Committee on Intelligence, *1989 Events in Panama: Joint Hearings before the Committee on Armed Services and the Select Committee on Intelligence,* October 6 and 17, December 22, 1989, 135.

Senator Nunn's warning to veil the phallus was itself contradictory because it was made from a feminine location — the joint hearings on the invasion. The term "joint hearings" recalls Irigaray's characterization of feminine lips that must be read but must not speak. I thank an anonymous reviewer for bringing this to my attention.
35. *Oxford English Dictionary,* quoted in Moi, *Sexual/Textual Politics,* 130.
36. Concerning the specter, recall the act of matricide in Lacan's mirror stage. As for the inversion of images in the speculum, see Irigaray, *Speculum,* 144.
37. Irigaray notes that physics's long-time neglect of fluids is related to its neglect of gender. See Irigaray, "The 'Mechanics' of Fluids," *This Sex,* 106–18, esp. 106. Also see Schor, "This Essentialism," 48–55.
38. The engendering of domestic and international spaces is occasionally reversed. Domestic space coded as "order" may be engendered as masculine and opposed to international space coded as feminine "anarchy." My analysis follows the domestic = feminine/international = masculine engendering scheme because it is the most common in international relations theory. As the concluding section's discussion of transvestite states suggests, it is less important how international relations theorists engender domestic and international spaces than it is that domestic spaces are described by only *one* gender and international spaces by the opposite gender. See, e.g., Elshtain, *Public Man, Private Woman*; Elshtain, *Women and War*; Grant and Newland, *Gender and International Relations*; Runyan and Peterson, "The Radical Future of Realism"; and Peterson, *Gendered States.*
39. George Bush, U.S. Department of State, *U.S. Military Action in Panama, American Foreign Policy Current Documents 1989* (Washington, D.C., 1990), 720.
40. *Foreign Broadcast Information Service,* May 9, 1989, 40–41; brackets in original.
41. Recall that it was the United States's wish to build a canal in Central America that led to the United States–supported independence movement of Upper Colombia (present-day Panama) against Colombia in the early 1900s.
42. *London Times,* December 21, 1989.

43. Senate Committees, *1989 Events in Panama*, 140.
44. Lawrence Eagleburger, "The OAS and the Crisis in Panama," *Current Policy* 1205 (August 24, 1989): 1–3, esp. 2.
45. Michael G. Kozak, "Panama Canal: The Strategic Dimension," *Current Policy* 1226 (November 2, 1989): 1–3, esp. 2.
46. Ibid., 2. In this particular speech, this Bush administration official repeatedly referred to the U.S. "broad" national interest.
47. Irigaray argues that the feminine lips cannot speak in a phallocentric discourse, although the lips simultaneously invoke language and the feminine.
48. Senate Committees, *1989 Events in Panama*, 137.
49. In the postinvasion discourse, "June" as a time/location serves as an embarrassing reminder that Bush's masculine subjectivity is unconfirmed. It was in June 1992 that Bush visited post-Noriega Panama, only to be greeted by "menacing stares and defiant thumbs-down gestures," as well as by a possible assassination attempt. See the *St. Croix Avis*, June 12, 1992, 35.
50. *London Times*, December 21, 1989.
51. *Newsweek*, January 15, 1990, 18. That Noriega sought sanctuary in the Vatican Embassy may suggest Noriega attempted to compensate for his own lack of a phallus by turning to his phallic mother (the Catholic Church). Thanks to a member of the audience at my Midwest American Political Science Association panel for suggesting this interpretation.
52. For an analysis of the relationship between state sovereignty and intervention, see Cynthia Weber, *Simulating Sovereignty: Intervention, the State, and Symbolic Exchange* (Cambridge: Cambridge University Press, forthcoming).
53. American Political Science Association, preliminary program, 1991.
54. George Bush, "Freedom and World Prosperity," *Current Policy* 1210 (September 27, 1989): 1–3, esp. 2.
55. Eagleburger, "The OAS," 2.
56. John S. Wolf, "UN Program Coordination and Narcotics Control," *Current Policy* 1219 (October 17, 1989): 1–2, esp. 2.
57. Eagleburger, "The Case," 2.
58. For a comparison of the U.S. invasions of Grenada and Panama, see Weber, *Simulating Sovereignty*.
59. Bush, "Freedom," 2.
60. Eagleburger, "The Case," 6.
61. Indeed, that the domestic = feminine/international = masculine dichotomy was ever meaningful is problematic, as are the dichotomies domestic/international and feminine/masculine.
62. Placing the terms *transvestite* and *transsexual* on a continuum rather than having them function in opposition to one another would draw attention to the sign function of both. Jean Baudrillard, in "Transpolitics, Transsexuality, Transaesthetics," in *Jean Baudrillard: The Disappearance of Art and Politics*, ed. William Stearns and William Chaloupka (New York: St. Martin's, 1992), 9–26, suggests that transsexuality marks a mutation within the symbolic order of sexual difference. Transsexuality is "not an anatomical difference but a

game of the communication of signs of sex" (Baudrillard, "Transpolitics," 19). "The transsexual is based on artifice whether it is a question of anatomy (changing sex) or a question of variations of dress, gestural or morphological codes which are characteristic of transvestites. In all cases, whether it is a surgical process or transvestism, it is a question of artifice" (Baudrillard, "Transpolitics," 20). On the symbolic importance of the transvestite-transsexual continuum for postmodernity, see Lisa Bower, "Transsexuals in the Cockpit: The 'Dangers' of Sexual Ambiguity" (paper presented at the meeting of the Western Political Science Association, San Francisco, April 1992); and Marjorie Garber, *Vested Interests*.

63. The disruptive logic of a "deviant" sexuality has been addressed most recently by "queer theory." See the 1991 issue of *differences* (vol. 3, no. 2), edited by Teresa de Lauretis. Writes de Lauretis, the work of queer theory is "intended to articulate the terms in which lesbian and gay sexualities may be understood and imaged as forms of resistance to cultural homogenization, counteracting dominant discourses with other constructions of the subject in culture" and explores questions "such as the respective and/or common grounding of current discourses and practices of homo-sexualities in relation to gender and to race, with their attendant differences of class or ethnic culture, generational, geographical, and socio-political locations.... 'Queer Theory' conveys a double emphasis — on the conceptual and speculative work involved in discourse production, and on the necessary critical work of deconstructing our own discourses and their constructed silences" (de Lauretis, iii–iv).

See also *Socialist Review* 22, no. 1 (January–March, 1992), special issue entitled "Queer Innovation: Transforming Gender, Sexuality and Social Movements," as well as Diana Fuss, "Fashion and the Homospectorial Look," in the *Critical Inquiry* special issue on identities, vol. 18, no. 4 (Summer 1992), 713–37; Jonathan Goldberg, "Recalling Totalities: The Mirrored Stages of Arnold Schwarzenegger," in *differences*, special issue on the phallus, vol. 4, no. 1 (1992), 172–204 (in the same issue, see Judith Butler's "Lesbian Phallus and the Morphological Imaginary," 133–71).

For the way transvestism as "veil" links sexuality to a discussion of the postcolonial, see Marjorie Garber's "The Chic of Arabia: Transvestism and the Erotics of Cultural Appropriation," in her *Vested Interests*, chap. 12. See also Emily Apter, "Female Trouble in the Colonial Harem," *differences* 4, no. 1 (1992): 205–24; and Kaja Silverman's "White Skins, Brown Masks: The Double Mimesis, or With Lawrence in Arabia," chap. 7 of her *Male Subjectivity at the Margins* (New York: Routledge, 1992), 299–338.

EIGHT

Gendered Troubles: Refiguring "Woman" in Northern Ireland

Heather Zwicker

In a recent article in *Critical Inquiry*, Cheryl Herr theorizes "The Erotics of Irishness."[1] Writing against the dominant trope of Ireland as a devouring hag demanding the sacrifice of her sons — a trope that begs explanation for the everyday disempowerment of actual Irish women — Herr postulates instead that Ireland is governed by a historical refusal to sanction womanliness in any but the most flatly mythological way. In fact the female body is rendered for all intents and purposes invisible because optically filtered by an "aesthetics of denial" that serves, in the context of Ireland's " 'over-identity crisis,' " to neutralize the body (Herr, 31, 6). The emphasis on Irish identity, a psychological and discursive concern, works to efface the multiplicity of Irish bodies and the relationships they might have to any kind of Irish mind.

Paradoxically, Herr argues, in a visual economy this neutralization works not by veiling but by scrutinizing the body — indeed, overscrutinizing it: the body is frozen in a photographic still that spawns "a reluctance to connect issues of shape and structure with cultural dialogue and possibility, and an unwillingness to recover at any level the physicality of the body in other than the most destructive and threatening sense" (Herr, 31). Representations of the body, especially the female body, become the site for an internal censorship that finds statutory articulation in Ireland's long history of legislative censorship.

In its attentive reading of a wide range of texts, Herr's essay is a model of interdisciplinarity. It also exemplifies responsible intercultural criticism: she opens her piece by considering some problematics of Irish studies in America.[2] It is in the spirit of such hybridity that I want to adopt some of Herr's arguments to discuss representations of women in the context of the Troubles in Northern Ireland.

Although "The Erotics of Irishness" refers to the Republic of Ireland, Herr intends her "psycho-logic" in part to explain the dynamics of Irish sectarian violence: it is not the omnipresence of the vicious mother, she argues, but the contradiction between the mythology of matriarchy and the miserable material conditions of women's lives that expresses itself violently.[3] As an explanation of violence, then, Herr's postulations can usefully be moved north of the border. Furthermore, an already hybridized approach like Herr's offers a way to dance through the minefield of Northern Ireland, where the feminist analytic category "woman" frequently finds itself caught between imperialist occupation, on the one hand, with its relatively liberal attitudes toward traditionally feminist platforms such as divorce, contraception, and abortion, and, on the other, the patriarchal nationalism of Republicanism, which links itself to one of the most conservative Catholicisms in western Europe.[4] The Troubles demand a supple feminism that can mutually imagine religious ethnicity and nation with gender.

On the matter of nation, Herr and I necessarily part company. As a point of national reference, the Republic is relatively stable. Not so with Northern Ireland (or Ulster, as the Protestants prefer). One way to read the sectarian violence of Northern Ireland is as the trace of an identity crisis. Tied to both England and Ireland yet owned by neither, Northern Ireland remains too deeply divided along religious ethnic lines to be (yet?) a nation per se. If we take the nation to be a patriarchal structure and the colonial centre to be matriarchal, Northern Ireland lives the awkward adolescence of postcoloniality.[5] Abandoned by either imperial Mother Britain or perennially sad Mother Ireland, depending on one's political perspective, Ulster has yet to accede to the law of the fatherland that would set its identity by giving it discursive credence as a nation.

What I have called the awkward adolescence of postcoloniality others call decolonization, one aspect of which involves constructing oppositional identity from within a colonial setting. Frantz Fanon describes this process as "the veritable creation of new men," a postulation that invites problematization along gender lines.[6] If men are created anew in the course of nationalist struggle, what about women? Specifically, what about women in a context where representations of women mediate particularly resilient nationalisms and, as Herr argues, a peculiarly Irish form of internal censorship? How, that is, are Woman and Nation interdependently produced and reproduced in the context of sectarian violence, and how can the tenacious dovetail holding them together be pried apart? In seeking answers to such questions, this essay will examine recent images of gender and nation in three media: murals in Belfast, Neil Jordan's recent film, *The Crying Game*, and Mary Beckett's two collections of short stories, *A Belfast Woman* and *A Literary Woman*.

The first thing to be said about both Protestant Loyalist[7] and Catholic Republican murals is that very few represent women at all.[8] However, the limited number that do offer a controlled insight into some important gender distinctions that arise from the disparate political platforms. Murals from Protestant districts, anxious to maintain colonial ties to Britain, read like cultural defenses of the status quo: ironically proximate to traditional Irish representations of Mother Ireland, Loyalist murals deploy the figure of woman in a straightforward pictorial allegory, in which she stands for the nation in a one-to-one substitution.

The mural in figure 8.1 celebrates the Ulster Volunteer Force (UVF),

Fig. 8.1 UVF for God and Ulster. Courtesy of the Ciaran MacGowan Collection of the Hoover Institution Archives, Stanford University.

a proscribed paramilitary organization with Unionist sympathies.[9] Painstakingly retouched year after year, the mural is a graphic analog to political conservatism. The left panel (fig. 8.2) emblematizes female figures as Nation.[10] Like the flag, the red hand, and the gun, the domesticated Irish colleen (note the apron and the church) stands for Ulster, calling men to arms in her defence. We are meant to look not at the woman herself, but through her, at what she stands for: a pastoral domesticity denied the UVF militia men, who, depicted without an artistic backdrop, represent only themselves. The female body in the mural is as inseparable from its ground as the archaeological remains that Herr discusses, and it is similarly neutralized — here, by the emphasis on abstract nouns in the slogan ("How is *freedom* measured? By the *effort* which it costs to retain it"). "Freedom," a vision encapsulated in the Union Jack held by domestic Jill, is represented by women but fought for and protected by men. Indeed, the slippage between the slogan's "retained" and "restrained," applicable from a Protestant Loyalist perspective to both women and Irish nationalism, is almost irresistible.

The right panel (fig. 8.3) puts essentially the same figure in a slightly different context. Although the caption, "Deserted! — Well, I can stand alone," appears feminist, it actually acts as the pivot over which the figure of Woman turns into the figure of Nation. Read as a statement by the female figure, the caption summons the history of women's suffrage, contested in Ireland as in England in the early twentieth century.[11] However, the mural's heading, "Ulster 1914," abrogates such narrative possibility by tying the iconography to a specific historical moment. The year 1914 commemorates the formation of Loyalist Ulster as such: in that year the Home Rule Bill, explicitly excluding four northern counties, was passed in British parliament without the support of Ulster Unionists.[12] This legislation was tantamount to desertion of the northern province, both by southern Irish organizations (for a few years before 1914 cautiously supportive of the UVF) and by its erstwhile British allies. It is not the woman figured, then, who mouths the mural's slogan, but the northern counties, divided from the southern, ready to fight against Irish Home Rule. In contemporary Irish politics the caption has a slightly different, though no less Loyalist, sense: it articulates the difficult position of Unionists who find themselves loyal to a Britain that is frequently indifferent, if not hostile, to the fate of its closest and most troublesome colony.

As a whole the Unionist triptych can be read as a graphic distillation of

Fig. 8.2 Left panel, UVF for God and Ulster. Courtesy of the Ciaran MacGowan Collection of the Hoover Institution Archives, Stanford University.

Fig. 8.3 Right panel, UVF for God and Ulster. Courtesy of the Ciaran MacGowan Collection of the Hoover Institution Archives, Stanford University.

past, present, and future, in which the nation freezes as a woman and as a moment. The woman, like the ideal of Ulster she represents, is vintage World War I.[13] The UVF militia men who protect her, on the other hand, are historically specific across time. The figure on the left represents the original UVF, opposite his modern inheritor. In the very centre of the mural is the Red Hand of Ulster, the abstraction toward which the UVF strives. Although the mural represents past, present, and future, the narrative possibilities of movement through time and space are curtailed by being set in an allegorical tableau that, to quote Herr again, is reluctant "to connect issues of shape and structure with cultural dialogue and possibility" (Herr, 31). The figure of the woman speaks only with the voice of the nation; to use a double blasphemy, she is an empty vessel filled with Loyalism.

If the irony of Protestant murals is that they use traditionally Catholic constructions of women to Unionist ends, the irony of Republican murals is that they do not, by and large, use the readily available iconography of Catholicism in their depictions of women. Catholic West Belfast features what is known as the Women's Wall. Murals painted on this wall are temporary, replaced periodically by new ones that are Republican in sympathy and feminist in perspective. Instead of recycling timeless, idealized images, this wall usually depicts contemporary women. One of the early murals (fig. 8.4), painted during the Irish Republican Army (IRA) revitalization of the 1970s, depicts the various roles Republican women play: one woman reads, another loads a weapon, and a third raises her fist in defiance. Shown in contemporary street clothes, the women are not straightforwardly emblematic of Nation: by comparison to the UVF mural, they are more similar to the militia men than to the feminized nation they protect. At the same time the women remain to some degree allegorical figures in a tableau dedicated to "Resistance," here defined by the Sinn Fein ideal of a united, socialist Ireland, represented by the Irish tricolour in the background. Graphically decontextualized, undifferentiated from one another, and remarkably androgynous-looking, the female figures are rendered invisible *as women* in their service to Irish Republican nationalism.[14]

In 1982 "Resistance" was covered with a mural that depicts the mutuality of gender and nation (fig. 8.5). Women from three nationalist movements – the Palestine Liberation Organization (PLO), the Southwest African People's Organization (SWAPO), and the IRA – are held within

Fig. 8.4 Resistance. Courtesy of the Ciaran MacGowan Collection of the Hoover Institution Archives, Stanford University.

the international sign for Woman. Just as the variety of movements represented saves the image from nationalist emblematism, the historical and ethnic specificity of the female figures saves the image from an overcorrective feminist emblematism. The point is not global (if revolutionary) sisterhood but, as the caption reads, "Solidarity between women in armed struggle." Nor is this duality of gender and nation totalizing: although the bodies of the women stay nicely within the limits of the sign, their weapons, representative of the revolutionary struggles in which they are involved, exceed its boundaries. In other words, an essentialist notion of woman will always be undone by the historical specificity of different women's lives.

The version of feminism depicted on the Women's Wall is rooted in positionality, a politics of location given perhaps its best articulation by Chandra Mohanty, who argues that "Women are constituted as women through the complex interaction between class, culture, religion, and other ideological institutions and frameworks" and that "our definitions, descriptions, and interpretations of third world women's engagement with feminism must necessarily be simultaneously historically specific and

Fig. 8.5 Solidarity. Courtesy of the Ciaran MacGowan Collection of the Hoover Institution Archives, Stanford University.

dynamic, not frozen in time in the form of a spectacle."[15] Murals necessarily limit dynamism to some degree: as iconographic art they tend to arrest figures in historical time and national-political space. But as spectacle they offer possibility as well as limitation. As "Solidarity" shows, women need not be seen through the distorting lens of an "aesthetics of denial"; rather, "woman" can be used as an optic filter through which to view specificities of history, nationalism, and ethnicity.

If spectacle inclines to stasis, narrative is its active Other, and film would seem to promise a productive hybridity. Neil Jordan's *The Crying Game*, framed beginning and end by a fable, is quite self-conscious of its status as narrative.[16] The fable goes as follows: there is a scorpion who wants to cross a river, but he cannot do it alone, so he asks a frog for a lift. The frog points out that it would be foolish for him to carry the scorpion across the river because the scorpion would sting him. The scorpion, in turn, states that it would be foolish for him to sting the frog, because then neither of them would make it across the river. After considering this logic, the frog agrees to carry the scorpion across the river on his back. Halfway over, the scorpion stings the frog. As they are going down, the frog asks, "Why did you do that?" The scorpion replies, "It's in my nature: I had to do it." And both drown.

The fable establishes an essentialism that the film goes on to problematize though never finally undercut. The story is first recounted by Jody, a Black British soldier held hostage by the IRA against the release of one of their volunteers. Jody uses the story to get his smothering canvas hood removed, but it also serves as allegorical evidence for the inevitability of his assassination. Because all Irish are, in Jody's words, "tough undeluded motherfuckers," they will have to kill him. His interpretation of the fable thus assumes essentialism: "a scorpion does what is in its nature," he concludes.

Inasmuch as Fergus does receive orders to shoot the prisoner, Jody's moral to the story is upheld. However, Fergus's assassination attempt is grotesquely aborted by a British saracen. This twist in the plot is characteristic of the film's ambivalence. On the one hand, *The Crying Game*'s semiotic richness lends itself to a critique of essentialism; on the other hand, the film repeatedly pulls back from the political possibilities of radical contingency. This ambivalence pivots around Dil — or, to be precise, around the revelation of Dil's sex. Her disclosure constitutes a moment of interpretive crisis that both shapes what will happen in the remainder of the film and demands a renegotiation of what has happened so far.

Though the pivotal quality of this moment is unarguable — time moves, in a sense, both forward and backward from this point — exactly what Dil reveals when she drops her robe remains an open question. The tone of secrecy observed by reviewers and audiences suggests something outrageous and maybe even unimaginable, but the secret they fastidiously protect works as a surprise only if one holds that although Dil appears to be a woman, she is "really" a man.[17] Such a view belittles the film's complexity by assuming the expressive unity of gender and genitalia. I would argue, rather, that Dil's penis, unimportant in and of itself, serves as a signifier — a phallus — that provokes interpretive possibilities. My reading seizes two of them. First, Dil's sex can be read as a sign that lays bare the machinations of a system of normative gender signification in just the way Judith Butler's *Gender Trouble* suggests, demonstrating that gender is made intelligible by launching generally recognizable codes within a heterosexual matrix.[18] Second, and consequent, even as Dil's sex reveals the instability of gender, it mystifies and reifies nation. These two moves take us to a newly inscribed, newly conservative, realm of subject construction that is explicitly not postcolonial in affiliation.

To review *Gender Trouble*, briefly: gender is not expression, but performance governed by a tacit, collective agreement that interpellates people into reproducing the signs of gendered identity on a daily basis.[19] Every time gender is enacted, the subject imitates previous performances of gender (though not necessarily an ideal or original version), which means that parody is possible at every moment of reproduction. Put simply, gender's discursive codes have to be launched again and again; the trick is to launch them a little bit differently. Although gender norms cannot be overthrown, they can be subverted through a "dissonant juxtaposition" of signifiers (Butler, 123). To return to *The Crying Game*, the "dissonant juxtaposition" of Dil's sex to her gender — the penis beneath the dress — mobilizes the subversive potential of gender performativity, making it possible to read the film's codes of femininity and heterosexual courtship as parodic, as signs that simultaneously recall and undercut dominant gender and sexual norms. The comic nature of Dil's visit to Fergus at work turns on exactly this juxtaposition: Fergus and the audience know that Dil is neither "tart" nor "lady" as Fergus's overseer sarcastically suggests. Gender subversion reaches its hyperbolic apogee in the film's closing scene, when "Stand by Your Man" accompanies Dil's visit to the prison. When this song is matched to the opening one, the film wryly agrees that "When a Man Loves a Woman," she "can bring him [much] misery."[20]

"Misery" might not be strong enough to account for Fergus's violent reaction to Dil's sexual revelation. When Dil drops her robe, Fergus hits her and then rushes out of the room to vomit. To call him homophobic is to state – or maybe understate – the obvious. The reasons for his revulsion and their implications are not so simple, however. Whatever Jordan's film might encourage a theoretically savvy audience to think about the instability of gender dichotomy, Fergus sees male genitalia and female gender as an unsustainable contradiction. For him, Dil's phallus reveals her immutable male sex ("You should have stayed a girl," he comments later) and, by association, his own immutable Irish identity. Fergus and Dil are obvious alter egos – both masquerade, both keep a secret – and Dil functions throughout the film as the object in relation to which Fergus negotiates his subjectivity. Masculine to Dil's feminine, white to her black, Fergus is also Irish/Scottish to her English, but this last characteristic constitutes a mask he creates by discarding the Irish nationalist overtones of "Fergus" for the archetypally English name Jimmy, which he then passes off as Scottish. When Dil disrobes she reveals – at least in Fergus's mind – the essential and inescapable nature of what is given to one at birth: her gender and his nation. Hence Dil's penis not only spoils her masquerade, for Fergus, but also precipitates a crisis in his own relational subjectivity. If she is not feminine, can he be masculine? Can he be straight? If she cannot successfully transgress gender boundaries, can he ever escape Northern Ireland? Can he ever be out of, or out in, the IRA?

The film's answer is a resounding "no." Heterosexuality is policed, in the most literal sense, by the IRA, and it is through this consolidation of sexuality and politics that the film's deconstruction of gender serves to reify nation. Suspecting that Fergus's friendliness with the prisoner might render him unfit to carry out the necessary assassination, Peter, the IRA commander, summons Fergus and asks whether he will be able to perform his duties. "I'm a volunteer, Commander," Fergus says stoically. "Good," responds Peter, "we've been having doubts about you over the last few days." He gets reinforcement from Jude, who has earlier expressed sexual interest in Fergus and, as the sole woman volunteer, is the only IRA member who can guarantee Fergus's heterosexuality. She adds, "You're not the only one." Doubts about revolutionary commitment collapse into doubts about heterosexuality and, if we follow through Butler's argument that heterosexuality is the matrix that gives meaning to gender dichotomy, doubts about Fergus's masculinity as well.

Good Foucauldians will immediately point out that policing is productive as well as prohibitive, and indeed the legislation of heterosexuality and its undoing by homoeroticism are evident — at least retrospectively — from the film's initial sequences. Again, though, *The Crying Game* shies away from radical politics. Think of the scene in which Fergus helps Jody urinate. Although the scene oozes homoerotic innuendo, our sympathy, held in the camera's gaze, is directed away from Jody's penis toward Fergus's uneasiness at touching it. Fergus's discomfiture gives the denial of homoeroticism a self-consciousness that necessarily recalls it even while disavowing it. This self-conscious denial of homoeroticism is compounded by the following scene, where Fergus and Jody bond — apparently safely, heterosexually — over the photograph of Dil, a shared object of desire. This affiliation is coded heterosexual because the men's sexual attraction is mediated by the sign of woman. After Dil disrobes, we realize that this avowal of sexual attraction is not simply heterosexual. On the other hand, it is not simply homosexual, either: to posit that would be to see Dil as a man in women's clothing. If we take seriously Butler's point about gender performativity, we have to grant Dil a gender identity that exceeds the binarism of male/female and grant Fergus an attraction that is similarly ambivalent: neither simply heterosexual nor finally homosexual.

We might grant Fergus such a sexuality; he does not. Although Dil's penis as phallus signifies that heterosexuality is always policed and always (already) exceeded, Fergus's revulsion at Dil's sex betokens horror at such transgressions. To put this in Fergus's terms, if the individual human body is almost infinitely permeable, how can the national body remain immutable? His reading is in some sense understandable. Although Dil could be said to inhabit an ambivalent gender identity, the urgency of the political situation in Northern Ireland admits no such liminality: the colony's borders are guarded by the British army. Gender, then, appears to be permeable in a way that nation is not.[21] But the naturalization of national identity as it collapses metaphorically into the human body is more problematic. In reading Dil's body as the symbol of his Irishness,

Fergus mistakes natality for affiliation: his secret is not his Irishness per se, but his IRA membership. To collapse the distinction between nationality and political affiliation is to deny the history that turns a given racial or ethnic or national identity into a political commitment. In the case of Northern Ireland, such a dehistoricizing naturalization of nation casts the nationalist struggle as inexplicably atavistic.[22] Somehow violence is immanent in Northern Ireland: to paraphrase Jody, "a scorpion does what is in its nature to do."[23]

Were Jordan to historicize Fergus's notion of Irishness, he would establish the possibility for solidarity between Fergus and Dil on the basis of a shared, though somewhat different, ambivalence to Britain — a postcolonial ambivalence mediated not only by gender and nation, but also by race. The film approaches this level of complexity around race early on, in the captivity scene. Although Jody is a British soldier, his relationship to Britain (England and Northern Ireland) is thoroughly permeated by his race: from Antigua via Tottenham, he has been sent to what he describes as "the only country in the world where they call you nigger to your face." At the same time, Jody himself voices considerable anti-Irish racism: he addresses Fergus as "Paddy" and mocks the Irish sport of hurling as "a game where a bunch of paddies whack sticks at each other."[24]

This scene suggests that the categories of white and black, British and Irish, cut across each other in complicated ways, but Jody's real insight — that racism works by flattening history into superficial appearances ("It does no good to tell them I'm from Tottenham") — gets forgotten in the latter half of the film. When the queers of Empire meet in the aptly named "Metro," they share only the coincidence of location. Though the space itself, as a "half-way house of racial and cultural origins," is reminiscent of Homi Bhabha's "unhomely," the Metro provides none of the "interstitial intimacy" between "private and public, past and present, the psyche and the social" that a meaningful postcolonial unhomeliness calls for.[25] Characters do not even talk directly to each other; all conversation is mediated by the ambiguous bartender, Col. What ought to be a queer space in the most enabling sense of that word actually downplays Dil's racial ambivalence in relation to Britain by fetishizing gender, barring her from the patriot game while making her the focal point of the crying game.

To put this another way, although the film plays lots of games, its play is peculiarly apolitical. Love is decontaminated of politics by simple intertextual substitution: "*The Crying Game*," song and film, blots out "The Patriot Game," song and trope. "The Patriot Game," an Irish Republican song from the nationalist revolution of 1916 to 1923, emphasizes that in political terms what matters is not one's given nationality but what one does with it, the part one plays in the political game. *The Crying Game* misses this point: in contesting filiation — how one's performance relates to one's identity — it ignores the politically urgent issue of affiliation — how one's actions relate to one's beliefs.

The treason that "The Patriot Game" invokes is displaced in *The Crying Game* from nationalist politics onto sexual politics, where it is blamed on women and ultimately shot to death. The film's use of a conventional love story to solve political issues could be lifted from a Victorian novel, even though its fetishism of gender is unmistakably postmodern.[26] Equally postmodern is the suggestion that organized militancy against the state is obsolete, implying that the really subversive work is going on elsewhere. But this is not necessarily the case: not in Northern Ireland, and not in *The Crying Game*. When gender and nation, love and politics, come together in the climactic bedroom scene, we are presented with an entirely conventional cast of female characters. Dil's penis makes no difference — in fact, to return to Herr's notion of an "aesthetics of denial," it is the film's fixation on this ambiguously signifying phallus that obscures the way gender is constructed narratively. Segregated in the love story, Dil is every inch the conventional heroine, driven by jealousy and frightened of being alone. Ultimately, so much blood is spilled — so much female blood, accompanied by Dil's shouts of "tits" and "ass" — that Dil's relationship to Fergus is more grotesquely hyperbolic than it is parodic of normative gender relations.

As for Jude, the only biological woman in the film: Jody says early on, explicitly distinguishing Jude from Dil, that she's "trouble." "Some women are trouble, Fergus. Now, Dil, she was no trouble at all." Jody's insistent application of the word "trouble" to women serves, like the trope of the game, to sexualize and sterilize what is already well politicized, the sectarian violence in Northern Ireland known as the Troubles. Once again, the opposition posed (here, between gender fetishism and state politics) is untenable. Seen from the outside, Jude manifests what Jordan denies: that the IRA has known about performativity all along.[27] If we take gender to be determined positionally rather than essentially, Jude's transformation from fairground tramp to executive killer is quite as complete as Dil's female impersonation.[28] However, the film tries to dissuade us from this reading of Jude by typing her throughout as an evil woman – evil *because* she is a woman who uses her body in the service of nationalism. The film at once naturalizes and demonizes political struggle by shaping it as a biological woman who simply "does what is in her nature to do." The all-too-literal femme fatale – named after Judas but ironically more like devouring, cruel Mother Ireland – can change her hair colour, Jordan implies, but her treachery remains constant.[29]

The constancy of nature brings us back to the story of the frog and the scorpion, which Fergus retells at the end of the film. The story this time around appears to have no moral implication but, in its exaggerated expressions and intonations, epitomizes the notion of textual play. At one level the story of the frog and the scorpion is about the act of reading, about what has meaning, and under what circumstances. The film cannot attribute meaning to the story this time because the filmic narrative has broken. Faced with the impossibility of reconciling love and politics, the film repudiates the project of reading altogether, and stories – the narrative possibilities that initially appear so much more promising than photographic iconography – become a way for Fergus to pass time in prison while he waits to come out.

In a sense, this refusal to mean is a foreseeable, if not an intentional, consequence of Butler's theory. Parody is based, after all, on deliberately flouting the well-established terms of a reading contract. However, because the effectiveness of parody relies on an interpretive pact, it is particularly vulnerable to co-optation. *The Crying Game*, marketed as a suspense film, is a case in point: to treat the subversion of discursive codes as an exotic exception is not to destabilize but to reinforce those codes. Gender, that is, can be detached from biology, only to be reinscribed misogynously through narrative – in this case, the love story. The effect is to detach performativity from its subversive ends.

The ends of subversion are important and (like IRA violence) connected to their cause: this is the point of Mohanty's insistence that subjectivity is a function of multiple vectors. In focusing so closely on gender alone, Butler's theory finds it hard to account for other competing and complementary axes of subject formation, particularly the material conditions of people's lives. In conjunction with Mohanty's feminism of positionality, however, the strategy Butler maps out can be productively adapted to talk about gender, nation, and class concurrently. If gender is performative, Mohanty reminds us that its very material dramas are played out in a theatre of history that is buttressed by "systemic networks of class, race, (hetero)sexuality, and nation" in addition to gender (Mohanty, 13). Such a theoretical hybrid offers productive reading possibilities.

Before we go on to explore what at least one of them might look like, let us review the argument so far. We started with a discussion of gender and nation in Ireland. Just as Irish identity is overdetermined by the rigidity of polarized subject positions in an obdurate war of decolonization, what Cheryl Herr calls an "aesthetics of denial" neutralizes the female body through overscrutiny. Pictorial representations of women's bodies from Loyalist perspectives seem to prove Herr's point: Woman stands for Nation in a simple metaphoric substitution. The fixed focus *on* woman, rather than *through* her, abrogates narrative possibility, a pitfall of iconography that the constantly changing murals on the Republican Women's Wall skirt. Both "Resistance" and, to an even greater extent, "Solidarity" show how the feminist analytic category "woman" can usefully shape history, nation, and ethnicity without becoming a totalizing term itself.

The Crying Game, ostensibly both narrative and pictorial, totalizes in a different direction. It ignores narrative constructions of gender even as it problematizes the visual. By fetishizing Dil and demonizing Jude, the film writes its own "aesthetics of denial" that censors nationalist struggles in Northern Ireland and, by extension, other former colonies of Britain. Furthermore, in splitting Dil's sexuality from Jude's nationalism, *The Crying Game* recycles tediously conventional representations of Irish nationalism as a devouring hag. If Herr is correct in arguing that it is not the omnipresence of the vicious mother but the contradiction between matriarchal mythology and the everyday immiserization of women that expresses itself in sectarian violence, it is to representations of the material conditions of women's lives that we must now turn.

Mary Beckett's two collections of short stories, *A Belfast Woman*, published in 1980, and *A Literary Woman*, published ten years later, describe the conditions of working-class life in Belfast.[30] Both collections invoke in their very titles the troublesome term *woman*. But this invocation need not essentialize or unify female experience. Rather, following Butler and Mohanty, it can be read as a parodic appropriation of the subject of feminism that is always necessarily destabilized by vectors of class and religious ethnicity.

Take the title story of *A Belfast Woman*, a fictional autobiography. The protagonist's retrospective narrative is triggered when she receives a letter warning her that she is about to be burned out of her house (a historical reference to Loyalist tactics against Catholics). The Troubles thus become a trope for social phenomena — like totalities of gender — that interpellate citizens into particular subjectivities. The narrative that follows delineates its stages with all the conventional markers of women's biography — childhood, marriage, childbirth, children leaving home, and so on — but the significance of these events has to do with life in Belfast, not with gender as such. The character's marriage, for example, precipitates a crisis in her family not because of sexuality or the threat of familial separation, but because she marries a Protestant. When she develops what is probably a prolapsed uterus, our protagonist cannot afford to have it seen to, given the risk that she will die and leave her children alone. The metaphor of human body for body politic, suggested by both Herr and *The Crying Game*, holds here, but with the important caveat that the relationship of subjectivity to body is necessarily mediated by material considerations.

A Belfast Woman, then, defies an understanding of its protagonist in terms of gender alone: the sense of "Woman" is always deferred because preceded by its significant modifier "Belfast." The gendered term constitutes a rubric over a more complicated subjectivity specific to geopolitical location and material conditions. Because these conditions are never fixed — because sectarian violence erupts into everyday life in working-class Belfast — subjectivity can never be static. This instability in turn evacuates the totalizing hegemony of the term woman, even as Beckett so self-consciously invokes it. Furthermore, a constant deferral of the meaning of "woman" resists fixture of either term or idea in a nostalgic, photographic still.

The constant danger of fixture in a discursive terrain as overdetermined as Northern Ireland is suggested by "Flags and Emblems," a cautionary tale with allegorical moments. The generative crisis in the story is that the five-year-old son in a devoted Republican family is seen, on the day of a British visit to Belfast, carrying a tiny Union Jack. A few paragraphs at the end of the story explain that the child was handed the flag, for a split second, after another child dropped it. This part of the story does not circulate in the Republican community; rather, the representation of child and flag rests, denarrativized, in a posture as emblematic as a UVF wall mural. The short story surrounds this emblem, dwelling on how it destroys the Republican credibility of the child's activist father, casting the family into mortal danger. Because our sympathy is drawn to the family, our criticism is drawn to the denarrativization — the substitution of the image of the boy with the flag for the story of how he came to pick it up — that results in their endangerment. Extrapolated, the story castigates any discursive emblematization: the reduction of a nation to a flag, of women's lives to a universal notion of gender.

Beckett's second book, *A Literary Woman*, attempts to correct the reductiveness implied in the term woman by addressing, obliquely, the construction of the literary woman. The short stories that make up the collection initially appear to have little in common. One of them follows a Dubliner to Belfast, another describes a couple adjusting to the husband's retirement, and still another portrays a woman dealing with the death of her infant. Despite the stories' apparent heterogeneity, a similar structure gradually appears: in several stories a character receives an anonymous, threatening letter. The husband who has retired, for example, receives a note that says, "You should know your wife is an alcoholic. She is being talked about all over the district. She hurries home in the mornings without talking to her neighbours and shuts herself in the house. Some of these days she will disgrace you" (112). Similarly, the woman whose infant has died receives a letter that reads, "Do the guards know you murdered little Rory by holding his face down under the water? They say you got depressed because you were expecting again but that is no excuse, is it? I will write soon" (79–80). These letters are signed "The Watcher" or "The Wellwisher," and it is not until the penultimate story in the collection that we learn the identity of this anonymous correspondent: she is the "literary woman" after whom the collection of stories is named.

The literary woman in the short story is Miss Teeling, and she is a wholly unsympathetic character: hateful, mean-spirited, envious, and petty. Born to a servant, she leads a childhood of grinding poverty punctuated by violence, a life she swears to escape as an adult. She makes her way in the world by letting rooms in the houses of wealthy old ladies. She ingratiates her way into nursing them and then, through malevolent neglect, manipulates them into naming her in their wills. By the time the story opens, Miss Teeling has amassed enough property that she has a flat of her own, but she still lets a room in the O'Reillys' comfortable suburban house. Her occupation is to be a malignant presence in a nice middle-class community. She sits in the window of her tiny upstairs room and watches the family and the neighbourhood, occasionally writing the people she sees anonymous, threatening letters — apparently unmotivated. But to look for motivation is to ask the wrong question. An impoverished woman in the house of plenty, Miss Teeling acts as a continual reminder of what nice middle-class communities exclude; as a literary woman, she is a kind of discursive sniper, firing off missives that disrupt people's lives.

One might extend the allegory of the literary woman to Mary Beckett herself: to be a literary woman from Northern Ireland is to be a troublesome presence in the house of first-world theory. In writing narratives that represent women in the context of the Troubles, where the instability of social conditions makes essentializing the category "woman" impossible, Beckett proves that category to be at once crucial and insufficient for characterizing the material conditions of women's lives. Beckett's work demands a hybridity of terminology that can imagine gender, class, race, and nation as mutual, so that every articulation of the word *woman* can be heard as a parodic repetition that points to what the term excludes. Her call finds its analogy in the "Solidarity" mural from the Women's Wall, which shows the sign of woman stretched by the heterogeneity it is asked to contain. If the term woman is parodic, that image captures its uneasy tension: its imperialism *as* a sign is continually exceeded and so undone. In 1987, before the Sinn Fein elections, the mural was painted over by a tripartite slogan reading, "Freedom, Justice, and Peace." Until these ideals are achieved, "woman" will have to be written over and over and over.

NOTES

I gratefully acknowledge the audience granted to an early version of this essay by Erin Carlston, Kim Gillespie, Brian Gore, Andrew Gunther, Marcia Klotz, Diana Maltz, Steve Martinot, and Gay Morris. A special thanks to Jennifer Schaffner for on-line, full-text newspaper searches.

1. Cheryl Herr, "The Erotics of Irishness," *Critical Inquiry* 17 (Autumn 1990): 1–34. Subsequent citations are in the text.
2. See Cheryl Herr, "Ireland from the Outside," *James Joyce Quarterly* 28 (Sum-

mer 1991): 777–89, for more interdisciplinary, intercultural work of the same calibre.
3. R. Radhakrishnan makes a similar point about the relationship between representations of women and nationalist struggle: "Unable to produce its own history in response to its inner sense of identity, nationalist ideology sets up Woman as victim and goddess simultaneously. Woman becomes the allegorical name for a specific historical failure: the failure to coordinate the political or the ontological with the epistemological within an undivided agency" ("Nationalism, Gender, and the Narrative of Identity," in *Nationalisms and Sexualities*, ed. Andrew Parker et al. [New York: Routledge, 1992], 85).
4. My expression is indebted, of course, to Annette Kolodny's important essay, "Dancing through the Minefield," *Feminist Studies* 6 (1980): 1–25; reprinted in *The New Feminist Criticism*, ed. Elaine Showalter (New York: Pantheon Books, 1985), 144–67. I deliberately echo a North American feminist because the main problem I am engaging here – namely, how to imagine gender in dynamic relation to other axes of identity like nation, race, and class – is relevant well outside Northern Ireland.
5. For an elaboration of Nation and Colony as patriarchal and matriarchal structures, respectively, see Marcia Klotz, "White Women and the Dark Continent: Gender and Sexuality in German Colonial Discourse, 1885–1945" (Ph.D. diss., Stanford University, in progress).
6. Frantz Fanon, "Concerning Violence," in *The Wretched of the Earth*, trans. Constance Farrington (1961; New York: Grove Weidenfeld, 1963), 36.
7. I use the terms *Loyalist* and *Unionist* interchangeably.
8. Bill Rolston has written broad and nonpartisan coverage of Belfast murals in three texts: *Politics and Painting: Murals and Conflict in Northern Ireland* (Rutherford, N.J.: Fairleigh Dickinson University Press, 1991); "'When You're Fighting a War, You've Gotta Take Setbacks': Murals and Propaganda in the North of Ireland," *Polygraph* 5 (1992): 112–35; and *Drawing Support: Murals in the North of Ireland* (Belfast: Beyond the Pale, 1992).
9. All figures are taken from the Ciaran MacGowan collection held in the Hoover Institution Archives, Stanford University, Stanford, Calif. I am grateful to Mr. MacGowan for permission to use a small number of his slides. The murals are, naturally, anonymous.
10. The mural's emblematic character is highlighted not only by the abstract centerpiece, but also by the mural above it (not pictured here), which shows the Red Hand of Ulster dancing on the Irish tricolour, flanked by British and Ulster flags. See Rolston, *Politics and Painting*, 32–33.
11. See Margaret Ward, *Unmanageable Revolutionaries: Women and Irish Nationalism* (London: Pluto, 1983), for a historical account of Irish feminism.
12. Significantly, 1914 does not mark the formation of the UVF itself (it was founded a year earlier), although it does commemorate its first successful military operation, gunrunning from Germany to Larne, and the planned UVF coup d'etat that was aborted by the outbreak of World War I. See R. F. Foster, *Modern Ireland, 1600–1972* (London: Penguin, 1988), 462–71, for

one account of this operation. A good introduction to the origin and early development of the UVF may be found in David Boulton, *The UVF, 1966–73: An Anatomy of Loyalist Rebellion* (Dublin: Torc, Gill & Macmillan, 1973). The UVF depended on the support of women: Ward reports that 234,046 Ulster women signed a female counterpart to the UVF's Solemn League and Covenant "to resist Home Rule by any means" (Ward, *Unmanageable Revolutionaries*, 89–90). Significantly, this mobilization of women was used specifically for nationalist, not feminist, ends.
13. The outer segments of the triptych are copied from World War I–era postcards.
14. This rendering invisible of femininity was corrected, so to speak, when the mural was repainted in the early 1980s: the middle figure was shown wearing a skirt, and the caption "We must grow tough without losing our tenderness" was added. See Rolston, *Drawing Support*, 34.
15. Chandra Talpade Mohanty, "Cartographies of Struggle: Third World Women and the Politics of Feminism," in *Third World Women and the Politics of Feminism*, ed. Mohanty, Ann Russo, and Lourdes Torres (Bloomington: Indiana University Press, 1991), 63, 6. Subsequent citations are in the text.
16. *The Crying Game*, written and directed by Neil Jordan, with Stephen Rea, Jaye Davidson, Miranda Richardson; London: Miramax Films, 1992. 112 min.
17. For representative reviews, see the *New York Times*, September 26, 1992, sec. 1, p. 2; *New Statesman and Society* 5, no. 226 (October 30, 1992): 35; *Film Comment*: FLMCA 28 (November–December 1992): 67; *The New Yorker*, November 16, 1992, 127–30; and *The Sunday Times*, December 13, 1992, 8–24. For a critique of the "surprise," see *The Advocate* 620 (January 12, 1993): 89. For a metacritical comment on keeping the secret, see *The New Yorker*, December 7, 1992, 50.
18. Judith Butler, *Gender Trouble* (New York: Routledge, 1990). Subsequent citations are in the text.
19. Butler's argument thus has much in common with Louis Althusser's "Ideology and Ideological State Apparatuses," in *Lenin and Philosophy*, trans. Ben Brewster (New York: Monthly Review, 1972).
20. I think that to this point my argument describes the way the film functions on a mass level. Perhaps to dissolve the connection between biological sex and gender, and to parody heterosexual courtship might be enough progressive work to ask of one cultural production.
21. Though the film's politics do not admit this reading, the IRA's recent attacks in England prove that national borders can be every bit as permeable as the limits of gender.
22. For the persistence of atavistic explanations of Northern Irish violence – and a thorough critique of them – see Tom Nairn, *The Break-Up of Britain* (London: Verso, 1981), 222–25.
23. Obviously, the allegorical relationship of the frog to Britain and the scorpion to Northern Ireland already strains credibility: what exactly is the free ride Britain gives its colony?

24. On anti-Irish racism, see Liz Curtis, *Nothing but the Same Old Story: The Roots of Anti-Irish Racism* (London: Information on Ireland, 1984); Ned Lebow, "British Historians and Irish History," *Eire-Ireland* 8 (Winter 1973): 3–38; Lebow, *White Britain and Black Ireland: The Influence of Stereotypes on Colonial Policy* (Philadelphia: Institute for the Study of Human Issues, 1976); and Nicholas P. Canny, "The Ideology of English Colonisation from Ireland to America," *William and Mary Quarterly* 30 (July 1973): 575–98.
25. Homi Bhabha, "The World and the Home," *Social Text* 31/32 (1992): 148.
26. I am indebted to Regenia Gagnier for this observation.
27. Ann Rosalind Jones and Peter Stallybrass put gendered Irish identity in provocative historical context, showing that Irish people have frequently used ambiguous gender codes to flout English colonial authority. See their "Dismantling Irena: The Sexualizing of Ireland in Early Modern England," in *Nationalisms and Sexualities*, ed. Parker et al., 157–71.
28. In addition to Mohanty's essay, see Adrienne Rich, "Notes toward a Politics of Location," in *Blood, Bread and Poetry* (New York: Norton, 1986); and Teresa de Lauretis, "Feminist Studies/Critical Studies: Issues, Terms, and Contexts," in *Feminist Studies/Critical Studies*, ed. Teresa de Lauretis (Bloomington: Indiana University Press, 1986).
29. I would not want this line of argument to be interpreted as necessarily or entirely a defence of the IRA; Republican policy and its implementation need constantly to be critiqued, especially from the perspective of women. Jordan's attempt, however, shortchanges both gender and nation.
30. Mary Beckett, *A Belfast Woman* (Swords, Co. Dublin: Poolbeg, 1980), and Beckett, *A Literary Woman* (London: Bloomsbury, 1990). Quotations will be included parenthetically in the text.

PART THREE

How Political Is Identity Politics?

NINE

The Crisis of Femininity and Modernity in the Third World

Rajeswari Mohan

At the Rethinking Marxism Conference in Amherst in November 1989, a roundtable discussion on "Marxism and Third World Women" ran itself into the ground, as happens ever so often, on the semantic niceties of the term *third world*. Most of the discussion circled around issues of representation: Could white American women speak for the third world? Can work expended on academic specialization in area studies earn one the ticket to represent a particular area's interests? How many women of color had to be put on the panel for the third world to be represented in all its heterogeneity? And so on. Suddenly, a member of the audience declared vehemently, "There are no third world women in this room." A look around the standing-room-only crowd, at least half of which was comprised of women from various parts of that third world, told us that the declaration was meant to call into question the grounds for our concern and knowledges. For the critic was talking about the "authentic" third world woman, "perhaps the peasant woman," in the face of whose superexploitation our passionate feminist arguments sounded like trivial chatter. Embarrassment, maybe terror, at being caught out of line one more time got the better of conference decorum. The faltering discussion came to a dead halt. I revisit this scene as a point of entry into the contentious discursive claims among which the project of third world feminism is articulated in the West and in one site of the third world, India.

In hindsight I realize that the discussion, already ensnared in the anxiety of authority and representation, had almost set itself up for the charge of inauthenticity. In general the question of political responsibility of feminist intellectuals, the issue of theory's responsiveness to the heterogeneity of women's concerns, and the recognition of the urgent need for globally articulated accounts of women's oppression have placed on feminist discourses enormous burdens, which prompted the 1985 National Women's Studies Association (NWSA) button "Sisterhood Is Trying." The invocation of authenticity short-circuits the delicate and wearying work of unpacking these burdens. The imbrication of "authenticity" in the discursive construction of the third world and the peculiar importance it assumes in configurations of modernity in the third world is one of the concerns of this essay. More specifically, the essay addresses the ways tensions and anxieties provoked by modernity in India find a focus in the figure of the liberated woman in political and filmic representation. As much as my analysis of K. Balachander's melodramas is motivated by these concerns, it is also spurred by the belief that the entry of third world issues into the domain of feminist inquiry will pose new theoretical challenges. For it is one of the distinctive advantages of third world feminist studies that they bring into sharper focus the epistemological and political contestations within feminism and third world studies in general. To this end the essay identifies points where Balachander's films press against the limits of feminist theory and analysis of melodrama, and in doing so the essay suggests areas of further inquiry.

In third world feminist discourses, calling attention to absent third world women often serves as an overcompensatory reaction to eager attempts to position the third world academic as the condensation of radical alterity to Western feminism and as the political and epistemological stand-in for the third world in general. In carrying out a similar function, the criticism of the roundtable discussion made visible a fairly typical strategy of containment that simultaneously acknowledges and disavows racial/cultural/historical differences.[1] By implicitly invoking the immense variations of class, caste, nation, and region, not to mention the various mutations of (neo)colonial experience, the criticism once again underscored the heterogeneous backgrounds and agendas of third world women. For those Western feminists naïve in the matters of other worlds, the comment presumably served as a disclosure of class politics in the third world, by opening up a brief insight into the ongoing exploitation and silencing of subaltern and working-class women in our various homelands and exposing the implication of our relatively comfortable academic lives, with their rote of seminars and conferences, in the deprivation we talked so much about. The analytical and political force of such moments of critical self-reflexivity for feminist and postcolonial scholars derives from a growing epistemological self-consciousness, from an understanding that the enabling conditions of knowledge include the suppression, as trace, of a marginalized other. The trace itself is seen as an inscription of hidden relations of exploitation and oppression enabled by the violent social hierarchies that directly facilitate the production of knowledge. Thus, the ongoing erasure of the supporting, secret sharer of knowledge is not merely unjust but works actively to perpetuate those hidden relations.[2] But this potential for critical introspection was elided by our critic into an accusation, long familiar, of introducing Western discourses into the third world context without considering their relevance or usefulness, of imposing our middle-class problems on women of widely varying class, caste, and religious backgrounds, and of assuming the mantle of neocolonialism and silencing the concerns and experiences of those far more numerous than ourselves. In response to such criticisms, third world feminisms have diversely agonized over the enabling conditions of political practice and vigilantly continue to negotiate between the heritages of Western feminism, middle-class nationalism, and subaltern activism to formulate a contingent political practice radically skeptical of traditional patriarchal as well as class, religious, and caste hierarchies.[3] The persistence of the charge of inauthenticity despite these efforts points to its continuing use as a strategy of silencing feminist discourses in the non-Western world.

Invocations of authenticity have a particularly disabling effect on discourses such as feminism that have only recently begun to examine their historical reliance on identity politics. Usually, the call to authenticity signals a movement toward containing and dismissing the political desires of the discourse in question, since the categorical indeterminacy of the authentic undercuts the possibility that a productive assessment of gains or realistic evaluation of agendas might follow the challenge to the authority of the discourse.[4] Instead, one is often left with gestures of tokenism ad infinitum, whereby a margin hurries to acknowledge a margin within the margin.

Even those instances where the criticism initiates an epistemological self-reflexivity are often mired in passive resistance to the implications of attending to alterity and difference. Often the discursive status quo ante closes over the self-reflexive hiatus, this time with the satisfaction that all the proper gestures have been duly made. Equally often, the position of knowledge is vacated for the other, now fetishized as having privileged access to the complete knowledge the center can never have, and in the process the unequal knowledge relations that occasioned the critique in the first place are introduced again, in inverse.[5] More recently, a tame pluralism has become fashionable under the banner of "diversity" or "multiculturalism" and has all but displaced a rigorous analytical understanding of the historically and culturally specific ways the tension between margin and center plays itself out across hierarchies constituted along the lines of class, gender, sexuality, and race.

The theoretical and political vacuity of such developments has increasingly become obvious, and we may be able to extricate ourselves from them by attending closely to the dialectic constitution of alterity and to the historical and contextual shifts in its value. That is, marginality or alterity is not a territory or birthright claimed on the basis of blood, skin, or body, but a relational configuration, invested with psychological energy, economic value, and political interest. As a general epistemological position, the margin provides a self-reflexive, critical, and antagonistic orientation to dominant structures of knowledge and associated social arrangements. Such a position would be especially valuable to an oppositional discourse such as feminism that, in seeking to overthrow existing social hierarchies, runs the risk of setting up new ones if it forgets its own historical and political contingency. But according absolute epistemological privilege to a margin (usually constituted in essentialist terms) is to reify and fetishize it and, ironically, to reconstitute it as center in a discursive system reigned by the symbolic capital of the oppressed. A somewhat different response has been to posit a proliferation of margins leading to a banal celebration of difference and a deferral of knowledge. In the face of exacerbated racial and gender oppression sanctioned by the rhetoric of "a thousand points of light" and the "new world order," the prominence granted to these responses in the academy suggests that an important compensatory and diversionary effect may be at work here as well.

This, then, is the political and intellectual context for third world feminists working in the West. Feminist investigations of the third world have demonstrated that women's empowerment — the enabling condition and effect of a thriving feminist discourse — has been achieved in the West at the cost of disempowerment and exploitation elsewhere in less visible sites of the third world.[6] So, while the work of stressing the implications of feminist theoretical interventions for women in the third world continues to be urgent, the uneven distribution of the benefits of modernity among third world women and the exacerbated exploitation of some groups of women under multinational capitalism have made it urgent that third world feminists resist being interpellated as fetishized margins or being dismissed as too modern to be authentic.

The ambivalent relations between third world feminism and its Western counterpart has a long and complex history.[7] In the nineteenth and twentieth centuries, organized and concerted struggles against women's oppression found their most influential expression in the contexts of nationalist liberation movements and drastic changes wrought by colonialism in the material and ideological conditions of women's existence. Western secular thought, education, print capitalism, and nineteenth-century Western feminism all played a part in the emergence of these struggles.[8] At the same time, as colonial policy sought to replace the authority of indigenous patriarchy with Western patriarchal discourses in the name of protecting "native" women, the nationalist elite saw these interventions as attacks on tradition and so responded by reaffirming women's roles and positions within indigenous patriarchal arrangements as essential to their nationalist integrity, not to mention cultural authenticity.[9] As a result, women were wary of making radical critiques of traditional structures and values for fear of seeming to undermine the anticolonialist cause. Thus, from the start the question of women's rights has been contradictorily linked to emancipation from political and cultural domination by the West. Women's rights have been seen as a mark of progressive, postcolonial politics even as feminists have been dismissed as aping decadent, bourgeois, Western fashions or critiqued for being divisive of larger antiimperialist and class struggles. In these contestations we see the beginnings of the line of argument followed by contemporary antifeminist criticisms in the third world.

These contradictions may be explored in detail in relation to India, where they have clearly restricted the scope and effectivity of feminist discourses even as they continue to be replayed, albeit with new inflections, in the context of the state's aggressive program of modernization. Dominated by a highly visible, educated, urban, middle-class intelligentsia, Indian feminism had, for a while, been more invested in maintaining its elite leadership than in mobilizing grass-roots opposition to the patriarchal state. Consequently it refrained from making radical critiques of the patriarchal ideology that works through religious and bureaucratic institutions. Middle-class ideologies of ideal Hindu and Indian womanhood were forged in contrast both to "feudalist" and "Westernized" gender identities and institutionalized through social reform and popular cultural productions in ways that anticipate the contemporary developments this essay will explore. Middle-class feminism's narrowly articulated agendas also blocked a potentially powerful alliance with labor and peasant movements and left out the interests of women from religious minority groups (Muslims, Christians, Parsis) and lower-caste, peasant, and tribal women.[10] Since the mid-seventies, however, an active and self-conscious attempt is being made to allow the subaltern activism of urban poor, tribal, and peasant women to shape the priorities and agendas of Indian feminism.[11]

Even from this sketchy discursive history it becomes clear that the project of feminism in India is articulated in the course of contestations among a multiplicity of discourses, of which Western feminist, colonialist, nationalist, indigenous patriarchal, and subaltern discourses have historically been the most important.[12] Notably muted or arguably even absent is a discourse of sexuality pitched against the institutions of marriage and heterosexuality. Even so, third world feminists have realized that the heterogeneous positions and interests contained by the category "woman" are becoming impossible to ignore. Responding to this realization, Kalpana Bardhan has argued that "in a society divided by economic inequality and permeated by hierarchy, women hardly constitute a collectivity with shared interests and needs. . . . In such a context, gender politics can hardly be a surrogate for class politics."[13] While the importance of Bardhan's admonition not to forget class politics cannot be emphasized enough, developments affecting Indian women in the eighties have made it abundantly clear that a feminist political practice is urgently necessary to maintain women's legal rights. A growing religious fundamentalism and a burgeoning commodity aesthetic that positions woman as the object of gaze have been highly influential in propagating a homogenized notion of woman. That is, while Bardhan is correct in drawing attention to the vast material differences in women's lives, there has been an ongoing countervailing attempt to discursively construct woman as a homogeneous, essentially defined entity on the basis of which an erosion of legal rights has been sanctioned.[14] Ironically, then, these homogenizing trends affecting women occupying differential class, caste, and religious positions have de facto provided a common ground for the emergence of a rearticulated feminism contesting the ideological positioning of women by dominant discourses.

My belated response to the critic in Amherst, then, would be that the third world woman emerges as a category in the context of constructions of "woman" and "the third world." That is, there is no collective will, visibly marked body of people, or community based on shared experience that inherently corresponds or exists anterior to the discursive configuration of the third world woman. The protean figure emerges in the thick of the contestations that inevitably accompany the move to name, demarcate, and identify, acquiescing neither to the call to conform demurely to the limits of otherness nor to the desire to assert a normative and coherent subjectivity. To the extent that discourses of alterity circulate inside and outside the halls of academia, in the Western and in the non-Western world, the third world woman passes through all these spaces, never the same, inscribing in her inconstancy the varied claims she negotiates. However, the slipperiness of this figure becomes an intolerable contradiction when the discourse of modernity enters the picture. While modernization is seen as the redemptive destiny of the third world, it severely strains the construction of third world women as embodiments of authenticity and tradition. Popular cultural forms, especially film and television, have played an increasingly effective role in disseminating a generalized awareness of the rights and options available to women as a result of the government's concerted effort to integrate women into development. In response to the perception that traditional patriarchal control over women has been weakened by these changes, conservative sections of the middle class have also used the media to gain support for an invented tradition of feminine submissiveness. Repeatedly, in the ongoing contest over representation, the invocation of authentic or traditional womanhood follows a pattern similar to those in the academic setting I described above. Pitting the traditional/authentic ideal against the figure of the modern woman serves to dismiss the latter, even though the invocation of authenticity is usually a reference to an absent, anterior figure that is never rendered substantive. Most of all, conservative outcries over a threatened and marginalized tradition gloss over the active and selective invention of tradition that is being achieved in and through popular cultural productions. This moment, when the shifting valence and significance of the components of the term "third world women" begin to show themselves, serves as a useful point of entry into an investigation of the interests served by configurations of the "modern woman" on the dual registers of left politico-intellectual discourses and popular culture in India.

THE THIRD WORLD, MODERNITY, AND WOMAN: A GENEALOGY

Implicit in the declarations of my academic friend in Amherst is an understanding of the third world in generative and filial terms as the home that defines and underwrites our political activities only as long as we live in it. Concomitantly, the task of carving out an epistemological position from which nationalist patriarchy can be critiqued simultaneously with neoimperialism is seen as divisive and wasteful violence by unruly or prodigal daughters. But the crucial point to be made about the third world is precisely one about the confusion between the discursive and the geographical. For the third world is neither a geographical space nor a specific economic entity even though territorial and economic interests are secured through its deployment. Instead, it can be argued that the third world is a concept metaphor, a discursive entity, and an imagined collectivity. Moreover, the category "third world" has a specific genealogy in which the production of knowledges in Western universities and research foundations in combination with the theory and implementation of modernization programs play a central role. In other words, the "third world" is a category whose primary sphere of deployment is precisely the academic spaces my Amherst friend wishes it to vacate.

The division of the world into three discursive entities or conceptual worlds was a direct response to the exigencies of the cold war and the realignment of global power following decolonization and the shift from Pax Britannica to Pecunia Americana. As Carl Pletsch and Nigel Harris have variously argued, this response has served as what Michel Foucault theorizes as a grid of specificity organizing the work of Western social scientists, aligning and allocating the labor of social scientific disciplines from the 1950s, and enabling the exploitation of the third world despite the avowed good intentions of everyone concerned.[15] Several points are of interest here. From its inception, the term *third world* was central to the emerging discipline of area studies, which was itself of strategic importance to Western intelligence communities at the end of World War II. Third world studies have thus been financed by the same governmental agencies and foundations that supported other branches of area studies whose strategic significance is more immediately visible — communism research and Soviet Union and Eastern European area studies. Furthermore, as Pletsch suggests, the concept of the three worlds is seemingly inseparable from strategies of containment targeting anticapitalist struggles: "It would have been simply impossible to explain the need for foreign aid and vast military expenditures in a time of peace with categories any more differentiated than those marshalled under the three worlds umbrella."[16]

The third world is that which is not the first or the second world, though precariously poised between and sometimes shuttling in and out of those spaces. That is to say, as a precipitate of the imperialist policies of the first two worlds it still carries the residual status of unaligned objects bearing the inscription of those orders it seeks to evade.

Teasing out the ideologies of alterity informing the structural divisions of the three worlds makes visible the contradictions threatening to explode the category "the modern third world." Within this schema, the defining characteristic of the third world is the dominance of the traditional (a euphemism for backwardness) over the modern (as in technological progress). The third world is seen to be ruled by religion, irrationality, superstition, backwardness, underdevelopment, overpopulation, and political chaos. Recent additions to this list are irresponsible nuclear proliferation and reckless destruction of the environment. The second world is modern and technologically advanced; it is rational to a degree but is dragged down by the inefficiency of its authoritarian and repressive government. Its potential is curbed by its ideologically weighted socialist elite. The first world is completely modern, running smoothly on the oiled wheels of scientific and utilitarian decision making. A technological miracle in its efficiency, freedom, and opportunity, it is "in short, a natural society unfettered by religion or ideology."[17] Within this schema, traditional societies are seen as earlier forms of modern societies, awaiting their destiny of modernization. That is, modernization is not incidental or tangential to the three-world scheme; it is a constitutive element of the scheme. It is unnecessary for me to point out the arrogance and ahistoricity of modernization theorists who see their problem-ridden societies as the universal end and goal of history, a view that is ably supported by the Hegelian teleological notion of history.[18]

The division of the world was matched by a corresponding division of labor in the production of knowledge and by a precise distribution of discursive modalities in the knowledges produced. In this ideological order of things, the third world — understood as a space of pure alterity — has been known mostly across the grids of ethnographic description. Consequently, as Pletsch points out, the third world has prompted an "exquisite description of otherness," to which priority theoretical inquiry has traditionally been secondary, especially in the United States and Britain. In contrast, the disciplines of economics, sociology, and political science have been thought to be "scientific" insofar as they "discover" the natural laws of human behavior through studies of the "natural" first world unconstrained by ideology (as in the second world) or erratic culture (as in the third world). Thus, theoretical knowledge is seen to apply only inadequately to the second and third worlds, which seem to demand so many contingent and complex adjustments and variables as to make theory impossible if not irrelevant.

Pletsch's explanation for this trepidation about the relevance of theory in the third world applies to the realm of cultural studies as well. The social scientist's dismissal of anthropological data as outdated and irrelevant to the scientific laws governing the advanced, "natural" societies of the first world translates into the first world cultural theorist's continued eurocentric refusal to deal with the third world. The sense that theory developed in the first world is inapplicable to the third world results in the dismissal of any attempt at theoretical analysis of third world cultures as a wrong-headed instance of cultural imperialism.[19] The rhetoric of resistance to the eurocentricity of theory has somewhat mystified the genealogical history and context that has given rise to the problem in the first place. That is, the problem comes into being at that point where one loses sight of the tropic and discursive histories of analytical categories. The diacritical value of the term third world is precisely to situate it in a postcolonial relation of simultaneous affiliation with and resistance to the first world. As such, the third world is neither radically "other than" nor essentially "the same as" the first world. This liminality does not so much obviate the theoretical enterprise in relation to the third world as demand that theory itself take up the rhetoric and form of the hybrid and the mutant. Such a hybrid theory may not only be more adequate to its object but may also initiate a critical interrogation of its parent stock. The disruption of this neat division of the world by the intrusion of modernity into the third world releases varied and contradictory responses. That is, the long-awaited, much-heralded entry of modernization into the third world precipitates an epistemological crisis that makes visible the ideological investments of the three-world scheme and constructs the modernized third world as a historical or logical contradiction that must be quickly resolved by whatever means necessary.[20] The questions to be asked, then, have to do with the interests served by such constructions of contradictory modernity in the global context and, for the purposes of this essay, in the local context of the emergence and consolidation of nationalist and cultural elites.

In India, discourses of modernization and progress have informed the nationalist agenda from the start. Modernity is seen as that which promises to launch the nation into its rightful place in the international order even as it threatens to disrupt tradition and thereby destroy the nation's distinctive cultural identity. More to the point, the oxymoronic tensions of the modernized third world have gathered around the figure of woman, long hailed as the custodian and symbol of tradition and culture. The problems that have been pointed out about modernization theories — the equation of modernity to Westernization, its inappropriateness to the third world or Indian context, its supportive function in multinational capitalism — have come to be directed against an emergent feminist movement seeking to change traditional patriarchal arrangements, both Western and indigenous. It seems that the hegemonic imbrication of modernization theory with third world studies has so completely taken over our imaginations that it is impossible to conceptualize change in terms other than modernization. So it is that in popular consciousness the chain of signification beginning with the equation of the modern to the Western yokes the urban middle-class woman to sexual stereotypes proliferated through Hollywood-inspired Indian films, "new wave" popular fiction, and advertisement. The modern Indian woman, in such constructions, is associated with a lifestyle that is distinctly marked as opposed to tradition: she is "convent-educated," sometimes even has a degree from a Western university, communicates in English, and is given to flamboyant behavior. In left political discourse, this construction is cross-hatched with the term "bourgeois" to denounce feminism as promoting corruption, idleness, decadence, conspicuous consumption, selfish individualism, and above all, a mindless aping of the foreign (neo)colonial master.[21]

The chain of signification I have just drawn out often signifies power, economic prosperity, and even progressiveness in representations of masculinity. It assumes scandalous proportions only when articulated with femininity. This double standard has prompted Islamic and Hindu fundamentalist revisions of ideologies of womanhood and has informed influential legal and political decisions as in the Shahbano and Roop Kanwar cases.[22] Implicit in conservative outcries against the changing roles of women is an idealization of precolonial India that ignores the feudal, monarchist, caste-based patriarchal societies of the past. Often it is claimed that in these societies women enjoyed rights and privileges they lost with modernization. In other instances such idealized precolonial societies are valorized in the name of order, social stability, and tradition. At this point it becomes clear that the popular denunciation of the Westernized woman secures social values that not only are repressive to women, but that sentimentalize oppressive caste and class hierarchies as well. Thus, the panic over the Westernized woman may well be the latest episode in the tradition of seeing control of women as the distinguishing feature of an ordered and "good" society, such that the management of female sexuality becomes a crucial factor in the maintenance and reproduction of inequality in the name of social order.[23]

MODERNITY AS MELODRAMATIC DESIRE IN K. BALACHANDER'S FILMS

I have suggested that the peculiar constellation of change, modernity, and Westernization around the category "woman" finds its most influential expression in popular cinema and advertising. In this section I would like to traverse quickly through a body of films produced between 1974 and 1989 by K. Balachander, a Tamil film maker who occupies the anomalous position of a director of box-office hits who enjoys a reputation for producing "socially conscious" films. Balachander is peripherally associated with what Aruna Vasudev calls "the new Indian cinema," a growing body of film that is experimental in form and adventurous in the range of issues with which it seeks to engage.[24] His films directly address the status of women in changing family structures; the potential for sexual freedom opened by women's increasing forays into the public sphere as career women, students, and consumers; and the tension between brahminical ideals of art, tradition, and purity, and populist ideals of culture, religious tolerance, and productivity. Balachander's films display all the conventions of melodrama — contrived plotting and coincidences, heavy musical support for dramatic development, and a sharply divided moral universe. They are also remarkable for consistently opening up a space of transgression where dominant ideologies of the patriarchal family, feminine sexuality, and class and caste hierarchies are suspended or even overturned temporarily. Typically, the films displace emblematic figures or symbolic moments of middle-class Indian life into estranging plot situations whereby latent anxieties triggered by social change are brought to the surface. The films thus offer a prolonged exploration of the pleasures and dangers of disorder in the course of which a more "natural" order is arrived at. Whereas in mainstream Indian melodrama the family romance revolves around a privileged male subject who is integrated into the moral universe of patriarchal ideology as a result of his passage through the transgressive experience, Balachander's films center on the position of female subjects in the overturned patriarchal order.[25] In many instances the accession of women into the privilege and power of modernity is set up as the inaugural or catalytic moment of social disorder. The narrative work of containing this disorder is thus not directed at feminine excess per se, but at an excess that is ostensibly fortified and encouraged by modernity. That is to say, melodramatic excess is figured in Balachander's films as the heady mix of the feminine and the modern.

The enabling condition of transgression is the real or symbolic absence of the father. In *Solathan Ninaikiren* (I wish to speak), the father of the three female protagonists is mentally unstable and therefore cannot hold down a job and provide for his family. In *Aval Oru Thodarkathai* (Hers is an unending story), the father has abandoned his family, and the oldest son, who traditionally would be expected to assume responsibility as head of the household, leads a life of drunken wastefulness. The main female characters of *Puthu Puthu Arthangal* (New meanings) and *Sindhu Bhairavi*, who are the most sexually adventurous of all of Balachander's heroines, are illegitimate children who have contact with their mothers but do not know their fathers. Even when tension develops between father and son, as it does in *Apurva Ragangal* (Unusual melodies) and *Unnal Mudiyum Thambi* (Brother, you can do it), it is pushed over the edge into crisis by the presence of fatherless women. The absence of the father is usually exacerbated by the absence of maternal authority as well. These absences clear a space for the destabilization not only of gender but also of age hierarchies. The chaos that ensues is significantly one that occurs in an excessively feminized universe where young women are left uncontrolled or unprotected.

But the transgressive space signified by the misrule of women is not merely one of excessive freedom. It is one in which women have been forced to assume the role of the father, for the films usually depict the women as driven by circumstances to assume responsibility for the family against their desires and indeed their natures. The anxiety generated by the violation of age and gender hierarchies is displayed in the contradictory portrayal of the women as "egotistical, arrogant, proud, vain, tyrannical and yet as life-sustaining as a banyan tree" *(Aval Oru Thodar Kathai)*. Significantly, these women are able to assume positions of power and responsibility because of their marketable education and their wage-earning capacities. At the same time the threat is ever present that they will be overcome by pride or temptation to take the paths of pleasure — conspicuous consumption and sexual freedom — made available to them by their economic independence. While considerable dramatic mileage is gained from this threatening possibility, the films always end with the reintegration of the feminine in its subservient position within the family. For instance, although Manjula, the heroine of *Solathan Ninaikiren*, supports her family and enjoys a certain degree of economic independence by working as a schoolteacher, she finds fulfillment only in marriage — albeit much beneath her class position — to an uneducated cook, a widower who marries her mainly so that she will look after his two children. Manjula's choice is driven by the same ideology Promilla Kapur has uncovered in her case studies of middle-class working women whose income-generating activities are accorded less value than their function as decorative, dependent, and untainted wives.[26] Their efforts as wives and mothers go virtually unrecognized as labor, even as their threatened accession to phallic authority activates the classic overcompensatory masquerade of hyperfemininity.

The anxiety produced by the absent father in the films parallels a growing sense of crisis in India over the status of the law as a code of inheritance and legitimacy. Upon the conventional understanding of the bourgeois woman as the medium of reproduction, legal institutions have established patriarchal authority over women and inscribed children as property bound by the patronymic. Seclusion of women and aggressive control of their movement in the public sphere have been ways of maintaining their role as conduits for property, ensuring paternity, and annexing their productive and reproductive labor to the patriarchal family. However, with the influx of women into the public sphere as workers whose incomes become necessary for family subsistence in an inflationary economy, the policing of women's sexuality becomes less tenable and gives rise to "cultural panic." This reaction is further fueled by recent challenges to existing laws of inheritance and succession, challenges that often call for a common civil code.[27] One outcome of cultural panic is mass sexual violence such as the Pararia rape in Bihar in 1988. As Gita Sen has pointed out, such violence works with chilling efficiency: "It punishes the militant women in the most direct and brutal manner, and it violates the militant men by appropriating the only arena in which they exercise authority — 'their' women."[28] In these and other alarmingly similar instances, the movement of women out of the home has extended and generalized patriarchal authority previously exercised by male members of the family, such that even men outside the kinship network feel themselves invested with the charge and authority to police women once they enter the public sphere. Another form taken by the panic is popular culture's obsession with narratives that underscore the dangers of feminine freedom. Films, in particular, combine the proscription of feminine freedom with a somewhat contradictory sexual objectification of women through gratuitous female nudity and sexual violence. Balachander's films scrupulously set themselves apart from such box-office formulas. Nevertheless, his films follow box-office hits in their rehearsal of narratives of aggressive male control of feminine sexuality.

Most often this control is exercised through marriage. While the ideal of companionate marriage gets short shrift in relation to women, it has come to gain more and more importance in Balachander's later films as an exclusively male need that may perhaps justify the temporary suspension of social and moral codes. *Sindhu Bhairavi* and *Puthu Puthu Arthangal* begin with male protagonists in unhappy marriages with wives who cannot offer them the support, companionship, and inspiration they need to grow in their musical abilities. In the former film the lack is figured as childlessness. In both cases help comes in the form of unattached women who devote themselves body and soul to the regeneration of the male hero's ability to create, procreate, and make money. Significantly the two heroines represent what may be described as modernization with a feminine face. They are educated, culturally informed, witty, and yet nurturing and selfless in their devotion. Having carried out their mission, both heroines voluntarily relinquish their claims and restore the heros to their wives, in one instance with the child the hero could never have in marriage. The ideological function of such narratives becomes evident in the light of feminist analyses that have shown that even when middle-class women rebel against the ideal of feminine domesticity by following careers, whatever prestige they attain as successful professionals, and all the wages they earn, accrue to the male-dominated family.[29] In the two films discussed above, even female transgression is recruited for the benefit of men despite its ultimately having to be cast out of the social and domestic circle.

Common to all of Balachander's heroines is the representation of their freedom, mobility, assertiveness, and above all, their economic independence in terms of the modernity-Westernization equation. All the films have emblematic moments when the heroine puts on lipstick, rides a scooter, or swears in English — all signifiers of Westernization and also of sexual freedom. The anxiety around female autonomy is thus refigured as the disruptive potential of feminine sexuality yoked to Westernization. The flip side of this configuration is the definition of sexual identity within the patriarchal order as authentic cultural identity, such that the woman who refuses to conform to the rules of sexual conduct is seen to reject her ethnic or religious identity as well. Thus, the integrative moment of marriage is usually marked by the heroine discarding her flamboyant signs of Westernization. In *Aval Oru Thodarkathai Kavitha* throws out all her lipsticks when she thinks she is going to get married. There is also a symbolic moment in the film when the hitherto brash heroine is transformed into a demure bride who publicly apologizes for her youthful swearing ways and adopts a respectful demeanor toward her new husband. *Sindhu Bhairavi* ends with the chastised heroine deciding on a self-imposed exile from her hometown and mother, after having given up her illegitimate child to its father. The firm and predictable exclusion of rebellious women from the social circle of family and community in these films parallels the erasure, in modern Indian society, of female subject positions that in earlier historical periods were part of an acceptable liminality. Without comforting links to class, caste, gender, or demarcated space, these positions seem to be too threatening for the modern world.[30]

In their figuring of feminine sexuality, the films also make visible the contradictory claims made upon women by patriarchy and commodity culture. With the growing importance of women's roles as consumers, there is some pressure to make adjustments in traditional constructions of the middle-class woman and allow for her existence as a creature of pleasure. Even so, the tendency is to code the female consumer as emotionally and socially dependent on men despite her economic independence and spending power. So it is that the narrative trajectory of desire, excess, and containment is triggered in *Puthu Puthu Arthangal* by an emblematic moment of the feminine gaze. Gowri, who is coded as a figure of avariciously conspicuous consumption, first sees the hero, Manibharathi, in a commercial for Solidaire TV. Her desire for him is set off by her acquisitive gaze as consumer and as economically able sexual subject. The fact that the object of gaze is male marks a departure from the typical melodramatic moment in which the feminine gaze serves to introduce self-conscious pressure points in the narrative, wherein the gazing woman recognizes herself in the object of her gaze and thereby loses her position as subject.[31] Here, woman as object of cinematic gaze does not provoke any such recognition, and it is the bold revocation of knowledge of woman's objectification compounded by the aggressive objectification of a man that provokes the melodramatic scandal. Gowri's mother goes about procuring Manibharathi for her with the same verve she displays in her shopping sprees. Through a series of ruses, Gowri succeeds in winning Manibharathi's affections. But his status as object of gaze — besides being a model, he is also a popular singer — spurs Gowri on to fits of jealous competition and rage.

As the couple becomes estranged, Gowri shifts her attention to Guru. This shift in interest is visualized as Manibharathi's displacement by Guru as the new Solidaire Hero. The new commercial, which shows Guru aggressively wielding a cricket bat, neatly encapsulates urban bourgeois cultural practices: through fetishized signs of colonialism and technology, the bourgeoisie puts in place gender relations appropriate to an emergent consumer culture, in the process securing its status over an upwardly mobile working class. Guru himself is the object of another woman's desires — he has been carrying on all the while with Krishnaveni, the servant girl in Gowri's household. The transgression of the codes of feminine decorum by Gowri's obsessive desire for Manibharathi is overdetermined in Krishnaveni's case by her class position. The new position of women as consumers whose gaze is encouraged by the commodity culture brings with it a fear that their sexuality may slip free of the tight patriarchal control exercised on them. Gowri's gaze is simultaneously "beneficial" in that she makes a desirable marriage and destructive in that having succeeded once she becomes a compulsive shopper, pursuing more and better objects of gaze. As for Krishnaveni, her gaze is not only a transgression of feminine modesty but also a mark of her danger as a social climber. She has transgressed the bounds of feminine behavior and also overstepped her class position by trespassing on Gowri's turf. The inadmissibility of her desire is evident in the class-inflected containment of feminine excess in the film. Gowri goes insane, gets institutionalized, repents, and is given a new lease on life by Manibharathi, who takes her back as his wife. Disappointed in love, Krishnaveni hangs herself. This incident underscores, albeit unself-consciously, the point that the gains of the upper-class woman are made possible by the extraordinary burden borne by her lower-class double. In making this point, the narrative logic makes visible a gap in feminist film theory that is a legacy of Freudian psychoanalysis. It is now widely acknowledged that the family romance in the Freudian schema is underpinned by specific class arrangements and that if psychoanalytic discourse is to further feminism's political desire, it needs to be infused with a theory of history and the social. The drama of sexuality played out within the heterosexual domains of bourgeois privilege is made possible not only by the suppression of homosexual desire, but also by the class hierarchies informing the Western nuclear family and its sexual division of labor. Because of a reluctance to explore these connections, psychoanalytic discourse has stayed with a more or less monolithic understanding of sexuality despite politically interested attempts to work out difference.[32] Several feminist attempts to engage with the heterogeneity of feminine sexuality have either incorporated the other or have firmly set it aside, as Helena Michie argues.[33] In other instances, as in Michie's own essay, alterity is textualized as a trope. Only recently have feminists begun the work of elaborating the roles of race and class in the construction of sexual subjects and tracing the effects of technologies of desire in constituting race- and class-specific sexual subjects.[34] The distinctly class-differentiated sexualities of Gowri and Krishnaveni attest to the importance of these theoretical interventions.

While the family arrangements and division of labor represented in Balachander's films share much with the Western bourgeois family model, the films are much more up-front about class hierarchies than the melodramas analyzed by Doane and others. Krishnaveni's position, as a member of the servant class whose body is value coded primarily as labor, is underscored early in the film when Gowri's mother shears off her long tresses so that she will spend less time preening herself and attend more fully to her work. This event, however, violently propels Krishnaveni into her other position — that of the master's sexual property. With short hair that makes her look as if she affects a fashionable hairstyle, she becomes doubly threatening: her looks transgress class-differentiated codes of feminine appearance more dramatically than before, and she becomes a rival for the affections of her mistress's fiancé. She is, in other words, the bad consumer who refuses to stay in her place as producer and whose desire is therefore simultaneously coded as social ambition and ressentiment. In contrast, the figuring of Gowri more simply centers around her transgression of marital decorum. The threat represented by Krishnaveni seems too powerful to be contained even by the trope of suicide. Krishnaveni stages her suicide on the marriage dais the morning of Gowri's wedding, prefiguring and precipitating Gowri's own psychic death in marriage. Strangely, the suicide scene is not given the time and prominence it usually receives in traditional melodrama. Instead, the almost documentary austerity with which it is presented disrupts the continuity of melodramatic emotion and introduces an affecting moment of social critique. That is, even though the film does not make any explicit commentary on the deeply rooted social arrangements that push Krishnaveni to her fate, and even though the film itself is implicated in these oppressive systems, the way the camera lingers on her body and the use of traditional mourning music catapult this scene out of the melodramatic frame. Fashioned this way, the scene becomes an aporetic moment whose emotional charge exceeds and escapes the narrative logic toward closure and reinstitution of the patriarchal order, as the extremity of Krishnaveni's fate resists justification.

Against such moments, Balachander's films manage feminine sexuality in such a way that "productive" sexuality is winnowed out from "unproductive" sexual pleasure. While the pleasures of unrestrained and forbidden sexuality are given free play temporarily, the salubrious effects of the play attach themselves only to the men. The feminine is always exiled at the end of the carnival. The value of modernity in woman — her salary, the improved standard of living she facilitates, and her intellectual stimulus — are shepherded into the fold of the patriarchal family. Equally, modernity is shown to give more grief than benefit when it is assumed by members of the working class. Repeatedly the grand narrative of the priority of family welfare over personal autonomy is rehearsed as the opposition between the modern and the traditional is superimposed on the public/private division. Thus, while the modern woman is permitted or even encouraged in her activities in the public sphere as worker or consumer, she is expected to maintain a traditional purity in her roles as daughter, wife, and mother in the private sphere. Critics have pointed out that melodrama posits not an advance into a revolutionary future, but a return to a glorious past.[35] Balachander's films, however, celebrate a modern technological future fortified by the patriarchal traditions of a sentimentalized past. In so doing they participate in what Ashish Rajadhyaksha has aptly termed the "feudalist modernism" of contemporary Indian culture.

Balachander's melodramas install their class-differentiated ideology of modern femininity in a context where cinema is seen not merely as entertainment but as information and education, as an essential support for a developing economy and progressive society. As such, film, in general, functions to create "an economic proletariat that is culturally lumpenized."[36] The specifically urban middle-class dilemmas and ideologies explored in Balachander's films are thus disseminated in universalized form among the urban and rural proletariat who comprise the majority of their audience. Without their economic and political support, these bourgeois ideologies heighten the oppression of working-class women. In sum, the consistent devaluation of female labor in these films affects not only the middle class but also feeds into the process traced by Kalpana Bardhan by which aggressive modernization in agriculture and industry has led to the feminization of the proletariat, has swelled the casual-labor work force, thereby driving down wages, and has tempered working-class insurgency by heightening job insecurity. In their class-selective allocation of feminine agency, Balachander's films foreground the connection between the deployment of sexuality and the value of women as producers, which mostly remains hidden in Western cultural productions.

FILM THEORY AND THIRD WORLD FILM— CRITICAL INTERROGATIONS

Various feminist theorists suggest that speaking and seeing are subversive and emancipatory gestures of and by themselves for women. However, my discussion of Balachander's films suggests that such gestures, at their best, momentarily make visible the interconnected networks of patriarchal and capitalist arrangements. The subversive potential of these gestures is transitory and localized, for as I suggest above, they often serve as cultural safety valves, as controlled explorations of women's changing social roles explicitly aimed at reconciling change with patriarchal values. Unless these moments initiate a critique of the far-spreading and interrelated systems between and within which women are caught, and until they bring forth radical and counterhegemonic narratives in film as well as in critical analysis, their political potential will be libertarian at best, collaborative at worst. This is an important limitation of existing theoretical analyses of melodrama thrown into relief by popular Indian cinema.

Feminist attempts to elaborate upon the ideological work of melodrama in interpellating acquiescent and resisting subjects of patriarchy have often stayed on the tracks laid by *Screen* theory. Starting with Laura Mulvey's important and influential essay, "Visual Pleasure and Narrative Cinema," *Screen* theory assigns a privileged status to psychoanalysis as a discourse uniquely suited for feminist investigations of cinema.[37] This emphasis has remained despite the inflections introduced by semiotics and Althusserian Marxism. Attempts to delineate the work of film apparatus in interpellating viewers and to elaborate the narrative codes of cinema have been underwritten by the Lacanian emphasis on the look and the gaze as constitutive features of the coherence of the subject in the imaginary. As a result, while filmic representation has been understood as a compulsive psychic mechanism cathected on the female figure, a full-blown account locating libidinal investments in relation to representation — understood as an ideologically effective social activity — has been slow in coming.[38] In film theory the universalist notion of the subject in psychoanalysis usually combines with the formalist and taxonomic preoccupations of semiotics to write out historical/cultural/racial difference.

A notable exception to this trend is Mary Ann Doane's *The Desire to Desire*, which sets out to analyze female spectatorship by drawing upon Freudian and Marxian accounts of fetishism. The resulting account exemplifies the wealth of material to be uncovered when one begins with the acknowledgement that films do not operate in some autonomous and isolated psychic space, but address women in diverse and specific social positions. But even here Freudian psychoanalysis's indifference to class- and race-specific constructions of identity seems to introduce a restrictive inertia. While Doane sets for herself the project of charting the historical mutations of the subject of film, her exclusive focus on the women's activities as gazers takes her only as far as to account for the intersections between women's positions as sexual objects and their emergent roles as consumers. Still in the shadows is the link between female spectatorship and women's class-differentiated value as producers following their historically significant movement into the workplace in the forties.

Long identified as a founding genre in Hollywood cinema, melodrama is significantly invested in framing the feminine. Doane's investigations of this genre lead her to conclude that over and over again the "tropes of female spectatorship are not empowering" in women's film of the 1940s because the female gaze is constituted in such a way that as a woman watches scenes of women gazing or being gazed at, she becomes the image she sees as a spectator.[39] That is, woman's position as object of gaze is reinforced by her participation in the spectacle as a consumer-subject. This erasure of a potentially empowering subject position and the repeated withdrawal of the space of active critical spectatorship results in female spectators continually finding themselves pushed into "non-places."[40] This movement is overdetermined by the narrative logic of melodramatic films that, with relentless predictability, develop ingenious and complex ways to obliterate violently woman's gaze. Insistently, female gaze is figured as leading to disastrous consequences and is invariably punished by disfigurement, insanity, death, or marriage. However, Doane does not explore the differences between the voyeuristic privileges of black women and white women, or for that matter between women regardless of race and black men. In the absence of a systematic reading of the melodramas in their full sociohistorical context, universalist assumptions of both Freud and Marx creep back into her arguments. Doane is thus left with the conclusion that female desire, regardless of its location in specific racial or class contexts, is cut off such that women are left with no position of voyeuristic knowledge within woman's film: "Woman's exercise of an active investigating gaze can only be simultaneous with her own victimization."[41] Judith Mayne echoes this argument in her analysis that the woman at the keyhole, looking inside or outside, always invites patriarchal suppression. Thus, in theories of melodrama, as in the melodramas themselves, the feminine is constructed as an excess, intransigent even to feminist desire for empowered agency.

An apparently opposing argument is advanced by Geoffrey Nowell-Smith and Thomas Elsaesser in their argument that melodramatic excess carries with it a radical potential to disrupt the smooth regime of the bourgeois-patriarchal discourses that constitute narrative cinema in general.[42] Thus, whereas Doane finds the situation uniformly hopeless for the female spectator, these theorists are equally and oppositely sanguine about the subversive potential of melodramatic film. They posit the feminine in melodrama as a radical alterity, inaccessible to patriarchal discourse. But in so doing they dematerialize "woman." Not only — as Doane, Mellencamp, and Williams charge — do they overlook the contradictory positioning of woman as supportive and disruptive of patriarchal interests, but they also stop short of wrestling with the more difficult issue of melodrama's effectivity as radical cultural politics. The question remains whether images of irrepressible feminine excess can bring about a critical consciousness of patriarchy and thereby move spectators from disruptive pleasures to a commitment to social change.[43] Common to both camps is the heritage of the universalist subject of psychoanalysis, which blurs the historical specificity each seeks and which forces a homogenizing construction of feminine excess.

As a consequence of this line of theorizing, feminist film theorists find themselves in a double bind that Doane, Mellencamp, and Williams have characterized as follows in their introduction to *Re-Vision:* "The choice appears to be a not very attractive one between a continual repetition of the same gesture of demystification (itself perhaps mystified as to its methodological heritage) and a possible regression to ideas of feminine identity which threaten to constitute a veritable re-mystification."[44] Feminist theory has been definitely moving away from the first choice over the past decade. In trying to avoid the second choice, feminist theorists have sometimes resisted attributing any single position or identity to woman and instead have celebrated a multiplicity and dispersal of difference. If the project of feminist theory is to create a space where feminist film and epistemology will flourish and oppressive sexual and gender hierarchies will disappear, then feminist film theory must enact an engagement with its margins rather than simply permit a proliferation of difference in a move reminiscent of the more obviously sinister policy of "benign neglect."[45] Attending to the historically and contextually shifting effects introduced by race and class into the filmic configuration of the feminine would, I suggest, permit a re-vision of the picture of feminine excess and its containment that steers between the two extremes of monolithic and dispersed feminine subjectivity.

On the other hand the movement of film theory into one such site of difference, the third world, has not been smooth. Critics of third world cinema have long resisted theories based on Hollywood film on the ground that they are inapplicable, if not irrelevant, to the alternative cinema into which third world cinema in general is often elided. While the charge of ethnocentrism is undoubtedly serious and cannot easily be set aside, all too often it serves to mystify the prior importation of Hollywood structures of spectacle, desire, and subjectivity through the apparatus of film into the third world. That is, it is somewhat belated to rail upon the theory for its ethnocentrism when the object that is elucidated — the narratives, traditions, and mechanisms of film, its material relations of production and circulation, and the modality of spectatorship it presumes — often install a subject closely modeled on the Western bourgeois male. In arguing that Western theory may indeed be useful to analyze Hollywood-inspired third world film, I am not making a truth claim for theory but only suggesting that its epistemological dependence on the films it elucidates makes it applicable to third world takes on Hollywood genres. It is also to be hoped that the theory will be reprocessed, rearticulated, and more finely tuned through its migratory movements such that it can better account for the workings of Hollywood cinema.

Rosie Thomas's important discussion of popular cinema in her essay, "Indian Cinema: Pleasures and Popularity," introduces *Screen* readers to one such negotiation between theoretical frameworks developed in the West and the social contexts of mainstream Indian cinema.[46] Arguing that it would be a mistake to superciliously dismiss the escapism of Indian films, Thomas draws out the relevance of *Screen* theory's emphasis on cinematic apparatus and mechanisms of pleasure to Indian cinema. The pleasure of Indian film, Thomas demonstrates, derives both from the proliferation of spectacle and from the reassuring familiarity of narrative structures drawn from mythological and folk traditions. Verisimilitude is not particularly striven for, and cinema moves the spectator through a variety of aesthetically prescribed emotional moments instead of providing a sense of realistic coherence. But what Thomas overlooks is that the disavowal of verisimilitude does not involve a concomitant abandoning of normative values. That is, pleasure takes historically specific forms and carries specific ideological content: for instance, the decrease in dream sequences based on mythological themes and the increasing popularity of dance sequences choreographed closely along the styles set by Michael Jackson, Madonna, and recently MC Hammer parallel the growing claims of American-style commodity aesthetics on the popular imaginary. Furthermore, mythological themes, when adopted, often serve as vehicles of social and political commentary. Pleasure also serves to mask gender and class norms, which are continually updated and disseminated through film.[47] In its emphasis on pleasure as an ahistorical constant, Thomas's application of *Screen* theory to Indian cinema stays close to the very ethnocentrism she sets out to critique.

Similarly, Ravi Vasudevan argues that melodramatic film is a genre that structures expectations and conventions in a fairly predictable manner and that it remained virtually unchanged between the years 1935 and 1982, a period during which the social formation in India was racked by partition, decolonization, rapid industrialization, and most recently by the consolidation of a consumer economy secured by the culture of spectacle. Like Thomas, Vasudevan begins by marking the differences between the aesthetic theory underpinning Indian cinema and the Aristotelian poetics associated with Western linear narratives. Relying heavily on psychoanalytic discourse and Peter Brooks's account of the emergence of melodrama as a counternarrative to realism, Vasudevan reads Indian melodrama as an unchanging narrative in which the male subject enacts transgressive fantasies primarily around conflict with the father.[48] The feminine, he argues, is always subordinated to a narrative logic that reinforces a narcissistic male subject. Furthermore, in a move that rehearses the subordination of the feminine he locates in the film, Vasudevan only attends to the figuration of the maternal. When forced by his cinematic texts to deal with the question of feminine sexuality, he argues that the spectacular demonstration of feminine sexuality, so often a central component of melodrama, assumes glamorous proportions and so slips free of the narrative's control. Thus, though the logic of melodrama demands that the spectacular display of feminine sexuality be punished or redeemed by death, the image of the sensual or the glamorous exceeds and outlives the narrative closure as an indelible erotic trace. This excess, Vasudevan asserts, constitutes a subversion of masculine privilege.[49]

Vasudevan's elision of history is based on a strategic misreading of Peter Brooks's account of the modern melodrama. Brooks traces the gradual process by which modern melodrama moves away from the metaphysical dilemmas characteristic of Victorian melodramas and toward tensions similar to those at the center of contemporary discourses such as psychoanalysis, medical ethics, politics, and feminism. That is, in Brooks's account, melodrama participates in the epistemic shifts associated with modernity. Similarly, in Indian melodrama, the generational conflict that Vasudevan ably traces between the bad father and his rebel son, the sacrificing mother and the selfish "other woman," must be seen as inflected with contemporary discourses on politics, education, work ethic, self-help, anti-Brahminism, and feminism, among others. Brooks claims that melodramas owe their success to their ability to make the world "morally legible" by drawing out into the open and articulating the fears, desires, and value systems remaining unvoiced in public discourse.[50] Furthermore, melodramas themselves encourage an understanding of their driving tensions as products of social arrangements rather than of private or individual motives. This imbrication of melodrama in social discourses makes it a site where the exploitative and oppressive structures of a society are particularly visible. My analysis shows that Brooks's notion of moral legibility translates invariably into patriarchal reaction in Balachander's films. Since female excess is rendered legible within patriarchal frames of intelligibility, the films participate in mystifying ideology as the moral and the natural order of things. The clear hierarchy of punishment in the narrative management of feminine excess in *Puthu Puthu Arthangal* makes visible certain nuances that all the theorists of melodrama we have seen so far are unable to bring out clearly. In contrast to Doane's reading of the operation of the gaze, we see in this film a significantly differentiated withdrawal of power from women on the basis of their class positions. Furthermore, the structure and logic of looking works in ways more varied than the securing or barring of woman as mother that Vasudevan has analyzed so convincingly. Balachander's films allow women various situations where they can look and know, suggesting that the concern has shifted away from a univocal proscription to a complexly nuanced range of control and permission of the feminine gaze. The varied trajectories of the gaze also suggest that the gender ideology informing films seeks to accommodate, acknowledge, and perhaps even feels some pressure to encourage women in roles beyond the maternal, roles that are nonetheless subject to patriarchal control.

The entanglement of the surreptitious look in the disciplining of everyday life was gender inflected for me, as I suspect it is for many women in my position, by stories from Hindu scriptures of women like Ahalya, who was turned to stone for unwittingly desiring the God Indra, who came to her looking like her husband; or of Renuka, who met a gruesome end in the hands of her axe-wielding son for momentarily admiring the reflected image of a gandharva. The pleasure and danger of looking emblematized in such scenes has been evoked and disseminated repeatedly in updated forms in recent times, their power and influence technologically augmented in television and film. However, the impulse to focus entirely on the ideological continuum such scenes derive from and consolidate runs the risk of mystifying the historically specific functions they carry out. And it is an interest in the changing political contents of such moments of forbidden gaze, especially as they are framed in melodramatic cinema, that guides the larger trajectory of this essay.

It must be acknowledged, however, that the meticulous logic of patriarchy is somewhat disturbed by what may be called the supplementary effects of the image. All the actresses who play the tragic heroines of Balachander's films have gone on to become stars, whose celebrity effect resists and overcomes the narrative suppression of their characters. The blurring of the distinction between star and character often results in certain figures attaining fame or notoriety despite being rigorously disciplined within the narrative logic. Dissatisfaction or disappointment at the narrative closure of a particular actress's role sometimes spoils the satisfaction offered by fulfilled expectation and patriarchal order. The reassurance offered by the restoration of order is also undercut by the residual effects of music and dance, where it is not the woman only who is the object of gaze. In almost all of Balachander's films, women's songs exceed and escape the repressive logic of the narrative.

The haunting effect of the songs, which assume a formidable life of their own as they linger on people's lips and crowd the airwaves, resists the containment of female voice and agency in the films. The insidious workings of songs about feminine desire, freedom, and power owe much to the centrality of music in Indian dramatic traditions. But augmented by technologies of broadcasting and replication, songs become meanings that move, in every sense of the word. And so they serve to open up the closures effected in the name of authenticity and tradition. In this we can see an encouraging analogue to the persistence and growing vitality of feminist discourses in India despite the various attempts to discredit them. In the wide spectrum of situations we have analyzed, the project of third world feminism is continuously harassed. The silencing of feminist voices by tokenizing invocations of the marginalized other, the construction of feminists as decadent and Westernized, the invention of female submissiveness as tradition, are all strategies that crop up in intellectual and political debate, strategies that in one way or another construct feminism as excess. These strategies are given even more emotionally compelling form in the popular cultural productions. Fending off these constructions, we find that we cannot always count on an easier time in our engagements with Western feminist discourses, whose reliance on the ideological preconstructions of third-worldism often undermines their attempts to deal with alterity in its modern aspects. Just as the three-world schema makes it difficult to engage with modernity in the third world in terms other than contradiction and crisis, so too do melodramatic constructions of femininity prevent the understanding of change as anything other than social disorder. The circulation of "authenticity" and "tradition" as normative values in both third-worldist and melodramatic narratives, and the association of these values with ideals of femininity, make the triangulated relations between "third world," "modernity," and "woman" an important area of feminist inquiry. What persists is the realization that the history of feminism is inseparable from the history of antifeminist politics. At the same time feminism's agonistic relation to various other political agendas suggests that feminist politics cannot be directed against patriarchy alone but must also take on other social arrangements positioning women. In following this political imperative, feminist modes of analysis can take inspiration from theories of reading variously described as "transdisciplinarity," "cognitive mapping," and " 'border' studies," all of which run the risk of seeming to "do too much," or to be excessively ambitious in trying to trace the connections between technologies of knowledge, technologies of desire, and the economic and political arrangements positioning gendered subjects.[51]

NOTES

I thank Priti Ramamurthy, Robyn Weigman, Laurie Hart, Samir Dayal, and the anonymous reviewer for *Genders* for their insightful critiques of this essay during its various stages of development.

1. See Homi Bhabha, "The Other Question . . ." *Screen* 24, no. 6 (1983): 18–36. Bhabha has advanced a suggestive account of the fetishistic construction of the "other" in colonial discourses whereby the psychic and ideological satisfaction of the fetish is simultaneously promised and withdrawn. Between the acknowledgment and disavowal of the other, Bhabha argues, a hybrid resisting subjectivity emerges that throws colonial discourse into disarray. Framing the question of alterity within feminism in terms of "women of color" has ironically contributed to a similar fetishism in academic feminist discourse, which simultaneously allows and refuses alterity: by privileging color as the overarching index of otherness, this move metonymically acknowledges the heterogeneity glossed over by the category "woman." At the same time the move merely defers the homogenizing impulse momentarily, because color serves as a metonymic shorthand for the complex articulation of class, sexuality, and nationality with gender. The struggles within NWSA conventions dramatize the resistance provoked by this oscillation as well as the agonistic emergence of a hybrid feminism that negotiates and reworks the oppositions white/colored, straight/lesbian, and bourgeois/working class. See *Bridges of Power: Women's Multicultural Alliances*, ed. Lisa Albrecht and Rose M. Brewer (Philadelphia: New Society, 1990), especially Gloria Anzaldúa, "Bridge, Drawbridge, Sandbar or Island Lesbians-of-Color Hacienda Alianzas," 216–31.
2. See Gayatri Chakravorty Spivak, "French Feminism in an International Frame," in *In Other Worlds* (London: Routledge, 1988); and Spivak, "A Literary Representation of the Subaltern: A Woman's Text from the Third World," in *In Other Worlds*, 241–68.
3. Kumari Jayawardena, *Feminism and Nationalism in the Third World* (London: Zed, 1986); Madhu Kishwar, introduction to *In Search of Answers*, ed. Kishwar and Ruth Vanita (London: Zed, 1984), 1–48.
4. I am grateful to Samir Dayal for pointing out the indeterminacy of the authentic and the consequent ineffectuality of any critique based on its value.
5. See Gloria Anzaldúa and Cherrie Morraga, eds. *This Bridge Called My Back: Writings by Radical Women of Color* (Watertown, Mass: Persephone, 1981). The continued relevance of these essays after a decade points, more than anything else, to the persistence of this problem, sometimes in new guises.
6. See Maria Mies, *Patriarchy and Accumulation on a World Scale* (London: Zed, 1986); Jennifer Wicke, "Postmodernism: The Perfume of Information," *Yale Journal of Criticism* 1, no. 2 (1988): 145–60.

7. In India, for instance, the linkages between metropolitan and third world feminist struggles were established as early as the nineteenth century, when attitudes of colonial policymakers were directly shaped by conservative reaction to feminist agitation in Britain. See Kumkum Sangari and Sudesh Vaid, introduction to *Recasting Women*, ed. Sangari and Vaid (New Brunswick, N.J.: Rutgers University Press, 1989), 7.
8. Jayawardena, *Feminism*.
9. For a suggestive discussion of the unexpected parallels between arguments about the Western origins of women's struggle and the linear stages of development narrative, see Barbara Harlow, "Commentary: 'All That Is Inside Is Not Center': Responses to the Discourses of Domination," in *Coming to Terms: Feminism, Theory, Politics*, ed. Elizabeth Weed (New York: Routledge, 1989), 162–70.
10. See Gail Omvedt, "Feminism and the Women's Movement in India," Working Paper no. 16 (Bombay: Shreemati Nathibai Damodar Thackersey [SNDT] Women's University, 1987); Madhu Kishwar, introduction to *In Search of Answers*; Jana Matson Everett, *Women and Social Change in India* (New York: St Martin's, 1979).
11. The feminist monthly *Manushi* and the recent collection of essays *Recasting Women*, ed. Sangari and Vaid, are influential instances of this discursive shift, wrought more by powerful instances of subaltern resistance and insurgency than by left critiques of bourgeois intellectual predilections. Also see Gail Omvedt, Chetna Gala, and Govind Kelkar, "Unity and Struggle: A Report on Nari Mukti Sangarsh Sammelan," *Economic and Political Weekly* 23, no. 18 (1988): 883–86, for an account of Nari Mukti Sangarsh Sammelan's attempt in 1988 to bring together in dialogue feminist groups occupying diverse political spaces.
12. While traditionally the role played by Western feminist, colonialist, nationalist, and indigenous patriarchal discourses in forging feminist discourse has received more coverage, recent studies have done much to draw attention to the histories of subaltern resistance and in doing so have altered the narratives of feminist politics in India. See, for instance, Indra Munshi Saldhana, "Tribal Women in the Warli Revolt, 1945–47: Class and Gender in the Left Perspective," *Review of Women's Studies, Economic and Political Weekly* 21, no. 17 (1986): 41–52; Peter Custers, *Women in the Tebhaga Uprising* (Calcutta: Noya Prokash, 1987); Stree Shakti Sanghatana, *We Were Making History* (New Delhi: Kali for Women, 1989).
13. Kalpana Bardhan, "Women: Work, Welfare and Status: Forces of Tradition and Change in India," *South Asia Bulletin* 6, no. 1 (1986): 3.
14. For a suggestive reference to the erosion of women's rights wrought by what is termed the "realism" of the law in Pakistan that shares many of the historical factors discussed in relation to the Indian context, see Sara Suleri, "Woman Skin Deep: Feminism and the Postcolonial Condition," *Critical Inquiry* 18 (1992): 756–69.
15. Michel Foucault, *The Archeology of Knowledge*, trans. A. Sheridan Smith (New

York: Pantheon, 1972); Nigel Harris, "Third Worldism," in *The End of the Third World* (Harmondsworth, Middlesex: Penguin, 1986), 11–29; Carl E. Pletsch, "The Three Worlds, or the Division of Social Scientific Labor, circa 1950–1975," *Comparative Studies in Society and History* 23, no. 4 (1981): 565–90.
16. Pletsch, "The Three Worlds," 575.
17. Ibid., 574.
18. For a thoughtful discussion of the philosophical and political ramifications of Hegelian theories of history and recent attempts to circumvent teleology, see Robert Young, *White Mythologies: Writing History and the West* (London: Routledge, 1990).
19. See Homi Bhabha, "The Commitment to Theory," *New Formations* 5 (1988): 5–24, for a discussion of this impasse of theory in debates on third world cinema. Indeed this impasse seems to be occasioned by a relatively greater theoretical self-consciousness than is found usually in analysis of the third world. For instance, several feminists have pointed out that Western feminist attempts to address difference have been deflected from their course by Eurocentric, universalist, and homogenizing constructions of third world women. See, for instance, Marnia Lazreg, "Feminism and Difference: The Perils of Writing as a Woman on Women in Algeria," *Feminist Studies* 14, no. 1 (1988): 81–107; Chandra Talpade Mohanty, "Under Western Eyes: Feminist Scholarship and Colonial Discourses," in *Third World Women and the Politics of Feminism*, ed. Mohanty, Ann Russo, and Lourdes Torres (Bloomington: Indiana University Press, 1991), 51–80.
20. For a quick summary of the many unsatisfactory attempts to explain and forecast modernization in the third world, see Nigel Harris, "Third Worldism." Harris's account suggests a counterpoint to metropolitan exasperation at the intransigency of the third world to systematic development. Instead of taking the dislocation of development efforts as a confirmation of the intuitive truth of the three-world schema, we may view this dislocation as a symptom of fundamental flaws in theories of development and modernization that were formulated in the West to account for a process of economic growth and rationalization that was fed to a large degree by the invisible flow of capital accrued through imperialist and neoimperialist practices whose residual mark is precisely the third world's supposed resistance to development. The repressed returns, and the other refuses to play by the rules and remain in uncontaminated alterity. The material consequences of the epistemological crisis provoked by the modernized third world were tragically demonstrated by the Gulf War, when Iraq's dramatic modernization drew retributory fire that, we were repeatedly assured, "bombed it back to the dark ages." This essay was written before the dramatic events in Eastern Europe. It remains to be seen whether the new world order is not a retooled three-world schema, since Robert Gates's confirmation and the storm over Bill Clinton's visit to Moscow indicate that the institutional and discursive apparatus put in place under that schema is not about to be shut down.

21. A striking instance of the recruitment of the image of feminism as an invitation to conspicuous consumption is the recent launching of an Indian cigarette for women, with the brand name Ms, the advertisement for which celebrates women who are "not subservient, not coquettish, not wily, not other-worldly pure . . . not as men have traditionally thought them to be." Such constructions seem to have provoked widespread panic reactions and have been invoked even within left intellectual circles to suppress feminist claims. See Kumari Jayawardena, "Some Comments on Feminism and the Left in South Asia," *South Asia Bulletin* 8 (1988): 88–91.
22. Fundamentalism, as an ideology that exerts particular influence on Indian politics and government policy, gathered strength at the same time that efforts to integrate women into development through education and vocational training brought them in large numbers to the workplace. As the exigencies of life and employment in an increasingly capitalist society weaken the hold of traditional patriarchal control over women's lives, fundamentalism reasserts traditional controls and in doing so recruits women's labor, fertility, and sexuality to serve capitalist and patriarchal interests. For a detailed account of the role of fundamentalism in India see Amrita Chhachhi, "The State, Religious Fundamentalism, and Women: Trends in South Asia," *Economic and Political Weekly* 21, no. 11 (1989), 567–78; for an account of two recent and much-publicized instances of fundamentalist intervention in state policy, see Imrana Quadeer, "Roop Kanwar and Shabano," *Seminar* 342 (1988).
23. See Sangari and Vaid, eds., *Recasting Women*, 5–10.
24. Aruna Vasudev, *The New Indian Cinema* (New Delhi: Macmillan, 1986).
25. For an account of box-office melodrama in India, see Ravi Vasudevan, "The Melodramatic Mode and the Commercial Hindi Cinema," *Screen* 30, no. 3 (1989): 29–50.
26. Promilla Kapur, *Marriage and the Working Woman in India* (New Delhi: Vikas, 1970).
27. See Indira Jaising, "Women and Law," in *A Decade of Women's Movement in India*, ed. Neera Desai (Bombay: Himalaya, 1988), 45–59. For an account of the various means by which patriarchal interests have repeatedly prevailed against legislation on the inheritance rights of women such that women of landowning classes as well as of the entrepreneurial urban educated classes have been, in effect, barred from property ownership, see Maria Mies, *Indian Women and Patriarchy* (New Delhi: Concept, 1980), 62–65.
28. Gita Sen, "Subordination and Sexual Control: A Comparative View of the Control of Women," *Review of Radical Political Economics* 16, no. 1 (1984): 139.
29. Joanna Liddle and Rama Joshi, *Daughters of Independence* (London: Zed, 1986), 89–112.
30. Sangari and Vaid, *Recasting Women*, 12.
31. See Mary Ann Doane, *The Desire to Desire: The Woman's Film of the 1940s* (Bloomington: Indiana University Press, 1987); Christine Gledhill, "Develop-

ments in Feminist Film Criticism," in *Re-Vision: Essays in Feminist Film Criticism*, ed. Mary Ann Doane, Patricia Mellencamp, and Linda Williams (Los Angeles: American Film Institute, 1984), 18–48; Judith Mayne, "The Woman at the Keyhole: Women's Cinema and Feminist Criticism," in *Re-Vision*, ed. Doane, Mellencamp, and Williams, 49–66.
32. For critiques of the limitations of the psychoanalytic concept of sexual difference in explaining racial and class difference in sexuality, and suggestive attempts to theorize sexuality in ways that overcome these limitations, see Jane Gaines, "White Privilege and Looking Relations: Race and Gender in Feminist Film Theory," *Screen* 29, no. 4 (1988): 12–27; Elizabeth Abel, "Race, Class, and Psychoanalysis? Opening Questions," in *Conflicts in Feminism*, ed. Marianne Hirsch and Evelyn Fox Keller (London: Routledge, 1990), 184–204.
33. See Helena Michie, "Not One of the Family: The Repression of the Other Woman in Feminist Theory," in *Discontented Discourses: Feminism/Textual Intervention/Psychoanalysis*, ed. Marleen S. Barr and Richard Feldstein (Chicago: University of Illinois Press, 1989), 15–28.
34. For two particularly compelling analyses along these lines, see Hortense Spillers, "Mama's Baby, Papa's Maybe: An American Grammar Book," *Diacritics* 17, no. 2 (1987): 65–81; Carolyn Kay Steedman, *Landscape for a Good Woman: A Story of Two Lives* (New Brunswick: Rutgers University Press, 1987).
35. See Ashish Rajadhyaksha, "Neo-Traditionalism: Film as Popular Art in India," *Framework* 32/33 (1986): 20–67.
36. Ibid., 31.
37. Laura Mulvey, "Visual Pleasure and Narrative Cinema," *Screen* 16, no. 3 (1975): 6–18.
38. For a sustained critical account of feminist film criticism, see Gledhill, "Developments in Feminist Film Criticism."
39. Doane, *The Desire to Desire*, 9.
40. Ibid., 12.
41. Mary Ann Doane, "The 'Woman's Film': Possession and Address," *Re-Vision*, ed. Doane, Mellencamp, and Williams, 72.
42. Thomas Elsaesser, "Tales of Sound and Fury: Observations on the Family Melodrama," in *Home Is Where the Heart Is: Studies in Melodrama and Women's Film*, ed. Christine Gledhill (London: British Film Institute, 1987), 43–69; Geoffrey Nowell-Smith, "Minelli and Melodrama," in *Home Is Where the Heart Is*, ed. Gledhill, 70–74.
43. Mary Ann Doane, Patricia Mellencamp, and Linda Williams, "Feminist Film Criticism: An Introduction," in *Re-Vision*, ed. Doane, Mellencamp, and Williams, 12.
44. Ibid., 9.
45. See Teresa Ebert, "The 'Difference' of Postmodern Feminism" *College English* 53, no. 8 (1991): 886–904, for an exploration of the ways difference has been recuperated by feminism.

46. Rosie Thomas, "Indian Cinema – Pleasures and Popularity," *Screen* 26, nos. 3–4 (1985): 116–32.
47. For a critique of the ways arguments about pleasure dehistoricize and therefore mystify the operations of power, see Rajadhyaksha, "Neotraditionalism."
48. Ravi Vasudevan, "The Melodramatic Mode"; Peter Brooks, *The Melodramatic Imagination: Balzac, Henry James, Melodrama and the Mode of Excess* (New Haven: Yale University Press, 1976).
49. Vasudevan, "Melodramatic Mode," 46.
50. Brooks, *Melodramatic Imagination*, 42.
51. See Fredric Jameson, "Cognitive Mapping," in *Marxism and the Interpretation of Culture*, ed. Cary Nelson and Lawrence Grossberg (Chicago: University of Illinois Press, 1988), 347–57; Paula Gunn Allen, "'Border' Studies: The Intersection of Gender and Color," in *Introduction to Scholarship in Modern Languages and Literatures*, ed. Joseph Gibaldi (New York: MLA, 1992), 303–19; for a discussion of transdisciplinarity, see Mas'ud Zavarzadeh and Donald Morton, "Theory Pedagogy Politics: The Crisis of 'The Subject' in the Humanities" in their *Theory/Pedagogy/Politics: Texts for Change* (Chicago: University of Illinois Press, 1991), 10.

TEN

Zero-Degree Deviancy: *Lesbians Who Kill*

Lynda Hart

> Murder is where history and crime intersect. . . . Murder establishes the ambiguity of the lawful and the unlawful.
> — Michel Foucault, *I Pierre Riviere, Having Slaughtered My Mother, My Sister, and My Brother*

In *Lesbians Who Kill*, Deb Margolin's wry philosophical bent creates a dissident space of mimicry for Split Britches butch/femme performers Peggy Shaw and Lois Weaver to play out their seductions. May (Weaver) and June (Shaw) abandon their house because it attracts lightning. While they wait out a thunderstorm in their car, they divine ways to kill time. "Making time" with men, their eyes are as "open as bulletholes looking right at" [each other] as they kiss the men they dream of killing. Wanting to be remembered, they "kiss for memory . . . before fall[ing] into history."[1] Their kiss marks the hope of being together in the impossible present tense.

History is being made all around them while their desire grows in the garden where May plants seeds in the middle of the night when she cannot sleep. By the railroad tracks they pick wild raspberries in the dark. Crouched down in the "mouth of an animal" where the raspberries are hidden, May sucks June's fingers bruised by the brambles. All of this reads like a dream for June, but May insists that she never dreams, and June tries to believe her.

Lesbians Who Kill carves out a space in which the impossible-real of May and June's desire is an article of faith that can almost be believed for the few hours that we are drawn into their performance. Almost, but always not quite. Something is always obstructing their/our vision. Vision itself is a barrier that reminds us that desire is always the desire of the Other. These lovers' desire is fueled by their rage against the repetitions of history into which they are inevitably falling. They kill time by playing a word game — "looks like/is like." It works like this:

> You pick a thing, and then you think of all the things that look like it or are like it, and if the other person doesn't understand why you think that, they can ask you for an explanation. And if you can make any sense out of it for them, they lose! You have to tell them: does it *look* like the original thing, or is it like that thing in some *invisible* way? And if you're on to something that they couldn't see, they lose! The minute it makes sense to them. They lose everything! And then you start up all over again.

Losing the game is the promise of continuance. The failure to see, and thus to know, insures their relationship. May and June depend on accepting each other's explanations on faith. The game both perpetuates their desire and demonstrates how it is constituted. Each pushes the other in turn to acknowledge her insufficiencies; and with the acceptance of failure, the hope of reciprocity and recognition is continually renewed. The always broken promise of the game is the promise of being, for the game always breaks down when the relationship between the word and the thing surpasses resemblance — looks like — which is intelligible to the senses, and depends on accepting the other's inexpressible interiority — is like. "Funny how one thing resembles another," May tells June. But resemblance is not really so funny; getting beyond it is the goal of the game.

Resemblance is the world of "reality" from which May and June outlaw themselves. Within it, they *are* outlaws. What is there in this world of simple division to separate them from the pathological discourse that displaces women's aggression onto the lesbian, that constructs and conflates the sexually "deviant" woman as a murderer? How can they know that if they leave their fantasies they won't be apprehended by the law that has put out an all-points bulletin for two lesbian killers, one blond, one brunette, who have left their traces on the Florida highways, "each signpost along the way, the body of a middle-aged white man riddled with bullets." May and June identify with Aileen Wuornos, the real killer in Florida who has been sentenced to death and labeled the "first female serial killer" by the FBI, and her lover, Tyria Moore, who was granted clemency for entrapping Wuornos to confess. May and June think they may be just as "guilty," for they haven't got an alibi. They too are one blond and one brunette; they too are lesbians. What more evidence, in a "reality" ordered by resemblance, might be necessary to convict them? They are, they know, always already the guilty ones in this symbolic order.

They can dream, however, of differences that multiply and affirm. The darkness gives them a reprieve from the incarcerating light of mimesis. They fantasize about murder but choose instead to make poetry. "I'm not a poet, I'm a killer . . . don't get them mixed up," June says in one of her performances for May. But they do get mixed up. Metaphor can go either way. Resemblance can be deadly. "Resemblance," Foucault writes, "makes a unique assertion, always the same: This thing, that thing, yet another thing is something else." Resemblance negates, denies, and insists on the unity of the One. But similitude, the affirmation of the simulacrum, "multiplies different affirmations, which dance together, tilting and tumbling over one another."[2]

Lesbians Who Kill takes place in only one space — the front and back seats of the car that protects them from the storm. Like Hamlet, they depend on their fantasies to transport them outside this "nutshell," where they might command infinite space. May insists that she never dreams, and June doubts her. But they are not the mistresses of their own fantasies; they too are invaded by bad dreams, which are not phantasmatic, but the stuff of their everyday waking reality. The voice of this reality enters their refuge by way of the car radio, which intermittently broadcasts reports:

Willis, who has been serving her sentence at a state prison . . . outlining some of her reasons for ordering the killing. ". . . I'm asking that you place yourself in my shoes, knowing you had to lay awake each night knowing that your children have been molested by the man that is their father and your husband."

They have spent most of their time as escapees fantasizing about murder and playing word games to pass the time, like children do on a long car ride. The final game that they play is a fantasy about their own deaths, and how many times it can be repeated.

May is thinking about math, about "number[s] for everything, . . . a number of times ... a number of times ... that we'll do things and say things ... let's say ... how many times we'll kiss":

JUNE: How many times we'll fight ...
MAY: How many times it'll rain ...
JUNE: How many times we'll say How Many Times.
MAY: Before we ...
JUNE: ... die.

May contemplates the longest division, dividing a number by zero — "like putting a white sheet over the number." June asks: "Like it's dead?" May responds: "Yeah, like it died in the hospital ..." There is not enough time for June to count the hairs on May's head (there's a number for them too); but there is time for June to divide May by zero, cover her in white, and lay her to rest. June asks if there is "a number how many times [she] can do that?" May answers: "Yes, ... but I don't know ..." June: "You don't know?" May: "No ... I don't know." This failure to know keeps them from falling into history. It is the promise of infinity that they embrace in a passionate desire for the perpetual present.

This final game, the fantasy of the indeterminacy of their own deaths, is figured through the act of division. In a performance that constantly refers to, but never names, the "real" lesbian serial killer — Aileen Wuornos — who circulates throughout the performance as an absent model, this emphasis on division in the end might be thought of in terms of the Platonic theory of Ideas, which, as Giles Deleuze describes it, is in the order of division:

The Platonic project emerges only if we refer back to the method of division, for this method is not one dialectical procedure among others. ... One could initially say that it consists of dividing a genus into opposing species in order to place the thing under investigation within the correct species. ... But this is only the superficial aspect of the division, its ironic aspect.[3]

The real goal of division, Deleuze argues, is the erection of a hierarchy, "selection from among lines of succession, distinguishing between the [true and false] claimaints, distinguishing the pure from the impure, the authentic from the inauthentic."[4] It is a secondary irony that characterizes Platonic division. Deleuze explains this other irony in the example of the *Phaedrus*, in which the myth of the circulation of souls (a closed system) tells the foundational narrative of "true love," which belongs to "those souls who have seen much and thus have many dormant but revivable memories; while sensual souls, forgetful and narrow of vision, are denounced as false claimants."[5] It is these false claimants who occupy the simulacra, "built on a dissimilitude, implying a perversion, an essential turning away."[6] Unlike the true claimants, the icons, copies, or good images, who are authorized by resemblance, the "false claimants" are not just likenesses. On the contrary, the false claimant, or simulacrum, lays her claim "by means of an aggression, an insinuation, a subversion, 'against the father' and without passing through the Idea."[7]

The simulacrum is postlapsarian, constituting a break in time, a rupture in history, a difference not of degree but of kind. Deleuze summarizes this theological passage: "God made man in His own image and to resemble Him [the good copy], but through sin, man has lost the resemblance while retaining the image [the simulacrum]."[8] If we are to understand in this passage the curse that falls on the false claimant, who comes to embody an "evil power," it is also here that desire is born in this fall, this turning away that is perversion of the good and the true. And it is Woman who effects this passage, through her seduction, interrupting the resemblance between man and his model, insinuating herself everywhere and instigating a brotherhood of rivalry. Or so the story goes of how women brought evil into the world. Without this narrative and its countless incarnations, one would have to create a different system of values, for life and for art, that did not raise reproduction to the pinnacle of these successive claims.

The simulacrum comes into being after the fall, or through the mirror stage, where aggressivity becomes constitutive of desire and where secondary identifications will henceforth be based on the oscillation between insufficiency and mastery. The simulacrum's model is the Other, and desire has become the desire of the Other. The chaos of what Deleuze calls the "Eternal Return" reigns and the "overthrow of the icons or the subversion of the world of representation is decided."[9]

By the end of the performance May and June have assembled quite an impressive collection of guns. They are prepared to use them, if necessary, to protect their love. They don't, however, ever emerge from the car, never enter into the storm shooting. But the possibility remains tangible. In this last scene May appears to succumb to the fantasy of June dividing her by zero and covering her over with a white sheet. Have they given up the fantasy of freedom? Not quite. Lacan writes:

Everyone knows that if zero appears in the denominator, the value of the fraction no longer has meaning, but assumes by convention what mathematicians call an infinite value. In a way, this is one of the stages in the constitution of the subject. In so far as the primary signifier is pure non-sense, it becomes the bearer of the infinitization of the value of the subject, not open to all meanings, but abolishing them all, which is different.[10]

Peggy Phelan elaborates:

Different too is the distinction between the abolishment of meaning and the abolishment of value. For while metaphor can be understood as the erosion and loss of "original" or "singular" meaning it does not follow that this erosion negates value. On the contrary, metaphor makes value. And perhaps nowhere more meaningfully than in the metaphoric values of sexual difference.[11]

Lacan explains that this is why one cannot understand "the relation of alienation without introducing the word freedom," for what "in effect, grounds, in the meaning and radical non-meaning of the subject, the function of freedom, is strictly speaking this signifier that kills all meanings."[12] This nonsensical signifier that kills all meanings and thus permits the foundational narrative of freedom is, of course, the phallus. The phallus, like the zero, is an integer — a whole number, complete in itself, entire, from the Latin *untouched*. The zero, as an integer, partakes of all these qualities but distinguishes itself from other "whole" numbers in that it signifies nothing. Its referent, if it could be said to have one at all, is a lack. If one is divided by any other integer there is either diminishment or amplification, both of which produce differences. Dividing by zero, on the other hand, merely produces an infinity of reproductions of the Same. Lacan reminds us that this signifier, which bears "the infinitization of the value of the subject" should not lead us to conclude that interpretation is therefore open to all meanings. This "non-sense" signifier "does not mean that interpretation is in itself nonsense."[13]

May and June understand these limitations. They know that there are only so many times that something can be repeated. This knowledge, however, does not preclude their desire for infinite returns. Nor does the reassurance that the phallus circulates without touching ground satisfy them. Perhaps the phallus reminds them too much of the ball of lightning that once got into their house and rolled around the top of the stove, sink, and kitchen cabinet. "Smelling hot, looking for somewhere to land. May said it was looking for [them]." That was when they "got smart" and decided to sit in their car. In their desire, they act out a psychic economy in which *no one* "has" the phallus. But they can't help noticing that in the world of "reality" most people believe that this phallus belongs to men, and that men, who are psychically enjoined, doomed perhaps, to attempt constantly to represent it, seize the women where they believe the phallus is embodied.

So May and June keep their guns loaded. June doesn't divide May by zero. Instead, she ends the performance with this fantasy: "I'd love to watch her *really* kill somebody. . . . Kill somebody by the railroad tracks in the wind while the trains went by, somebody with a beard of thorns and a crotch as soft and bitter as an unripe raspberry. Y'all know anybody like that?" Who might this "somebody" be? Let's hope that it is not someone who merely resembles the One.

May and June know that they are the false claimaints, the sensual souls who introduce doubt into the conception of models and their copies. They know that they are "fallen women," but they like where they have landed. They reinhabit the "femme fatale" with a difference. Opening with a lip-sync parody of the classic noir film *Deception*, Shaw's Claude Raines is taken by surprise by Weaver's Bette Davis, who confronts him with the gun he bought her for protection. He treats her like a child, or a hysterical woman, and demands that she hand over the gun: "Give me that nonsensical object! I've seen this kind of thing before. Give it to me!" Failing to secure the promise that she wants from him — "I'll swear nothing! I'll do what I please, see whom I please, say what I please" — May kills him.

The "nonsensical" object can indeed change hands. Becoming the phallus, in this case, fulfills its threatening potential. The wager man makes in making woman embody the phallus is that he might be reassured or murdered. *Lesbians Who Kill* both reminds him of the perils of that bargain and hopes for a place to play that is indifferent to it.

NOTES

This essay is the epilogue to my book, *Fatal Women: Lesbian Sexuality and the Mark of Aggression* (Princeton, N.J.: Princeton University Press, 1994). I wish to thank Deb Margolin, Lois Weaver, and Peggy Shaw for generously sharing their work with me in various stages of the production of *Lesbians Who Kill*.

1. Deb Margolin, *Lesbians Who Kill*. All quotations are taken from an unpublished script generously made available to me by Margolin.

2. Michel Foucault, *This Is Not a Pipe* (Berkeley: University of California Press, 1982), 46.
3. Gilles Deleuze, "Plato and the Simulacrum," trans. Rosalind Krauss, *October* 27 (Winter 1983): 45.
4. Ibid.
5. Ibid.
6. Ibid., 47.
7. Ibid., 48.
8. Ibid.
9. Ibid., 54.
10. Jacques Lacan, *The Four Fundamental Concepts of Psycho-Analysis*, trans. Alan Sheridan (New York: Norton, 1981), 252.
11. Peggy Phelan, *Unmarked: The Politics of Performance* (New York: Routledge, 1992), 24.
12. Lacan, *Psycho-Analysis*, 252.
13. Ibid., 250.

ELEVEN

Macho Sluts: Genre-Fuck, S/M Fantasy, and the Reconfiguration of Political Action

Ian Barnard

(But since I don't have the boy or nerve or weapon, I just sit here scribbling, jerking off. That's what my left hand is doing while this one is writing. But inside my head the most spectacular violence is happening. A boy's exploding, caving in. It looks sort of fake since my only models are splatter films, but it's unbelievably powerful.)

— Dennis Cooper[1]

As a culture we accept the idea that men can write about women, but it's much less common for women to write about the intimate part of men's lives. If your thing is getting fist-fucked or whipped or tied up, it may not matter so much who's doing that to you as long as they know what they're doing. I've done these things with gay men; I have tied them up, beaten and fucked them. I have direct experience here.

— Pat Califia[2]

In this essay I "read" lesbian S/M neither directly out of the debates around it among feminists over the past two decades, nor through a perverse or reclaimed psychoanalysis, but rather from Pat Califia's 1988 collection of "erotic fiction," *Macho Sluts*.[3] By hypostatizing S/M as a process of reading, this less-traveled route circumvents the binarisms and impasses that have characterized other positionings of S/M. It also enables us to rethink the framing of the S/M debates themselves to the extent that they have ignored the crucial role that textual production plays in any (representation of) S/M.

Because the "sex" in *Macho Sluts* primarily is constituted as S/M, this sex explicitly treats its production by and of various texts. This is not to say that S/M sex is any less "real" (or any more representational) than any other sex. Indeed, apologists for S/M have stressed the continuities between S/M and vanilla sex.[4] Vanilla sexual etiquette is as much derived from societal socializations and media representations, and enmeshed in dynamics of domination, submission, power, violence, fantasy, and role-playing (the colloquial characteristics of S/M) as S/M is. However, while these elements are usually disavowed in vanilla sex, in sex that represents itself as S/M they are foregrounded.

There is in *Macho Sluts* a politics of sex, a politics of text, and, most tellingly for my purposes, a politics of sex-text. This last nexus crucially unravels its preceding (and enabling) dichotomy (sex versus text). The unraveling itself generates unexpected strategies for an unconventional sexual politics. And if, as feminism, psychoanalysis, and queer theory urge, sexual politics necessarily is an index of other processes of subject formation, the unraveling will also inf(l)ect our understanding of politics per se.

I read *Macho Sluts* as a specific evocation of the politics of reading, and the politics in reading, in the text's delineation and materialization of an array of communities and subjectivities, and of strategies of resistance both to dominant institutions and to oppositional political theory that has been the hegemonic inscriptor of these same strategies of resistance.

To ask the question, Why use a text — literature — to elaborate/enact/climax "theory"? does not leave me with a comfortable binarism ("applying" "theory" to "literature," or "using" "literature" to "illustrate" "theory") that could invoke a rationalization for working on "Literature" in this way, since the text in question confounds its own status. Cover and title page bill *Macho Sluts* as a collection of "erotic fiction," and the twelve fictions thus described are framed by an opening "Introduction" and a closing "Note on Lesbians, AIDS, and Safer Sex." However, the distinctions in *Macho Sluts* between the fiction and its frame are not as clear as they appear. Concomitantly, the "fiction" itself continually violates the bound(arie)s between the pornographic, the erotic, the literary, and the textual.

The elusiveness (and allusiveness) of Califia's text situates it within a number of traditions, genres, and categorizations, and yet destabilizes all of them. *Macho Sluts* could be said to "belong" with other S/M texts, with other pornography, with Califia's other work, with the writings in the theoretical sex wars among feminists, and so on. Since Califia identifies as a lesbian and enjoys many affiliations with various lesbian and gay communities, and since most of the characters in the stories are lesbians, and the stories are written and presented from lesbian perspectives, the book also appears in lesbian and gay book catalogs and in the lesbian section of progressive bookstores — notwithstanding the fact that some of its most vocal critics have been lesbians who object to its S/M and to the men in some of the stories.

Varied levels and fields of violence suffuse *Macho Sluts:* violations of the integrity of identity (of genres, characters, readers, and communities), the psychological and physical violences that constitute the book's evocation of S/M, and the appropriations that the text suggests for a male critic.[5] These planes of violence inform and enable each other. To the extent that Califia's descriptions of sex between gay men and lesbians arouse my own lesbian interest, my celebration of Califia's (necessarily violent) dissolution of boundaries between male and female is framed by but also a violation of *Macho Sluts*. In some ways Califia explicitly gives gay men access to a lesbian feminism, gives us a way in. Not only does she indicate that she does not object to nonlesbian readers "enjoying" her book (17), and include gay male characters in some of the stories, but she also has a special relationship with gay men outside this text. She is a well-known advice columnist for the *Advocate*, a magazine directed almost exclusively at gay men, and one of *Macho Sluts*'s stories ("The Spoiler") was originally published in the *Advocate*. In addition to her other writings, Califia has penned gay male pornography. Furthermore, since there was until recently no lesbian S/M "community" to speak of, Califia's S/M identification has led her to align herself in telling ways with gay male leather communities (as well as with other S/M groupings), and she has on occasion written and spoken about engaging in sexual activities with gay men herself.[6] Her apparent disdain for biologically determined communities fosters my own stake in models of micropolitics based on notions of affiliation rather than founded in predetermined bodies.

I feel that she is challenging gay men (or so I tell myself). Is it now time for me to reciprocate, to pay back? For me not to write about Califia would not be a way out. For me to write (about) her is hardly a way in.

The S/M in *Macho Sluts* breaks down barriers/boundaries (between Self and Other, between surface and depth, between skin and bone, between genders) and so contributes to the intensity and sense of being at an edge (of definitions of pain, pleasure, body, self, consciousness) that the characters experience and that is often a part of the experience of reading *Macho Sluts*. The rituals of S/M pull at and pick open socially constructed niceties. Because S/M discourses and other S/M practices expose and publicize the invention, enactment, and parody of the power relations inherent in all "sex" (as "sex" itself produces and is produced by a context of historically determined social institutions), they appropriate and interact with and between already constituted modalities of domination (and violence) and the identities that comprise these.[7] S/M's flaunting of its contamination by these relations of power has been a continuing source of criticism of S/M. Some leftists see the costumes (leather, uniforms) and rituals of domination in some S/M as a hankering for and (re)enactment of fascism. Some feminists denounce lesbian S/Mers as victims of false consciousness, arguing that S/M celebrates and reproduces sexist and heterosexist social relations: since the domination of women is almost characteristic of heterosexual male sexuality, any practice that is organized around domination and submission is colluding in shoring up this misogynistic heterosexuality.[8] Furthermore, the argument goes, the rituals of bondage and submission practiced by many S/Mers recreate the abuses inflicted on people of color in this country, both historically and in the present.

My own intention in appealing to S/M in this article is not to deny the institutionalization of heterosexual sexuality, and thus its constitution in essentially sexist (and heterosexist) forms, as if sexuality existed in a vacuum independent of other social forces. I am not convinced that any heterosexual sexuality can be fully dislocated from the institutions of compulsory heterosexuality,[9] despite the intentions of some of its participants to effect such a dislocation. Andrea Dworkin and other feminists (for instance, the Leeds Revolutionary Feminist Group) have argued persuasively that heterosexual penile-vaginal penetrative sex is the socially sanctioned veneer for rape.[10] But in the last decade work by "pro-sex" feminists has posited an increased possibility for women's agency and empowerment by complicating these analyses in order to speak of women as desiring subjects in patriarchal contexts.[11] Even if one were to concede that conventional heterosexuality always enforces violence against women, it does not follow that there is some other sexuality that can escape this violence. Just as heterosexual sexuality cannot completely remove itself from its institutional antecedents and manifestations, so any nonheterosexual sexuality cannot fully sever its ties to the heterosexual consciousness that must contaminate it and to the forces that inform that heterosexual consciousness. No one is independent from the materialities of national and world economic and political systems, and no one is free from socialization, whatever its particular permutations in any individual subject; to the extent that it is hegemonic, heterosexuality constitutes its Others as every center produces the margins that it relies on for its sense of self.

To condemn S/M for perpetuating systemic inequities is to imply that it is possible and desirable to separate sexuality from other social formations. I see no such possibility or desirability. With Foucault and post-Foucauldians (Judith Butler, for instance), I insist on the futility of seeking spaces outside of existing power relations (and outside of language and discourse) whence "subversion" of that order must originate. It is naïve to hope either that a sexual order free from the valences of power and domination can be called into existence, or that such a hypothetical order would inevitably be more desirable than one suffused with power. On the contrary it is the parody, appropriation, and shatterings of particular embodiments of power, not the denial of their force, that render those powers vulnerable. Furthermore, any prescription for political oppositionality must be suspect if it would deny access to power to those who historically have been denied power anyway, (re)ghettoizing, for instance, women and African Americans to a place of Pure and Different Femaleness, Blackness, etc.

The formative contexts of material power relations necessarily particularize my own argument: it engages with a specifically lesbian S/M, and I would neither pursue it nor would it carry the same meaning or force in the context of, for instance, heterosexual or gay male S/M. It is telling, for instance, that popular gay male representations of desirable gay male S/M seldom interrogate narrow and essentialist assumptions of gay identity and hardly ever invoke the gender-bending ethos that informs much of Califia's text, and that is characteristic of other lesbian S/M work, too.

In fact gay male S/M often relies on codes of hypermasculinity set up in opposition to effeminate gay men (and hence as a put-down of women). Here I share Leo Bersani's suspicion of the "nonsubversive intentions" and "problematically subversive effects" of gay male machismo.[12]

In the case of a written text that expresses a marginalized lesbian subjectivity, and for the critic-writer who analyzes that text, language itself can only describe and appropriate an already-existing reality and the fantasies that negotiate with and are the excess of that reality. Language cannot stand outside reality, since it is a product of and itself produces that reality. Thus we need to ask *how* various representations of S/M (and S/M practices "themselves" as representations) penetrate and work power relations, rather than to search for a model of utopic sex or to condemn S/M for its apparent collusions with established forms of domination. Representations of S/M construct sites for investigating the changing meanings of political effectivities precisely because, like debates around the significance of discourses of sexuality, continuing battles around lesbian S/M among feminists have retained as unresolved even the question of whether S/M should be politicized at all. Some African American feminists have argued that even to ask whether S/M is "liberatory" or "oppressive" and whether its cast of slaves and masters are brutalizing is to trivialize the literal sufferings of people of color and the history of slavery in the United States.[13] Califia, in turn, appears to be annoyed at the academification of the S/M debates and reminds debatees that people practice S/M for sexual arousal and fulfillment, and not because they are bent on pursuing a radical politics in the bedroom. She does not believe that any single sexual practice is in itself more liberatory than any other and doubts, in fact, whether any kind of sex has any liberatory consequence. In her introduction to *Macho Sluts* she insists, "I do not believe that sex has an inherent power to transform the world. I do not believe that pleasure is always an anarchic force for good. I do not believe that we can fuck our way to freedom" (15).

However, while S/M does not automatically have a transformative power in the arena of social relations, it does not stand outside that arena either. Although Califia herself usually acknowledges that the sexual does carry political meaning, that the possibilities and meanings of all sexual practices are determined by a variety of socializations, many S/M apologists respond to condemnations of S/M with a libertarian rhetoric of "free choice," urging that everyone has the "right" to choose/fulfill their sexual desires provided that they bring no harm to others. These justifications assume that desire is accidental to or inherent in every subject and unrelated to political and social forces, and hence that S/M desires are arbitrarily inscribed onto a subject who is a tabula rasa. The liberal defense of S/M denies its interactions with its constituting and effected contexts. A more responsible analysis suggests that while the dominations and submissions of S/M are not exactly congruent with social and political power relations, they are not entirely independent of them either.

"Jessie," the first story in *Macho Sluts*, illustrates S/M's complex imbrication in existing structures of language and power. The piece begins with the story's protagonists, Liz and Jessie, at a women's dance. Liz, the first-person narrator, is mooning over Jessie, the enigmatic bass guitarist and singer from the band The Bitch. Jessie returns to the bar after the other members of the band have left, and, much to the narrator's delight, invites her to dance. Jessie dances Liz into a dark corner of the bar, where she kisses, caresses, pinches, and squeezes her. She tells her, "You're so turned on, I think I could make you come right now, in front of everybody." The narrator continues, "She began to call me names — slut, bitch, whore, cunt — and they were rich and resonant in my ear, like an incantation" (37). Both women reclaim the words (and the images that these words evoke) that historically were used and still are used to demean women and, by extension, to insult others. They reclaim the words and images not only from overtly misogynistic contexts of male threats, insults, and violences to women, but also from the heterosexual sexual scenario that these violences produce; in such a scenario men commonly use and invoke these images and words as a titillatory accompaniment to heterosexual sexual intercourse. Later, Jessie drives Liz to her house, where they spend the night. The narrator relates, "She teased me, calling me a pussy-kisser, a cunt-lapper. Yes, something inside me said. I am all those things. And right now that's all I want to be. I ached to redeem myself. My mouth heated, watered, hurt with the need to service her" (50). In the case of Liz and Jessie, the epithets "pussy-kisser" and "cunt-lapper" conjure up the possibility of insults directed at lesbians, in particular, but this potential is immediately appropriated in the service of a lesbian erotics. The epithets become words of praise, affirmation, and celebration.

"The Finishing School," the piece following "Jessie" in *Macho Sluts*, articulates and enacts this process of appropriation even more multivalently. This story turns on the S/M interrelationships among three women, Berenice, her daughter, Clarissa, and their maid, Elise. After Clarissa invites Elise to begin an apparently predictable and regular ritual of storytelling, readers discover that Elise and Berenice are, in fact, sisters. As a girl, Berenice had taken care of Elise, and the two had become enmeshed in an intense and satisfying S/M relationship. This relationship continued until Berenice was ejected from the household and disinherited by their mother, who came upon Berenice whipping Elise with a handful of long-stemmed roses, having "stuffed a peeled persimmon up" her sister "before beginning the flagellation" (81). Elise subsequently became wealthy and sought out her sister after their mother's death. When the sisters found each other they "switched roles." Clarissa summarizes the events in her request to Elise for the "story": " 'Tell me about you and Mother and how she enslaved you and you lost her and found her and laid your fortune at her feet so you could wear a maid's uniform every day and she had me, and you both decided to bring me up without any of the flaws that were present in your early education and — " ' (77).

"The Finishing School" and Elise's story-within-the-story are replete with clichés in plot, language, and dialogue. These clichés heighten the sense of disjunction created by the story's plot reversal, the shift from a scenario of a decadent moneyed class (Berenice) exploiting a servant (Elise) to an improbably utopian revelation of "justice for all" (the wealthy Elise becomes poor, the poor Berenice becomes wealthy). The clichés parody not only an ahistorical Victorianism in which such S/M stories are popularly intuited to be set, but also the genre of melodramatic pornography that uses the accoutrements of this mythical Victorianism to produce its well-codified narrative of Desire. The story's alienation from itself is thus also an essential (and conventional) ingredient of its effectiveness (and of the effectiveness of its genre). This conventionality is underscored by the method(olog)ically unsurprising nature of the story's "surprise reversal" (the poor Elise was wealthy; the wealthy Berenice was poor): the about-face in "The Finishing School" cannot be altogether unexpected, given the story's setting within the genre of S/M that conventionally relies on "roles" and "inversions" and the pleasures of these roles and inversions. This is not to say that these stories are any less titillating for their readers because of the unsurprising nature of their surprise, or the conventions of genre, or that Califia's version of them is any less so as a parody. On the contrary, the irreconcilable mixtures of surprise and predictability, spontaneity and parody, and collusion and rebellion, are themselves the loci of arousal.

The present-tense plot of "The Finishing School" points to the complex composition of this arousal. This layer of the story centers not only around Elise's narrative of the past, but also around Clarissa's imminent separation from her beloved mother in order to attend "finishing school." Mother and daughter's final night together climaxes in Berenice's passionate caning of Clarissa, after which she exhorts her daughter, "You must show your headmistress and teachers the same respect and cheerful obedience that you give me. I'll read your reports every month.... If they are satisfactory, when you return I will deflower you, if that is your wish and your maidenhead is still intact" (72). Berenice apparently promises to reward Clarissa for cooperating with a disciplinary regime (institutionalized schooling) that claims to be hostile to exactly the kind of reward Berenice has in mind — educational institutions officially are inimical to any kind of sexual activity, but even more so to lesbianism, S/M, incest, and intergenerational sex. Yet, in appearance, the educational apparatus institutionalizes the dynamic of Clarissa and Berenice's relationship, too (discipline, intergenerational authority, caning, suppressed/expressed lesbianism/homoeroticism). Official schooling also provides one of the institutional homes for a practice that appears to imitate the Clarissa-Berenice dynamic but which is, in actuality, not present at all in Clarissa and Berenice's relationship — sexual abuse.

These interstices in "The Finishing School" generate at least two possible trajectories of power: an idea of school is being recreated by subjects who/that would usually have no power to do so; an imaginary school is being recreated in fantasy (in order to bring Clarissa up "without any of the flaws that were present in [Elise and Berenice's] early education"). In both cases Clarissa's "cooperation" with the headmistress will be similar to her "punishment" from Berenice and also different from it precisely in that sameness. The title "The Finishing School" thus refers to two finishing schools, Clarissa's school away from home and her S/M education at home. While the perverse S/M "school" gets its erotic charge by playing off the institution of schooling, the latter also has been irrevocably contaminated by the former's appropriation of it.

Berenice's advice to Clarissa in "The Finishing School" and Jessie's murmurings to Liz in "Jessie" are simultaneously parody and not parody, separatist and not separatist, derivative and original.

The magnitude of Califia's lesbian desire finds its most elliptical expression at a tense moment in "The Calyx of Isis," the celebrated, long, and central set-piece of *Macho Sluts*. In this story the character Alex arranges for her lover Roxanne to be disciplined and pleasured by a team of outstanding dominatrixes at a lesbian bathhouse (The Calyx of Isis) in San Francisco. As the women who are disciplining Roxanne become aroused, one of them orders her reluctant lover to perform fellatio on Michael, the dildo-packing lesbian chauffeur to Tyre, the owner/madam of the Calyx: "See, you don't want to suck it because you figure that makes you pussy, but welcome to the twentieth-century, EZ, where it takes a real man to suck cock. Blow it" (162). Rather than trying to avoid men and cocks, these lesbians preinvent the lesbian man-cock. It's a punishment and a reward. The most powerful vehicle to out-lesbian lesbianness is, paradoxically, the lesbian man, the sucking of lesbian cock. This lesbianism is both inside and outside man, inside and outside cock. Because it's all lesbian, it's also a wor(l)d according to lesbians, a lesbian wor(l)d. Many hours later, as Roxanne is acquiring rings in her ears, breasts, and labia as signs of her success as an initiate, and of her and Alex's love for one another, Tyre tells her, "They'll remind you that you belong to women. In the outside world, you are a particularly despised brand of female: a cunt who rejects cock, a slave who rejects the masters of currency and armies. But we prize you for what the world despises. You make us wealthy" (170). These words neither repudiate nor transcend the earlier injunction to EZ to "suck cock." In fact, each moment enables, safeguards, and concentrates the other. The marks and rituals of patriarchal ownership of women here reserve lesbian place as a deep rejection of that patriarchal order.

The multivalent location of desire and of particular desires' resistances to institutionalized legitimacy is always homeless (in exile), constantly in search of articulation. The "Epilogue" to "Jessie" illustrates the final irresolution of Califia's reversals, their ultimate and necessary habitation of a no-man's limboland between the legitimate and the illegitimate, between the dominant and its impossible, inexpressible, undesirable Other. In this epilogue Jessie and Liz enact a bathetic parley of suburban conversational set-pieces after their night together: " 'So go get a Sunday paper and I'll cook. There's a mom 'n' pop grocery in the next block' " (60), etc. Because this suburban morning follows a night of decidedly unsuburban passion (the burning wax and caressing beatings that mark its climax are a far cry from the suppressed familiarity of domestic violence), it cannot but take on an aura of parody and menace. As they struggle to articulate their feelings and plans, Liz and Jessie recognize that this mundane and sanctioned morning-after will always recall and recoup their night of illegitimate passion inadequately: " 'It was the best,' I shrugged. My voice was high and unconvincing. 'It was the best ever,' I repeated firmly. 'I guess that's what makes today so difficult' " (60).

The utopian revelation in "The Finishing School" that the maid, in fact, was the madam, and the madam the maid, invites us to ask whose fantasy this story is. The identity of its agent(s) is especially brought into question by the story-within-a-story format of the piece (Elise narrates the "reversal" to Clarissa) that explicitly defines the central narrative climax as a production of fantasy and a construction of story-telling. Various planes of agency are intricated here: I am describing Califia describing a narrator describing Clarissa describing Elise telling the story of the "reversal." Each of these figures has a stake in this story, and each could be said to be fantasizing it, too. The institution of the school and its disciplinary regimen is appropriated in the service of Berenice and Clarissa's relationship, and for the titillation of Elise, and of Califia's readers. As the story of the "reversal" is appropriated not only by the participants in that story, but also by those for whom this is a story, so control moves from institutional oppressor, to S/M dominatrix, to fantasy creator, to writer, to reader, to critic.

In "Jessie" a parallel slippage in authority/authorship occurs in the passages where Jessie calls Liz "names."[14] Whereas the narrator and/or writer begins the first passage by using quotation marks to indicate that she is relaying Jessie's exact words, the appellations "slut, bitch, whore, cunt" appear between dashes rather than quotation marks and, as such, could be exact quotes — with the dashes standing in for quotation marks — could be paraphrases, or could be the narrator's invention (as, of course, they are by definition the author's invention). Similarly, Jessie's words later at her house are reported by the narrator as if they were being quoted but without actually being quoted: "She teased me, calling me a pussy-kisser, a cunt-lapper." The absence of quotation marks around "pussy-kisser" and "cunt-lapper" marks these crucially affirming and arousing lesbian appropriations as the narrator's appropriations and creations (and, by extension, the reader's projections) as much as they are a supposed recreation/repetition/reenactment of Jessie's words to her. Further down the same page the narrator describes another such instance of agent-confounding naming: "She clamped my head to her, shook and bucked, crying my name." Here not only are "Jessie's words" not enclosed within quotation marks, but the words themselves — the narrator's name, "Liz," for instance — are not given at all. In fact, the narrator's name is only mentioned once early in the story when she first meets Jessie and introduces herself. Her namelessness here imbues her with the potential to be Anyone, and, specifically, Any(lesbian)reader, facilitating the projection onto her of readers' fantasies, the introjection into her of readers' identities. Events and the words that articulate them are posited as the narrator's/protagonist's fantasy/creation, and readers are invited to collude in this phantasmatic by creating/providing the unspecified words and by sharing the protagonist's/narrator's pleasure in her fantasy-projections. Readers hence play a correlative role to that of the author/narrator, and of the players of the S/M "roles" within the stories.

In *Macho Sluts*, as the lines between characters slip away and the anchors between the dimensions of characters and author and between characters/author and readers loose their parallel but never crossing moorings, so, too, genre loses its definition. In fact it is largely because of the slippage between author/character/reader and between author/narrator that the status of the text is confounded. Given Califia's eloquent plea on behalf of S/M in her introduction to the book, it is impossible to decide whether *Macho Sluts* is a theoretical text justifying a certain type of fiction or fiction illustrating theory. Since Califia authors both the stories and their framing "Introduction" and "Note on Lesbians, AIDS, and Safer Sex," it is impossible to tell whether she or her text are for real or not. She disrupts the self-sufficiencies of genre with the "Introduction" and the closing "Note." Neither of these is coded as "fiction," but even if one were to read them as part of the fiction (as, say, teachers of canonical literature tell students to read the "Letter from Capt. Gulliver" and "Note from the Publisher" that begin *Gulliver's Travels*, or the preface to *Robinson Crusoe*), they would surpass it. They would still explicitly interact with the contexts that escape the confines of their text: Califia's other writings (her advice columns and essays, for instance) where Califia as author purports to speak as Califia the real person, the history of debates among feminists about pornography and lesbian S/M, the reality of AIDS, and so forth. It is difficult to read *Macho Sluts* without implicating it in these extra-textual debates. Not only does *Macho Sluts* begin with a theoretical introduction and end with Safer Sex advice, but the "theoretical" questions also appear to be embedded in the "stories" themselves. "The Hustler," for instance, is an extended exegesis of feminist debates around sex, and sex workers in particular, and a damning indictment of those feminists who have aligned themselves with "antisex" and "antiprostitution" rhetoric; the absence of any "sex" in the story estranges it from its pornographic context (that is, the stories that surround it).

The text thus further eludes stability as its tentative affiliations with pornography stretch the limits of both itself and the pornographic and insofar as pornography itself is never definitive. Given the uncharacteristic narrative elaborations in most of the stories (and the apparent absence of anything coded as "sex" at all in "The Hustler"), is *Macho Sluts* pornographic? Is it erotic rather than pornographic, given its subtitle, "Erotic Fiction by Pat Califia," and the heretofore decidedly male and often misogynistic character of what is popularly thought of as "pornography"? Yet in feminist debates around pornography Califia has clearly positioned herself in opposition to those who would make binary and classist distinctions between "erotica" and "pornography" in order to validate the former category and denounce the latter.[15] In any case, pornography per se continually evades its own generic bounds. The pornographic, as a genre and a medium, is unstable in its production of moments in which calls to action intersect with the fantasies of such calls to action. Butler sees the pornographic as always a deferral: "If the phantasmatic remains in tension with the 'real' effects it produces — and there is good reason to understand pornography as the erotic exploitation of this tension — then the 'real' remains permanently within quotations, i.e., 'action' is suspended, or, better yet, pornographic action is always suspended action."[16] Part of pornography's erotic appeal is precisely the fantasy that pornographic representation is reality. Yet such a reality would only serve to heighten the fantasy. The demand for definition can never be fulfilled.

As pornography exposes the impossibility of Desire's fulfillment, so it also practicalizes this impossibility in a variety of fulfilling ways. Pornography is peculiarly practical (which is not to imply that other texts are "only" texts). Among consumers of nondocumentary film genres, porn viewers are unique in their demand that the action represented "actually" be taking place. Viewers of conventional thriller movies do not customarily expect "real" chases, robberies, and murders to be a part of the filmmaking, but in the case of pornography, consumers are assumed to want "proof" that the characters/actors are "actually having sex" (hence the high premium men place on male cum-shots — "money shots" — in male porn films). But "pornography" makes other incursions from the "textual" into the "real," too: its aim is almost always to turn the reader/viewer/listener/participant on. Its financial profit is taken to indicate the extent to which it achieves this aim. Well-established traditions materialize this urging: voyeurism is not a satisfactory sign of engagement with the film, and so viewers themselves, inspired by the pornographic representation/actuality, frequently provide a further proof of sex, often in the form of private or public masturbation or other sexual activity, either while consuming the pornography or soon afterward.

Representations and referents (as this dichotomy itself is constructed in the service of cordoning off the "public" from the "private," "reality" from "fantasy," "essence" from "artifice," and so forth) mutually constitute each other, and because of the pornographic's liminal status between genres and dimensions it functions as a how-to guide as much as it embodies its consumers' preexisting fantasies. Linda Williams has described the genre's utopian "problem-solving" intent in its popular narrative formula that addresses the "curing" of characters' (and viewers') sexual "problems," and Gertrud Koch notes that some pornography even sees itself as contributing toward research on sexuality.[17] A tellingly unoutstanding scene from Mike Nichols's 1991 film *Regarding Henry* points to pornography's synecdochal role in virtualizing sexual realities: the film's title character has supposedly lost all memory of his former self after being shot in the head, but his heterosexuality is soon recreated in a straight porn cinema; although he stares at the film in disbelief and remarks "I don't know if I can do that," he makes love to his wife soon afterward. The porn movie's fictions socialize him — teach him how to "make love."[18] Gay male pornography, in turn, has been an important means for gay men to validate our sexualities, and, in the AIDS crisis, pornography has become a central vehicle for teaching gay men about "safe sex," for teaching us to eroticize "safe sex" — for inspiring us to unlearn our sexuality and learn a new gay sexuality. The recent boom in pornography by and for lesbians has affirmed the fact of lesbian sex and the variety of lesbian sexual practices, realities that have often in the past been denied by most men, by many heterosexual feminists, and by some lesbians. It has also initiated the possibility of new lesbian sexual practices for many lesbians.

Pornography's transgressions, inversions, and deconstructions of hierarchies and oppositions effect a number of productive contradictions in *Macho Sluts* itself. Neither Califia nor her book are pure (fiction). At the conclusion to her "Note on Lesbians, AIDS, and Safer Sex," she writes, "This book isn't a sex manual. It can't be used as a guideline for how to have safer sex. It can't be used as a manual for how to do safe S/M, either. Some of the things that go on in these stories are in fact risky to do" (296). But if the book is "pure fiction," why is there a need for the safer sex note in the first place? Surely the note is an acknowledgment that this "fiction" has some material interrelation with reality? Califia's publisher seems to agree: if the book is "pure fiction," why did he refuse to publish it unless it described only "Safe Sex" (17)? And how does one reconcile an understanding of the book as pure fiction with Califia's description of it as a "recruitment poster" (10) and her conclusion that porn industry profits are an indication of "how badly people want to learn about sex and get turned on" (11)? Surely Califia does not hope to "recruit" only new *readers* of S/M, but is thinking of recruiting new practicing S/M lesbians, too? And what does it mean that people will use something that is "pure fiction" to "learn about sex"?

In *Macho Sluts*, disjunctive juxtapositions within pornography and between fiction and nonfiction are "resolved" in the sphere of fantasy, as the phantasmatic variously circles in and out of reality, before and beyond reality, escaping reality but also tied to it as "before" and "beyond" are always before and beyond something else. In her essay "The Force of Fantasy: Feminism, Mapplethorpe, and Discursive Excess," Butler takes antipornography procensorship feminists to task for their tendency to see fantasy (in this case, pornographic images) as causing actions that are injurious to women. But while Butler defines herself as a feminist in opposition to these feminists, she is not willing to concede fantasy to the realm of the "unreal." Butler argues that because the "real" is itself a construct (that is, that which is determined to be "real" is not necessarily more "real" than that which is designated as "unreal"), the "real" is always determined in relation to fantasy.[19] As the political is a category designed to distinguish the forces that determine and effect changes in material power relations, so there is a political stake in the methodologies and epistemologies that produce the real, and that the real itself constitutes. Since fantasy is that which is excluded from the real in order to construct the real, and fantasy thus continually contests the borders of the real, fantasy "informs political discourse in ways that often defeat the very purpose to which political discourse is put."[20] It prods political discourse into expressing exactly the fantasies that this political discourse claims to want to suppress.

Furthermore, fantasy suspends action and "in its suspension, provides for a critical investigation of what it is that constitutes action."[21] Because fantasy is always a part of yet never exactly congruent with action, it enacts, it is enaction, and it can also stand outside that action. Because of the cross-identifications and dispersals of identifications that take place around it (in fantasy, women can identify with male characters, lesbians can identify with straight characters, a fantasizer can identify with the fantasy itself rather than with a particular character in it, and so forth) and its emphatic retention of the repressed, the phantasmatic yokes the past, the possible future, and the junction of the past and the future in the present.

It is reductive to conflate a text with that which the text "represents" (which is not to say that "representation" is self-explanatory; "readers" learn — and often naturalize — particular codes that signify representation). In addition, because S/M is so explicitly concerned with "fantasy," because *Macho Sluts* is a fantasy (text) about S/M, and because the text itself foregrounds its status as fantasy about fantasies with numerous stories-within-stories and fantasies-within-stories, the stories are not anything more/other than "fiction." Fantasy is central to *Macho Sluts* because S/M practices often openly foreground it. But *Macho Sluts* explicitly represents itself as a *text* about/of S/M. This text, then, cannot be conflated with S/M practices (which is not to say that S/M practices aren't texts themselves). Its textuality represents a further level of fantasy at which *Macho Sluts* is removed from the "real." Moreover, the fantasy and storytelling within the text that often frame the fantasies about S/M (fantasies) establish yet another level of remove from the "real." Because *Macho Sluts* so clearly represents itself as a *text* about S/M, these removes are not repressed in the text but rather are emphasized in it. The multiple fantasy frames of *Macho Sluts* allow for expanded possibilities of identification and cross-identification. Those who denounce pornography often have assumed a far too easy causal chronology between fantasy and reality that ignores the fact that the unconscious manifests itself in translations, transformations, transferences, displacements, and projections. The stories in *Macho Sluts* illustrate a more complex working of fantasy, identification, and control than an essentialist representational model would require. Not only can women be men and men be women, but women can also do men, and vice versa, although what the women do as men will not be the same as what men do as men, and so on.

In her introduction to *Macho Sluts* Califia reassures her (lesbian) readers about the presence of men in the book by explaining that many people "do not fantasize about the kind of sex that they actually have" (16). The fantasies might be a central component of the sex, without the sex literally reenacting the fantasy. Furthermore, the fantasies themselves might constitute a kind of "sex," or might have no relation at all to "sex." The disjunction between fantasy and reality might be what makes fantasy (and so its transformations of realities) feasible in the first place: a particular fantasy is often only possible because it is unlikely to occur in reality.[22] Lesbian fantasies about men do not necessarily indicate lesbian desire to have sex with men or even to see men having sex. These fantasies might achieve their effect precisely due to their status as taboo but "unreal"; they might, moreover, fuel specifically lesbian and women-only sexual practices as these incorporate, transform, and disavow those "men."

Califia also prepares her readers for the male characters in some of the stories by explaining that her own (lesbian) sexual fantasies include (gay) men.[23] Given Califia's lesbian positioning of herself, her text, and her readers, and the distinction she draws between fantasy and "actual sex" in her introduction, all the gay men in the book are fantasies produced by this lesbian imaginary — are, in fact, lesbians. They are lesbians because they are participants in the book's lesbian desire and lesbian sex. In "The Spoiler," the *Macho Sluts* story with all-male characters, lesbian desire r(es)ides in the lesbian presences surveying and orchestrating the gay male sex as much as in the "actual" gay male sex. My intervention on behalf of and in the name of the "gay men" in Califia's text is as much an accession to lesbian identity on my part as it is an index of the extent of Califia's power of control, naming, and authority/authorship. My own earlier placement in quotation marks of words and phrases that I claimed Califia had refrained from quoting, and my own furnishing (invention) of words that were missing altogether in her text indicate a multiplication of the levels of collusion and participation that a "reading" of this text solicits.

Much recent work in queer theory has treated the expansion and production of lesbian sexualities in the wake of AIDS under the influence of gay male sexual practices as lesbians have come to scrutinize and talk of these practices to contest rampantly antigay and antisexual responses to the AIDS crisis. Little has been said of the potential for lesbians to construct and control gay male subjectivities as Califia has done. She has created me in her image.

Thus, fiction and fantasy do impinge upon the real, and vice versa, but the relationship is not a literal imitation. The libertarian argument that assumes that fantasy has no material effects ignores the role that representation and socialization, words and images, play in shaping people's experiences. For Butler, the "psychic reality" and "semantic excess" of fantasy makes it "precisely that which haunts and contests the borders which circumscribe the construction of stable identities."[24] We can say, then, that the phantasmatic *will* determine realities and reality-paradigms, but in a variety of dispersions that are often highly mediated and modulated manifestations of a fantasy, or that are consequences of the phantasmatic that might be quite far removed from the immediate superficial content of an actual fantasy.

As I insist on neither a literal and predictable correspondence between fantasy and "action," nor on a nonrelation between the phantasmatic and the "real," so, too, I neither want to imply that the violations and uses of violence in *Macho Sluts*, or in S/M, are no different from their physical enactment, nor that they are "just" fantasies. To relegate them to the realm of "mere" fantasy would not only deny the very real violences that words and texts can embody and inspire, but also, more specifically, would deny the characteristic inscription of S/M *practices* by and in fantasy and hence would sanitize and domesticate Califia's text.

In *Macho Sluts* the complex relationship between fantasy and reality is mediated and modulated in the act of "reading." A telling feature of many of the stories is the manner in which processes of reading are themselves lodged in the narrative thematics. One of the stories, "The Surprise Party," presents Don, a gay highway patrol officer, and his henchmen, two gay cops, repeatedly "raping" a lesbian protagonist. It is important to the erotic charge of the reading and fantasizing of (")The Surprise Party(") that readers only discover at the end of the story that the protagonist is in fact previously acquainted with Don and that the entire incident was arranged by her lover as a birthday surprise for her. Until this final page the narrator gives no indication that the protagonist knows Don, leaving readers with the embarrassing/titillating task of having to explain — albeit within the "safe" space of (lesbian) fiction/reading — what appears to be a rape, and, worse/more still, that the protagonist (and, presumably, any reader) "enjoys it." However, like the "discovery" in "The Finishing School," the "about-face" at the end of "The Surprise Party" is an S/M genre convention, and given the context of the rest of the book and Califia's own explanations of S/M as consensual and safe, a "real" rape is unlikely to be represented in the story. In addition, "The Surprise Party's" unlikely combination of highway patrolman with city policemen in one car (an anomaly that the protagonist herself remarks on) is a clue that all is not what it appears, and the story's title foreshadows its final revelation. It is precisely the *fantasy* of not knowing that the "rape" is really consensual (concomitant with the *knowledge* that it is) that mobilizes the story's intricate network of arousingly illicit desire.

Yet if fantasy orders/authors S/M, and, in fact, the fantasy of rape is precisely a part of "The Surprise Party's" titillation both for readers and the protagonist (even in her unconscious — as represented by the interior narration in the story — she doesn't let on that she knows Don), how does one account for the story's final revelation? Surely the story would maintain its integrity as S/M fantasy/text even without explicit assurances that the "rape" wasn't "real"? Readers would still know that they were reading a "story" and "reading" S/M and wouldn't assume that the "rape" in the story or in the S/M was equivalent to a real rape. One could argue that Califia merely includes the final revelation in order to pacify those who need to be reassured that S/M is "safe," "respectable," and "consensual." But given the fact that other clues in the story already alert readers to the consensual nature of the "rape," I want to suggest that the explicit revelation that the "rape" was, in actuality, a "surprise party" also enacts a crucially paradoxical "twist" to the already complex relations of fantasy to reality and text to action in *Macho Sluts*. The paradox is that the story's metafictional frame actually serves to bring its reality into relief. For the revelation at the end of (")The Surprise Party(") not only reforegrounds the story's fantasy (re)framings, but also adds a very down-to-earth how-to component to the story. By explaining that the sex orgy was planned as a surprise party, Califia suggests to her readers how they might go about creating such an orgy. Without this ending readers might be at a loss as to how to create a similar scene for themselves. The fantasy frame grounds the story in reality.

The "revelation" at the end of "The Surprise Party" further blurs the borderlines between fantasy/reality and fiction/nonfiction and problematizes any easy sense of teleology from the phantasmatic to the real, or vice versa. Which comes first? Which causes the other? Which is more material than the other? What does it mean that fantasy is more real than reality? The more the story emphasizes its fantasy framework, the more real it becomes, and the more urgent is the reader's quest for agency. The more insistently the author bemoans her death, the more tellingly does she demand recognition. Whose (collective?) fantasy is "The Surprise Party," then? Califia's? The narrator's? The protagonist's? Her lover's? Don's? The reader's? The critic's? The gay man's? Is the protagonist's/narrator's response to the "rape" a fantasy? Is the sex a fantasy? How is a reader implicated in the story *while reading it*, before reaching the ending that confirms that the protagonist might not have been raped after all? And how do multiple rereadings of the story reauthorize readers to (re)fantasize the story without or with the ending that they already know awaits them (that they knew all along awaited them)? In the context of the S/M in *Macho Sluts*, the practice of reading is only reading, but also is a unique mode of action and a disarming act of violence.

The inversion of fantasy and reality in the book is rehearsed in another startling irony: the stories only depict Safe Sex in the scenes involving men, possibly because no discourse of lesbian Safe Sex existed at the time the book was published. The absence of lesbian Safe Sex in the stories, whatever the reasons for this absence, has the effect of assigning the greatest degree of "reality" (Safe Sex) to the most fantastic elements of this lesbian book (gay male–gay male and gay male–lesbian sex), of making these elements more "real" than the reality of their lesbian readers.

My intention, then, in drawing attention to the phantasmatic and fictional overlayerings of Califia's text is not to dismiss its violence, to make it "safe." I do not want to ignore the fantastic elements in the S/M of *Macho Sluts* by conflating its representations with some "real" enactment of violence. Yet I also do not want to deny the unsettling potential of the gender and other disruptions in, for instance, "The Surprise Party" by situating them solely as the fantasy of Califia and/or her narrators/

characters/readers and as hermetically enclosed within a lesbian imaginary that I construct as definitive and confined. Even if these are "just" stories, they do still have some kind of effectivity, though this might be in a realm that does not appear to be a direct translation of its representation. Because S/M is so closely associated with fantasy, violence and fantasy cannot be comfortably dissociated. Because S/M is fantasy, to say "it's only fantasy" is not in any way to diminish the reality of its violences that disrupt hierarchies and oppositions and rupture the self-containability and integrity of genres, genders, and realities. In this case violence is fantasy and fantasy is violence. Although Califia distinguishes between fantasy and "actual sex," in (her) S/M the point is precisely that fantasy is the real sex. From one perspective the text cannot be conflated with S/M *practices*, yet, from another, because S/M practices are so commonly emphasized as texts (fantasies, roles, mimicries), this text *is* S/M, and to engage with it is to take up violence, to participate in such S/M. Conversely, S/M is this text — S/M imagines and authors it.

Because the S/M in *Macho Sluts* occupies so many subject and object positions, it encompasses more than a logic of inversion. It doesn't merely permit the "rich" to become "poor," the dominated to dominate, the victim to authorize, and so on. A mere reversal in meaning of an existing set of offices would be too easy, too pat — unconvincing and untrue. Any explanation of S/M as such a reversal is bound to suppress the complexities, contradictions, and particular pleasures of S/M. Furthermore, such an explanation robs S/M of its potential to confound definition and dismantle binaries inasmuch as such a reversal's accession to an existing binary relation (even by inverting it) solidifies the terms of that relation. Inversion depends on a binary. *Macho Sluts* complicates any such simple opposition: in its doubling, doubled, and troubled S/M, it creates and encompasses reversal, but it also fractures that inversion with replications, reenactments, inventions, combinations, "stases," the "reenaction" of acts not yet enacted, and the reformulation of the meaning of the already-acted. Moreover, it is especially in the intersections and contradictions of these various practices that the text eludes essentialist-constructionist binarisms, marginalizing models of oppositionality, and the ensuing political deadends of these binarisms and oppositions. The "roles" of any S/M relation are not infinitely fluid — tops and bottoms don't often switch — but the relative power and shifting meanings invested in each role are.

These powers and meanings proliferate infinitely uncontrollably. A switch represents one defined reversal. A multiplication within the hierarchy of the original relation dissolves the relation itself.

In the *Macho Sluts* story "The Spoiler," lesbian desire conceives of its most extensive sweep of power by removing all women from the narrative. Lesbianness is undone by a lesbian extreme, destroys itself. This destructive force is immensely unnerving but also immensely powerful because it is so unnerving. Because S/M must always be straining at boundaries and limits, when it's good it outdoes itself. In this story the mission of the male protagonist — known only as "the spoiler" — is to top other topmen. If S/M already involves processes of reversal, here even the roles of the reversal are undercut; S/M's own fixity — a fixity that itself is a confounding founded on ritual, role, and definition — is further undermined. If S/M tops and bottoms rebel against vanilla sexual etiquette and its social underpinnings, the mission to top a top rebels against S/M itself, even as it is assigned from within and made meaningful by S/M. The spoiler inhabits a space of impossible and inarticulable desire: "We are raised to think that everything in the world occurs naturally as a set of paired opposites. It is almost impossible for us to know what anything is if we cannot locate and define its counterpart. The spoiler was an anomaly. The same system that created him found that he threatened its premises. And that system was not known for dealing with irritating matter by making pearls out of it" (280). Desire is always destined to remain unfulfilled, since once the spoiler has topped a top, the (ex-)top no longer qualifies as a top and thus no longer is desirable. The spoiler has a profound, indeed, a life-changing effect on those with whom he comes into contact. Some of his targets become (impossibly) obsessed with him: one begins wearing a harness under his business suit, repeatedly leaving his desk at work, and eventually leaving his job.

The fragility of Califia's S/M is rehearsed in "The Calyx of Isis" when the petulant EZ is dragged to a padded horse for a caning, fuming "This is not consensual!" (162). Here and elsewhere in the book Califia toys even with the notion of "consent" that forms the crux of her defenses of S/M, in order to extend and intensify her S/M by undercutting it. If "consent" is a critical component of her defense of S/M, and as S/M gains its desirable intensity precisely by pushing against limits and boundaries, so there must be a continual tension between this "consent" and this "S/M." S/M repeatedly outdoes/undoes itself. By definition, S/M defi(n)es itself out of existence, is nothing, and everything, is always itself, is never itself.

The various discourses of and about S/M assign S/M to spaces between the political and the "nonpolitical" and in excess of dominant social relations. "S/M" thus illustrates the means by which politics and dominance may be constituted and itself constructs strategies for contesting domination outside of self-perpetuating binarisms and insulating compartmentalizations. This contestation considers and negotiates desire, socialization, and politics together as a totality (though not as a coherent or linear unity). To uncritically celebrate desire is to fail to grasp its place in a full sociality. To academify and coherently theorize Desire is to mask its enigmas (to ignore the unconscious). When cultural productions are expected to portray a political correctness that reduces this complexity, as if political conscience can always be mapped unhesitatingly onto desire, a part of what these productions could reveal and create of political praxis is suppressed and wasted.[25] Butler, for instance, is sometimes unable to resist the temptation to map culture directly onto politics, hence reducing the complexity and unpredictability (and thus productivity) of the interfaces between these two realms. She writes of power dynamics in lesbian and gay sexualities and the drag and butch-femme identities in lesbian and gay cultures, "The replication of heterosexual constructs in nonheterosexual frames brings into relief the utterly constructed status of the so-called heterosexual original.... The normative focus for gay and lesbian practice ought to be on the subversive and parodic redeployment of power rather than on the impossible fantasy of its full-scale transcendence."[26] This injunction does not account for the many complex and contradictory reasons that inform these practices. Just as practitioners of S/M aren't necessarily primarily motivated by political altruism, so drag queens and butch dykes might not be intent primarily on "the subversive ... redeployment of power." While I value Butler's discoveries of parody and resistance in mimicry, I find her readings of these components of lesbian and gay cultures too binary (heterosexual versus nonheterosexual, collusion versus subversion, imitator versus imitated, original versus parody), too confident (as if we all know what is "subversive"), too determined to make forbidden desires submit to a singular revolutionary regimen, too evasive of the multiplicities that demand a reenvisioning of even that revolutionary program. This reenvisioning must recognize the reformist impetus that will inhere in any relation of oppositionality (since to speak in opposition is to maintain the center-periphery relation that produces binary oppositionality in the first place) and the potential of the unconscious to disrupt such oppositionalities. S/M's much-criticized investment in power and violence, together with its indeterminate relationship to the "political," demand a rethinking of an entire arena of oppositional politics and of any contestatory political imaginary.

The spaces between the intersections of fantasy and reality point to the uncontainability of desire and the indeterminacy of politics; in its uncontainability and indeterminacy the politics of desire resists containment both by institutional oppression and subaltern fixity.

The relation of fantasies of desire to the political is simultaneously very convoluted, highly charged, and significantly formative. In exploding the distinctions and borders between the phantasmatic and the "real" by showing how it is exactly the phantasmatic that produces ever heightened realities, I demand that these distinctions cannot — and should not — hold in the realm of political action either. This is not to repeat quietist assurances that revolutionizing *language* or *imagining* a different order is sufficient political work, but rather to adumbrate a way of thinking through the phantasmatic that will access political work to a full range of social realms, including those in which the unconscious "contradicts" the logic of conventionalized political linearity. This is to recognize the place of the unconscious in the political.

NOTES

I am grateful to S. J. Mitchell, Molly Rhodes, Page duBois, Andrea Slane, Anne Shea, Kayann Short, Maggie Sale, Abou Farman, Judith Halberstam, Mónica Szurmuk, Rickie Brown, Bruce M. Abrams, Carol Siegel, C. D. Moore, Kate Cummings, and an anonymous reviewer for *Genders* for assisting me with this essay.

1. Dennis Cooper, *Frisk* (New York: Grove, 1991), 54.
2. Pat Califia, qtd. in Jim Merrett, "Do You Know Who You're Jacking Off To? A Look at Women Who Pen Gay Male Porn," *Advocate*, May 19, 1992, 58.
3. Pat Califia, *Macho Sluts* (Boston: Alyson, 1988). I will include further references to this work parenthetically in the text. For some examples of writing in the feminist (lesbian) S/M debates, see the following: Pat Califia, "Feminism and Sadomasochism," *CoEvolution Quarterly* (Spring 1982): 33–40; Califia, "A Secret Side of Lesbian Sexuality," in *S and M: Studies in Sadomasochism*, ed. Thomas Weinberg and G. W. Levi Kamel (Buffalo: Prometheus,

1983), 129–36; Califia, introduction to *Macho Sluts*, 9–27; Linda Williams, *Hard Core: Power, Pleasure, and the "Frenzy of the Visible"* (Los Angeles: University of California Press, 1989); Samois Collective, ed., *Coming to Power: Writings and Graphics on Lesbian S/M*, 3d ed. (Boston: Alyson, 1987); Gayle Rubin, "Thinking Sex: Notes for a Radical Theory of the Politics of Sexuality," in *Pleasure and Danger: Exploring Female Sexuality*, ed. Carole Vance (Boston: Routledge, 1984), 267–319; Judy Simmons, "Out of Bounds," *Ms.*, April 1989, 65–67; Susan Ardill and Sue O'Sullivan, "Upsetting an Applecart: Difference, Desire and Lesbian Sadomasochism," *Feminist Review* 23 (June 1986): 31–57; Bev Jo, Linda Strega, and Ruston, *Dykes-Loving-Dykes: Dyke Separatist Politics for Lesbians Only* (Oakland: Battleaxe, 1990); Robin Ruth Linden et al., eds., *Against S/M: A Radical Feminist Analysis* (East Palo Alto, Calif.: Frog in the Well, 1982); Irene Reti, ed., *Unleashing Feminism: Critiquing Lesbian Sadomasochism in the Gay Nineties* (Santa Cruz: HerBooks, 1993).
4. See, for instance, Califia's "Feminism."
5. See Alice Jardine and Paul Smith, eds., *Men in Feminism* (New York: Methuen, 1987).
6. See, for instance, Pat Califia, "Gay Men, Lesbians and Sex: Doing It Together," *Advocate*, July 7, 1983, 24–27; and Jim Merrett, "Do You Know Who You're Jacking Off To?"
7. Rather than following the distinction between "sex" and "gender" developed by some feminists, I use "sex" to denote sexual practices and "gender" to refer to constructions of maleness and femaleness.
8. For example, in the book *Dykes-Loving-Dykes*, Bev Jo, Linda Strega, and Ruston title their chapter on S/M "S/M = Sadism & Masochism = Heterosexism."
9. See Adrienne Rich, "Compulsory Heterosexuality and Lesbian Existence," *Signs* 5, no. 4 (1980): 631–60.
10. Andrea Dworkin, *Intercourse* (New York: Free, 1987); Leeds Revolutionary Feminist Group, *Love Your Enemy? The Debate between Heterosexual Feminism and Political Lesbianism* (London: Onlywomen, 1981).
11. See, for instance, Joan Nestle, *A Restricted Country* (Ithaca: Firebrand, 1987); ed. Vance, *Pleasure and Danger*; Marion Bower, "Daring to Speak Its Name: The Relationship of Women to Pornography," *Feminist Review* 24 (October 1986): 40–55; Varda Burstyn, ed., *Women against Censorship* (Vancouver: Douglas & McIntyre, 1985); Caught Looking, Inc., *Caught Looking: Feminism, Pornography and Censorship*, 3d ed. (East Haven, Conn.: Long River, 1992); and Ann Snitow, Christine Stansell, and Sharon Thompson, eds., *Powers of Desire: The Politics of Sexuality* (New York: Monthly Review, 1983).
12. Leo Bersani, "Is the Rectum a Grave?" in *AIDS: Cultural Analysis, Cultural Activism*, ed. Douglas Crimp (Cambridge, Mass.: October–MIT Press, 1988), 207.
13. Karen Sims, for instance, feels that the entire S/M debate is "a white women's issue" and comes out of a luxury (of leisure, contemplation, and distance) that

she doesn't enjoy: "it does not speak to building a stronger movement of Third World women, it does not speak to the racism within the women's movement. It does not speak about the homophobia in the women's community—it doesn't progress us." See Karen Sims, Rose Mason, and Darlene Pagano, "Racism and Sadomasochism: A Conversation with Two Black Lesbians," in *Against Sadomasochism*, ed. Linden et al., 99. Some African-American feminists have similarly suggested that arguments about pornography should be a "low priority" for feminists. See, for example, Tracey A. Gardner, "Racism in Pornography and the Women's Movement," and Luisah Teish, "A Quiet Subversion," in *Take Back the Night: Women on Pornography*, ed. Laura Lederer (New York: Morrow, 1980), 105–14, 115–18.
14. Califia, *Macho Sluts*, 37, 50.
15. For articulations of the class permutations in arguments around pornography, see, for instance, Samuel Delany, "The Possibility of Possibilities," interview by Joseph Beam in *In the Life: A Black Gay Anthology*, ed. Beam (Boston: Alyson, 1986), 207–8; and Andrew Ross's chapter on pornography in his *No Respect: Intellectuals and Popular Culture* (New York: Routledge, 1989). The recent release of a handful of "feminist" porn videos by Femme Productions has illustrated the class-bound nature of feminist debates over pornography. While these movies appear to be less phallically driven than the usual man-made porn and have been praised by some feminists (Williams, for instance), their conceptualization of feminism seems to draw from and be confined to a tradition of bourgeois romanticism and monogamous, married heterosexuality. For example, in *Three Daughters* (dir. Candida Royalle, 108 min., Femme Productions, 1986, videocassette), the refreshing portrayal of sexual activity in a wide variety of age groups is undercut by its restriction to white heterosexual couples (where each character is roughly the same age as her or his partner) who are married or about to be married (the one instance of explicit lesbian sexuality is presented as "practice for" and a prelude to "the real thing"). Sexual activity takes place against a backdrop of chandeliers and shaggy carpets, often with close-ups of dinner-party silverware for titillatory montage. This restrictive version of acceptable sexuality is inimical to feminism for those feminists who want to see women's sexuality expanded and diversified beyond the bounds of patriarchal traditions of middle-class heterosexuality, marriage, and monogamy. In defending S/M, Califia writes, "I didn't join the feminist movement to live inside a Hallmark greeting card" ("Feminism," 39).
16. Judith Butler, "The Force of Fantasy: Feminism, Mapplethorpe, and Discursive Excess," *differences* 2, no. 2 (1990), 113.
17. Williams, *Hard Core*, 154; Gertrud Koch, "The Body's Shadow Realm," trans. Jan-Christopher Horak and Joyce Rheuban, *October* 50 (Fall 1989): 14.
18. *Regarding Henry*, dir. Mike Nichols, prod. Scott Rudin and Mike Nichols, written by Jeffrey Abrams, 107 min., Paramount, 1991.
19. Butler, "Force," 106.
20. Ibid., 108

21. Ibid., 113.
22. Ross, *No Respect*, 200.
23. For further discussion of lesbian male fantasies see Trish Thomas, "Dykes and Dicks," *Sandmutopia Guardian* 12 (1993): 18–21.
24. Butler, "Force," 108.
25. See, for example, bell hooks's criticisms of the film *Paris Is Burning*, as elaborated in her article "Is Paris Burning?" *Z Magazine*, June 1991, 60–64.
26. Judith Butler, *Gender Trouble: Feminism and the Subversion of Identity* (New York: Routledge, 1990), 31, 124.

TWELVE

Ideology, Poststructuralism, and Class Politics: Rethinking Ideology Critique for a Transformative Feminist Politics

Mas'ud Zavarzadeh

POSTMODERN FEMINISM AND ITS OPPOSITION TO IDEOLOGY (CRITIQUE)

In its new orthodoxy, postmodern feminism has responded to Jane Flax's old (rhetorical?) question, "Do Feminists Need Marxism?"[1] with a resounding "No!" Consequently, in its more recent ludic articulations, feminism has become more and more antagonistic not only to the Marxist labor theory of value, but also toward such Marxist concepts as "ideology" and "ideology critique," which provide the modes of oppositional knowledge of gender and sexuality enabling social transformation. While there are several historical and theoretical reasons for such a growing antagonism, the broad historical situation in which it is located is, of course, the reemergence of the cult of individuality and the free market under the new guise of the subject-as-active-agent, which is itself part of the larger "triumph" of capitalism and its neoliberal ethics in the West as well as in Eastern Europe.

The most important theoretical factor in the rejection of the concept of "ideology" in postmodern feminism, however, is that "gender," as a historical and materialist production of sexual difference, is displaced in ludic feminism by the idea of "sexuality." "Gender," in short, is seen as too deterministic and thus not very conducive to the idea of "agency," whereas "sexuality" — as a postgender notion that marks the "excess"ive play of desire — is considered to open up more room for the aleatory workings of the subject and its freedom.[2] This shift in postmodern feminism and recent queer theory from "gender" to "sexuality" is itself part of a larger shift in social theory and the rearticulation of the very ideas of the "social" and of "social change."

The "social" is reunderstood in postmodern feminism and queer theory along a "ludic" line proposed by such poststructuralist and post-Marxist social and cultural theorists as Michel Foucault, Ernesto Laclau, Donna Haraway, Chantal Mouffe, Teresa De Lauretis, and Judith Butler. In spite of some local variations and disagreements over details in their writings, these theorists model their idea of the "social" after the notion of "difference." The "social" is seen as an ensemble of incommensurable differential (language) games and, as such, a decentered set of processes without any definite closure or end. (Thus the displacement of "gender" — which is seen as a "closural" determinateness — by "sexuality" — as an open-ended language game that Butler calls "performance").[3] In such an understanding of the social, "social change" itself becomes a process of nonclosural negotiations that such ludic theorists as Richard Rorty and Flax have called "conversations"; social change, to be precise, is regarded to be the effect of the emergence of new "discourses" that modify the limits of intelligibilities and re-form representations not by any determining external force (such as labor or economics, for example) but by immanent communal "consensus."

The name of this postmodern consensus in neoliberal cultural theory is "hegemony" — the revival of the Gramscian notion by Laclau and Mouffe to designate a conversational agreement without grounds or center.[4] "Hegemony" and its effects, as developed in the writings of Laclau and Mouffe, is broadened and rearticulated as "ethics" in the writings of J. F. Lyotard and many postmodern feminists who deploy the term as a process of normative evaluation without norms: a case-by-case "reading" of individual practices without any totalizing and overarching theory of "justice."[5] "Ethics" therefore, like discourse, becomes a space of opposition to "politics" and "ideology" — concepts that are seen to represent a total theory that attempts to ground local practices.

The most widely known embodiment of this ludic feminist social and cultural theory is, of course, the allegory of the "cyborg" narrated by Donna Haraway in the "New Age" accents of "experience," "technoculture," and "indeterminacy." "Cyborg" is a figure whose eclectic body and coalitionist outlook normalizes all the social contradictions of late capitalism and presents the incoherence of life under the regime of wage-labor and capital as the mark of living on the advanced frontiers of emerging new life forms, "the boundary between human and animal ... between animal-human and machine ... between physical and nonphysical." "Cyborg," in (post)modern feminist and queer theory, is the negation of "ideology" — normativity — it is a figure whose very existence signifies the polysemic performance of the excessive play of sexual difference and absolute indeterminacy ("affinity"). "Cyborg," in short, is a ludic sign for the ever-expanding horizons of freedom of the subject of the postcausal "social" founded upon conversation, coalition, and hegemony. "Cyborg" is the queer figure of the postideological and postlabor.

In contrast to the postmodern notion of "discourse" (as an indeterminate operation of immanent laws of signification, nonidentity, and difference — the cyborg), postmodern feminist theory has posited "ideology" as theory of determinism that, by its inherently epistemological concerns, limits the "free" play of the cyborg and thus reduces the freedom of "sexuality." Ideology, in short, is perceived in these theories as the repression of desire: a concept reductive of free individuality and agency. By representing "ideology" as an obstacle to individual freedom and free play, postmodern feminist theory has effectively shifted the focus of ideology and ideology critique.

In contrast, ideology critique, in a materialist theory and praxis, produces a knowledge of the social and historical contradictions that enable one class (the owners of the means of production) to exploit (not simply dominate) another class (those who own nothing but their own labor power). To deploy ideology critique in understanding the social is to develop active knowledges of these class relations and social contradictions and consequently to engage in those forms of praxis that overthrow the social structures producing such contradictions and naturalizing them. Ideology critique is above all a historical knowledge of social totality. Such a knowledge is in direct opposition to the class interests that are now represented by ludic feminism and its figure of unbounded desire and the spirit of free enterprise, the "cyborg."

Another orthodoxy in feminism has been the erasure of class or at least the rendering of class as irrelevant to sexual difference. In her classic essay, "Feminism, Marxism, Methods and the State: An Agenda for Theory," Catherine MacKinnon wrote, "Sexuality is to feminism what work is to Marxism: that which is most one's own yet most taken away."[6] Although Haraway, in her figure of the cyborg, opposes the very analytics from which MacKinnon is writing, both share the view that sexuality is indeed what matters most — in fact this has become the commonplace of feminism. Indeed sexuality, like work, is always taken away, but that is not the question: the question is rather, How is it taken away and what are the social structures by which this taking away is put to an end? In other words, sexuality is always historical: it is produced historically, and it is taken away historically. One does not know sexuality immanently, although this is what feminists based in experience have always advocated. Sexuality is produced and taken away by the operations of ideology, which itself acts in the interests of the ruling class. Sexuality, in short, is not experienced in a historical vacuum but is always part of the way in which social relations of production reproduce and distribute economic resources. Whether sexuality is theorized as the mode of reproduction or, as is more common in ludic postmodern theory, as that experience of jouissance fracturing cultural codes and liberating women, it is always the effect of class and labor. The ruling class, in order to justify its appropriation of surplus labor, uses gender and sexuality (as it uses race and other "differences") to naturalize, to justify, and to render unquestionable its exploitation of social labor and to continue the regime of profit. In doing so, it defers the revolutionary praxis that can put human need in place of profit. In a society formed around human need (not profit) one's sexuality is not taken away.

As I elaborate in the following pages, the construction of "ideology" as an epistemological view of the social (truth/untruth) and as a reductive understanding of "desire" is part of a larger class politics in which postmodern feminism is complicit. The ludic feminist theory produces ideology as a repressive concept, and the effect is to conceal the historical practices of exploitation that have maintained the present social relations and to enable them to continue without any crisis. Such postmodern feminists as Michele Barrett obscure the class politics of their opposition to ideology by resorting to a cognitive game, by in fact hiding behind "epistemology." Barrett, finally, justifies the (concealed) class politics of rejecting ideology critique by appealing to "philosophy" (not, I must emphasize, *economics or class)*. In a seemingly disinterested discussion in which it is assumed that ideology is primarily concerned with sorting out "truth" from "falsehood" (thus Barrett's preoccupation with "false consciousness"), she argues that since the grounding of all truths has become so problematic in postmodern theories of knowledge, ideology is irrelevant to any serious discussion of social reality because, among other things, ideology "occludes the question of the body."[7] The "body" in Foucault, whom Barrett is quoting here approvingly, is, of course, the last frontier of the postmodern subject who was "killed" in early structuralist theory and is now being resurrected in poststructuralist thought. The "body," in short, is a transhistorical physicality that asserts the unique aleatory individuality of an enterprising post-Cartesian self who has lost its "consciousness" but gained an autonomous body. Through the figure of the body, ludic feminism brings together the postmodern theory of the social as an ensemble of differences and its opposition to historical materialism (= ideology). The body not only becomes the trope of subjectivity but also the embodiment of materiality itself, and history is no longer perceived as the history of class struggles and the divisions of labor but the history of the body itself. Historical materialism is thus supplanted by what Judith Butler calls "the materiality of women's bodies, the materiality of sex."[8]

The "other" of ideology in postmodern feminist theory, as I have already implied, is "discourse." Discourse, in ludic cultural theory, is seen to be free from the phallocentric preoccupation with "reason" ("truth"), and as such it is capable of offering an understanding of the situation of "women" in advanced industrial democracies — one that is nondeterministic and more relevant to the new world order. "Discourse," unlike "ideology," is considered to empower women by enabling them to intervene in social representations. Since the social is itself conceived as a set of discourses (representations), such discursive interventions are assumed to be freeing, but the social does not in any way address the problem of emancipation from exploitative social and labor relations.

It is, of course, important to note that postmodern feminism, which often locates itself on the "left," shares this antagonism to "ideology" as an occlusion of "individual freedom" and "agency" with right-wing advocates of a deregulated market and free enterprise. In both, the ideas of a just social collectivity and the struggle to eliminate class inequalities are supplanted by the notions of a community of people who share "experiences" and conduct "conversations" about those experiences. Conservative social and cultural theorists such as Daniel Bell and Francis Fukuyama — to take two figures who represent different generations of rightist theorists — have, like Donna Haraway and other ludic feminists, argued for abandoning ideology critique. For them, too, ideology is a "modernist" notion that has exhausted its possibilities and cannot provide reliable knowledge of the complexities of post-al societies: technoculture societies that have crossed the boundaries of the modern Fordism and entered post-ality — the condition of being postcollective, posthistorical, postindustrial and, above all, postclass.

There is in fact a telling convergence between the ludic theories of a postmodern feminist such as Donna Haraway and a right-wing theorist such as Camile Paglia (who claims to be the only "real" feminist around) in their opposition to ideology critique. Both, in obviously different languages, argue that any deployment of ideology critique in understanding the situation of women now leads to producing women as nonactive agents (in Paglia's commonsensical language, as "victims"). The notion of the subject-as-active-agent (in the face of the actual historical domination of the subject by the ruling class relations) is, of course, part of the class politics that I have alluded to. To posit the subject-as-inherently-active is to ignore the historicity of the subject formations in class societies. The views put forth by both Haraway and Paglia, in short, are repetitions of the traditional American notions of self-help and voluntarism celebrated by theorists of petty bourgeois conservatism such as Ronald Reagan and Margaret Thatcher.[9] Class societies are binary societies, and the binary will not be dissolved simply by the "volition" of the free, active agent but requires a collective praxis grounded in the historical knowledge of the social totality. To advocate agency in a vacuum is nothing less than lending support to the most reactionary social theories in which the subject is posited as the origin and source of the social. Ideology critique makes the class politics of such "theories" clear and displays their operation, in various local languages, on all levels of social practices — from the cultural left (the subtle ludic notion of the subject-as-body) to the outrageous right (the subject-as-consciousness). The opposition to ideology and ideology critique is an opposition to such class knowledges.

The convergence of postmodern feminism and right-wing theories is therefore not surprising. Both represent class interests that find it necessary to think of the social and the social division of labor (power) as the outcome of the free expressions of free individuals and to obscure their reality as the effect of the systematic working of labor relations. Ideology critique, as I have argued in the following pages, shows this "freedom" to be a historical construct and demonstrates its necessity for maintaining the ruling social order and for the normalizing and managing the existing social contradictions. For feminism to be a transformative force in bringing about the structural change of gender relations in capitalist societies, it needs not to reunderstand ideology as simply repressive of the agency of the subject but rather to engage ideology critique as the means for producing the historical knowledges that enable the dialectics of agency and the praxis of social revolution.

My focus in this essay is on a sustained theoretical investigation of the ludic assumptions and presuppositions about "ideology" and their overall class politics rather than on the specific forms of postmodern feminist antagonism to ideology and opposition to ideology critique (on these specific questions see the rigorous theoretical work by Teresa L. Ebert, Rosemary Hennessy, and Donald Morton).[10] I am, in other words, addressing here the question why "ideology" has become the "dirty" word in postmodern social theory in general, and not only in feminist theory and (post)modern sexual theories.

LUDIC AND RESISTANCE POSTMODERNISM

Like all concepts deployed for culture analysis, "postmodernism" is not a stable one but a shifting site of social struggle. Even though one may consider certain local features of the contemporary to be "postmodern," postmodernism is not an ensemble of free-floating, "positive," and autointelligible lineaments. Instead, its meaning is the effect of a global frame of intelligibility, a system of articulation, in which various traces and marks are interrelated. This frame of intelligibility is neither in the phenomenon itself, as empiricists propose, nor is it simply a matter of "writing," as textualists insist. It is rather produced historically through social struggles. Thus there are many contesting ways of constructing it — with each construction having a different social effectivity.

Following Teresa L. Ebert's reading of postmodernity,[11] I shall name as "ludic postmodernism" the understanding of postmodernity as a problematics of "representation" that conceives of "representation" itself as a rhetorical issue, a matter of signification in which the very process of signification articulates the signified. Knowledge of the "outside" — if we can mark such a zone of being — is, according to ludic theory, traversed by the rifts, slippages, and alterity that are immanent in signifying practices and, above all, in language. Representation, in other words, is always incommensurate with the represented because it is the subject of the law of "differance."[12] Ludic postmodernism, therefore, posits the "real" as an instance of "simulation" and in no sense the "origin" of a "truth" that can provide a ground for a political project.[13] Differance, in ludic postmodernism, is the effect of the unending "playfulness" (thus the term *ludic*) in signifying practices of the signifier, which can no longer acquire representational authority by anchoring itself in what Derrida has called the "transcendental signified."[14]

Contesting the understanding of "differance" as an effect of rhetoric, "resistance postmodernism" articulates it as the effect of "labor," focusing on congealed and alienated labor as private property. Labor, and not language, I argue, is the social grid of intelligibility that determines the regime of signification and the ensuing "representation" of the real. (In my argument here, I differ from Ebert, who does not privilege "labor" in her reading of resistance postmodernism.)[15] Furthermore, I question the political effectivity of theorizing an excess to labor whether one calls it the "Real,"[16] "jouissance,"[17] or the "Sublime."[18] Language and all other semiotic processes are articulated by the social division of labor and the relations that derive from it. Difference, in short, is a "materialist" praxis produced through class struggle, and not a "rhetorical" effect. Thus, while ludic postmodernism seeks its own genealogy in Nietzschean texts, resistance postmodernism is articulated in the writings of Marx.

THEORIES OF IDEOLOGY

Depending on how "ideology" is articulated with economic and social class structures, the concept of ideology produces different political effects. To stage the deconstructive conflict between ludic postmodernism and the (radical) concept of ideology as the differential of social "difference," I propose a fourfold schema to account for the main understandings of ideology in contemporary discourses.

(1) Theories that see ideology as a historical system of social intelligibility that naturalizes the economic interests of the ruling class by producing a political imaginary ("false consciousness") for the "subject" and thus interpellates the subject within a social zone in which the social contradictions of the relations of production are reversed and the interests of the dominant class are seen as logical, universal, inevitable, and there-

fore as part of the natural order of the world — the way things are and ought to be. This, I would argue, is essentially a Marxian — as distinguished from a Marxist — view. In this radical notion ideology is an imaginary solution to the social contradictions that cannot be solved in practice: the erasure of the contradictions of capital and labor relations.[19]

(2) Political theories that regard ideology to be an ensemble of practices that are, as in the Marxian view, closely related to the material conditions of the mode of production but not specifically tied to the interests of one single class (ruling class). For such theorists as Lenin and Gramsci, there are proletarian (and other) ideologies coexisting with the dominant ruling class ideology at any given historical moment. The "proletarian ideology" does not produce "false consciousness," but quite the opposite. Ideology in this sense, then, is a generalized understanding of the world related to the class position of the subject, but it can be emancipatory (proletarian ideology) or oppressive (bourgeois ideology).

(3) In the writings of Louis Althusser and others, V. I. Lenin's and Antonio Gramsci's expansion of the notion of ideology — to include modes of political intelligibility other than the ruling one that reverses social relations — loses its specific class ties and its involvement in class struggle. It becomes more a set of material practices and forms of knowing that, in Nicos Poulantzas's words, constitute a "relatively coherent discourse which serves as the horizon of agents' experience."[20] Ideology, which in Marx's theories is part of the knowledges and practices of class societies, justifying the economic relations of exploitation, becomes a postclass and panhistorical process: Ideology is eternal; it has no history, in the sense that all societies, as a condition of their existence, secrete ideology. There is no "outside" to ideology. Although Althusser himself maintains a notion of class in the form of specific ideologies, his theory provides a new frame for the complete depoliticization of ideology. Under the kind of epistemological pressures that ludic discourses put on ideology (which I shall examine later in this essay), the concept of ideology, after Althusser, is completely depoliticized. It becomes an innocuously descriptive form; something like this: "ideology is not a system of true or false beliefs and values, a doctrine, so much as it is the means by which culture represents beliefs and values." The emphasis, in other words, is shifted from "why" ideology does what it does to "how" it does it: a shift from the political to the rhetorical, from the explanatory to the descriptive — a

dissolution, in short, of ideology into "discourse." As such, it grounds one of the ludic dogmas that there is no "outside" to ideology.

(4) The radically ludic pronouncement on ideology, however, goes much further than a depoliticized Althusserian reading of representation and subjectivity. It is most clearly articulated in the writings of Gilles Deleuze and Felix Guattari, who, for instance, in their *A Thousand Plateaus: Capitalism and Schizophrenia*, write: "There is no ideology and never has been."[21]

I regard the Marxian and Deleuze-Guattari concepts of ideology to be "radical" in the sense that both address the root issues. In this essay I attempt to foreground the conceptual crisis of "ideology" brought about by the encounter of ludic and Marxian discourses in the postmodern moment. I shall briefly map out the points of contestation between the ludic and radical (Marxian) views of ideology, because such a comparative reading will shed light on a range of issues that are discussed in this book. I will focus on such recurring questions in reading ideology as "truth," "totality," "causality," "subjectivity," and the like. Throughout the essay, however, whenever I talk about the "radical theory of ideology," it is the Marxian view that I have in mind — the Deleuze-Guattari, ludic erasure of the Marxian notion is radical only in its opposition to the Marxian theory. Its social and political consequences are extremely conservative. The marking of these two political sites as "radical" and "conservative," of course, marks my own discourse and its own conditions of possibility: I find the radical (Marxian) concept of "ideology" necessary for producing political "knowledge" for the purpose of social transformation and the building of a multicultural democracy founded upon economic (and not merely discursive and semiotic) equality. The ludic notion of ideology as discourse, I believe, will provide, at the very most, the "experience" of "pleasure" for the subject who might deploy "jouissance" as a mode of opposition to the dominant cultural policy and subsequently as a means for opening up a more flexible space ("freedom") for the "enterprises" of the "ethical" subject. I find the "ethical" — as an erasure of the political — to be a return to immanent reforms in the dominant social arrangements and not a radical transformation of the enframing structures of exploitation. I will come back to this issue several times through my discussion of the "outside" of ideology. From a ludic perspective radical ideology's claim to an "outside" to ideology (a classless society) amounts to a metaphysical fiction: a claim to have access to a coherent truth, and such a claim, it is believed, necessarily issues from a theory of the theory of signs that is founded upon the possibility of the "proper" — the literalness that lies beyond the reach of "differance."[22]

THE LUDIC READING OF "IDEOLOGY" AS EPISTEMOLOGICAL AND THE QUESTION OF "TRUTH" AND "FALSEHOOD"

This is one reason why "ideology" is the repressed concept in the discourses of ludic postmodernism. The "quarrel" of ludic postmodern — as the regime of difference and reflexivity — with the radical concept of ideology begins with a reading of ideology as a mastering mode of understanding. In this ludic reading, radical ideology suppresses difference by attributing it to the "other" and thus erasing it within itself in order to construct an identitarian truth and its corollary, selfsame falsehood. The concept of ideology, in other words, is seen in the ludic discourses as another repetition of a familiar logocentric story. This view is itself, of course, a repetition of a familiar story: Karl Mannheim's narrative in which the radical theory of ideology is regarded as being interested only in examining the opponent's position and not its own. Ideology, according to him, protects its own "truth" by constructing a coherent "other" and thus obtains its own "identity." For Mannheim the radical concept of ideology provides a unified account of the world from the perspective of a privileged subject (the proletariat) whose own position is never put in question. In a move that anticipates the ludic notion of ideology as the all-pervasive discursive horizon of cultural intelligibility and not as a class device for reversing social contradictions, Mannheim writes that ideology cannot "remain the exclusive privilege of one class. ... It is no longer possible for one point of view and interpretation to assail all others as ideological without itself being placed in the position of having to meet that challenge."[23]

Mannheim, clearly, demands that ideology be read reflexively so that its reading of the world includes itself. As if responding to this demand, the ludic reflexive reading, by inscribing the "other" in ideology, deconstructs the radical political use of the "concept" as identitarian in Marx's texts, among others,[24] and reduces it to "discourse" — the ineluctable matrix of all social utterances. The decentering of "ideology" by "discourse" is part of a larger theoretical move in ludic postmodern theory, the purpose of which is to put under erasure the Hegelian idea of "concept" as "giving the essence of the real"[25] that is, as an epistemological closure, a self-identical proximation to truth. From the perspective of ludic postmodernism, ideology's claim to truth locates it in the Hegelian project. It is thus, like all other logocentric concepts, "textualized" into "discourse," where it is traversed, as a differential representation (of "truth"), by its "other" ("falsehood") and thus is un-founded and de-centered.

The ludic decentering of the "truth" of ideology — by including in it its seeming opposite, "falsehood" — is ultimately founded upon a theory of language derived from Ferdinand de Saussure. In his *Course in General Linguistics*, Saussure writes, "In language there are only differences *without positive terms*" (emphasis in the original).[26] The philosophical and political ramifications of such a theory of the sign are many, but perhaps the most important, at least in Jacques Derrida's radical reading of it, is that there are no self-possessed, identitarian concepts that can be said to be "present" to themselves and as such self-standing and without intertextuality. Seemingly positive, coherent, and unitary concepts such as "nature," "truth," "goodness" are part of what Derrida calls the (Western) "metaphysics of presence" and its affiliated regimes of logocentrism and phallo-logocentrism. Each of these putatively self-possessed concepts is an instance of "differance": its excluded opposite is not in its "outside" but is, in fact, inscribed in its "inside," undermining its claim to a coherent identity. This is another way of saying, of course, that the boundaries of inside/outside are also part of the regime of logocentrism. The coherent concept, in short, like the (linguistic) sign is internally divided and marked by the "trace" of other signs — its identity is enabled by its intertextuality and not through a direct participation in the "reality" that it is said to signify.

"Nature," for example, cannot be conceptualized without its binary opposite, "culture," and in this sense it can be said that "nature," far from signifying a moment of plenitude and fullness, is constituted by its excluded "other" — culture, in short, by what it is not supposed to be, by its own "absence." As such it is not a "decidable" category whose meaning is "present" to itself; instead it actually means through its supplementary relation with culture. Culture, in other words, is the "differance" of "nature" from itself — its nonpossession of reality that it seems to signify — the "differance" banished to nature's "outside," which marks absence and fallenness. By the same token, culture is also a differential concept whose meaning is not in itself but falls between itself and its other, nature. Both nature and culture, like all other categories of intelligibility, are then "undecidable." It is important to remember that the purpose of ludic deconstruction is not a simple reversal of nature/culture, truth/falsehood but a destablization of both. In short, like linguistic signs, all seemingly self-coherent concepts derive their meaningfulness not from their own positivity but through their supplementary, differential relation with other signs and concepts that are always "present" in them by their "absence."

According to the ludic notion of supplementarity and trace, therefore, "truth" in the radical theory of ideology — its proposal that the social is produced by the historical interests of the ruling class but represented in the dominant ideology as the transhistorical and universal truth derived from the very structures of actuality — is not an instance of "positivity" (self-coherence). Rather it is constituted by its excluded "other" (the falsehood of bourgeois ideology). As such, it is not a self-constituted and self-identical truth that can provide a reliable ground for such political and social actions as "revolution." The truth claimed by the radical theory of ideology is, in ludic terms, an undecidable truth. To disregard the rhetoric of truth — its textual difference and tracefullness — is, according to the ludic logic, to "essentialize" truth and to be "reductive" and "totalizing."

In his "Structure, Sign, and Play in the Discourse of the Human Sciences," Derrida provides an authorizing account of the dissolution of concepts, as centered totalities, into the differential play of discourse. The "truth" of a proposition, according to Derrida, is not centered in itself and thus is not reliable because:

the center had no natural site. . . . It was not a fixed locus but a function, a sort of nonlocus in which an infinite number of sign-substitutes came into play. *This was the moment when language invaded the universal problematic, the moment when, in the absence of a center or origin, everything became discourse* . . . that is to say a system in which the central signified, the original or transcendental signified, is never absolutely present outside a system of differences. The absence of the transcendental signified extends the domain and the play of signification infinitely.[27]

To see the full implications of Derrida's observations for a theory of the social in which ideology is a reflexive discourse, we need first to take a detour and briefly examine the outline of a social analytics based on

Derrida's deconstruction of ideology through his notions of difference, play, and discourse.

In his exemplary text "Transformations of Advanced Industrial Societies and the Theory of the Subject,"[28] Ernesto Laclau offers a post-Marxist analysis of the growing complexity of the postmodern social by rejecting the Hegelian theory of mediations, which interprets this complexity as a mere diversification of an originary totality, in favor of an analytics of "articulation." "Articulation," he later writes, is a "practice establishing a relation among elements such that their identity is modified as a result of the articulatory practice. The structured totality resulting from the articulatory practice we will call *discourse*."[29] The postmodern social complexity — by which he seems to mean the historical situation since the French Revolution, in which bipolar social antagonism, Laclau believes, appeared for the last time — is thus only understandable as being constitutively differential and discursive. "The social," he maintains "is that which is always already there, as a possibility and as a terrain for constitution of differences."[30] Differences, for him, are not "positivities" between two selfsame entities, but, like Saussure, he understands them to be constitutive of the phenomenon. There is no outside to "difference." Thus any understanding of the social in terms of a totality is reductive and leads to the dissolution of "politics" into "economics" and, furthermore, brings to an end the tension between the "logic of equality" and the "logic of difference"/"liberty" that is constitutive of a radical democracy. Democracy, unlike totalitarianism, is seen as a constant hegemonic negotiation of the "tension" between the "same" and "different." The social, he writes, is identical with "an infinite play of differences in relation to which there is no privileged point of entry."[31] In fact the "social" itself, as the object of such disciplinary knowledges as "sociology," does not exist (the "impossibility of society") because it cannot provide a reliable and firm ground for analysis: "The incomplete character of every totality leads us to abandon, as a terrain of analysis, the premise of 'society' as a sutured totality. 'Society' is not a valid object of discourse ... there is no single underlying principle fixing — and hence constituting — the whole field of differences."[32] In other words, the social is not a determinate totality but follows the logic of the "sign," and as such its relations are identical with those of the sign. It is a "type of relationship between elements in which each of the elements points towards the rest without this relationship being predetermined by the nature of any of them."[33] For Laclau, to conceive of the social as the "articulation of differences" is to conceive of it as "signifying relations;"[34] and as such it is subject to the laws of the sign and thus, following Saussure, is marked by arbitrariness.

The implication of such an analogy between the social and the sign is that social relations, far from being determined by a structure of necessity, always "exceed" such a structure and rupture its laws of representation. One can never explain existing social relations, for example, in terms of relations of exploitation, because such an explanation, according to Laclau, refers "the social order to a transcendental principle."[35] In the absence of any underlying totality or even originary difference,[36] the social is reduced to a series of conjunctural sites that are autointelligible: they make sense in and of themselves without any necessary structural connections with others. And because there is no law of "necessity," *experience* itself provides the grid of intelligibility. Opposition to "necessity" is, of course, by now, a founding component of the postmodern commonsense.[37] Like signs, elements of the social may have connections with one another, but this connection is by no means predetermined. The social, in short, is produced, in Laclau's theory, as a plurality that is not only not predetermined but also reversible. In post-Marxist thought, then, social relations become "language games," to use Lyotard's term:[38] incommensurate with one another, they are mere contingent associations. When the social is the site of reversible differentiality and contingent articulations, then the conception of "politics" itself changes into the "politics of the signifier."[39]

The modern concept of ideology from its initial articulation in the writings of Destutt de Tracy (*Element d'Ideologie*, 1801–1815) to the texts of Antonio Negri (*Marx beyond Marx: Lessons on the Grundrisse*)[40] and Gilles Deleuze and Felix Guattari (*A Thousand Plateaus: Capitalism and Schizophrenia*),[41] has been, in Stuart Hall's words, "shadowed by its 'Other' – Truth, Reason, Science."[42] The ludic critique also reads the radical concept of ideology epistemologically as an instance of logocentrism. In Paul Hirst's words, "The concept of ideology as part of an epistemological discourse has always involved the distinction of true and false (ideological) knowledge of reality."[43] Such an epistemologization of the radical theory of ideology is itself a ludic strategy of containment: the radical concept of ideology is primarily a political construct aimed at articulating the power differential (and its consequent exploitative relations) and thus an apparatus in class struggle. It is not, in other words, a calculus of truth and falsehood in the ludic sense.

The claim to "truth" that ludic postmodern theory finds implicit in the theory of ideology is regarded to be unfounded because it requires the correspondence between "knowledge" and "being" — a theory of representation that differential postmodernism finds highly problematic. Therefore, to designate any discourse as "ideological," according to this view, is to set up a logocentric binary, the purpose of which is the erasure of "differance," since to point to "falsehood," ineluctably, is to point simultaneously to a region that is free from error: an instance of plenitude, transparency, and truth — a moment that is, in other words, free from "differance." The truth of ideology, it is said, is "founded" on nothing less than a claim to have access to an "outside": a space of knowing that is natural, transtextual, and beyond the systems of cultural (linguistic) representations. It is this "outside" (truth) that ludic postmodern theory posits as determining, in the last instance, the "falsehood" of ideology. Ludic theory, after Derrida's "The Outside Is Inside,"[44] finds such a claim to truth to be not only epistemologically unviable but also ethically unacceptable: it is an instance of the violence of the will to truth/power and as such is repressive and totalitarian. This (repressive) "truth" of ideology, for ludic theorists, is seen to be founded upon the presupposition of a sutured "totality" as the unity of the social.

The ludic assault on the radical theory of ideology, then, is, in the first instance, focused on the notion that the radical theory posits the ideological as the domain of error and distortion ("false consciousness"). Moreover, the radical concept of ideology embodies, in the words of Alessandro Fontana and Pasquale Pasquino, a "nostalgia for a quasi-transparent form of knowledge, free from all error and illusion ... knowledge without deception,"[45] and because such distinctions are baseless, the concept of ideology itself is meaningless. Foucault's own privileging of a Nietzschean understanding of truth (like Hirst's advocacy of a Nietzschean ethics) is in fact founded upon a similar argument. For him the main problem with the concept of ideology is that "it always stands in virtual opposition to something else which is supposed to count as truth." The interesting issue for him is not simply drawing the line between "truth" and "falsehood" in a discourse but, more importantly, "seeing historically how effects of truth are produced within discourses which in themselves are neither true nor false."[46] Here Foucault not only erases social conflicts in the interest of the neutrality of (the libertarian) discourse, but more significantly he denies the possibility of any distinctions between truth and falsehood. In his essay "Nietzsche, Genealogy, History" he is more specific about the aporia that writes both terms of the binary (truth/falsehood): "Truth is undoubtedly the sort of error that cannot be refuted because it was hardened into an unalterable form in the long baking process of history."[47] By reducing ideology to a mere epistemological issue, Foucault constructs the concept of ideology as presupposing the possibility of a disinterested truth as an instance of plenitude and presence. Such a reading of the radical theory of ideology is, of course, founded upon Foucault's libertarian view of "power" as nonrepressive: a view that underlies his proposal to replace ideology critique with a genealogical (apolitical and nonconflictual) analytic of power (as enabling) and (existing) truth. Such a project removes ideology critique from the scene of political contestation and installs in its place a cognitive inquiry into difference.

In ludic theory, the radical theory of ideology is thus narrated as the story of a reification of truth that posits the critic of ideology as the person of truthful consciousness and places him outside ideology as the absolute subject of knowledge. This is the absolute subject of the metanarrative of Lyotard, who claims to have access to history and through such a knowledge to have obtained an (infallible) understanding of the social "totality." Once again the postmodern critique of the concept of ideology leads back to its injunction against totality and totalization.

IDEOLOGY, TOTALITY, AND TOTALIZATION

The postmodern–post-Marxist rejection of totality/totalizing is not founded simply on the assertion that totalization is the conceptual equivalent of totalitarianism or that the social is a series of incommensurate language games without any necessary links. Rather it is based on a further "turn" on the question of "language." If, as Laclau elaborates,[48] the logic of the social is that of the sign, then a total knowledge of the social is as impossible as a total knowledge of the sign. Here, as elsewhere in his theory of the social as discourse, Laclau draws upon Derrida.

Derrida's argument against totality, although related to those of Lyotard and all other postmodern theoreticians of language (games), is not identical with them. While Lyotard's argument is, like those put forth by Deleuze and Guattari, a somewhat empirical argument for "specificity" based upon the incommensurability of specific instances, Derrida's discourse against totality is founded upon the the unmasterable (nontotalizable) play of the sign itself. In the text I have already referred to, "Structure, Sign, and Play in the Discourses of the Human Sciences," Derrida engages Claude Lévi-Strauss's "Overture" to his *The Raw and the Cooked*, in which he refers to the impossibility of making an "exhaustive inventory (totalizing) of South American Myths before analyzing them" in defense of his own antiempiricism. Empirically, Lévi-Strauss believes, it is not possible to undertake such an inventory because "The total body of myth belonging to a given community is comparable to its speech" and thus infinite. Therefore, "unless the population dies out physically or morally," the act of "totalization" of its myths is never complete. In other words, totalization is an empirical impossibility because the data is infinite and beyond the understanding of the subject of knowledge. However, Lévi-Strauss's argument acquires a new turn when he states that even if it were possible to "totalize" the myths belonging to a given community, he would not feel "constrained to accept the arbitrary demand for a total mythological pattern, since as has been shown, such a requirement has no meaning."[49] Lévi-Strauss then, in Derrida's reading, argues that "totalization" is both impossible (on empirical grounds) and useless (theoretically). Lévi-Strauss arrives at the same antitotality position held by Lyotard and post-Marxists, such as Laclau and Mouffe, as well as many other ludic postmodernists. His observations lead back to the question of the subject: totality is not thinkable without an absolute subject of knowledge, and such a subject is neither available nor desirable — it is meaningless. Derrida's critique of Lévi-Strauss, as might be expected, is not that Lévi-Strauss argues against totality and totalization but that his argument is not radical enough. The absolute knowledge (of the subject) is not possible because of the immanent play of the sign and its intrinsic "negativity" — not because of empirical or theoretical considerations:

If totalization no longer has any meaning, it is not because the infiniteness of a field cannot be covered by a finite glance or a finite discourse, but because the nature of the field — that is language and a finite language excludes totalization. This field is in effect that of *play*, that is to say, a field of infinite substitutions only because it is finite, that is to say, because instead of being an inexhaustible field, as in the classical hypothesis, instead of being too large, there is something missing from it: a center which arrests and grounds the play of substitutions.[50]

Totalization is not possible because our knowledge is textual and subject to the laws of difference. Any attempt to totalize, therefore, amounts to excluding some parts of the totalized because there is always already an "excess" that the totalization cannot account for. Totalization is thus, in Lyotard's language, a violence toward the unrepresentable and as such a totalitarian act. To posit a total truth, through the true consciousness of the subject of knowledge as the "other" of "false consciousness," for ludic theory, is thus a violence that the radical theory ideology commits in its attempt to make sense of the social.

"FALSE CONSCIOUSNESS," LUDIC POLITICS, THE "AUTONOMY" OF THE IDEOLOGICAL, AND CLASS STRUGGLE

The theory of knowledge that produces the binary of "truth" and "falsehood" on the assumption of the identity of "knowledge" and "being" is, according to ludic epistemology, founded upon the erasure of differance and, consequently, upon a notion of signification as representational — a notion that is deeply rooted in a logocentric empiricism. Empiricism/representationalism posits knowledge as a representation or, even more forcefully, a "reflection" of the truth of the object itself in the consciousness of the subject. Language simply "represents"/"reflects" that which is presignificatory and unconstrained by textuality: a truth in its fullness of identity. Knowledge, then, is not the effect of the means of representation (signifying practices) but lies in the object itself. Consequently, "truth" is a correspondence (correct representation) between the represented and its representation, while "falsehood" (misrepresentation) is a lack of such a correspondence. The represented, in other words, exists "outside" the process of representation. The empiricist theory of knowledge and its concomitant representationalism, as I have already implied, posit knowledge as the experience of the subject, thus leading to the notion of ideology as "false consciousness": a misrepresentation and an illusion.

Ludic discourses, on the other hand, regard knowledge to be the effect of the means of representation themselves. All knowledges, in other words, are fallen (constrained and textual) knowledges produced by signification (that is, in the last instance, by "interpretation") and not of representation. In Hirst's words, "the means of representation determine the represented."[51] Knowledge, in short, is a "discourse," and as such its truth is "significatory" (immanent to its signifying practices and internal semiotic regime) and not "representational." Such a theory, as we shall see, has an important implication for the relation between the "economic" instance/class and ideology.

The notion that knowledge is representational and consequently the idea that ideology is a misrepresentation, as ludic postmodernism claims, has led to a theory of ideology as illusion: a misrepresentation. Such a view of ideology as the experience of (false) knowledge by the subject — false consciousness — denies the "materiality" of ideology as a set of social practices. Ideology, accordingly, will not have a reality of its own, and its (ir)reality is a mere reflection/representation of an "outside." To say that ideology is an illusion, a mere refection of social reality, is to question the possibility of ideological struggle as a means of intervention in the dominant social arrangements. If ideology is a mere illusion and a simple false consciousness, then it is not so much a part of social reality — open to intervention — but a mere reflection of it. No ideological struggle is possible — and to that extent the range of radical politics is restricted — since ideology is a shadow knowledge, "a pure illusion, a pure dream i.e. ... nothingness."[52]

"Differance" in ludic theory is the trope of a superstructuralist politics: the ludic politics of the signifier, which privileges "ideological struggle" — directed and controlled by the upper (middle) classes, who have access to modes of signification (media, culture, industry, universities, publishing networks) — over "class struggle." The notion of ideological struggle has acquired considerable prominence among the professionals of ideology (intellectuals?) in first world postmodernism because of the commonsensical belief that the new forms of deployment of capital rely more than ever on the strategic uses of ideology for their effectivity. In fact, the very notion of politics and political struggle is so rearticulated in ludic postmodernism as to render "ideological struggle" identical with emancipatory practices by erasing revolutionary "class struggle." The tenet of postmodern superstructuralism is perhaps best articulated by one of its precursors, Mikhail Bakhtin, in his framing of the logic of signification: intelligibility is produced, he writes, "Not from the thing to the word, but from the word to the thing; the word gives birth to the thing."[53] Bakhtin's ludic politics — whose popularity among first world intellectuals is one of the symptoms of the "cold war," during which his writings were deployed as the grand strategy for the containment of radical practices — is the trope for the global reversal of the relation of "production" and "consumption" in the ludic logic of the social. This logic also informs such other local reversals as Jean Baudrillard's positing of the "exchange value" as producer of "use value," Roland Barthes's shift in the relation between denotation and connotation, and Foucault's "genealogy" (as the discourse of immanence), and it shapes the central principle of Derridean "differance," which traverses all binaries and marks them as the effects of a protoform (archewriting).

Superstructuralism — as the regime of the reversal of the relations between the material base and cultural and political productions through a privileging of politics and culture over the economics — is the archelogic of ludic postmodernism. In its philosophical and theoretical practices, such as poststructuralism, deconstruction, Lacanian psychoanalysis, new historicism, neopragmatism, mainstream feminism, and various forms of experiential "cultural studies," it produces the social frames of intelligibility that most effectively construct the political and economic "obviousnesses" needed by advanced capitalism under the sign of the postmodern. In his address to the joint session of the United States Congress on February 21, 1990, Czechoslovak President Vaclav Havel announced the death of socialism and the triumph of capitalism by appealing to the ludic logic of the superstructuralist common sense when he declared to the cheers of his ecstatic American audience: "Consciousness precedes Being, and not the other way around as Marxists claim."

However, "ideological struggle," in the radical theory of ideology, is an integral part of class struggle. As Nicholas Garnham argues,

The very notion of ideology and ideological struggle related to it, derives from a notion of class and of economic and not vice versa.... That is to say the concept of ideology was developed for specific purposes, namely to explain how a specific structure of material imbalance reproduces itself. The theory of ideology is thus the product of a theory of social formations which are ultimately determined at the economic level.[54]

The ludic notion of "ideological struggle," on the other hand, is an apparatus for deconstructing the logic of economic determination in order to produce a notion of the social as an ensemble of free-floating discourses, each autonomous and self-determining. It is a theory that ends up reproducing the historically necessary social relations of production in advanced capitalism.

For ludic postmodernity, radical politics is therefore not so much a matter of providing access to the means of production for all (economic democracy as the foundation of rights) but access to the means of signification. Because, in spite of its ostensible erasure of all forms of determinism, ludic superstructuralism sees "culture" as the determinant of intelligibilities, radical politics is thus rearticulated so as to mean an intervention in cultural "meanings." The most "radical" form of this intervention is, according to ludic deconstruction, an "obscuring" (by rendering "undecidable") of the established meanings of the old common sense — the bourgeois common sense that is no longer historically relevant to the unimpeded movement of capital. The jettisoning of the traditional (humanist) common sense, in the name of a "radical politics," in other words, is itself a subtle maneuver to remove from the scene of philosophy those frames of intelligibility that have lost their economic relevance to the relations of capitalist production. Barbara Johnson formulates the major premise of superstructuralist radicalism when she writes, "Nothing could be more comforting to the established order than the requirement that everything be assigned a clear meaning or stand."[55] In the writings of Foucault, Derrida, and particularly Lyotard, then, "radical politics" becomes more a matter of locally obscuring the "obviousnesses" of the dominant common sense and thus problematizing its "certainty" about the real, than a way of globally transforming social arrangements and providing access to the means of production for all. Lyotard goes so far in this "obscuring" of meaning as to equate any coherent collective cultural meaning with "cultural policy" and to regard "cultural policy" to be a form of "totalizing" and the effect of an underlying totalitarianism.

In the antitotalitarian, democratic ludic politics, "parody," "pastiche," "irony," "pun," Bakhtinian "carnavalesque," and their archewriting — "laughter" — are used as devices through which the connection between the signifier and the signified is deferred and the "obviousnesses" of "cultural policy" — established meanings — are "obscured." Obscurity is thus conceived to produce a radical effect because it empties the world of ready-made meanings. The way the emptied world is charged and made to resignify, however, is politically of significance.

In opposing radical ideology, ludic politics grounds itself upon the notion that language is not a reliable means of access to the "truth" of the world because, as Derrida has argued, any "representation" of the real is subject to the laws of signification: it is marked by slippage and gaps and is thus undecidable. Representation, in the post-Marxist articulation of Paul Hirst, is "the product of the practice of signification."[56] If indeed there is no signified that exists prior to its signification, then the social itself, as a language effect, is an ensemble of "differences" — the product of ludic "writing," and as such it always "exceeds" any "totality." Ludic politics is, in other words, a postpolitics that announces the death of the social "totality."

It must be added, however, that the ludic critique of ideology as false consciousness — illusion determined by material forces and, consequently, a move away from "class struggle" toward "ideological struggle" — is, as my previous reference to Althusser indicates, also inscribed within the discourses of the radical theory of ideology itself. In his various texts Althusser argues for ideology as "a representation [narratives, images, signifying practices] of the imaginary relationship of individuals to their real conditions of existence."[57] Ideology, in short, to use Althusser's words again, "has a material existence."[58] In annotating Althusser, Hirst argues that the proof of "materiality" (non-illusionary) of ideology is "how can something which has effects be false?"[59] Hirst's notion of nonfalsehood is a rather simplistic one: capitalism is the regime of the "effective" false. The question, for ludic politics, is not that ideology has a material existence but rather, What is the relation of its material existence to other instances of material existence: the contestations over ideology are only secondarily about its "material existence." What is at issue is the logic of the social: the order of determination/indeterminacy. "Material existence," in the ludic discussions on ideology, is a trope for "autonomy" — the self-governance of ideology by virtue of its own immanent laws of intelligibility and cognitive properties. In order to claim the autonomy of the ideological, assert the necessity of ideological struggle, and justify the understanding of politics as an intervention in signification (jarring the gap between the signifier and the signified and deferring the fullness of clear meanings), ludic postmodern theory needs to argue for the reality of ideology as an autonomous reality in itself and not as a mere representation/reflection of the forces of production.

If politics is conceived as an intervention in the means of signification without reference to the modes and means of production, then the question of the relation of ideology to other social instances acquires a different aspect. In the radical theory of ideology, ideology has always been seen as closely related to the mode of production. This connection, which Hirst, Laclau, and Mouffe call "economism," is what post-Marxist/postmodernist theory has set out to deconstruct, because such a model, in Chantal Mouffe's words, misrecognizes "the distinct *autonomy* of politics and ideology" (emphasis added).[60]

"CAUSALITY," BASE, SUPERSTRUCTURE, AND THE (RE)TURN TO THE "AUTONOMY" OF IDEOLOGY

In their text "Recasting Marxism: Hegemony and New Political Movements" Laclau and Mouffe articulate the theoretical/political space of the ludic postmodern as it displaces the radical theory of ideology and reunderstands ideology as the discourse of a differential inclusivity and a libertarian and reformist politics so passionately defended by Hirst and Barry Hindess and Hirst.[61] The radical theory of ideology, they believe, should be abandoned because it is founded upon the (classic Marxist) theory of the "base" and "superstructure" and the (causal) logic of determination (from the "outside") that it entails. "The economistic problematic of ideology," Mouffe maintains, consists in "seeing a causal link between the structure and superstructure and in viewing the latter purely as a mechanical reflection of the economic base. This leads to a vision of ideological superstructures as epiphenomena which play no part in the historical process."[62] Similarly, Laclau interprets the explanatory power of the "base" as being identical with the force of natural causal laws and thus essentialized as a nondiscursive "origin." He therefore concludes that in radical theory, "the ensemble of signifying practices constituting the field of discourse could only be conceived, by definition, as belonging to the realm of superstructures. 'Ideology' was synonymous with 'forms of consciousness' and the latter were necessary reflections — or at least representations — of a causal movement which transcended them."[63] Ideology, for Laclau and Mouffe — who read Gramsci's texts, in the wake of Althusser, as a postmodern site for a new theory of the social — is not a body of ideas/false consciousness "caused" by the economic instance but an autonomous discourse, the "truth" of which is the effect of the discourse's very own immanent laws of signification. It is an "organic and relational whole embodied in institutions and apparatuses which weld together a historic bloc around a number of basic articulatory principles."[64] Such a theory, they maintain, "precludes the possibility of a 'superstructuralist' reading of the ideological."[65]

Laclau and Mouffe's proposal for ideology as an autonomous instance of the social is, of course, an extension of Althusser's rejection of the Hegelian notion of the social as an "expressive totality." Althusser reunderstands the social as an overdetermined totality in which different social instances — the economic, the political, and the ideological — enjoy a degree of "relative autonomy." However, this is not an absolute autonomy because all are, "in the last instance," related to the economic something that ludic political theory finds unacceptable.[66] In Althusser, in other words, the instances of the social are affected, in a hierarchical fashion, by those (economic) social contradictions that are prior to others. The postmodern/post-Marxist theory of the social first of all attacks the notion of social totality and its hierarchical determination. In rejecting the proposal of the radical theory of ideology that there is indeed a necessary relation among all the instances of the social, determined in the last instance by the economic, post-Marxist theory posits (at least in one of its interpretations) that there is, as Stuart Hall argues, "necessarily no correspondence . . . that nothing really connects with anything else."[67]

Contesting Hall's reading as a misrecognition of his (post-Marxist) position, Paul Hirst theorizes the social without reference to any "totality." He is arguing, he explains,

for the rejection of the concept of totality itself, and, therefore, the rejection of the problems of the relations of the political, economic, and other "instances" in terms of hierarchy of causal effectivity, relative autonomy etc. In our position, political, economic and other social relations are unified into a whole and subject to its limits.[68]

Political forces, ideological formations, and other social practices, in other words, are not subject to general laws or concepts "stemming, say, from the necessities and effects of capitalist mode of production." In other words, there is, as far as post-Marxism/postmodernism is concerned, no possibility for a theory of ideology. Ideological effects should be "read" conjuncturally. Hall's own position — which is not argued politically or even philosophically but is a "pragmatic" solution — is that there are no "guarantees" and that the truth lies somewhere between "necessary correspondence" and no correspondence. Hall's eclectic and pragmatic solution is, at the present moment, the most pervasive one on the (generic) left. It is a more philosophically complex (but still politically eclectic) version — a position for which Fredric Jameson has argued[69] — and attempts to bridge the gap between the radical Marxist theory of ideology and ludic postmodern theories by adopting a version of Althusser's "structural causality."

The post-Marxist position on ideology and the problematic of causality are very much an expansion and elaboration of Foucault's objection to the radical theory of ideology in which, according to him, "ideology stands in a secondary position relative to something which functions as its infrastructure, as its material, economic determinant."[70] Foucault's solution is, of course, to displace ideology by that form of discursive practice that he calls, at various points in his thinking, "archaeology"/"genealogy" — a noncausal and conjunctural "thick description." Similarly, in the neo-Nietzschean stance of Hirst, Hindess, Laclau, and Mouffe, ideology is cut off from a material base/determinant and reduced to a self-determining discourse that operates by its own laws of signification and is governed not by causality but by the tropic regimes of rhetoric — the logic of the sign. Such a move has a profound political role in the organization of the postmodern social because it effectively erases ideology as a marker of "conflicts" (for instance, "class struggle") and reinscribes it as discourse — the space of a nonconflictual difference. Since, in the ludic postmodern turning away from ideology, all social relations are posited as discursive difference, "the basis for the distinction between base and superstructure," according to Laclau, "collapses and with it disappears the only terrain on which the concept of ideology made sense."[71] The logic of the social in ludic politics is, in the last instance, a species of rhetoric: association by tropes.

THE "SUBJECT" OF/IN IDEOLOGY

If the radical theory is read as essentially a theory of ideology as "false consciousness," then the subject itself in this theory will be seen as standing outside the "discourse," beyond the reach of the laws of difference. As Foucault puts it, "The concept of ideology refers, I think necessarily, to something of the order of a subject."[72] The theory of the social as *atotality* and thus as a theater of the incessant play of difference dismantles such a notion of the subject and proposes the subject as discontinuous. In her essay "Hegemony and Ideology in Gramsci," Mouffe maintains that what she calls an economistic theory of ideology presupposes not only a linear causality between economic and ideological instances, but also a theory of the subject as being determined by its "position ... in the relations of production."[73] The subject, in the radical theory of ideology, as far as ludic postmodernists are concerned, is pregiven and preconstituted by its class position. In the postmodern moment marked by increasing social complexity, Laclau believes, the continuous subject, whose ideological position is an extension of its class and economic situationality, is displaced by a hegemonic subject — a "dislocated" subject of diverse and contradictory positions that traverses social classes and thus is post-"class." It is, he maintains, only by such a view of the subject as an ensemble of heterogeneity that one can account for such complex postmodern subject behaviors as, for example, "the linkage between the degree of union militancy of a white worker in the workplace, on the one hand, and his attitude towards racial conflicts in his neighborhood, on the other."[74] The relations among these subject positions, he believes, are by no means determined (by economic/class interests) but rather, as instances of the social as discursive practice, follow the arbitrary logic of the sign. The conception of the logic of the social as that of the sign, as we have already implied, posits the social as contingent and discards the logic of "necessity." The post-Marxist social analytics — which most pointedly articulates the discontent of the postmodern with ideology — essentially marks, as Laclau and Mouffe put it in their *Hegemony and Socialist Strategy: Towards a Radical Democratic Politics*, the "dissolution" of the revolutionary "Jacobin imaginary" and the consequent refounding of the liberal imaginary.[75]

Hirst's critique of the subject in the radical theory of ideology is an extension of his contestation of the empiricist theory of knowledge and representationalism that he sees implied in that theory. If ideology is "false consciousness," according to him, it means that "knowledge" is an "experience" of the object by a subject that is always already constituted and is thus beyond the reach of the discourses of ideology. "The subject," in the radical theory of ideology, Hirst believes, "constitutes what it knows, it is the origin of what it knows, and therefore experience is the return of origin to itself."[76] Because in such a theory "Ideology is ... a function of the structure of reality itself; the places that are created by social relations generate the ideologies that follow from them, through the mechanism of experience."[77] However, in the absence of "totality" and the necessary determinations among social instances that such a totality presupposes, the ideological position of the subject is far from being determined by its class. Referring to Althusser's notion that the structure of ideology is "specular" and his theorizing ideology as an "imaginary relationship of individuals to their real conditions of existence,"[78] Hirst proposes a view of the subject by annotating Althusser's "imaginary" in the following terms. "The 'imaginary' is a concept which supposes recognition; it is both an *image* (object or recognition) and a spectral reality (it is only itself, it 'reflects' nothing but itself). The 'imaginary' is not the *imagination* of the subject; as if the subject were prior to the 'imaginary', imagination being an action of the subject." "The subject," Hirst concludes, "exists through the imaginary relation — in recognition it becomes a subject."[79] The subject, therefore, is not the preconstituted one that is, because of its economic position (proletariat), an "all knowing" subject but rather the subject produced in signifying practices. In ludic theory, as Hirst elaborates, "signifying practices do not 'represent' anything outside them, they cannot serve as a means of class interests or of (functional) mis-recognition of social relations."[80]

In Mouffe's words, commenting on Gramsci, "the subjects are not originally given but are always produced by ideology.... This implies that ideology has a material existence and that far from consisting in an ensemble of spiritual realities, it is always materialized in practices."[81] However, the attack on the radical theory as a theory of the essentialized subject goes beyond theory of ideology and in fact becomes a basis for displacing the radical theory of "alienation" and "alienated labor," which are also interpreted as positing an essentialized subject and which, along with "ideology," form the radical concepts for critique of capitalism.

CRITIQUE OF IDEOLOGY

One of the effective means that the radical theory of ideology has developed in its critique of capitalism has been "ideology critique." Radical ideology critique from the writings of Marx to the present time has been an inaugural device for emancipatory social practices: but only an inaugural one since the critique of ideology in itself is not enough for social transformation. Ludic politics displaces ideology critique by diverse forms of discursive genealogies — variously called "cultural critique," "critique of institutions," and the like. The argument of ludic theory against ideology is that it is a closural "reading" — it establishes "causes" for social practices and as such is a reductive reading. As I have argued at length,[82] the notions of "closure" and "process" are ideological alibis for occluding any sustained understanding of the global logic of domination that underlies the seemingly heterogeneous (and "autonomous") practices of capitalism.

In his *Critique of Cynical Reason*, Peter Sloterdijk attempts to strengthen the case of ludic politics against ideology critique by again focusing on ideology as false consciousness. He argues that the emergence of a postideological consciousness (a false consciousness that is self-reflexive and thus aware of its own falsehood) has made ideology critique historically redundant. What we are witnessing, he proposes, is the formation of a postmodern cynical consciousness that is immune to ideology critique. Consequently, Sloterdijik argues, radical ideology critique has become useless. In other words, ideology critique as a device for social change has lost its effectivity because "false consciousness" itself is eroded by the emergence of cynical consciousness.

Cynical consciousness is an *enlightened false consciousness*. It is that modernized unhappy consciousness, on which enlightenment has labored both successfully and in vain. It has learned its lessons in enlightenment, but it has not, and probably was not able to, put them into practice. Well-off and miserable at the same time, this consciousness no longer feels affected by any critique of ideology: its falseness is already reflexively buffered.[83]

His argument, in the last instance, amounts to a reversal of Marx's notion of ideology as an unconscious practice: "They do not know it, but they are doing it." However, as Slavoj Zizek points out, the notion of a reflexive and enlightened postmodern false consciousness does not change the effects of ideology. The only difference is the shift in the site of ideological misrecognition: the subject of false consciousness now knows its "falsehood." The knowledge, however, does not affect the practices because the enlightened false consciousness now adopts an "ironic" attitude toward itself: It knows what it is doing but it still does it! "Even if we do not take things seriously, even if we keep an ironical distance, *we are still doing them.*"[84]

Ideology critique for radical theory does not lose its effectivity in the moment of the postmodern; it simply becomes a more necessary practice: a practice that now has to become more vigilant and take into account the dissimulations of the enlightened false consciousness — the false consciousness of transnational capitalism — and show that "false consciousness" has never been the "other" of "true" consciousness, as idealistic and cognitive theories of ludic postmodernism have represented it. "False consciousness" in the radical theory of ideology is the sign of a lack, an absence: the lack of "class consciousness." The radical theory of ideology and its practices, such as ideology critique, are aimed at analyzing the political economy of this absence and making the invisible visible as an inaugural move in moving beyond ludic ethics.[85]

NOTES

1. Jane Flax, "Do Feminists Need Marxism?" in *Building Feminist Theory*, ed. Charlotte Bunch et al. (New York: Longman, 1981), 174–85.
2. Gayle Rubin, "Thinking Sex: Notes for a Radical Theory of the Politics of Sexuality," in *Pleasure and Danger: Exploring Female Sexuality*, ed. Carole S. Vance (New York: Routledge, 1984), 267–319.
3. Judith Butler, *Gender Trouble: Feminism and the Subversion of Identity* (New York: Routledge, 1990). For a clear articulation of the ludic model that underlies Butler and other postmodernist feminists and queer theorists see Ernesto Laclau, "Transformations of Advanced Industrial Societies and the Theory of the Subject," in *Rethinking Ideology: A Marxist Debate*, ed. Sakari Hanninen et al. (Berlin: Argument-Verlag, 1983), 39–44.
4. See Ernesto Laclau and Chantal Mouffe, *Hegemony and Socialist Strategy* (New York: Verso, 1985).
5. Nancy Fraser and Linda Nicholson, "Social Criticism without Philosophy: An Encounter between Feminism and Postmodernism," in *Feminism/Postmodernism*, ed. L. Nicholson (New York: Routledge, 1990), 19–38.
6. Donna Haraway, *Simians, Cyborg, and Women* (New York: Routledge, 1991), 149–81. For MacKinnon's comments see "Feminism, Marxism, Method, and the State," *Signs* 7, no. 3 (Spring 1982): 515–44.
7. See Michelle Barrett, *The Politics of Truth* (Stanford: Stanford University Press, 1991), 139.
8. See Judith Butler, "Contingent Foundations: Feminism and the Question of 'Postmodernism,' " in *Feminists Theorize the Political*, ed. Butler et al. (New York: Routledge, 1992), 17.
9. See Mas'ud Zavarzadeh, *Seeing Films Politically* (Albany: State University of New York Press, 1991), 31–89. For Camile Paglia, see her *Sex, Art, and American Culture* (New York: Vintage, 1992).
10. Teresa L. Ebert, "Ludic Feminism, the Body, Performance and Labor: Bringing *Materialism* Back into Feminist Cultural Studies," *Cultural Critique* 23

(Winter 1992–93): 5–50; Rosemary Hennessy, *Materialist Feminism and the Politics of Discourse* (New York: Routledge, 1993); Donald Morton, "The Politics of Queer Theory in the Moment of the (Post)modern," *Genders* 17 (Fall 1993), 121–50.

11. Teresa L. Ebert, "Writing in the Political: Resistance (Post)modernism," *Legal Studies Forum* 15, no. 4 (1991): 291–303.
12. Jacques Derrida, *Margins of Philosophy*, trans. A. Bass (Chicago: University of Chicago Press, 1982), 1–27.
13. Jean Baudrillard, *Simulations*, trans. P. Foss et al. (New York: Semiotext(e), 1983), 1–79.
14. Jacques Derrida, *Of Grammatology*, trans. G. Spivak (Baltimore: Johns Hopkins University Press, 1976), 20.
15. I might add here that Ebert's reading of "resistance postmodernism" does not emphasize "labor" in the way I have done here because her reading of Marx's labor theory is more focused on those discourses of Marx that foreground the abstractness of labor under capitalism and thus the erasure of difference among the heterogeneous. She, in short, accents Marx's notion of capitalism as itself a form of totalization.
16. Jacques Lacan, *The Four Fundamental Concepts of Psychoanalysis* (New York: Norton, 1980), 53–78.
17. Roland Barthes, *The Pleasure of the Text*, trans. Richard Howard (New York: Hill and Wang, 1975).
18. A. Benjamin, ed., *The Lyotard Reader* (Oxford: Blackwell, 1989), 155–68, 196–211.
19. Karl Marx and Friedrich Engels, *Collected Works*, vol. 5 (New York: International, 1976), 27–93.
20. N. Poulantzas, *Political Power and Social Class*, trans. T. O'Hagan (London: Verso, 1978), 207.
21. Gilles Deleuze and Felix Guattari, *A Thousand Plateaus: Capitalism and Schizophrenia*, trans. Brian Massumi (Minneapolis: University of Minnesota Press, 1987), 4.
22. Derrida, *Margins of Philosophy*, 207–71. See also Jacques Derrida, *Signsponge* (New York: Columbia University Press, 1984).
23. K. Mannheim, *Ideology and Utopia* (London: Routledge, 1972), 66.
24. Derrida, *Margins of Philosophy*, 216–17.
25. Barry Hindess and Paul Hirst, *Modes of Production and Social Formation* (London: Macmillan, 1977), 11.
26. Ferdinand de Saussure, *Course in General Linguistics* (New York: McGraw-Hill, 1966), 120.
27. Jacques Derrida, *Writing and Difference*, trans. A. Bass (Chicago: University of Chicago Press, 1978), 280.
28. Laclau, "Transformations," 39–44.
29. Laclau and Mouffe, *Hegemony and Socialist Strategy*, 105.
30. Laclau, "Transformations," 30.
31. Ibid., 39.

32. Laclau and Mouffe, *Hegemony and Socialist Strategy*, 111.
33. Laclau, "Transformations," 40.
34. Ibid.
35. Ibid., 41.
36. Ibid., 39.
37. Mas'ud Zavarzadeh, "Theory as Resistance," in *Pedagogy Is Politics*, ed. M. R. Kecht (Chicago: University of Illinois Press, 1992), 25–47.
38. J. F. Lyotard and Jean-Loup Thebaud, *Just Gaming*, trans. W. Godzich (Minneapolis: University of Minnesota Press, 1985), 50–51. Lyotard, of course, adopts this term from Wittgenstein.
39. Laclau, "Transformations," 42.
40. Antonio Negri, *Marx beyond Marx*, trans. H. Cleaver et al. (South Hadley, Mass.: Bergin and Garvey, 1984).
41. Deleuze and Guattari, *A Thousand Plateaus*.
42. Stuart Hall, "The Hinterland of Science: Ideology and the Sociology of Knowledge," in *On Ideology*, ed. Bill Schwartz (London: Hutchion, 1978), 10.
43. Paul Hirst, *On Law and Ideology* (Atlantic Highlands, N.J.: Humanities, 1979), 11.
44. Derrida, *Of Grammatology*, 44–56.
45. Michel Foucault, *Power/Knowledge*, ed. Colin Gordon (New York: Pantheon, 1980), 117.
46. Foucault, *Power/Knowledge*, 118.
47. Michel Foucault, *Language, Counter-Memory, Practice*, ed. D. F. Bouchard (Ithaca, N.Y.: Cornell University Press, 1977), 144.
48. Ernesto Laclau, "Transformation of Advanced Industrial Societies and the Theory of the Subject," in *Rethinking Ideology*, ed. S. Hannienen (Berlin: Argument Verlag, 1983), 40–41.
49. Claude Lévi-Strauss, *The Raw and the Cooked* (New York: Harper and Row, 1969), 7–8.
50. Derrida, *Writing and Difference*, 289.
51. Hirst, *On Law and Ideology*, 53.
52. Louis Althusser, *Lenin and Philosophy*, trans. B. Brewster (New York: Monthly Press Review, 1971), 159.
53. Gary S. Morson, ed. *Bakhtin: Essays and Dialogues on His Work* (Chicago: University of Chicago Press, 1986), 182.
54. Nicholas Garnham, "Subjectivity, Ideology, Class and Historical Materialism," *Screen* 20, no. 1 (1979): 125.
55. Barbara Johnson, *A World of Difference* (Baltimore: Johns Hopkins University Press, 1987), 30–31.
56. Hirst, *On Law and Ideology*, 73.
57. Althusser, *Lenin and Philosophy*, 162.
58. Ibid., 165.
59. Hirst, *On Law and Ideology*, 38.
60. Chantal Mouffe, "Hegemony and Ideology in Gramsci," in *Gramsci and Marxist Theory*, ed. Mouffe (London: Routledge, 1979), 168.

61. See Hirst, *On Law and Ideology*, 15–17, and Hindess and Hirst, *Modes of Production and Social Formation*.
62. Mouffe, "Hegemony and Ideology in Gramsci," 169.
63. Ernest Laclau and Chantal Mouffe, "Recasting Marxism: Hegemony and New Political Movements," *Socialist Review* 66 (1982): 97.
64. Laclau and Mouffe, *Hegemony and Socialist Strategy*, 67.
65. Ibid.
66. Ibid., 97–105.
67. Stuart Hall, "Signification, Representation, Ideology: Althusser and the Post-Structuralist Debates," *Critical Studies in Mass Communication* 2, no. 2 (1985): 94.
68. Hirst, *On Law and Ideology*, 18.
69. See Hall, "Signification," 94–96, and Fredric Jameson, *The Political Unconscious* (Ithaca, N.Y.: Cornell University Press, 1981), 23–41.
70. Foucault, *Power/Knowledge*, 118.
71. Laclau and Mouffe, "Recasting Marxism," 98.
72. Foucault, *Power/Knowledge*, 118.
73. Mouffe, "Hegemony and Ideology in Gramsci," 169.
74. Laclau, "Transformation of Advanced Industrial Societies," 43.
75. Laclau and Mouffe, *Hegemony and Socialist Strategy*, 1–5.
76. Hirst, *On Law and Ideology*, 31.
77. Ibid., 23.
78. Louis Althusser, *Lenin and Philosophy* (New York: Monthly Review, 1971), 162.
79. Hirst, *On Law and Ideology*, 57.
80. Ibid., 70.
81. Mouffe, "Hegemony and Ideology in Gramsci," 186.
82. Zavarzadeh, *Seeing Films Politically*, 31–89.
83. Peter Sloterdijk, *Critique of Cynical Reason*, trans. M. Eldred (Minneapolis: University of Minnesota Press, 1987), 5.
84. Slavoj Zizek, *The Sublime Object of Ideology* (New York: Verso, 1989), 33.
85. See Mas'ud Zavarzadeh, *Posttheory, Pun(k) Deconstruction and the Ludic Political Imaginary* (Washington, D.C.: Maisonneuve, 1994).

Contributors

IAN BARNARD teaches in the Department of English and Comparative Literature and in the Department of Rhetoric and Writing Studies at San Diego State University. His previous publications include articles on South African politics and literature and on the relation of gay men to lesbian feminism. He currently is working on a book on queer theory's disruptions of liberal pluralism, of which the present essay is a part.

JONES DERITTER is an assistant professor of English at the University of Scranton. He has published articles on Aphra Behn, Henry Fielding, and George Lillo. The chapter included in this volume is part of a larger project tentatively entitled *The Embodiment of Character: The Representation and Enactment of Physical Experience on Stage and in Print, 1728–1749*.

MARGARET A. EISENHART is professor of education at the University of Colorado, Boulder, and coauthor, with Dorothy C. Holland, of *Educated in Romance: Women, Achievement, and College Culture*.

ELISABETH A. FROST is a Ph.D. candidate in English at the University of California, Los Angeles. Her dissertation, "The Feminist Avant-Garde in American Poetry," explores the connections between linguistic experimentation and gender politics in the work of women poets from Gertrude Stein to the present. Her poetry and reviews have appeared in *The Women's Review of Books*, *The Massachusetts Review*, *The Denver Quarterly*, and other journals.

LEAH HACKLEMAN is a Ph.D. candidate in the American Culture Program at Bowling Green State University, where she holds a teaching fellowship through the Women's Studies Program. "Plastic Man versus the Sweet Assassin" was the inspiration for her dissertation, which will examine the cultural construction of gender in 1968.

LYNDA HART teaches performance, feminist theory, and lesbian and gay studies at the University of Pennsylvania. She is the editor of *Making a Spectacle: Feminist Essays on Contemporary Women's Theatre*; coeditor, with Peggy Phelan, of *Acting Out: Feminist Performances*; and author of *Fatal Women: Lesbian Sexuality and the Mark of Aggression*. She is currently completing *Between the Body and the Flesh: Performing Lesbian Sado-Masochism*, to be published by Columbia University Press.

NANCY R. LAWRENCE is a Ph.D. candidate in the Department of Education at the University of Colorado, Boulder.

RAJESWARI MOHAN is assistant professor of English at Haverford College. She is currently working on a book entitled *Between Two Worlds: British Modernism and the Crisis of the Empire*. Her previous work has appeared in *Textual Practice, College Literature, Rethinking Marxism,* and *Mediations*.

LORA REMPEL is a Ph.D. candidate in art history at the City University of New York Graduate Center. Her work on late-eighteenth-century British prints entitled "Carnal Satire and the Constitutional King" is forthcoming.

TALIA SCHAFFER is a Ph.D. candidate in the English Department at Cornell University. Her dissertation argues that 1890s aestheticism, far from being an all-male movement, was actually dominated by women and shaped by elements of women's popular culture. Her article "A Wilde Desire Took Me: The Homoerotic History of *Dracula*" is forthcoming in *ELH*.

CYNTHIA WEBER is assistant professor of political science at Purdue University. Her research focuses on the relationship between sovereignty and intervention practices in international relations theory and practice (see *Simulating Sovereignty: Intervention, the State, and Symbolic Exchange,*

Cambridge University Press, forthcoming) and on the role of desire in U.S.–Caribbean relations.

MAS'UD ZAVARZADEH writes on Marxist political and critical theory. His published books include *The Mythopoeic Reality*; *Seeing Films Politically*; *Theory, (Post)modernity), Opposition* (coauthor); *Theory, Pedagogy, Politics* (coeditor); and *Theory as Resistance: Politics and Culture after (Post)structuralism* (coauthor). He is, along with Teresa L. Ebert and Donald Morton, one of the editors of a new journal, *Transformation: Marxist Boundary Work in Theory, Economics, Politics and Culture* (first issue to appear in fall 1994).

HEATHER ZWICKER teaches English at the University of Alberta. A postcolonialist by training, her research and teaching interests encompass cultural studies, feminism, and interdisciplinary cultural theory.

Guidelines for Prospective Contributors

Genders welcomes essays on art, literature, media, photography, film, and social theory. We are especially interested in essays that address theoretical issues relating sexuality and gender to social, political, racial, economic, or stylistic concerns.

All essays that are considered for publication are sent to board members for review. Your name is not included on the manuscript in this process. A decision on the essay is usually reached in about four months. Essays are grouped for publication only after the manuscript has been accepted.

We require that we have first right to any manuscript that we consider and that we have first publication of any manuscript that we accept. We will not consider any manuscript that is already under consideration with another publication or that has already been published.

The recommended length for essays is twenty-five pages of double-spaced text. Essays must be printed in letter-quality type. Quotations in languages other than English must be accompanied by translations. Photocopies of illustrations are sufficient for initial review, but authors should be prepared to supply originals on request.

Place the title of the essay and your name, address, and telephone number on a separate sheet at the front of the essay. You are welcome to include relevant information about yourself or the essay in a letter to the editor, but please be advised that institutional affiliation does not affect editorial policy. Since the majority of manuscripts that we receive are photocopies, we do not routinely return submissions. However, if you would like your copies returned, please enclose a self-addressed, stamped envelope.

GUIDELINES FOR PROSPECTIVE CONTRIBUTORS

To submit an essay for consideration, send *three* legible copies to:
Thomas Foster
Genders
Department of English
Ballantine Hall 442
Indiana University
Bloomington, IN 47405